FOOTSLOGGERS

PREVIOUS TITLES BY PETER HART

Gallipoli
The Great War: 1914–1918
The Last Battle
Voices from the Front
At Close Range
Burning Steel

FOOTSLOGGERS

AN INFANTRY BATTALION AT WAR, 1939–45

PETER HART

P
PROFILE BOOKS

First published in Great Britain in 2023 by
Profile Books Ltd
29 Cloth Fair
London
ECIA 7JQ

www.profilebooks.com

Copyright © Peter Hart, 2023

1 3 5 7 9 10 8 6 4 2

Typeset in Dante by MacGuru Ltd
Printed and bound in Great Britain by Clays Ltd, Elcograf S.p.A.

The moral right of the author has been asserted.

All rights reserved. Without limiting the rights under copyright reserved above, no part of this publication may be reproduced, stored or introduced into a retrieval system, or transmitted, in any form or by any means (electronic, mechanical, photocopying, recording or otherwise), without the prior written permission of both the copyright owner and the publisher of this book.

A CIP catalogue record for this book is available from the British Library.

ISBN 978 1 80081 070 9
eISBN 978 1 80081 072 3

This book is dedicated with grateful thanks to Harry Moses, a true friend and chronicler to the 'Faithful Durhams'. And all the men of the 16th DLI who answered their country's call.

Thank you to you and all your comrades.

CONTENTS

Preface   xi
1. Close Encounters   1
2. Learning their Trade   5
3. The Great Adventure   38
4. Battle of Sedjenane   58
5. Advance to Tunis   78
6. Landing at Salerno   105
7. Naples and River Crossings   145
8. Monte Camino   174
9. Across the Garigliano   193
10. A Middle East Sojourn   202
11. Gothic Line Horrors   212
12. The Battle of Gemmano Ridge   233
13. More Bloody Ridges   246
14. Could *You* Have Coped?   280
15. Last Rites at Cosina   306
16. Grecian Odyssey   322
17. What a Relief, 8 May 1945   349
18. End of Days   375

Acknowledgements   390
Picture Credits   390
Notes   391
Index   406

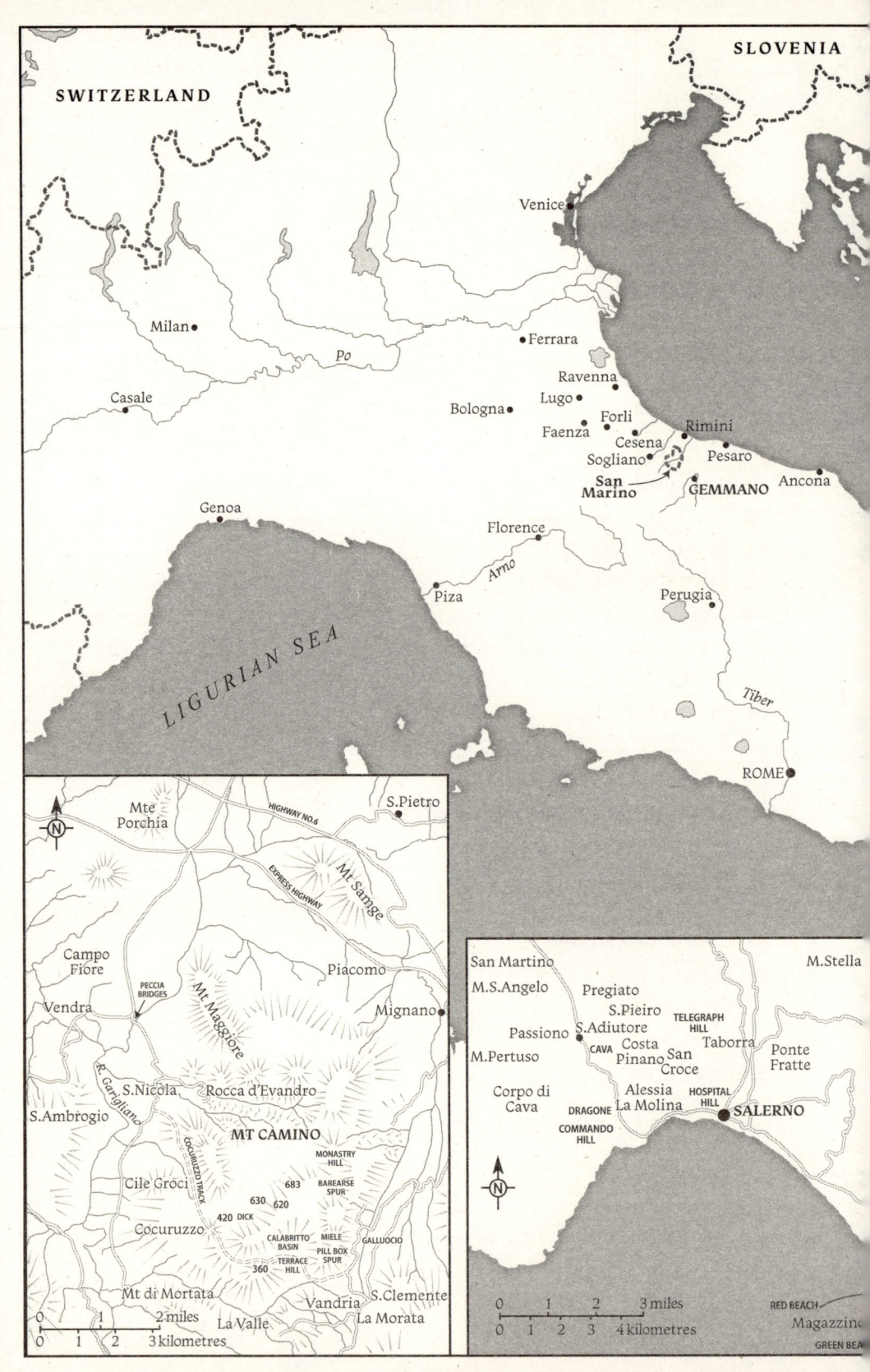

PREFACE

AS YOU WALK THROUGH DURHAM MARKET SQUARE your eyes are drawn to an imposing statue, cast in bronze to represent the men of the Durham Light Infantry. Unveiled in September 2014, it is a permanent reminder of all those who fought in the regiment's ranks; a timely gesture, as the actual flesh and blood veterans of the Second World War were even then fast dwindling in numbers. We have become accustomed to thinking of those few that remain as 'frail old men', but once they were hale and hearty, full of the joys of spring, ready to embrace all the challenges of life. Then they volunteered, or were called up, to fight for their country. Far too many of them would be cut down in their prime: dead long before their time. Their names live on now on war memorials, in family archives and the recorded memories of comrades fortunate enough to survive.

This book is an attempt to bring back to life the spirit of the living entity that was a battalion at war. The hopes and the fears. The life of monotonous tedium shot through with wild excruciating moments of mind-shredding terror. The twin imposters of military success and failure. But most of all the comrades cherished and lost, then and since.

The 16th Battalion, Durham Light Infantry (16th DLI) was the result of dire necessity – one of the sixty Dunkirk battalions raised across the UK in the immediate aftermath of the humiliating retreat of the British Expeditionary Force from Europe in June 1940. They were mainly made up of conscripts, soaking up some of the huge increase in those called up – growing from 70,000 to 345,000 in just a couple of months – as the 'Phoney War' ended abruptly with the German 'Blitzkrieg'. It was thus not a 'regular' or 'territorial' battalion carved out from the Durham heartlands, but one thrown together from drafts drawn from all over the country. With no obvious proud heritage to call on, the 16th DLI did not have a unit title with the potential to ring down across the centuries. It might be said that they were an 'ordinary' battalion, but there was nothing ordinary about the experiences they collectively faced in the war against fascism. Most of the men were civilians until the onset of war threw them into the maelstrom; few of them ever considered themselves as natural soldiers. They had to learn from scratch the fundamentals of military discipline and acquire the manifold skills required of the infantryman. Some learnt quickly and prospered; far more struggled in this harsh environment, enduring untold privations and humiliations. But most did in the end become effective soldiers, capable of facing their opponents serving the Third Reich.

The parent regiment was the DLI, the origins of which lay back in 1756 when an expansion in the army was ordered during the 'Seven Years War' with France. Thus the 23rd Regiment of Foot raised a second battalion, which two years later was renamed the 68th Foot. By 1760, the new regiment was based at Tynemouth and so began its connection with the northeast. It served in North America and the Caribbean before returning to Tynemouth and, by 1808, had been designated as the 68th Light Infantry, which meant marching at a faster pace – something of an enduring source of pride throughout the generations. After service in the ill-fated Walcheren Expedition, they took part in the later Peninsula War campaigns in Spain. After a period of quiet garrison duty, the battalion was despatched to fight in the Crimean War, where it distinguished itself at the grim Battle of Inkerman in 1854. In the army reforms of 1881, the DLI was formally created and its battalions would serve in the Sudan, India and in the Boer War, 1899–1902. During the Great War, 1914–18, the regiment raised some forty-two battalions, of which twenty-two saw active service, mainly on the Western Front, but also in Italy and Salonika. By dint of their efforts over the years, the DLI had acquired the honorific of 'The Faithful Durhams'. Now it was the turn of a new generation to go into battle.

This book results from the DLI Project conducted by the Imperial War Museum Sound Archive from 1986 to 2010. I was just one of a team of interviewers that included Harry Moses, Michael Moses, Tom Tunney and Conrad Wood. While conducting a Great War programme of interviews in the early 1980s, I realised that we had left it far too late to get a close-up, in-depth picture of any single battalion. Yes, we interviewed lots of individual soldiers, but that was not enough to really understand what was happening, or to prevent a few individuals dominating the narrative for the thousands who served in that one unit. To prevent the same happening with our Second World War interviews, I was encouraged by Margaret Brooks (the Keeper of the Sound Archive) to begin a huge project carrying out hundreds of interviews with the Second World War veterans of the DLI. Why that regiment? Well, I suppose in some ways it was a subjective choice, as my family come from County Durham; but justification was easily found in the distinguished service of the DLI battalions on most fronts during the war. I was also fortunate in the enthusiastic support of the DLI Regimental Association, the DLI Museum and the crucial assistance right from the start of Harry Moses, to whom I have dedicated this book. Harry was instrumental in locating and interviewing many of the veterans and he will be greatly missed. But why the 16th DLI in particular? To me their story seemed to most encapsulate the 'everyman' nature of the war. We also had the opportunity to interview nearly all the company commanders, something impossible in the 'older' regular or territorial battalions. I was also greatly abetted in my research by the assistance of Tom Tunney, whose interest was triggered by the service of his father, Thomas Tunney, with the battalion. He recorded many fine interviews and went on to create his own digital archive and website on the 16th DLI – to be found at http://16dli.awardspace.co.uk/

This is not the book to read if you want a potted history

of the campaigns; you should read this if you want to know what it was like to be a 'footslogger' at war. An infantry line battalion is not an overtly glamorous or elite corps. If you scan the histories of the various Italian campaigns, you will see scant references to the 16th DLI, but such 'ordinary' infantry battalions were the real 'bread and butter' of the British Army. The massed bombers of the RAF and the blazing guns of the Royal Artillery might pound the Germans almost to submission, while the armoured regiments smashed through gaps in their lines, but it is the infantry that had to take and hold the ground. It was – in the end – a matter of 'boots on the ground'. They would then have to face the onslaught of determined German counter-attacks that followed as night follows day. Shelled by artillery and mortars, threatened by air attack and panzers, they had to hold back their opposite numbers in the German infantry. It was a grim attritional battle. Pawns on the battlefield they may have been, but they were pawns that would ultimately decide the day. We owe them our thanks.

1

CLOSE ENCOUNTERS

THE SHOCK OF BATTLE was something for which no training could really prepare men. The 16th DLI had been training back in England for the best part of three years, building up their physical strength, getting used to the privations of military service, mastering their weapons, learning the battle drills that might keep them alive. But the first contact with the Germans could still be a fraught experience. For Lance Sergeant James Drake, the first real test was at the Battle of Sedjenane which began on 26 February 1943. During the fighting, he and the rest of the Carrier Platoon were ordered to carry out a flank approach into the hills in support of an attack by the rest of the battalion. It resulted in a small skirmish that does not appear in the regimental history, but which meant everything to the men involved.

> There was a machine gun in one of the hills at the back, which was causing a lot of damage to our troop as they advanced. There was also a mortar – a six-barrelled mortar – so they could keep 'popping' them in. They were pretty efficient on their mortars. They were throwing mortars down on to the plain below and covering the bridge – and so was the machine gun – which our troops had to cross. We could see the rifle companies moving backwards and forwards on our left. They hadn't the chance of attacking on the right, because they couldn't get across. We got the orders that we were to take the Vickers up the first hill on the right-hand side, apparently it wasn't occupied, and we had to go up the face of this hill and deal with

> the machine gun on the face of the hill in front of us – and the mortar which was down between both the hills.¹
>
> Lance Sergeant James Drake, Carrier Platoon

At this point an officer came up and cancelled the orders. They checked by runner with headquarters and were told as far as they were concerned the attack was 'still on'. It was becoming clear that something was wrong.

> The officer had been at Dunkirk and he'd gone through a lot. As soon as he came to action his body wouldn't take it – it's understandable. As soon as he saw a German his nerves went. That's all there was to it!²
>
> Lance Sergeant James Drake, Carrier Platoon

With that resolved, they set about moving up into the hills. This was not easy.

> The Vickers being a heavy gun, they provided a mule. We loaded it on the mule. We went as far as we could where the mule could go. Then we unloaded it and we proceeded to go further up the hill. In the meantime, Sergeant Doorman and one section of the Carrier Platoon went round the right-hand side of the hill – if they fired, we'd know the Germans were coming round the side. We made our way, dragging the Vickers. Just 25 yards before we got to the top of the hill, I went on to the left face and set up the Vickers. We could plainly see where the German machine gun was situated behind rocks on the side of the hill – every time he fired it the smoke came off – so we knew exactly where he was. I set the Vickers up to engage this machine gun – first puff of smoke I was there with the Vickers, letting as many rounds as I thought necessary. It was all going very well. Next puff of smoke I was there again – keeping it quiet. He didn't seem to be firing as much, so Lieutenant Lax went behind our gun – he knew how to fire it. I then took the Bren gun from one of the privates. I said, 'I'm going to crawl forward higher up, so I can look down into the valley below!'³
>
> Lance Sergeant James Drake, Carrier Platoon

Drake was intent on making sure that the way was clear for the main attack. When it came to the crunch, he was willing to risk his own life in an effort to 'make the difference'.

> I crawled forward on my belly. Sure enough, there was the mortar, plain as day. I could see the Germans all round it feeding it. I looked on the side of the hill opposite and there were two spotters. I turned the first magazine on the two spotters and put them out of action straight away! Then I turned my sights down to the mortars down below. It was no difficulty to put them out – that didn't operate any more I can assure you of that. I crawled back then to Lieutenant Lax.[4]
>
> Lance Sergeant James Drake, Carrier Platoon

Having achieved his mission, Drake sent back a runner for more instructions. However, his activities had attracted the vengeful attentions for the Germans.

> Suddenly grenades started coming over the top of the hill. I swung the Vickers round on a swinging traverse. I fired the gun and silenced the first lot coming over. I shouted to everybody to, 'GET OUT!' The lads all got out, but Lieutenant Lax said, 'I'm staying with you!' I said, 'You'd better not!' I gave him a few choice words and off he went. It was just my way – in these tight situations – you react – and mine was for him to get out. He was more important than I was. At the back of my mind, I used to think, 'Well, if I kill twelve Germans before I get killed, then at least I'll have done my duty!' I kept my head and I knew what I was doing! I stayed behind the gun. I was laid flat on my back operating the gun from over the top of my head! A grenade would have had to drop on me to do any damage! Two or three waves came over, throwing their hand grenades. They were right close too – between 10 to 15 yards – that's all! I couldn't miss them! I was there behind the gun, until the belt had gone through – I'd nothing left! I whipped the lock out of the gun and rolled down the hill. It was fairly steep – so I got a good roll on! I got to the bottom and then I heard shots coming from behind me. I did a zigzag course and dived straight into

the riverbank where I knew I was safe. I hadn't even got a scratch, which was most unusual.⁵

Lance Sergeant James Drake, Carrier Platoon

He had been lucky, but the combination of intensive training and his own soldierlike qualities had seen him through. There would be many more battles to come for the 16th DLI.

2

LEARNING THEIR TRADE

We always had kit inspections. Your blankets had to be folded square, everything else had to be folded square, your shirts, your socks. Your boots polished – studs uppermost to see if there was any missing. You just accepted it and just did your best. I never resented anything – I used to say to myself, 'Tom, you're here; you may as well make the best of it!'[1]

Private Tom Turnbull, 'E' (Training) Company

LET'S START AT THE VERY BEGINNING. The 16th DLI was created in July 1940, when Lieutenant Colonel Joseph Morrogh Bernard was appointed as the first commanding officer (CO). Originating from Hull, he had previously served with the East Yorkshire Regiment and spent some time in India. A smart-looking chap, he was very much a man of his time, who sported a big handlebar moustache. The 16th DLI, along with the 14th DLI and 17th DLI were all 'Dunkirk' battalions, raised following the evacuation of Dunkirk a month earlier. The three new DLI battalions formed the 206 (Independent) Brigade.

The 16th DLI was first established in the wide open fields of Norton Hall, just outside Edinburgh. A cadre of experienced instructors was included, with a large draft sent from the Bedfordshire and Hertfordshire Regiment Depot at Kempston Barracks, Bedford, a region which to most 'Durhams' was the far south. One of this original Beds and Herts draft was Wyndham (Jimmy) James who was the son of a publican in Ebbw Vale. He had a good education and secured work as sales clerk with Metropolitan Railways housing estates in Rickmansworth in 1936. He had been called up and completed his basic and continuation training, before specialising as a signaller, after which he was promoted to lance corporal and posted to the 16th DLI. At first, he found it was hard graft as they were required to erect tents and sort out latrines before the main body of recruits arrived.

> We had to put up marquees and bell tents in this field and get things organised. In addition to this nucleus of the Beds and Herts, suddenly Durham Light Infantrymen appeared. The draft of civvies was brought in from Princes Street. Men from all over the country, not just the north of England. If they were casualties, it wouldn't all happen in Durham. They had to be kitted out. The quartermaster's marquee was already there with all the uniforms, and they were kitted out as they came in. They were documented at another documentation tent, the NCOs there seeing to every man that came in and giving them an army number. They were allocated with eight men to a bell tent. I felt sorry for them because they weren't coming to a depot – they were coming into a field![2]
>
> Lance Corporal Jimmy James

Other drafts came directly from the DLI Depot at Brancepeth Castle, and many men were sent straight to Norton Hall straight after call up. One of the new arrivals was Gordon Gent, the son of a carpenter working on the Stanwick Estate in North Yorkshire. He was slightly older than most of the new drafts, working as a butcher and married with two children. He found his reception an intimidating introduction to army life.

> We were met by a bunch of Beds and Herts Regiment. Dyed in the wool Cockneys – we hardly knew what they were talking about! We were all Yorkshire and Durham lads. They knocked seven kinds of hell out of us verbally! Bawling and shouting – we didn't know what they were talking about. Knocking you into line! We weren't soldiers then! Some of them were drunk! It was chaos. The language that these NCO Cockneys used!

> We thought, as village lads, that we knew a few bad language words, but we didn't know anything until we heard these fellers! They really were disgusting! Vulgar isn't the word for it really! They were obscene![3]
>
> Private Gordon Gent

But it wasn't just the people that caused Gent distress. He found the tents to be grossly uncomfortable.

> There were big grass fields with rows of trees. They chopped a few trees down to get these tents in. The first night – oh dear me! Straight from 'Civvy Street'. There was a bit of a slope, and there was eight men in a tent with their feet in the middle – and I had a tree stump in the middle of my back! Nobody slept that night I can tell you. It was too uncomfortable.[4]
>
> Private Gordon Gent

Another conscript was James Drake, one of the nine children of a miner from Hemsworth in West Yorkshire. He had been working as a council driver. He had a hardly lived in the lap of luxury, but he found the conditions of service under canvas were appalling.

> It was very inclement weather; they called it Scotch mist – but I called it rain! It rained for a fortnight, it never seemed to stop. We couldn't do any drilling because the field was like a quagmire! There was a big marquee put up for the medical officers. He took the opportunity in the first two weeks of giving us all jabs in the arm! We had about five different lots all pumped into us. One big, tall, thin lad out of our tent, every time the orderly got hold of his arm – he used to faint – go down onto the floor. But they used to follow him down and still put it in! So, it wasn't a very pleasant two weeks – he finished up with his marquee full of invalids coming round after the injections. We were still in our civilian clothing. Believe me after a fortnight in them conditions you were damn glad to get the army clobber on! To feel a bit warmer at least than ordinary civilian clothing![5]
>
> Private James Drake

The issue of uniforms and kit was not a subtle or scientific process, as was vouchsafed by Sidney Shutt, who had been previously employed in the rather more sedate surroundings of a Cooperative store in Thornley.

> They were dishing the uniforms out! Just thrown at you! They just looked at you and guessed! The tin plates were thrown at you! This, that and the other! Then they threw a rifle at me! It must have been in the last war – thick with grease! 'Get that cleaned up!' Everything was just flung at you.[6]
>
> Private Sidney Shutt

Thomas Atkinson was from a poor background in Sunderland where he had been working on his brother's market stall before he was called up to serve 'King and Country'. He soon realised that he just had to make the best of it – the defining feature of an army uniform was that it was the same for everyone in the 'other ranks'.

> You got boots, which killed you when you'd been used to wearing shoes! You thought, 'I'll never get used to these things!' Funnily enough, after a few route marches, they were alright. You had your woolly vests, a couple of khaki shirts, khaki pullover, and a greatcoat. Your battledress. Your kitbag and everything. You packed your civilian clothes up and sent them home.[7]
>
> Private Thomas Atkinson

Many of the early arrivals were originally issued with Canadian P14 and P60 rifles, as there was a temporary shortage of the standard Lee Enfield .303 rifle. To the army instructors this was by far the most important part of their kit.

> We got our own rifle; that was going to be our best pal! That was more important than your wife – that's the instructions we got. Which could be so – depending on circumstances![8]
>
> Private James Drake

Having been kitted out, they had to learn how to lay it out in the approved fashion for the time-honoured ritual of the kit inspection: the ultimate military expression of a place for everything – and everything in its place. And woe betide the soldier whose kit was not perfect.

> We used to spend a hell of a lot of time in the evening spit and polishing! We had a brass button stick which you put behind the button and cleaned them with a little brush. It was there to protect your uniform. We got blanco issued for the webbing. You had to do your boots every night. Every time you went on parade, they had to be polished, sparkling! We got a very, very good shine on the boots.[9]
>
> Private Thomas Atkinson

They also soon realised that not everyone of their new comrades was strictly honest. Things would soon go 'missing' if they didn't keep a close eye on their kit.

> Although you were in a bell tent, you still had to pack everything neatly, and almost every morning the orderly sergeant used to come round and check everything was all there. If you had any equipment missing you had to report it. You kept 'losing' equipment. They taught you it seemed to be a general thing in the army: if you lose a hairbrush, you take somebody else's, and he'll take somebody else's! It went on like that. I must have been too honest![10]
>
> Private Thomas Atkinson

The tenets of basic training had not changed much in a hundred years – and have not really changed much since. It was a process designed to break the men's spirit, then rebuild them in the image of perfect trained soldiers – tough, capable of coping with great privation, obeying orders without hesitation or question and skilled in their weapons. But perhaps some of these men would have been capable of far more if they had been left 'unbroken'.

> They put you through the blooming muck! The infantry was noted for what we called 'bullshit'. It might have been all right

> in peacetime, all the fancy drill and that! But they were training us to fight a war! We'd come from responsible jobs. I'd been in charge of a butcher's business for several years – I was twenty-nine years old! They treated you as if you were all ignorant! But they said that was discipline! You had to be knocked into some kind of a working unit, but they carried it too far! Some of the NCOs loved being nasty – they loved it! They should have been Germans some of them. At first, we were full of enthusiasm, but they knocked that out of you. You couldn't see the necessity for half of the little piddling things that they would pick on you for! They did break your spirit of enthusiasm. That was wrong I thought.[11]
>
> Private Gordon Gent

Gent may have been right, but it should be remembered that the army did not have the time or inclination to tailor the training to an individual's needs; with millions being called to service it was of necessity a somewhat crude 'one size fits all' approach.

One tedious element was the endless drill sessions, training to move as formed bodies of men, to obey orders and to give experience of working together against a common enemy – in most cases the drill sergeant! Inevitably some uncoordinated men just could not keep in time.

> We used to do drill, drilling up and down. From the very beginning we were on light infantry pace. Lining up, making sure you got in line, how to stand easy, the commands of, 'Left turn!' and, 'Right turn!' It was pretty amazing how many people didn't know the difference between left and right. They weeded some of them out, because they should never have been called up in the first place. Nitwits – as thick as posts![12]
>
> Private Thomas Atkinson

It was of course crucial to improve men's standard of fitness. The army knew just how to achieve that at minimal cost.

> We went on route marches. About an hour and a half. The early ones used to kill me round the ankles, where the boots went

round. It didn't take long to get acclimatised. The marches got longer! You carried a hell of a load – everything but your kitbag! After every fifty minutes they used to stop for a ten-minute smoking time break. Everybody used to light up, didn't they! If you didn't smoke, you felt out of it! This is when I started smoking – to my regret![13]

Private Thomas Atkinson

Gradually standards of fitness improved.

It was not long before the battalion moved from Norton Hall into billets in the Dunfermline area. Jimmy James found himself in an old carpet factory under the gentle tutelage of a typical NCO of the 'old fashioned' sort. It proved an unforgettable experience, much though he might have wanted to forget it!

I was with Sergeant Harry Stern in Dunfermline. He was Beds and Herts, about forty, he was ex-Indian Army, long-service. He had a wonderful soldierly bearing. He loved his booze; he had a purple face through booze. He was a character – a Cockney. He used to say, 'I'm Harry Stern by name and stern by bloody nature!' Sadly, he didn't have any brains, he couldn't read a map, he couldn't read a compass, he couldn't do anything like that! He'd got his promotion through his ability to drill men – he was a good drill sergeant. He was drilling these men on the road outside the carpet factory, giving them what for! His word of command was really very, very loud, 'Left right! Left right!' There were houses nearby and a woman pushed up a bedroom window, 'You bloody great bully! You wouldn't teach my son like that! I've never heard anything so awful in my life!' He said, 'Lady! I've got a job to do! Send your old man down!' She slammed the window. Nobody would laugh – he really was a terror![14]

Lance Corporal Jimmy James

However, there was another side to the story. Many of the new recruits needed firm discipline and had no idea what they were doing. This could be dangerous.

> We were on guard, lined up, half a dozen of us. We used to have to pick up our rifles in a position so we could pull the bolt back. The officer used to come and inspect that you hadn't got one 'up the spout'! You had to press the bullets down when you closed the bolt. He used to say, 'Right, close your bolt!' Sometimes he'd look down the barrel, to see if it was clean. Then as he passed you, he'd say, 'Right, press down the bullets, close your bolts, fire the trigger!' This lad pulled the trigger – but he'd shoved one up the spout! It went right through the roof. It went through one bloke's shoulder, right up top, hit the roof at the top, the slates, came down – and landed back in his shoulder! He had to be whipped into hospital. There was a bit to do about that![15]
>
> Private James Drake

They had by this time come to grips with the light infantry speed of marching, which was 140 paces per minute, with a 'double' time of 180 paces. Once they were used to it, they were not shy of showing a fresh pair of heels to other units they encountered on the road.

> There was a heavy artillery mob close by – and I think we deliberately used to wait while they set off before we set off to the church parade on a Sunday morning. Then we used to pass 'em on the road! Sticking our chests out as much to say, 'What are you doing labouring?' As we were speeding past them![16]
>
> Private James Drake

The battalion embarked on an intensive programme of training. However, some night exercises in Carnegie Park exposed the inexperience of many of the young officers.

> We were doing night manoeuvres in the park at Dunfermline. We had our rifles and blanks. It was one lot against another. Next thing I knew, was a young lieutenant coming with a stick. I told him to , 'Halt!' and he didn't! So, I fired my blank, didn't I? He got a hell of a shock! He said, 'You could have bloody blinded me, you bloody fool!' I said, 'You should have stopped, Sir!'[17]
>
> Private Thomas Atkinson

Learning their Trade

Appropriate individuals were allotted to specialist roles, which meant some extra training. Thomas Atkinson was posted as one of the stretcher bearers with Headquarters Company.

> They taught us all the St John's manual of first aid. We were trained to do bandaging and to do splint work putting splints on broken limbs. Your job was to stop any bleeding – if possible – by packing the wound. Field dressings – that's all you had. Then taking him back to the first aid as quickly as you could, so that a doctor could get to him.[18]

Private Thomas Atkinson, Medical Section

New equipment was also beginning to arrive and James Drake, who had been promoted to corporal was posted to the Carrier Platoon and ordered to collect the battalion's first Bren carrier.

> I went to collect the first carrier from somewhere round Ayr. I went into this factory, and they brought it out into the field – and I had two to three hours with it. It was just a matter of getting used to how to drive it. The fellow from the factory showed me – it was simple enough. It was like driving a car except for one difference: when you came to anything like a sharp corner you changed down, put your foot down, got your 'revs' up, so you could get round the corner – because when you turned the steering wheel right it braked the right-hand side-track, so you got round a right-hand corner. Same on the opposite side. You'd stall the engine if you didn't have enough 'revs' on. Then I drove it back to the battalion. It was my job to teach everybody in the Carrier Platoon – forty-two men – how to drive it! There were three on each carrier: the driver, the Bren gunner, and a rifleman. As I handled it more, of course, the more I could do, I could turn it round on a sixpence! Our job, as far as the rifle companies were concerned, was that if they needed some speedy assistance, then the carriers would move quickly to where they were being troubled. A quick response to any situation.[19]

Corporal James Drake, Carrier Platoon

The Bren carriers were organised into a platoon with three sections each of three carriers.

After a few more weeks, in December 1940, the battalion moved on to Dalkeith. The battalion was put under the command of Lieutenant Colonel A. S. P. Murray, a former Grenadier Guards officer. He was a tall striking figure who set a fine example to his men. As might be expected from a Guards officer he was a forceful individual who was keen on enforcing a good turnout across the board and he would later introduce distinctive shoulder flashes to mark out his men. By this time, Jimmy James had been promoted to the dizzy heights of company quartermaster sergeant.

> Captain Ponder issued the regimental shoulder flashes, the Durham Light Infantry, red letters on a green semi-circle. We were issued with one set each and we had to carefully sew these on to our shoulders. When we were walking about, we were very proud. Durham Infantry – like guardsman![20]
>
> Company Quartermaster Sergeant Jimmy James, Headquarters Company

The inculcation of pride in unit is all important in preparing a battalion for combat. Flashes, badges, insignia all play their part in creating team spirit.

It was not long before the 16th DLI were removed from the 206 (Independent) Brigade, to replace the 9th Sherwood Foresters in 139 Brigade. (16th DLI, 2/5th Sherwood Foresters and 2/5th Leicestershire Regiment). It thus became an integral element of the 46th Division, which was made up of territorial battalions from the Northwest Midlands and West Riding area.

As a part of the 46th Division, this meant the first 'big' move for the 16th DLI, as they travelled by road and rail to a tented camp and billets around Thetford in Suffolk, with the battalion headquarters at Abbey Farm. Here they were put through a series of brigade and divisional exercises to accustom them to being part of a larger formation capable of working together in the field. This started with the basics in movement exercises, practising deploying from one place to another, a more complex process than might be imagined, and which uncovered many breakdowns in organisation and traffic control.

The battalion plunged into a seemingly never-ending programme of training, which embraced drill competitions, route marches, weapons, signals and tactical exercises. Intensive work was carried out in the deployment and use of Bren carriers, mortars, smoke bombs, hand grenades, Bren guns, Thompson submachine guns and many other specialist weapons. A start was even made on working with tank formations. Gas training was also given considerable priority, for there was still the chance that the Germans might use gas – after all, they had done so twenty years before. Bridging exercises and assault craft work prepared the way for future river crossings. Work on various types of listening, reconnaissance and fighting patrols was carried out. By July 1941, the men had moved on to live firing exercises, where everyone really had to know what they were doing or fatalities could ensue. As it was, Captain N. Metcalfe suffered severe foot wounds while searching for a Bakelite Mk 69 grenade that had failed to detonate – and then did.

During the whole of 1941, a programme of battalion, brigade and divisional field exercises was designed to test various aspects of the battalion's ability to operate as a coherent whole, and within a larger formation, in a hostile battlefield environment. Situations of 'German' sea or parachute invasions were practised, with the battalion variously practising holding river lines, defending bridges, crossing rivers and retaking captured airfields. They also took part in operations against 'German' forces intent on 'delaying' any advance and thus requiring attacks across rivers, on hilltop positions and in villages. Their performance was closely monitored by staff umpires assessing their success or failure – and the level of 'casualties' suffered. Soon this would be all too real. After-action reports and briefings using cloth models examined what had gone wrong – and what had gone right. There were recommendations issued to ensure proper reconnaissance, using small patrols to ferret out the exact locations of the 'enemy'. Plans for attack were to emphasise surprise, mobility, the importance of heavy covering fire, the use where possible of infiltration and an avoidance of too much rigidity in the planning process. It was evident that on the surface at least the basic lessons of warfare were being learnt. The question was whether the officers and NCOs could keep their heads to carry them out under the stress of real combat. That would be a very different matter.

In July 1941, the 16th DLI was sent with the rest of 139 Brigade to replace 113 Brigade on static beach defence duties in the North Norfolk area. They would take over for a month, while their predecessors were trained in more mobile operations. The 16th DLI was made responsible for 7 miles of sea front and the immediate hinterland north of Great Yarmouth. The defences were set up with platoon areas shared with the local Home Guard and based on pillboxes which would allow enfilading fire to rake across the heavily mined and wired beaches. Rapid response arrangements were brought in – and practised – to counter any possible parachutist incursion. As well as these duties they were employed in adding to anti-tank defences, establishing and testing a system of interlinked observation posts, erecting ever-more barbed wire and digging support positions. While they were there the Luftwaffe attempted to make them welcome, as several bombs were dropped, but there were only a few minor civilian injuries and the Durhams escaped unscathed. Previously, Great Yarmouth had been heavily bombed, so most of the inhabitants had been evacuated and many of the men were given comfortable hotel billets.

They were not there long before most of the battalion moved to new tented camps at Worstead Park and Scottow. The battalion were providing working parties to help establish the camp sites and they were plagued by continuous downpours. There was mud everywhere and the men were soon wet through. As ever, the British soldier did not complain; he just observed in a very traditional fashion, with senior NCOs acting as a lightning rod for the men's grievances.

> If you want to find the sergeant major, I know where he is
> I know where he is, I know where he is
> If you want to find the sergeant major, I know where he is
> He's hiding behind the shithouse door.
> I saw him, I saw him
> Hiding behind the shithouse door.[21]
>
> Company Quartermaster Sergeant Jimmy James, Headquarters Company

During this whole period, there was a rapid turnover of officers and NCOs as the regiment was 'shaken out' to get ready for active service. The old and more frail were edged aside to be replaced by younger, fitter men. One such newcomer was Henry Harris, the son of a farmer from just outside Tunbridge Wells. He had attended Officers Training Corps at Tonbridge School, before a period as a gunner on 3.7-inch guns with an anti-aircraft regiment, after which he was selected for a commission and trained as an officer at Falmouth. He had applied for his local Kentish regiments but found himself dispatched to join the 16th DLI. His reception was somewhat disconcerting.

> When I joined the battalion, the CO, Colonel Murray, said, 'Well, Harris, you'd better forget everything you learnt at Officer Cadet Training Unit. A complete waste of time! Forget it! Whatever you've got to learn, you'll learn it with us!' I had a platoon sergeant, a little chap – nought foot high! He jabbered like nobody's business at me! I couldn't understand him to begin with – it was a sort of foreign language. My batman I couldn't understand either, I used to say, 'Jack, what the hell are you talking about!' Well, I got used to it I suppose![22]
>
> 2nd Lieutenant Henry Harris

The mutual incomprehension caused by the regional accents between 'southerners' and the men of Durham and North Yorkshire would be an enduring theme throughout the life of the battalion.

On 17 November 1941, the 16th DLI moved into Risborough Barracks, Shorncliffe Camp at Folkestone, where the 139 Brigade was replacing the 169 Brigade of 56th Division on coastal defences. The whole of 46th Division was now under Southern Command. In winter the barracks were a welcome relief from the misery of sodden tents in a muddy field, perhaps even counterbalancing the inevitable increase in 'spit and polish' that barrack life encompassed.

By this time most of the 'Dunkirk' battalions were being used as training and reinforcement battalions, sending out drafts as required to other units. These departures were noted by John Lewindon, who grew up as part of a family dairy business in East Finchley. He had been called up for basic training with the Beds and Herts, and was one of the original draft sent to Edinburgh. He took a somewhat cynical attitude to the motivation of officers in picking out the men for drafting away.

> We lost people. Whilst we were at Folkestone, there were three small drafts taken out of the battalion – sent to other units as reinforcements. They were just picked out. That was the ideal opportunity for the company commander to get rid of undesirables![23]
>
> Private John Lewindon, Headquarters Company

In return, the 16th DLI received several large drafts of untrained men. This changeover of personnel meant a continued concentration in individual training. The idea was to raise the military standards of every soldier, while at the same time seeking to build up the reserves of specialists such as signallers, machine gunners, drivers, and, of course, junior NCOs. One of the new arrivals was Tom Turnbull, the son of a shipyard plater from Monkwearmouth, Sunderland. After a brief period as a rivet catcher in the shipyards, he had been working on property repairs as a builder. He had already settled down to married life and had a daughter. After being called up in January 1942, he was surprised to be posted straight to the 16th DLI.

> I was called up 8th January 1942. When I got my papers, when I saw Durham Light Infantry, I said to my wife, 'I'll be going to Brancepeth!' Till I read further down! I had to report to Shorncliffe Barracks in Folkestone, Kent. There was about 120

Learning their Trade

> of us all ex-tradesmen, from the building trade, we all went in together and formed 'E' Company – we did our training actually in the 16th Battalion, DLI.[24]
>
> Private Tom Turnbull, 'E' (Training) Company

They were well behind the rest of the battalion and had a lot of ground to make up in a very short time. It was certainly hard work.

> PT every day, mostly gymnasium work and physical training drill, we had a proper physical training instructor and fully equipped gym! I always wanted to keep myself fit before I went in the services, but you really found out you weren't as fit as you thought you were! Route marches were bloody awful – about 15–20 mile – ten minutes rest every hour. Sometimes when you sat down you found that you could hardly get up! At first you were blooming sore and your feet blistered, until you got used to army boots.[25]
>
> Private Tom Turnbull, 'E' (Training) Company

Then there was the weapons training – there was a lot to learn.

> I'd never shot anything before – apart from a rifle at a fairground. First, they had a sort of stand that they fixed the rifle in, and you were taught how to sight: you were told the front sight and the back sight – line them up and that was it! Then we went straight on the .303 range at Hythe with live ammunition. Most of your training is firing lying down, feet spread out in line, you just adapted that way. You learned how to keep the rifle tight in your shoulder, or you'll get a kick – it was a pretty hefty kick but you learn by trial and error! Bayonet training you started with the bags on the ground and on the frame charging with the fixed bayonet. Shouting just anything that come into your mind! We were fully trained on the Bren: stripping it down. You could do it in the dark! You fired it on the range – a very accurate weapon – it certainly was. You can put it on single shot or automatic. If it's automatic, you're taught to fire in bursts of five – which was pretty quick, just like a press of

> the trigger and release it and that was it. It was a good weapon. The 'Tommy gun' – the Thompson. We trained on them as well! It was a good little weapon. It had a stopping power. You were taught that if you wanted to hit anybody in the chest you had to fire at the knees – because it jumped. We liked it! You were trained on the Mills bomb. First of all, how to take the detonator in and out. Then training on a dummy grenade, to get used to throwing the distance – then they give you a live one. You pull the pin out and had the handle gripped in your hand. When you threw it – overarm – you saw the handle come off and that was it – you got down sharp. We were trained on the 2-inch mortar. One man dropped a bomb down a tube and the other man turned the handle on the side and fired it; it's fired by the striking pin on the base plate The range was judged by the elevation – you got that used to it you could more or less tell by the angle of the barrel to the base plate how far it would fire.[26]
>
> Private Tom Turnbull, 'E' (Training) Company

Only after they had passed out as a trained soldier were they assigned to a 'proper' company. Even then many were still inexperienced in the 'ways' of the army, as was recalled by Oswald McDonald, the son of shipyard riveter who had been working as a bricklayer building air raid shelters before he was called up.

> You were quite green – you'd volunteer for things that you should never have volunteered for! Because never volunteer in the army! 'Can anybody play the piano?' 'Yes!' 'Well, you go and clean the cookhouse up!' Things like that![27]
>
> Private Oswald McDonald, 'B' Company

Everyone still had a lot to learn. There was another series of tactical exercises, this time practising repelling a German invasion of Kent under various scenarios, each designed to test endurance, communications and leadership. The newer recruits were being taught basic fieldcraft – how to live in the open; how to prepare and occupy defensive positions. Meanwhile, the officers were despatched on courses to study anti-tank measures, tank-infantry cooperation, aircraft recognition, gas warfare and liaison with artillery observation posts. Demonstrations were organised on the right and wrong way of giving orders and the importance of following the correct battle procedure on first contact with a German force. Mistakes were difficult to put right once the fighting had started.

In January 1942, the battalion moved out of their barrack winter quarters and into hotel billets in Folkestone. Here many of the men found themselves on guard duties in the harbour area. One such was Thomas Lister, the son of a probation officer from Durham. He had been working pre-war as a travelling wholesale fish salesman, which meant he could drive.

> Being one of the only ones who knew anything about diesel engines, they pushed me almost every night operating a 90mm searchlight, in a sandbag emplacement, right on the end of the jetty on the east side of the harbour. There was this engine shed and there was this massive old two-cylinder Lister diesel; it must have come out of the ark! There was no starter motor, you had to start it by hand. When it finally decided to 'cough' you were in danger of being thrown up onto the roof! It took a lot of starting, but once it ran it was remarkably smooth, but it made an awful noise, 'Thump! Thump! Thump! Thump!' The Germans must have heard it 20 miles away! There were quite a lot of raids then. They came in low over the sea, so they weren't detected. They were Dornier, largely. The searchlight crew were our own blokes who knew little or nothing about it! They were armed with rifles and they had a Bren gun. A sergeant was in charge. This fairly cloudy night, I could hear this damn thing flying in. You hadn't to put the light on, unless you were told. The main searchlights, which weren't under our control, stab the skies, and this bloody thing came in lower down, you could actually see it coming! This bloke that was manning the searchlight panicked, pressed the wrong button – and put the light on – and it made a beeline straight for us. It was rattling away with its machine guns. I beat a hasty retreat behind a load of packing cases and hoped for the best. It didn't drop any bombs, just fired a load of bullets at us and

zoomed up and continued its journey. I think the bloke got a right dressing down![28]

Private Tom Lister, MT Section, Headquarters Company

It is interesting that during his stay in Folkestone, Lister felt himself a victim of the great 'north/south' divide in English society.

> We didn't find we were particularly well received by the civilian population. I got the impression that anybody north of the Watford Gap was a savage! A lot of them didn't even know where Durham was – they thought it was in Scotland somewhere! When you went in the pubs some of them wouldn't even serve you, 'You can't get served in here! We've just got enough for our own locals!' Even if you were perfectly quiet and reasonable. It didn't cause me any trouble, but certain types of blokes would resent it and show it by getting nasty – fighting locals.[29]

Private Tom Lister, MT Section, Headquarters Company

Some things never change!

On 16 March 1942, the 16th DLI moved along the coast to the Rye and Winchelsea area of East Sussex in a coastal defence role, responsible for the sea front stretching from Fairlight Cove to Rye Harbour. A strong defensive position was established in close collaboration with the local Home Guard on Rye Hill. Once ensconced in their new billets, the battalion began the usual series of intensive exercises, practising for every eventuality. But they also had to provide patrols and guard parties all along the coast. This was a regular duty for George Forster, the son of a shipyard joiner from South Shields, who had worked as an apprentice joiner before the army claimed him and he ended up in the 16th DLI.

> We used to do guards on the harbour at Winchelsea. You did two hours on, four hours off for forty-eight hours. There were holiday chalets at the bottom of the hill, and we used to be in a pillbox at the entrance to the chalets. We had sandbags and

a Bren gun! There were two guards on at a time. One used to stand in the pillbox and the other one walked around the chalets looking out to sea. It was all mined on the beach.[30]

Private George Forster, 'C' Company

It could be tedious beyond belief, as nothing ever seemed to happen.

On 9 May 1942, Colonel Murray was posted away as the second in command of the Support Group of 42nd Armoured Division. He had been a popular colonel and was considered to have achieved a high standard of training, despite the handicap of losing drafts to units serving overseas, largely to the 6th, 8th and 9th DLI serving with 151 Brigade in North Africa. The new commanding officer was Lieutenant Colonel Richard Ware, one of their own, a regular DLI officer who had won a Military Cross late in 1918. He was a smart somewhat stocky figure, affable, who by this time in his life was seen by some of the men as more of an 'administrative type' than a 'fighting officer'. But few questioned his professionalism, and as the training programme further intensified with a series of testing exercises, his analytical skills proved invaluable in detecting problems and working towards realistic solutions.

★

LIFE FOR THE DURHAMS in Rye and the surrounding villages was not at all unpleasant. They were mostly in comfortable billets and there was some time left after guard duties and training for some well-earned rest and relaxation. Some of the men found Winchelsea to be rather genteel.

> Don't forget that Winchelsea was a largely posh area – they had very big houses – and they didn't seem to want to know you! They would nod to you, but they wouldn't converse with you. We used to go in the pub occasionally. They were all right because they were farmworkers – they'd play shove halfpenny with you. There were two old ladies – in their eighties – in the

> main street opposite 'C' Company offices, and they used to make tea and home-baked cakes – it was quite cheap for a nice cup of tea and home-baked scones! Very nice![31]
>
> Private George Forster, 'C' Company

However, this led to some rather amusing confrontations between those two staples of British comedy: sergeant majors and little old ladies.

> We were doing drill parade and the Regimental Sergeant Major Thomasson was standing on the pavement cursing and swearing at the lads! And an old lady walked up to him, she taps him on the shoulder, and she says, 'We don't have swearing in our village!' He was speechless![32]
>
> Private George Forster, 'C' Company

Most of the men found themselves a pub that 'suited' them and had a reasonable supply of beer. In many of the interviews these sessions come across as relatively calm and pleasant affairs with nothing more untoward than a few pints. The men naturally sought out what female company they could, and dances were extremely popular.

> There was a little hall behind the New Inn – in a field – the village hall. George Broadhead was keen on organising dances. He decided to contact the ATS girls who were living in Ore, a little place just outside Winchelsea. They were informed that we had a pianist, a trombonist and a drummer. CQSM George Gaines was the kingpin because he created the tempo – he was a marvellous pianist – he could play any damn thing. He was the 'Mighty Atom' because he was about 4 foot 11 inches tall – he was a funny little bugger from Leeds – he was really broad Yorkshire! George Broadhead was the announcer – the 'Master of Ceremonies'. We would send over 15cwt trucks to bring these ATS girls to Winchelsea for the dance. I must say they were a very happy crowd. I couldn't dance for toffee. Who can with hobnail boots on? I'd go into the New Inn and have a couple of pints. Then somebody might say, 'Away to the dance!'

So we'd go along to the dance hall. An ATS girl had her eye on me. She came up and said, 'Come on, let's have this dance!' She said, 'I'll teach you!' She tried to teach me but with my great big boots I walked all over her! I did eventually learn the waltz and the slow foxtrot but couldn't do anything else. We had the odd song sung. There was one particular singer who was in 'D' Company, his name was Anderson, he had a bloody lovely silver, tenor voice. He gave one or two songs. He would sing ballad songs. The one that will always stick in my mind was:

'Just a little love, a little kiss
I would give you all I have for this'

He'd sing it beautifully, take his time and get applause. Poor chap was killed.[33] Quite a few liaisons sprang up.[34]

Company Quartermaster Sergeant Jimmy James, 'D' Company

An inevitable result of the 'liaisons' was a rise in venereal diseases. Here Thomas Atkinson was at the 'sharp end' as he was a medical orderly running the medical inspection room.

Crabs you can see, and they only attach themselves to your pubic hair; get rid of the hair and you've got rid of the crabs. Scabies, they are much smaller, you can't see them with the human eyesight. They burrow under the skin and then lay eggs. Then they itch like bloody blazes. They're horrible things. People scratch and they start getting impetigo – that's why they put the blue unction on – they were causing infection by scratching. We had the job of painting them from head to foot with some sort of benzine sort of petrol – I think if you'd put a match to it they would have blown up! That used to cure them of the scabies. There was the odd case of VD, they would be whipped away to hospital. Gonorrhoea and syphilis, both of those were very serious, especially syphilis. They used to say that it was a self-inflicted wound. If you got syphilis, you were out of action for two years; you were a liability, but I don't think we came across much of it, but there was some.[35]

Lance Corporal Thomas Atkinson, Headquarters Company

★

LIFE MAY HAVE BEEN RELATIVELY PLEASANT for the men of the 16th DLI during their period at Rye and Winchelsea, but there was a constant threat of German air attacks as the Luftwaffe bases were just a few miles across the Channel.

> There were quite a few air raids at Rye; usually hit and run daytime raids. A lot of skirmishes between Spitfires, Hurricanes and Me109s, Me110s. The Focke-Wulfs were a tremendous nuisance because they were very fast and comparatively quiet – they sneaked in wave high and dropped their bomb, fired their cannons, and whizzed off in a flash!³⁶
>
> Private Tom Lister, MT Section, Headquarters Company

The sudden roar of German fighter engines often came as a huge surprise – sometimes at the most inconvenient times.

> General Montgomery, he started PT before breakfast. You had to get your PT kit and run about doing all these exercises, first thing. We were at Camber one time – we had our white PT vests on with navy blue shorts and plimsolls. We were running about the beach. We had to run into the sea, because the saltwater does your feet a power of good. We got in there and we were about waist deep – and a German aircraft came over! The sea at the best of times is cold! When you get there first thing in the morning just after six or half past six – it's bloody cold! We couldn't get out of the water – we had to stay there until they flew away. We were in that water for quite some time! When we got out, we ran like hell to get out of the cold and into the warm baths and got changed.³⁷
>
> Private Oswald McDonald, 'B' Company

Tom Tunney was the son of miner and trade union activist in Thornley. He was working as an apprentice bricklayer when he was called up and posted to the 16th DLI in billets at Winchelsea. He clearly remembered one German air raid when he was on guard duty.

> Standing orders were to shoot at any aircraft approaching from the sea at less than 100 feet. If you were on guard during the night, you were on picket during the day, it was a twenty-four-hour job. We had this sentry box where you used to do your guard duty. There was a road that went down to the beach and the main road went along the coast. Two of you used to stand at this sentry box to stop anybody going down onto the beach. There was a Bren gun mounted on a tripod and you could fire it up a height. This plane came over, it was a Jerry, he was about 1,500 feet up off the coast and the ack-ack was firing at him. I said, 'I'm going have a go at the bugger!' I fired a full magazine off, thirty-odd rounds! The plane just sailed straight over! I had to report to the 'Black Rat', Company Sergeant Major Arthur Pearson, so nicknamed on account of his smart 'patent leather' haircut – amongst other reasons! He says, 'You never in the world tried to shoot that plane down? You couldn't have hit it with a Bofors gun, never mind about a Bren gun!'[38]
>
> Private Tom Tunney, 'C' Company

In most cases, despite aircraft recognition lectures, it was incredibly difficult to determine the nationality of fast moving low-flying aircraft. They had just seconds – and a mistake in identification either way could be fatal. One who could testify to this was Charles Palmer, who was the son of the poet Herbert Palmer from Batley. Although he had done OTC training at St Albans School, on call up he was rejected for a commission and had ended up in the ranks of the 16th DLI on intelligence duties. At 13.40 on 28 September 1942 he was on duty at an observation post on the hill at Rye when several German fighters attacked.

> These two planes came over – and we said, 'Oh, that's all right – they'll be ours!' Being in the Intelligence Section we were supposed to be able to identify aircraft, but when they're down low, flying across, it's difficult. Suddenly, 'BOOM!' Machine guns! They hit the cinema.[39]
>
> Private Charles Palmer, Intelligence Section, Headquarters Company

Four bombs were dropped, and one scored a direct hit on the Regent Cinema in Cinque Ports Street. It all happened so fast.

> They demolished the cinema in the main street one Saturday lunchtime – it was almost opposite our garage. I was standing talking to the MT clerk, Lance Corporal Jock Fisher, just outside. The window was like a big shop window, 12 feet high, taking up the entire front of the garage, except for the entrance. Suddenly there was this terrific roar and cannon fire. I grabbed Jock and banged him down into the gutter. We tried to get as close to the earth as we possibly could! The bomb dropped on the cinema virtually dead centre. The whole thing just disintegrated. There was bricks, glass and God knows what flying and showering down around us. Miraculously neither of us got a mark on us! And it didn't even break the glass in the garage window! It was truly fantastic. As soon as it had gone, we jumped to our feet, pretty shaken I can tell you! All I could see was a leg sticking out of the ruins on the opposite side. We shot across and by then a few more blokes that had been in the garage came out. We started to chuck debris away to try and get in – reasonably carefully. We were working on it for about five to six minutes, then the ARP people came. They found the remnants of the woman cashier. I don't like to contemplate whether her leg was still attached to the rest of her. It affected me very much, I'd never been in such close contact with a bomb, and I was shaking for days! A forty-eight hour thing, I thought I was never going to feel right again, but it went! The following week, the feature film, believe it or not, was to be 'Gone with the Wind'![40]
>
> Private Tom Lister, MT Section, Headquarters Company

One reported fatality was the relief manager from London who had been sent to Rye to get a respite from the London bombing. More fortunate was a woman and her baby who were pulled alive from the shattered foyer where they had taken shelter as the German aircraft appeared above. In all, four civilians were killed and twenty-six were injured.

On 7 October, the 16th DLI held an efficiency competition

to analyse the overall status of the battalion. It was simple in conception. Each platoon had to march 10 miles in two hours in full service marching order, then fire their Lee Enfield rifles, Bren guns and Thompson submachine guns at figure targets, before a session of scaling cliffs using ropes. Every platoon was allotted 500 points from which penalties would be deducted as follows: for each minute over marching time – minus five points; for every man failing to complete the course – minus twenty points, for any shot missing the target – minus one point; and for each man failing to scale the cliffs within ten minutes – minus five points. The winning platoon did well, suffering only 114 penalties. Overall, their colonel was satisfied, but sought to hammer home the lesson of why they were all there.

> The spirit of determination and grit of the men was grand, and I was very much heartened to see it. I am quite sure we have much to be proud of here – and we must make sure that we direct this grand spirit in the right way; and see that it is devoted towards the proper end – the winning of this war and the defeat of evil. Yesterday the men sweated their guts out to see their platoon win and not let their own show down. We must feel the same about our cause and country.[41]
>
> Lieutenant Colonel Richard Ware, Headquarters Company

He was particularly interested in the levels of leadership his NCOs had demonstrated – or not, as was sometimes the case.

> Most leaders came out well in a fairly severe test. Not all the leading was judicious, but this could in many cases be accounted for by lack of experience – but the main point was that they had the men behind them; so that they would have done all they humanly could whatever was asked of them. But – and it's quite a big but – there was also some bad leadership; cases in which commanders and their men were obviously NOT working together. In one platoon of 'D' Company this was very apparent, and I hope the officer commanding the company will have realised this if he saw the platoon. There were other cases of sergeants shouting and blasting their men

> to get them there – particularly in the rope climbing. Whilst in a few cases this works because of the personality of the leader, in many more it fails and the north country man as a rule responds marvellously to good leadership and will give the most extraordinary loyalty and devotion to a leader he respects, but he merely becomes fed up and 'bloody' obstinate if officers and NCOs attempt to drive him. I don't mean by this that the spur is never necessary; of course it often is, but some leaders are all spur![42]
>
> Lieutenant Colonel Richard Ware, Headquarters Company

He was also more than a little concerned that most of the penalties across the board were for shooting deficiencies.

> Even making allowance for physical condition at the end of the march, the shooting was nowhere good and in many cases rank bad. The range was less than 100 yards and nearer 50 yards – the targets were large and stationary – there was simply loads of time – good [firing] positions and the men were in no way hustled. If we are going to get such poor results in these conditions, what is going to happen in battle?[43]
>
> Lieutenant Colonel Richard Ware, Headquarters Company

He resolved to prioritise shooting practice over the next few weeks to improve matters as quickly as possible. Given his remarks above, it is to be hoped that Ware would have been pleased with the attitude shown by Russell King, formerly an apprentice bricklayer from a village near Durham, whose platoon had come a narrow second in the competition. He certainly seems to have had a firm grip of what was required from a sergeant.

> My responsibilities were to the platoon. To see that they operated as an efficient unit. To look after their welfare as well as making sure they were adequately trained. As far as you could. That was the main thing. We used to instil on them that the training was the thing. If they listened to what they were told – and did everything that they were told. Particularly when

we were doing field training. If they kept well apart and didn't all bunch up together, looked for camouflage, the ground, the basic ethics of military training there was less chance of them getting ruddy shot! That was it! You had to instil in them that it was for their own protection.[44]

Sergeant Russell King, 'D' Company

It is interesting to contrast the approach of Charles Bray, whose platoon came second from bottom. Bray was the son of a publican from Buckingham, who had been a solicitor's clerk before his call up. He had been in the very first draft from the Beds and Herts to the 16th DLI and had got rapid promotion. But enough was enough! He was resolved to do his bit – but equally determined to survive the war!

> When I was in Winchelsea, I was called to an interview with Major Balance, to see if I wanted a commission. I said, 'No, I didn't want a commission!' So, he said, 'All right, well, off you go then!' I was being entirely cowardly. I thought, 'Well, when you are a lieutenant and you go abroad, and you lead your troops gallantly into action – the first person to be shot is usually the lieutenant!' I didn't want that to happen to me! I thought, 'Well, I'll be the chap just behind him!' That's why I didn't want any more promotion.[45]
>
> Sergeant Charles Bray, 'D' Company

In the event both King and Bray proved to be very competent NCOs.

On 21 October, several of the men were witnesses to a dramatic incident when an aircraft identified as a JU 88 flew in from the south-east at an altitude of about 500 feet. All the local light anti-aircraft guns opened an enthusiastic barrage, among them some of the Bren guns of the 16th DLI.

> If an aircraft came in low, you had to open fire because the British aircraft had instructions to come over the coast at a certain height. This day I was on duty with another chappie, Jack Poole. He said, 'Aircraft coming in!' And it was spinning

over the sea. We got the Bren gun and fired at it and there was smoke coming from it – I couldn't tell whether we hit it or not, but it came down the other side of Winchelsea – it then dived into the ground – it was a Beaufighter. For our trouble we had to guard it all night! It was hit before we fired.[46]

Private George Forster, 'C' Company

It was a Beaufighter night fighter from 29 Squadron based at RAF West Malling. Unfortunately, it seemed that the RAF roundels were difficult to pick out against the predominantly dark night camouflage. The aircraft crash-landed south of Watlands Farm at Udimore and the crew, Sergeants Alfred Akester[47] and Harold Wright,[48] were both killed.

★

BY THIS TIME, against all the odds, it had been decided that the 16th DLI was ready for active service. This was remarkable as they would prove to be the only one of the sixty 'Dunkirk' battalions raised across the UK to be chosen to fight as a formed body against the Germans. The rest all had a vital role, but they were either broken up, or carried on providing drafts to the end of the war.

The first stage came in early December 1942, when the battalion was embussed to Camberley. Here they settled into billets in unoccupied houses. The battalion had no operational role; its main focus was on getting everyone away on embarkation leave before they went overseas. There was secrecy over their destination, so in the absence of facts the rumour mill went into overdrive.

It was all very 'Hush! Hush!' We left without being able to notify anybody. We just sort of upped sticks and that was it. I don't think anybody had any idea where we were going. Of course, you got the usual rumours – that they'd seen Arctic clothing![49]

Sergeant Russell King, 17 Platoon, 'D' Company

By this time the various disparate drafts had gelled together to form a coherent whole.

> We all wanted stay with the battalion. None of us wanted to leave because we had a good set of lads and you're all 'mucked in'. We were damned good pals. I wouldn't have liked to have left a battalion. When we got eight days we knew something was in the wind that was a hint that we were going somewhere. There were rumours flying around that we were going up to Scotland. I told my wife when I was on my eight days, 'I'll be seeing you – we will be getting a leave from Scotland!' But I didn't![50]
>
> Private Tom Turnbull, 'B' Company

Their embarkation leave was often a bitter-sweet experience. The Great War had left no one under any illusions as to the vicious nature of combat – and of the dreadful casualty lists that resulted.

> We had our home leave – it was December. It was so damn near to Christmas! My family was so distraught – everybody was in tears. Christmas was the sentimental part of the year – supposed to be such a happy time – yet it was a sad time. It was a goodbye occasion, but I was determined to show them that I was happy, to make it easier. So, I was 'a smiler' and left full of good spirits. They were all out looking at me – and I turned around and gave them a good wave – and they waved. That was it.[51]
>
> Company Quartermaster Sergeant Jimmy James, 'D' Company

Not everyone was willing to go. Some were paralysed by fear at the thought of not seeing their loved ones again. The stress did strange things to their thought processes and there was at least one case of a self-inflicted wound.

> There was one guy on the top floor. We knew that some time – it was official – we were going to go abroad. He had just got married and he was determined not to go abroad! It was a Saturday afternoon, and he decides to shoot himself in the foot.

> He got his rifle, put it on his foot and pulled the trigger. The guy in the room below was lying on his bed, fortunately had his legs like this [apart] and the bullet went straight through his bed! A lucky escape there! He gave him a right old rollicking! We never saw the bloke no more – he was put on a very serious charge. But they had to whip him off to hospital.[52]
>
> Private Oswald McDonald, 'B' Company

There was also a case of desertion by a regular defaulter and troublemaker who had already had several clashes with Sergeant James Drake.

> He used to abscond, absent without leave. He always admitted he'd been a rogue all his life. He once said to me, 'They say crime doesn't pay, but I've always made it pay!' What answer is there to that? I said, 'Well, it doesn't pay in the long run!' They put him on emptying all the toilets – he didn't like that job – so he went missing. Next thing we knew, about a month after – he was doing a civilian job. He'd got himself into trouble with the police and finished up with so many weeks jail. Then they'd say, 'Right it's time for him to come out!' They used to telephone, and we used to have to send somebody to go and escort him back to the battalion. Why didn't they get rid of him? He was a fit man – he was A1! He would probably have been a good man in action – you never know! You can't tell how you're going to react to a real battle.[53]
>
> Lance Sergeant James Drake, Carrier Platoon

This bad character was also an accomplished escape artist who made several ingenious escapes during his many arrests and imprisonments. He managed a final escape from Camberley just before they went overseas.

The battalion was up to its neck in final preparations. Every soldier's uniform and kit was inspected, worn clothing was replaced, and equipment made good for any missing, or faulty, items. Everything needed had to be packed away and any extraneous baggage despatched. Then on the afternoon of 18 December, they had the honour of an inspection by George VI.

> We were given the date and the hour. The big day came. The bands were there, the DLI band came down to Camberley. The whole of the division was going to be inspected by King George VI. We were in battledress, spick and span – no arms except for the white belts and the bayonet. Boots really polished! We marched down through Camberley to the band. This military band was wonderful, they were playing 'The Army of the Nile' – it's a stirring march. Solders marching in step, they really were, everybody was marching upright, arms swinging, left, right, nobody out of step at all. We arrived at the place of inspection.[54]
>
> Company Quartermaster Sergeant Jimmy James, 'D' Company

The King's inspection may have been intended to swell their patriotic feelings before they went off to 'face the foe'; but the gallant Durhams did not respond well to the experience. As was so often the case with army ceremonial inspections, their patience had been tested by a long wait in the cold miserable weather.

> We were all drawn up on the parade ground and the King came round and inspected us. He was done up like a bloody shilling dinner. He passed quite close to me – he was powdered up, seemed to have a lot of makeup on! He didn't say anything to anybody! He just walked round, that was it – end of story. It wasn't impressive at all to be honest! A lot of us thought it was a complete waste of bloody time, they'd all been stood there for hours.[55]
>
> Sergeant Russell King, 'D' Company

This was a common response to the experience.

> We were standing there for ages before he came – an endless age. At one time I thought I was going to 'see black'. I was standing for so long and you daren't move – the blood just leaves your head. Fortunately, I recovered. I remember thinking, 'God, I'll be glad when this is all over!' When the King approached in front of me, I could see him coming from

my left. I was just looking straight ahead, but peripheral vision gave me the King. He had his best uniform on and was 'made up to the nines' with rouge and powder and paint. With his entourage – he had the brigadier and colonel with him. He stood in front of every man – didn't say anything to anyone. I don't think he spoke a word – because he stammered.[56]

Company Quartermaster Sergeant Jimmy James, 'D' Company

Several of the men noticed that the King was wearing face powder and possibly lipstick. In fairness, he was not a strong man, and his health was generally precarious. The makeup was probably to give the illusion of good health.

> We stood in some park near Camberley for about three and a half hours in the cold, whole of the 46th Division. Then after the King had walked up down and inspected the troops, he got in a car to drive off and the regimental sergeant major shouted, 'If you want to run to the roadway and cheer, you can!' Well, it was that cold that hardly anybody moved. It was perishing cold! It was December. That was the reception he got![57]

Private George Forster, 'C' Company

It is interesting to note that the regimental diary, always a somewhat dubious beacon of honesty when it comes to the reputation of the regiment, recorded that:

> His Majesty walked along the ranks and spoke to a number of the officers and men, before the regimental band played the battalion back to the billets, the men cheering continuously, lined the road along which the King drove away. A memorable day.[58]

It is up to reader to decide where the truth lies.

The main body of the battalion left from Farnborough station in two trains on the night of 21 December.

> We marched to the railway station, got on a troop train at approximately seven o'clock in the evening. We travelled all night. No one knew which destination we were going! It was

just getting till daylight as we pulled into a big town and one of the lads, he was from Liverpool, says, 'Oooh, there's our house!' And we realised we were in Liverpool! We went straight through on to the docks. We never got a chance to look or see anything. They shepherded us from the train straight on to the boat. A matter of 10 yards. Military police were everywhere – there was no chance of anybody absconding![59]

Private George Forster, 'C' Company

By 12.30 on 22 December, the men were nearly all safely aboard the troopship *Staffordshire*. But where were they going?

3

THE GREAT ADVENTURE

> Get your head in your trench. Keep down and hope to God that they didn't drop a mortar bomb anywhere near your position. There was shrapnel flying everywhere! It's really frightening! But everybody stuck to their jobs, whatever they had to do.[1]
>
> Private George Forster, 'C' Company

HOW DID THE GREAT ADVENTURE START? As usual in the army there was a fair amount of hurry up and wait. The men were rushed aboard the troopship *Staffordshire,* which then moved only as far as the middle of the Mersey – where it then sat still for the best part of three days. The ship was crammed to the brim with soldiers.

> We found our bedding and a 'bed' – the lads were sleeping on tables, on hammocks, on the floor! I ended up sleeping on the dining table. There was that many troops – it was full of troops. It was not very comfortable. We happened to be right at the very bottom of the ship – and with the engines throbbing you couldn't get any sleep.[2]
>
> Private George Forster, 'C' Company

They set sail at last at 11.00 on Christmas Day, 25 December 1942, a day that in peacetime they would normally have spent at home with their loved ones. It was a poignant moment, as they were going to war – and they were well aware that some of them would not be coming back.

At last, the ship's anchor was drawn up and it moved downstream towards the open sea. Nearly all the troops on board were lining the ship's rails and no doubt, like me, they all wanted to see as much of dear old England as they could before she faded from view – perhaps for ever. I was leaning over the rail of the port side and was feeling pretty miserable. My thoughts were of the folks at home. Suddenly I was startled by the sound of loud cheers. The noise came from the starboard side, and I made my way across to find out what it was all about. After a struggle, I managed to get to the rail and saw a little British destroyer steaming close alongside us. She was displaying a big white sheet and printed on it in block letters was a message of good will: 'A HAPPY CHRISTMAS TO ALL ON BOARD'. I shall remember that greeting as long as I live.[3]

Company Sergeant Major George Gates, Headquarters Company

The officers tried their best to comfort their men, with religious services and a splendid dinner of pork, two vegetables and plum duff. The King's speech and festive programmes were broadcast round the ship from the wireless. The brigadier even wirelessed a special message as recorded in the war diary: 'Good luck lads, good hunting and a safe return for next Christmas.' The reply was sent, 'Many thanks. Will do best assist get bloody job over'.[4] As soon as it got out into open waters, the ship started to pitch and roll. It was only a slight swell, but these men were not natural sailors.

We went up the Irish Sea towards the Clyde. There was a big convoy coming out and we were joining it. We got up there and I was all right – but I felt a bit queasy! I stayed on deck! And by gum it was a rough sea! I was at the back of the boat and I'm watching the ship coming up, I thought, 'It's never going to stop going up! I'm sure I'll see the propellor any minute!' Then down she used to go! I stayed up as long as I could – I didn't want to go below. I had to go to the toilet. Well! The toilets! It was a great trough along one side, running water all the time, you used to cock your bottom over that trough! I got halfway down this short flight of stairs to the heads, and it hit me! Oh,

> dear me! I was bad! I never got in to have a meal. I nearly died of seasickness! I was useless. I finished up in the sickbay. It was days before I got on to my feet.[5]
>
> Private Gordon Gent, MT Section, 'A' Company

It wasn't just the restless movement of the ship. Everything seemed to conspire against their queasy stomachs.

> The *Staffordshire* was old, and it wasn't as clean as it might have been! Despite denials by the captain there was oil getting into the bilges somewhere. Depending on which deck you were – the lower down you got in the ship – the more the stench was! I was on the third deck down. It didn't do anybody any good! This oily stench all the time.[6]
>
> Private Tom Lister, MT Section, Headquarters Company

Of course, some bright sparks were impervious to the nausea that afflicted the majority. The last thing one would expect in the army is sympathy.

> Believe me, I've never seen so many violently sick in all my life. They were throwing up all over the place! When I was relieved of duty, I went down into the sergeants' mess deck for breakfast – and I upset one or two by asking them if they wanted a nice piece of pork fat! I enjoyed a good breakfast because there was that many sick so there was plenty of food that morning! As much as one could tackle![7]
>
> Lance Sergeant James Drake, Carrier Platoon

Most of the men began to feel better after a couple of days. The officers and NCOs organised PT sessions and some marching up and down around the decks to try and keep up their fitness levels. The officers were given special instructional lectures in various useful topics such as minefields, intelligence reports and the use of the American phonetic alphabet, which they were to adopt to avoid confusion in working with the US Army. As for recreations, there was very little to do. Many resorted to cards to while away the weary hours.

> Gambling was the main pastime. You could only get the cards out and do a bit of the usual card games. Some used to play 'Solo', but my soft spot was the old 'Three Card Brag'. We got quite a few schools going on that amongst the lads. I came out very, very well; I won quite a bit of money![8]
>
> Lance Sergeant James Drake, Carrier Platoon

Many of the men walked on deck, looking round at all the other ships in the large convoy. Then, on 28 December, there was a submarine alarm and a swathe of naval escorts leapt into frenetic action.

> I recall the destroyers were running fast round the whole of the convoy. We had two submarine scares – they were at full speed ahead dropping the depth charges from the rear of the destroyer. You could see the depth charges going up into the air, dropping into the sea. And then two or three minutes after, a big spout of water coming up when it exploded! Although the German submarines were there, they managed to keep them out.[9]
>
> Lance Sergeant James Drake, Carrier Platoon

None of the men had much idea of where they were going, and it remained a popular topic of discussion. After all it really was a matter of life or death to these men. Each theatre of war had its own perils, its own disadvantages.

> I was really sure we were going out into the Far East. But when we got into the Mediterranean, everybody was surmising where we were going! Some said Eighth Army; some said the Far East; nobody ever dreamt that it was going to be the First Army in Algiers! We passed Tangiers and it was all lit up at night! Somebody shouted, 'Come on – there's some lights out here!' Everybody dashed up – one mad rush – it was only for about half an hour and then back into darkness. The next thing it was dawn and there were all these white houses on land! We still didn't know where we were! And we pulled in to what we learnt later was Algiers![10]
>
> Private George Forster, 'C' Company

They arrived at Algiers at 13.00 on 1 January 1943. By the time they disembarked on to the quayside it was late afternoon. They were informed that they would have to march to a transit camp only 3 to 5 miles away. What happened next lingered long in their collective memory.

> We formed up and we had to do a march to our destination, which was a place just outside Algiers. I'll never forget that march! We walked, carrying your full kit: big pack on your back, your small pack on side, your rifle, a Bren gun distributed among three of you! We trudged along. Five minutes before the hour we stopped. We were absolutely leg-weary. Some sat down on the side of the road, and they couldn't get up – we had to pull them up with their rifle! It seemed cobblestones all the way and it was terrible on your feet.[11]
>
> Lance Sergeant James Drake, Carrier Platoon

Their ordeal lasted for what proved to be fifteen long painful miles. To make matters worse it started to rain.

> We marched and the officer in charge, he kept saying, 'It's only about 3 miles!' The longest 3 miles I've every marched! It was raining that hard we had gas capes on. We were soaking, absolutely soaking!![12]
>
> Private George Forster, 'C' Company

At last, they staggered into their destination, the Eucalyptus camp at Maison-Carrée. The term camp was perhaps a euphemism, for it was just an empty vineyard warehouse, with no concessions to comfort.

> Eventually we got to this vineyard. It was concrete floors and there was some straw there and we were lying on greatcoats trying to get a bit of sleep but it wasn't very comfortable! In our group I was the first one up and I walked outside the door and crikey, there was grape vines and orange groves! I went back and shouted to the lads, 'There something to eat and drink here!' We went out and filled our battledresses with oranges. That soon stopped, because the Frenchman that owned it, he

complained to the CO that the lads were stealing his fruit. They wouldn't give you anything; they gave you the impression that didn't want you there really![13]

Private George Forster, 'C' Company

The men spent the days checking their kit, especially their weapons and going on route marches to bring them up to peak fitness. The Bren carriers were also collected from the docks. Then in the evenings liberty trucks were laid on to take men back to Algiers. What happened there was not 'nice', but it was an understandable reaction from young men going to war.

There were three places for 'exhibitions' – bordellos shall we call them? They were very opulent: one was called the Black Cat, another the Number Twenty-Two, the other the Half Moon. Most of the battalion – and every other regiment in Algiers – were queuing up four deep waiting to go in – a queue three-quarters of a mile or a mile long! The married men – they wouldn't think of it! They were newly out of England; they'd just said goodbye to their loved ones! But for the unmarried, the footloose and fancy free – soldiers are soldiers and sailors are sailors! There were military police at the entrances to keep order and arrest any miscreants! You had to pay to go in to see the exhibitions. That was what I wanted more than anything else! You had to go inside, you paid, and they had hundreds of red plush seats. Chandeliers everywhere! And mirrors and chrome! They were palaces. If you wanted to sit in the seats, the available ladies were walking about in circles – in front of you! If anybody fancied one of those, he'd tap her on the shoulder, and she'd take him away! The ladies were inspected and 'passed' several times a day by service doctors. To go to the exhibitions, one had to ascend the stairs. There were queues for that as well! It was like live theatre done by lesbians. You wouldn't see it anywhere else in the world. There were officers there, drinking beers and senior naval officers. Seeing these people – [we knew] it was condoned! It was not broadcast, and nobody talks about it! We were going up to the line in two or three days.[14]

Company Quartermaster Sergeant Jimmy James, 'D' Company

Going 'up to the line' was what all the training had been about. But were they really ready for war? They would soon find out.

*

NORTH AFRICA HAD BECOME THE FOCUS of British and American efforts in 1942. Winston Churchill was sceptical of any chances of a successful invasion of mainland Europe in 1942, a view reinforced by the total failure of the Dieppe Raid on 19 August 1942. However, he was also under severe pressure to launch a 'Second Front' to help Soviet Russia, which was engaged in a titanic battle with the main force of the German Army. In response, Churchill pressed hard for a concentration on the Mediterranean theatre of war in accordance with his long-standing belief in seeking out a 'soft underbelly' to attack, notwithstanding the utter failure of such a strategy in the Great War – as highlighted by the Gallipoli, Salonika and Mesopotamia campaigns. He wanted to clear the Germans out of North Africa, clear the Mediterranean and assault Italy. The Americans grudgingly fell in with his view, believing they were only postponing the invasion until 1943, and they certainly harboured doubts about any future invasion of Italy. In the end, the real assault on 'Fortress Europe' would have to wait until 6 June 1944.

The path was set: an offensive would be launched by the Eighth Army (General Bernard Montgomery) which would push out from El Alamein and drive the Panzer Army Africa (General Erwin Rommel) through Libya and right back to Tunis. While thus distracted, on 8 November 1942, the Americans, under the overall command of Lieutenant General Dwight Eisenhower, would make a series of landings in French North Africa: the Western Task Force at Casablanca on the Atlantic coast of Morocco; the Central Force at Oran on the Algerian coast; the Eastern Force at Algiers.

After an initial resistance, the French first signed a truce and then joined the Allies, provoked by the German move into the hitherto unoccupied area of Vichy France. As the Allies began to push the Germans eastwards, they formed the First Army under the command of General Kenneth Anderson and consisting of the US II Corps, the British V Corps and the French XIX Corps, while Eisenhower set up his Supreme Headquarters in Algiers.

Initially successful, the First Army had made rapid progress pushing eastwards towards Tunis, assisted by British subsidiary landings at first Bougie and then Bone. However, the Axis resistance stiffened, as Hitler decided that Tunisia had to be held at all costs. The Germans took up strong defensive positions on a line centred on three large hills: Green Hill (Dj Azzag), Baldy Hill (Dj El Ajved) and Sugar Loaf (Dj Azag). Not all North Africa is desert, and pouring rain marked the onset of winter, reducing the roads to mud filled ruts, and rendering life a misery for the troops up on the hillsides. Further south the Germans counter-attacked on 1 December and soon First Army was locked in a static battle reminiscent of the Western Front in 1914–18.

*

THE 16TH DLI JOURNEY TO THE FRONT BEGAN when the men and then the Bren gun carriers were entrained to take them forward some 500 miles as a small part of the 46th Division (128 Brigade, 138 Brigade and 139 Brigade) under the command of Major-General Harold Freeman-Attwood. It proved to be a tiresome uncomfortable journey as the trains travelled at what seemed a snail's pace.

> We seemed to be on this train for ever and ever! I think you could have bloody marched faster than what the train was going! The train stopped and I said to this bloke, 'Go and get me some water – I'll have a shave!' The engine driver wouldn't give him any water. I went up to this engine driver and I'm trying to talk pidgin French to him about, 'Wanting l'eau!' and he was from bloody Crook[15] – a postman! I couldn't believe it! He was in the Royal Engineers and was driving the train.[16]
>
> Sergeant Russell King, 'D' Company

The Durhams finally arrived at Ghardimaou on 15 January. Here they met the lorries and other vehicles which had been driving for the last four days. They then moved by lorry to the reserve lines at Sedjenane. The senior officers went forward to examine the positions they were to take over from the 5th Royal East Kent Regiment (The Buffs). Plans were laid for the relief operation on the night of 17 January.

> In the early morning, we moved, and everybody had to be quiet as we went – no shouting, no loud speaking. It was dark when we went into these positions and out comes the Kent lads and all they said was, 'The best of luck to you!' We took over their positions facing in Green Hill. Slit trenches everywhere. You could get two men, or three men in, depending how long they were. About 7 or 8 foot long and as deep as they could get down – most of them are about 3 foot 6 inches to 4 foot. At the most about 3 foot wide. After we'd been there a while we went [scrounging] and we found some steel and we put that over the top so that if any mortars dropped, or shrapnel, it hit the steel plates. We used to use 'compo' boxes put them together to make a bed.[17]
>
> Private George Forster, 'C' Company

The slit trenches were facing the Germans who were up on Green Hill and Baldy Hill. In front of the British positions there was barbed wire and a minefield across the road that wound through the valley. A railway line ran through the ridge and towards the German positions. Initially, 'A' Company was on the right of the plateau to the south of the railway line, 'C' Company was on the left occupying the ridge on either side of the railway tunnel, 'B' Company was acting as a flank guard on the right, 'D' Company was in reserve, while the Headquarters Company was based in the tunnel.

> Everything was quiet. We used to get the occasional mortar shell across. Morning 'stand to' was just about an hour before daybreak till daybreak. Everybody went in the slit trenches – and you were on the alert. You didn't know what was going to happen. The officer or NCO would be moving around to

see if everything was all right. During the day somebody was always on guard in the trenches for about two or three hours at a time.[18]

Private Tom Turnbull, 'B' Company

The men not in the forward slit trenches would be 10–20 yards back in dugouts made by previous units on the reverse slopes of the ridge. The 4th Royal West Kents were to their left, but they too were relieved on the arrival of the 2/5th Sherwood Foresters on the night of 18/19 January. The 2/5th Leicesters were in the reserve area further back. There were some grim signs of the previous fighting in No Man's Land.

> There were three or four Bren carriers on the road, which belonged to the Argyle and Sutherland Highlanders. We could see them in the bottom – and the Germans could see them from their positions. There were dead soldiers in them – and they'd been there for a few weeks. We tried to get in to fetch the bodies out, but every time we got anywhere near, they used to open up artillery, mortar fire and machine-gun fire, so we never did get them out.[19]

Private George Forster, 'C' Company

The days stretched by slowly for the men up on the ridge.

> There was no activity, no troop movements, or anything like that. Not in daylight. You just lay down. You slept during the day. Very boring. There was no risk of being shot at because we were on the backside of the hill. There was only the two chaps up on top with a periscope. When it was our turn for duty, we used to go in a big slit trench right on the top of the hill. Officers used to come around and you weren't allowed to smoke during the night. Because when you lit a match – the Germans could see it! Sometimes, if you got in your slit trench and put a coat over, you could have a smoke in the back, but you weren't supposed to! You had a periscope, and you could see all the German defences down below about 1,000 yards away. They were dug in in the hillside. On a morning, at dawn,

you could see them coming out and shaking their blankets. We told our officer and next thing we knew was the Royal Artillery officer came up, stayed the night with us and he saw them. He was on a field telephone, and he directed the guns where to fire. It was fantastic.[20]

Private George Forster, 'C' Company

The supporting artillery was provided by the twenty-four 25-pounder guns of 70th Field Regiment, (277 Battery, 279 Battery and 449 Battery). The gunners would be a vital part of the 16th DLI story throughout the campaigns to follow.

The 'B' Echelon was located back at Sedjenane. This was the logistical heart of the battalion, where was held the MT, the food supplies, the kit and ammunition. There was also an old tobacco factory which acted as a rest centre for the men coming back from the front line.

> The tobacco factory was empty. It was two corrugated iron buildings on a hill, it wasn't too steep. The bottom one had a loading bank about 6-foot high. The inside of the two buildings was all open, but from the outside they appeared to be two separate buildings. That was used by us for sleeping, for chaps coming back and getting deloused, the occasional bath or wash. There the [Quartermaster] Bert Newman was very crafty, he didn't go near the bloody place, he was over in the woods with all his trucks, with trenches dug! It was an open-air store with camouflage nets with all his transport under cover.[21]

Company Quartermaster Sergeant Jimmy James, 'D' Company

Driver Gordon Gent was one of those located in the thick cork woods which hid them from prying eyes above. He and the rest of the 'B' Echelon personnel had a vital role, indeed the men at the front could not have existed long without the food and ammunition supplies brought up every night by lorry. It was not an easy drive.

> The mud! Dear me! We had to plough through – on our Canadian trucks we had very good heavy chains to put on the

wheels. They were meant for use for ice and snow, but they were invaluable in mud. Because we were in and out from this laager area up the line each night with food, carrying the rations for the lads. Ammunition as well. Every night there was a convoy went up – no lights on – hairpin bends! A Don R led the convoy, he was the only one with a little light on his motorbike! We had no lights at all in front. You were just following a little tiny light on the differential at the back of the truck in front of view – it was like a fag-end! When I saw that road in daylight that we'd been travelling up my heart nearly stopped. You couldn't see the bottom – no fences or anything![22]

Private Gordon Gent, MT Section, 'A' Company

The trucks could only get so far forward. Then it was all down to the muscle power of ration parties sent back from the companies in the line.

> The rations came up at dusk. They were brought to about a mile or so behind the lines – and we had to detail a party to carry these 'compo' boxes. Each man needs to carry one. Seven-man rations for one day. There was a tin of fifty cigarettes, tins of cheese, tins of jam, tins of rice pudding. Biscuits – hard tack! Tea, sugar and milk all in one powder. You just took your mug to the cooks and they topped you up. You got tins of Maconochies meat and veg stew. It had to be warmed up and a little bit further back from us a petrol blower, like a primus stove to warm it up. They used to warm it up and carry it up to the lads in a haybox. Quite palatable – it filled an empty hole![23]

Private George Forster, 'C' Company

Plain, simple food, that was all that the army offered, but it was also all the men needed in active service conditions. What was important was to ensure that the food always arrived on time, and the simplicity of the 'compo' system certainly facilitated that.

> I liked the 'compo' rations. They were all packed in individual cartons within the wooden box. Marked 'COMPO 'A', 'B' or 'C'

> whichever they were! You never really knew what was in them until you opened them. They had large tins of stew to be shared between so many. Or, alternatively, if you were lucky, which you weren't often, tinned chicken. They had tins of bacon, sometimes the fat greasy English bacon, then again if you were lucky, the Australian streaky bacon, which was much superior. Smaller portions of tinned cheese, tinned jam or marmalade. Hard tack biscuits. Tins of dried tea and milk. Five cigarettes a man, in round fifty cigarette tins. Tins of fruit, tins of rice pudding, or steamed puddings – ginger puddings or 'spotted dick' in tins. I found they were quite good. The only trouble was getting them heated up properly.[24]
>
> Private Tom Lister, MT Section, Headquarters Company

The water supply was limited, although they did find a small stream on the reverse slope that allowed them to have a wash and shave. But they were still afflicted by a pest that their fathers could have warned them about from their Great War service.

> I was lousy – I caught the buggers! I was given by Bert Newman a great big tin of carbolic anti-louse powder. It was called AL63! Well, I put some of that on my balls! And I jumped a mile! I thought I'd ruined my bloody self! I went to the Doctor, and he laughed his head off! He said, 'You silly bastard, balls are sweaty! You'll be all right, they won't fester and drop off!' Having the time, I took my shirt off and used to have a cigarette lighter, get the flame up, and I'd go right up the seam of my shirt, under the arms as well. I wasn't long enough to burn the shirt, but it would burn the lice – swell them up and burst them! and I bloody 'popped' the lot , 'POP! POP! POP! POP! POP!' All these lice![25]
>
> Company Quartermaster Sergeant Jimmy James, 'D' Company

Another pest familiar to their forefathers in Flanders was the rats, although they seem to have come in several varieties.

> Great big, coloured rats used to come around the place. Stripey ones, big ones, little ones! Some men when they went to sleep,

put lit candles by their head to keep these rats away from them. Then they used to put some biscuits from the roof, suspended by a string. We used to watch the rats crawl up the side, go along the top and then dive into the basket of hardtack biscuits. They'd do that several times, until they tore a hole in it, then they would all congregate in the middle of the hut eating the biscuits – then we would bang at them with our bayonets![26]

Lance Corporal Thomas Atkinson, 'B' Company

Meanwhile, on most nights a combination of standing, recce and fighting patrols were out in No Man's Land feeling their way to determine the exact location and strength of the German defences.

Seven of us and the NCO. 'You, you, and you!' The NCO would say, 'Try and see if you can find what's behind that part of the hill!' We used to blacken our faces, we used to get the cork from the cork trees at Sedjenane and burn it – it was like charcoal. We wore plimsolls and denims. Your rifle or your Bren gun. You were probably out two hours, across into enemy lines, seeing what you could pick up, see what you could find, take any prisoners you could catch. We used to walk in single file, no talking, no noise whatsoever. It was all whispering. The first one, when we got back, we'd lost a man – he'd been taken prisoner. We must have passed a German platoon – they collared the back one! We knew nothing about it. After that, we devised a method of some thin string. It used to be round everyone's arm and you could feel if anybody was taken – but it never happened after the first time! We'd get right up to their front line – 20 to 25 yards away – sometimes you would hear them talking. If they spotted you, or thought they spotted you, they used to fire Very lights and start firing mortars and machine guns. We would just drop flat and stay there for probably quarter of an hour. And then make your way back to our lines.[27]

Private George Forster, 'C' Company

It was a tense business. At any moment they could be ambushed

– and it certainly did not help when they knew they were meant to provoke a reaction.

> There was a standing patrol and they got up on this hillside, where they had observation of all the German area. Their job was to pinpoint where all the German fire was coming from. We on the fighting patrol were told that we were going to try and attract the fire, which wasn't very pleasant. We made our way along this hillside, all cactus and bad going. There was the company commander in front, I more or less adjacent to him. I went to go through this gap, and he pulled me back, quite quickly, because he must have seen they had a trip wire across this gap! We all stepped over it then, told the blokes to step over this trip wire. We hadn't gone, maybe about another 50 yards – this big German stood almost right in front of us and shouts, 'Hände hoch!' Bugger! All hell was let loose. It was like bloody Guy Fawkes Day! All the bloody German Army went to panic stations! Talk about attracting fire, I think we attracted all the bloody fire that there was! We made our way back rather hurriedly! When we got back, we had a count – and there was two blokes missing. O'Leary, the mortar man, was one of them – and his mate! No doubt about it; we should have counted them up before we started back! It's one of those things! The company commander said, 'We'll have to go back for them!' Him and I went back. By that time the bloody place was alive! You couldn't move for shellfire, mortar fire, odd rifles and Spandaus going off! All sorts! We went back to where we'd been. Couldn't find them! Couldn't find a bloody trace of them. We got back to our own lines; it must have been three or four o'clock in the morning. As far as we were concerned, they were missing. Lo and behold, the next night O'Leary came in as bold as brass – he'd walked right in front of the minefield in front of us. He'd got lost in the pandemonium and been laid up in the cactus all that day.[28]
>
> Sergeant Russell King, 'D' Company

There were also occasional Bren carrier patrols going out to check the wider area.

> A section of three carriers would patrol the road for about 3 miles down to a junction where there was a bridge over the river in case German troops in small numbers would come up during the night and lay land mines. We used to go over the bridge, turn round and then rest up for ten minutes! Have a cigarette and then come back. We never heard any of our own planes; we thought we hadn't got any in that area. On two occasions, we heard Messerschmitts coming over, machine gunning the road, dropped a couple of small bombs, then turn round and strafe the road again. You could see all the dust flying up from the bullets! As soon as we saw the planes, we ran off the road and got underneath the carriers. Got the Bren gun ready as they passed; then we could have at least a fire at them from the rear. You didn't get a lot of rounds off, because they were too fast. We didn't fetch any down! But we might have put one or two bullets in them! I don't recall them ever hitting one of the carriers.[29]
>
> Lance Sergeant James Drake, Carrier Platoon

On one occasion a foot patrol was sent out to check the crash site of an aircraft shot down by a German fighter. For Oswald McDonald it was a horrific experience.

> We had an idea of where it had landed in No Man's Land. Sergeant Dowell and myself had to go and find out what had happened. Dowell said, 'You go down there, I'll stand back and give you covering fire in case anyone comes!' [The pilot] was in the cockpit, I'm trying to move him about, looking for his identification disc – and as true as I'm sat here – his eyeball was hanging out like on a string – moving about! He was a South African bloke – and he didn't have any disc on him. But they used to have on the back of your shirt was your army number, to distinguish whose it was. I had to get my jack-knife out and cut the collar to take that so they could recognise who he was. It was really dreadful with his eye moving about. At the time it didn't worry me at all. We went back and about two hours after I was trembling, couldn't control it, panicking. An aftershock I suppose![30]
>
> Private Oswald McDonald, 'B' Company

Most of the men were coping well with this introduction to war. But there was at least one case of what the authorities considered to be a self-inflicted wound. Even for those men who knew the man concerned, it was difficult to tell what had really happened.

> I had one man there, a young lad, eighteen or nineteen, blew his finger off. He said, 'It was an accident, Sarge! I couldn't help it!' He'd put his rifle behind the trench, he'd reached out to get it, got hold of it by the muzzle to pull it – and the grass or something must have got caught in the trigger and it went off! I said, 'Well why the heck didn't you have the bloody safety catch on?' He said, 'I cleaned it and forgot to put it back on!' The lad was upset his bloody hand was all powder burns and a finger missing. It could have been an accident; he could have done it on purpose! I don't know – I don't think he did myself. They took him away and he was on a charge for a self-inflicted wound. I never heard what happened to him.[31]
>
> Sergeant John Douglass, 'C' Company

On 22 February 1943, the 'B' Company Headquarters came under German mortar fire. This came as a total surprise to Thomas Atkinson.

> I was wrestling with this chap, Johnny Fox, we were having a bit of fun, then this mortar came over and a piece hit him. I had to have a look at it and he had a huge hole in his kidneys. We did what we could for him, but it was hopeless. I tried to put a field dressing on, but he was dead within seconds.[32] It didn't seem long. It was rather a shock to all of us. That night we got orders to withdraw into Sedjenane. As it got dark, I and one of the other stretcher bearers got on this pickup truck and they took us back in the dark to collect the body. It was quite heavy work, because it was over rough country, and the truck was about 2–3 miles away and we had to carry this body back. Took him back to Sedjenane and then we had to dig a grave and bury him.[33]
>
> Lance Corporal Thomas Atkinson, 'B' Company

The companies would take it in turns to hold the line and to have rest periods back at the Sedjenane tobacco factory.

> We went back down to Sedjenane for a bath – clean-up and a good wash! A change of clothing! One or two of them had lice – it was just one of those things. The Royal Engineers made showers of a sort. It was a 50-gallon drum with water in, you pulled the handle – and you got a shower. There were toilets there as well in the woods – a wooden pole across a big pit. It was a bit uncomfortable![34]
>
> Private George Forster, 'C' Company

The Germans knew exactly where the Durhams' rest area was and would frequently launch sudden air raids. The cork trees provided excellent cover, but they were certainly not bullet proof.

> Every day they were over strafing these woods! On the outskirts of the wood, they put watch people who had whistles. If they heard or saw aircraft approaching, they blew their whistles violently and warned us. Everybody took whatever cover they could find. They used to come belting over, low over the tops of the trees. Before you knew where you were the damn things were over the treetops. Machine guns belting – cutting a swathe through the damn trees. They couldn't maybes see you, but they knew you were all in there! It was frightening, by gum it was! There were lots of casualties.[35]
>
> Private Gordon Gent, MT Section, 'A' Company

One raid came just as a 'D' Company was about to commence a delousing parade. Lice could itch and give you a nasty nip, but these flying pests were deadly.

> The whistles blew – that was the signal if there were aircraft! Army whistles were blowing all over the bloody place! We were told that if there was any aircraft coming over – and danger of attack – troops must remain within the buildings and not show themselves outside. Let them think the place was empty! I was standing in the middle of the tobacco factory, with all these

troops, Everybody, dashed to the edge of the buildings, all the way round! I was sitting in the centre with the Regimental Quartermaster Sergeant Golightly, I had to get down there, because the bombs started falling. Moaning, screaming Stukas going round and round in a circle like eagles. They came down one by one, dead down on the buildings, firing everything they had, we were the target, we knew because we looked up at the corrugated iron roof and we saw thousands of daylight holes appearing. And the bullets were bouncing around the concrete floor. Most of the troops were around the perimeter inside the building – not a soul left the building – that was the discipline. The old ack-ack outside stood their ground – and they were very vulnerable these ack-ack chaps, 'BUM! BUM! BUM! BUM! BUM!' Non-stop! It must have been firing right into the eyeballs of the German pilots! Bloody bombs came down, 'BOOOOOOM!' I counted thirteen bombs all around! Still the bloody bullets were coming through. And we weren't hit! I was so frightened that I scraped the concrete with my nails trying to get under the bloody thing! I made my fingers bleed! That was the terror! Suddenly no more sound – nothing – instant silence and dead blackness! A bloody bomb had dropped so near – that was the fourteenth bomb! I thought, 'I'm dead!' I felt my body all over, 'No, I'm not!' I got on my knees; there was all these lads, but there was dead silence. I said to the RQMS, 'Are you there? He said, 'Yes, Jimmy, I think we're buried!' I said, 'No we're not! I'm on my knees!' He said, 'Reach out!' Our hands met and he said, 'Now, let's get up! And for Christ's sake walk slowly, Jimmy!' He was a mature chap, must have been in his middle-forties! 'Let's take small steps. I don't know what the hell this bloody blackness is!' We were in the smoke cloud of the bomb, the cordite, it was pitch black. We walked through; it was many feet in diameter. We stepped out of it like stepping through a wall into blinding sunlight! We looked at each other and we were covered like flour men! Absolutely covered – every bloody thing – in the white dust! There were nine dead men – just there. The bomb had dropped where they were. One had his guts removed. One had one in his forehead! I recognised them – they were signallers. A Roman Catholic padre, a young beefy-faced Irishman, appeared on the scene. He knelt down and he gave them the 'Last Rites'.[36]

Company Quartermaster Sergeant Jimmy James, 'D' Company

On 23 February 1943, the battalion's period holding the front line came to an end, as the whole of 139 Brigade was withdrawn to become the IX Corps reserve. The 16th DLI was concentrated at Sedjenane. A few days later the storm broke.

4

BATTLE OF SEDJENANE

After that first day, the rumours coming around, that such and such a one's got killed. Your mates who you knew were missing – either captured or killed. It's a blow all right – you'd been with them two or three years in training. In a matter of a couple of days, you've lost quite a few of them. We had the job of burying the dead. Well, the ground was bone hard, and we just got them under the ground and put a bit of topsoil on them. That's all you could do.[1]

Lance Corporal Thomas Atkinson, 'B' Company

BOTH SIDES WERE PLANNING TO ATTACK but the Axis forces struck first. They had been reorganised when von Arnim's Fifth Panzer Army was combined with Rommel's Panzer Army Africa to form a single Army Group Africa under Rommel's command. On 14 February 1943, the Germans launched a concerted attack on the Kasserine Pass, where they caused mayhem among the relatively inexperienced – and initially outnumbered – American defenders. The Germans broke through the mountain pass and smashed their way some 40 miles forward with the intention of splitting the US II Corps from the rest of First Army to the north and cutting its main supply line along the Tebessa road. It took a while to sort themselves out, but eventually the Allied resistance firmed up and Rommel withdrew from the Kasserine Pass to turn his attention to Montgomery's imminent offensive on the Mareth Line.

Then on 26 February 1943, the relative peace and calm to the north of the First Army front was broken when the Germans launched two more offensives, which were in essence spoiling attacks, aimed at forcing a temporary Allied withdrawal, or at the very least delaying any planned advance towards Tunis. Operation Ochsenkopf (Ox Head) was a three-pronged attack: the northern group were to advance to capture Béja; the second to envelop the British at Mejez El Bab; and the third to carry out a pincer attack in the Bou Arouda valley before an advance on El Aroussa. A subsidiary operation Operation Ausladung (Bulge), proved to be a more direct threat to the 16th DLI. The Germans planned to use an improvised division (commanded by Colonel von Manteuffel), to outflank the British troops in their strong ridge positions facing Green Hill and Baldy Hill by attacking along the coastal strip to the north which was only weakly held by the Corps Francs d'Afrique. The German intention was to cut the communications from Jefna to Djebel Abiod and to cover the northern flank of Operation Ochsenkopf. Manteuffel's troops included motorised infantry of the Luftwaffe Fallschirmjäger Barenthin Regiment, and the Italian 10th Bersaglieri Regiment. The surprise attack broke through the Free French forces and drove on to approach Sedjenane from the north, which meant that the Axis forces were now behind the British positions and fast approaching the 16th DLI in their reserve positions.

> The first thing we knew, the French troops came streaming past us, saying, 'Allemand! Allemand!' Everybody got dressed, stand to, then we went into action. The Germans had broken through the French on the flank, and we were sent in to stop them, because they'd have come round behind the division.[2]
>
> Private Tom Turnbull, 'B' Company

Everyone was caught on the hop – but most of all poor Colonel Richard Ware who – all oblivious to the imminent threat – was engaged in a recce accompanied by all his company commanders in preparation for the battalion's planned move to Teboursouk. This left the battalion under the command of Major David Bannerman and the various company second in commands. This was not ideal to say the least and the situation was very confused with no clarity as to either how many Germans were attacking, or indeed their current location. As a first response, the battalion moved out of their tented camp to take up positions around the MT lines. That night Bannerman reported to brigade headquarters to get orders. When he returned early next day, he brought the news that the 16th DLI, accompanied by two troops of No. 1 Commando, were to launch a counterattack with an intended Zero Hour of 05.30 on 27 February. They were to advance northwards, to take possible German positions on the Bordj des Monopoles hill supported by the guns of the 70th Field and 5th Medium Regiments, Royal Artillery. They would advance along the Gap Sherrat road into the Sedjenane valley: 'A' Company would be leading, then the forward battalion headquarters, followed by 'B' and 'D' Companies, with 'C' Company acting as the reserve. When they reached the bridge over the river, 'A' Company would continue pushing forward up the valley; 'B' Company would move along the high ground to the left, accompanied by two troops of No. 1 Commando, with 'D' Company on the right of the valley. The men were given a rum ration, a comparatively rare event in the Second World War. It was issued by Jimmy James.

> The rum came in gallon jars from the quartermaster. I was told that at breakfast, they were to come back with mugs, in groups of eight, and they'd have a pint of rum between eight men. I supervised the issue of breakfast. I said, 'Rum ration! Get yourselves in eights!' And I dished out the rum ration. I filled the mugs right up to the brim with rum. They went away and they sipped it! I said, 'There's no good coming back for more!' George Broadhead said, 'Jimmy, I'll confide in you, I don't feel much like going into battle, give me an extra drop of rum!' I said, 'George, you don't drink do you! There's your ration!' He took hold of the jar – and he went, 'Glug! Glug! Glug!' I took the bottle – he must have had a good half pint of rum. I saw them go into battle.[3]
>
> Company Quartermaster Sergeant Jimmy James, 'D' Company

Delays meant they only moved forwards at 06.10 and 'A' Company crossed the bridge at 07.00. As they did so an intensive rifle and machine gun fire poured down from Ben Ihren, a small hill on the left, from the slopes of Djebel Sincira and Djebel Rachtouil to the right, and from directly ahead. No one seemed able to determine the strength of the Germans, but the fire was damaging. 'A' Company could make no real progress up the valley, while 'B' Company also suffered casualties.

> I'll never forget it – we were pinned down and the corporal said to one of the lads, 'Hand me the Bren gun – I can see where they're firing from!' And as he got up to get behind the Bren gun, a sniper put one through his wrist. Another lad at the other side said, 'Give the Bren gun to me!' And the sniper did exactly same to him – put one through his wrist! They were more or less on a hill in front of us, but they didn't show their positions. You could just see the smoke and that! Then we got orders, 'Drop back! Fall back!' Company Sergeant Major Hetherington was organising the way out! We were crawling, two or three of us along the ground; I got a burst alongside of me – right down the full length of my body – I could feel it! I didn't stop there very long – I was off! Two of us were running across an open space, to jump into a trench. The lad in front of me, he stopped one in the arm that crippled him. We got him into this slit trench.[4]
>
> Private Tom Turnbull, 'B' Company

Thomas Atkinson was on stretcher bearer duty, helping evacuate the wounded. It was a dangerous business.

> Jimmy Brown, who was on the other end of my stretcher, he fell to the ground – hit! I looked at his chest and could see his white vest, I saw a hole in battledress pocket. I thought, 'Well, it's gone through his chest!' I looked and there wasn't a bit of blood on his white vest. The bullet had gone through his jacket pocket and through his forearm and out the other side. That's all he had – an injury to his arm. I started taking him back to the riverbed, got him back, then he was taken from me

> by somebody else. I jumped into the riverbed and there was the second in command. He says, 'Have you seen the sergeant major?' I said, 'I haven't, Sir!' 'Well, get over the top and see if you can find him!' I went and there was hell let loose. I made a beeline down the top of the riverbed and jumped in further down. I didn't go back very far, because I'd heard that the best part of the sergeant majors had been killed. I was looking for somebody that wasn't there.[5]
>
> Lance Corporal Thomas Atkinson, 'B' Company

The Germans were evidently well forward of their imagined positions on the Bordj des Monopoles; indeed, they were in the hills just 2 miles north of Sedjenane.

On the right, 'D' Company managed to get up on to Djebel Sincira, but encountered some serious resistance.

> We had to get the men spread out, carrying the rifles at the high port, 4–5 yards between the men. We went up this bloody hill. Never saw anything. Blokes were walking up saying, 'Bloody hell! No bugger here! A waste of time! We've dashed all this way back!' I was trying to keep a bit of discipline, 'Come on, get yourselves on!' We got over this crest – and it was a false crest! There was another plateau; gullies and wadis, leading up to the peak. We got really bloody hammered. Machine guns, mortars, getting strafed. We were sitting ducks. Everybody went to ground and started crawling up into these wadis. One of the first lads I saw fall was Broadhead,[6] the sergeant major. We were really in trouble down in these wadis. Very low cactus. If you put your head above this cactus – that was it! Absolutely withering fire coming across. The snipers were taking pot-shots. We were stuck in these wadis. We'd been there quite a while, nobody seemed to know what the hell was going on. There seemed to be no overall pattern. What the hell were we supposed to do next? We laid there; you couldn't move anyway for the fire. I was with the platoon headquarters. Just in front of us, was one of our company platoons – I think it must have been 16 Platoon – the Germans rounded them all up, about 20 yards in front of where we were. You couldn't do anything! If

you stuck your head up it was shot off. We really got hammered. When things calmed down a bit, one of the lieutenants shouted, 'Lay low, where you are until it's dark!' I think it was Lieutenant Duffy. We laid in the cactus until it was dark then we went back down the hill. Like the Duke of York's men: marched up the bloody hill and marched down again! The initial count when we got back was twelve of our company! Then overnight they started straggling back in, but not a lot came back.[7]

Sergeant Russell King, 'D' Company

On the left, 'C' Company started to move forward, but then it was decided to pull both 'B' and 'C' Companies back to the bridge. It was difficult for Major Bannerman to exert any real control over events. At around 12.00, Colonel Richard Ware arrived, to find utter confusion. He too was in a very difficult position, but after assessing the situation, he organised a renewed assault, timed for 14.00. This time, 'C' Company and the 1st Commando would attack on the left flank towards Djebel Guerba and Djebel Galb Sour. Meanwhile, a strong fighting patrol, organised from Headquarters Company personnel, were sent further out to the left flank to move up Mosque spur and then move to the east. In the centre, 'B' Company had the thankless task of pushing straight up the valley, while 'D' Company were still marooned up on Djebel Sincira and Djebel Rachtouil.

As 'B' Company moved forward they came under heavy fire from machine guns and mortars. Enfiladed from both sides, they had only gone a couple of hundred yards when it became obvious it was hopeless.

> I thought, 'Well, I don't know, this is suicide, this!' There didn't seem to be any sense in it! I wished to hell we knew what we were doing, because I didn't! The enemy was on both sides of us and also in front of us. We looked to be marching into the 'Valley of Death' to me. You forget about home and ordinary life; you completely forget it. You're in a different world, somehow or other. If you started thinking about life back home, you would do nothing. 'Well, we're in this, so do the best you can!' There was artillery or mortars coming from both sides.

> We lost a hell of a lot; there was a lot of dead. It seemed to me that the artillery support was more after the first hour or so than it was beforehand. At that time, we could have done with some smoke to get out. That's why there were so many taken prisoner. They were outflanked. As I lay down that morning, I could hear the Jerry stalking. I mustn't have been more than about 30 yards from the German dugouts. You just lay there – you dare not move. There was artillery and mortar shells going over. Caught in the open, lying flat on your stomach, hoping for a little bit of cover, some smoke to get you back to your lines. There was a hell of a lot of artillery coming over – and the bulk of it was ours – dropping amongst us. You could hear the stuff falling around you. We lay pretending to be dead. Wishing it would turn dark, so I could get the hell out of it![8]
>
> Lance Corporal Thomas Atkinson, 'B' Company

Most of the men would be pinned down in that open ground until nightfall allowed them to trickle back. It was during this failed advance that Tom Turnbull's luck ran out.

> That was when I got hit! We heard the mortar shells coming, what we called the 'Moaning Minnies', a six-barrelled electric mortar. The shells used to explode in a circle – bloody terrible! We dove down – I was wounded and lifted off the ground by the blast and shrapnel in my back just below my left shoulder blade! It felt as if somebody had had a hell of a running kick at me! I looked up at two of the lads, bent over and I said, 'I'll catch up!' I was in pain then. I loosened my blouse and I looked down, and all my vest, my shirt and everything was all blood. I must have passed out. Then I knew no more till I saw two pair of legs coming towards us! It might sound boastful, but automatically I was grabbing for my rifle! It was a mortar sergeant and a little Frenchman. They pulled me up, took us behind a hillock, cut my blouse and put a dressing on. Major Hillis, the company commander, he walked towards me, where I was kneeling, He looked at me and he had tears in his eyes. He says, 'Drop further back, Turnbull. How many have I got left of the company?'[9]
>
> Private Tom Turnbull, 'B' Company

Turnbull was evacuated as walking wounded to a dressing station in a railway tunnel. He would spend time in hospital at Philippeville and near Algiers, then a convalescent camp before he rejoined the 16th DLI at Blida in July 1943. Thomas Atkinson was taken prisoner.

> It was getting dusk. The Germans suddenly appeared beside us! They knew we were there. We were surrounded by them, there were maybe half a dozen heavily armed Germans, who just took us 20 to 30 yards into this round hole, not slit trenches. We had a wounded chap with us – nasty – his thigh had been hit; all we could do was put a field dressing on him. He was moaning, he was in pain, but we couldn't do much about it. We carried him with us. They turned out to be rather friendly in a way – after they'd pinched our cigarettes. Next morning, we started moving back – to their medical inspection tent. We got the job that morning of bringing in casualties – Germans as well as ours. They evacuated them in priority, the more serious ones, it didn't matter whether they were English or German.[10]
>
> Lance Corporal Thomas Atkinson, 'B' Company

Meanwhile, Tom Tunney was with 'C' Company as they moved to the left accompanied by two troops of Commandos. They too were plagued by vigorous fire from the heights above them.

> Everybody dropped. Then, 'Up!' Got up and just carried on. At the bottom of the hill there was like a cliff – it was about 10 or 12 feet – and we all ran into that. You couldn't get up! Further along, each side, it was sloped. You could get up there and he was on the top only about 200 yards in front. We were crawling up through the grass and bushes. The bloody bullets were flying all over! You could see where the firing was coming from – and you'd have a pot shot. You couldn't see them. Word got round that the people on the top of the hill were French. The Commandos who were with us, these two Commandos, one of them got his rifle and his bayonet and put a white flag on, somebody's vest or something like that, and they went up. They were talking and you could see them shouting.[11]
>
> Private Tom Tunney, 'C' Company

Research by Tom Tunney (son of the Tom Tunney quoted above) has revealed that the two commandos with the white flag attempting to communicate with the 'French' were Captain Davidson and his batman. Sadly, it was the Germans that responded to the overtures.

> I think this bloody Jerry had a shot at them. He was only a few yards away – he was a sniper. He had us pinned down. If he saw a piece of grass going, 'Pssst!' The bloody bullets were coming over, you daren't move! I was about 15 yards back and I went up, crawled up and this commando he was lying there. We couldn't do anything with him. Couldn't put a tourniquet on him or anything.[12]
>
> Private Tom Tunney, 'C' Company

On the left the Durhams had made no real progress, but they managed to capture and retain Ben Ihren (which was named Jobey's Bump after their company commander, Captain George Jobey) and some of the lower heights on the left.

That night the tattered remnants of 'B' Company and the Headquarters Company were ensconced in a very small Arab village just north of Sedjenane; 'C' Company was still holding on to Jobey's Bump, while 'A' and 'D' Companies were amalgamated and pulled back into the Sedjenane cork woods. The next day was spent in reorganising, as the battalion had been badly knocked about. Colonel Ware reported back to 139 Brigade, only to find he was ordered to begin the preparations for a major counterattack at 05.00 on 2 March.

> We were all lined up and Colonel Ware was up and down the line talking. We were going in tomorrow. He says, 'You'll have the artillery behind you! Nothing really to worry about! Lobbing in front of you; advance follow the shells! Anybody that feels like falling out, now is the time! If you can't take it!' Well, there's nobody going to fall out; probably we'd all like to fall out at the time – it was only natural! Because we knew what we were in for![13]
>
> Private Sidney Shutt, 'B' Company

On the left, 'C' Company would push forward from Jobey's Bump to take Djebel Guerba, 'B' Company were to move up Mosque spur to attack Point 231 on Djebel Galb Sour, while 'D' Company would follow up behind 'B' Company along Mosque spur and then attack Mraf spur. The 6th Lincolnshires would move to hold the start lines as a firm base once the 16th DLI had attacked. All told, an extremely dangerous series of tasks had been assigned to the 16th DLI, as the Germans were by this time present in considerable strength. That night, the Durhams readied themselves for the challenges ahead. Sydney Shutt was in the platoon commanded by Lieutenant Dorian.

> We got a bit of a meal; there was a touch of rum, very little mind. We set out, crossed that river in the dark and lined up. I was with the officer and the sergeant major. The watches were synchronised. Dorian says, 'Now, we'll hear the first shot from the artillery, that's the sign to move forward!' There we were, standing static. Silent, not a word. Just waiting for that. Watching the watches. Off goes the gun! One shot! Dorian, 'Right, that's the signal, Advance, steady!' And we marched forward. The shells were dropping. It was muddy; it was rough![14]
>
> Private Sidney Shutt, 'B' Company

The 'creeping' barrage line of shells moved slowly forward ahead of the attacking infantry.

> This barrage started. The artillery and our own mortars. They started about 40 or 50 yards in front of us and it went up the hill, all the way up. Jerry, he was on the top, he just had to bloody run back about 50 or 100 yards. Then when the bugger stopped, he just ran back again to where he was! We followed it up and a sergeant he came crawling over to me. He says, 'There's a bloody machine gun over there, can you see it, Tunney?' I says, 'Aye!' He was firing up our arses! We were going up the hill and he was down here and he was firing, crossways, upwards. The sergeant says, 'Have a go at him!' and I had a go with the Bren – I got him. That's when my mate got

hit, Forster. He was lying alongside us. He says, 'Argghhh, I've been hit!' He got up and he was away down the bank![15]

Private Tom Tunney, 'C' Company

As can be imagined, it was a terrible shock to George Forster.

> I got hit by a machine gun or whatever it was from the right on the hill. It hit me in the stomach and came out the side, through my ribs on the left-hand side. I just felt a searing pain and I went down on my knees. That was the end of me. I can't remember any more. I came to – and I looked – and everybody had gone. I had boots on, and the blood was oozing out through the eyelets of my boots. I thought, 'Oh!' Then somebody fired a mortar bomb and it dropped 50 yards away! I thought 'If that's come from that way, I'll go this way!' I could just about stand. I turned round and staggered away! There was nobody about! Not a soul![16]

Private George Forster, 'C' Company

He went back towards Jobey's Bump and set off towards the Sedjenane road.

> I met another man from 'D' Company; he was a bit shell-shocked, what you called 'bomb happy'. He didn't know where he was or what he was doing! He helped me across the river on to the other side and the RAMC blokes were coming up then – and they picked me up and put me on a stretcher on a donkey. Took me back to Sedjenane – to a tunnel. They told me later we lost nearly all our men. I hadn't a clue! Not till afterwards. Quite a bit of pain. There were big bright lights. I kept saying, 'Can I have a drink?' And they wouldn't give me a drink with stomach wounds? They kept putting cotton wool on me mouth to moisten my lips. The next thing I knew, they were wheeling me in and there were loads and loads of stretchers and men lying. I had an operation in the tunnel, they sewed me up, I was bleeding in my stomach, they had to operate, or it was curtains! I came to when they were lifting me into an ambulance to take me 15–20 miles further back. The Germans were getting closer to the field ambulance.[17]

Private George Forster, 'C' Company

Meanwhile Tom Tunney and the remains of 'C' Company were still trying to fight their way up on to Djebel Guerba.

> I had a lance corporal, from Bishop Auckland, he took over as my No. 2 and I says, 'We better get up there and get o'er the top!' Instead of coming back as we should have done, we went up, towards them! I thought our lot were in front, that they'd gone over the top. But they'd all been bloody knocked out. They were knocked out and took prisoner and there was any amount killed and wounded. I gave him the Bren, I says, 'I'm sick to bloody death of pulling this bloody thing about! Here, have a go at this!' We were going up through the grass, crawling away up, and I heard these voices. You could hear them getting nearer and nearer. I said, 'Here, they're coming. There's somebody coming. If they pop their heads over have a go!' I had his rifle and this head comes over the top! I pulled the trigger and nothing happened. If that rifle had been cocked, I'd have gotten him, but there was about six or seven of them and we would have had it. They wouldn't have taken us bloody prisoner if we knocked one of their mates out! We would have got killed there and then in the heat of the moment. They said, 'Stand up!' We had to get up. One of the Germans picked up the Bren gun, he burned his hand on the hot barrel chucking it down the hillside! He actually said, 'For you, Tommy, the war is over.' He actually said it![18]
>
> Private Tom Tunney, 'C' Company

Tom Tunney would spend the rest of the war as a prisoner, first in PG66 and PG53 in Italy, before being moved to at Stalag IV B in Germany, where he was sent out to a work camp in a brickyard at Bad Schmiedeberg. John Douglass had a very similar experience as he too was taken prisoner.

> I had casualties, yelling, 'I'm hit, Sergeant, I'm hit!' But you cannot stop. When you're in an attack you've got to go. We got up on to this slope. Heavy machine gun fire. We were lying down, 'Get your heads down!' Trouble was, when you lay down, you couldn't see anything because there was about 18

inches to 2 foot of thick scrub. I was hit by a piece of shrapnel – it caught us on the thumb – I was bleeding – I couldn't use my hand. The next thing they put a counterattack in. They came down the slope and they were on us before we knew they were there. We'd used most of our ammunition – I think I had two rounds left – some of the lads had none. I was lying there – I looked up and I saw this [German soldier]. He would have put the bayonet through us! I twisted and I got it just across my backside. He pulled back and I said, 'No! No!' He didn't! There was me and five of the platoon left who were taken prisoner.[19]

Sergeant John Douglass, 'C' Company

The 'C' Company attack had degenerated into utter failure, with high casualties and many of the men taken prisoner. One witness was Harry Craggs, acting as a forward observation officer (FOO) 70th Field Regiment, who had been attached to 'C' Company with George Jobey.

I left my OP party at a suitable point near the end of the defile and set off alone to recce an OP. I had walked about 20 yards into the open when two Bosche with an MG opened up at me at a range of about 50 yards and out of the corner of my eye I saw British soldiers being rounded up as prisoners about 200 yards away. I didn't stay long to investigate but ran back to my party, told them to grab the wireless sets and leave hastily and independently for a rocky area which I pointed out about 200 yards away to the SE. We did this, chased by four Bosche with two MGs (as far as I can remember there were four of us with one rifle and one revolver). We carried water bottles strapped to the back of our webbing, that is covering the small of the back. My OP assistant felt a blow in that part and dropped as though dead: he had been smoking a cigarette which he continued to hold. The Bosche walked past him and as the remainder of us got under cover they walked away. He rejoined us and rattled a bullet in the inside of his now empty water bottle. After this it became a standing order with my party never to be relaxed, that water bottles would always be carried in that position. By this time there were no other British soldiers in sight, and it was obvious that the enemy had successfully counterattacked and mopped up.[20]

Captain Harry Craggs, 70th Field Regiment, Royal Artillery

To their left, 'B' Company pushed up Mosque spur aiming towards Point 231 on Djebel Galb Sour. At first all went well, as they kept right up to the barrage of bursting shells, but then the German fire burst upon them, scything through their ranks. A chain of mutually supporting machine gun posts caused most of the damage, but the Germans also had troops close to hand ready to make a counterattack.

> All of a sudden, it was hell let loose. I've never known owt like it. The bullets were flying, the shells were dropping, and some were dropping short; dropping on our own lads as we were advancing! The sergeant major was killed. We weren't getting very far. You couldn't see any of them. You didn't know where they were coming from, they were set in there. On we went and it was getting worse. As soon as you got up you were an open target for a rifle; you were above the bushes. The shells were still dropping. I could hear this young lad, shouting for his mother, 'Mother! Mother!' It was terrible. He'd been hit. I walked over the top of him in our next advance. He was 'out'. He was only a young lad. My sergeant, he came over and dropped beside me, he says, 'You can't see a bloody thing! If you get up – you're down!' They were chipping the leaves off the top of the bushes.[21]

Private Sidney Shutt, 'B' Company

During the advance, Oswald McDonald ran into a belt of thick cactus scrub which made matters even worse as they struggled forwards.

> We were going up the hill. You had to spread out as much as you can and when you're spread out, you can only see what's in front of you! You're only looking after yourself or the next guy who's with you. We were more or less sitting ducks! We came to a wall of cactus. I took my bayonet off my rifle; I was

hacking my way through this cactus. Captain Bavington-Jones gave me a dressing down, 'Put that back on! We're just going to batter our way through!' I think he wanted to get it over with, he was very impatient, 'Let's get there! Let's get it over with!' Which we did, we forced out way through. I managed to get a big cactus spike right inside my knee! It must have been 4 or 5 inches inside my knee! It was very, very painful but nothing compared to hot lead! We went on! Bavington-Jones got shot – he went down – he was lying there. Lieutenant Dorian says, 'I'm afraid we'll have to give ourselves up! We've no chance!' I could see a German coming towards me, I saw another German coming round. We stood up together, put our hands up and shouted, 'Kamerad! Kamerad!' The German says, 'Tommy, for you the war is over!'[22]

Private Oswald McDonald, 'B' Company

Captain Jeffrey Bavington-Jones[23] had been hit in the thigh and died in the following days, despite receiving medical treatment from the Germans. Oswald McDonald had a miserable period as a POW at PG 66 and PG53 Camp in Italy, before he escaped after the Italian surrender in September 1943. He got back to England in December 1943, but then retrained and served as a driver with the Royal Army Service Corps in Italy and Austria.

The situation steadily worsened as at 10.00 the Germans launched an attack on the defensive positions which had been established by the 2/5th Sherwood Foresters some 5 miles to the east of Sedjenane. By nightfall, they had broken through, rendering Sedjenane vulnerable from both east and north. The 6th Lincolnshires were defending the town of Sedjenane with one company forward at the Mosque at Si Mansoor, alongside 'D' Company of the 16th DLI. The few survivors of the assaulting 'A', 'B' and 'C' Companies of 16th DLI had filtered back to the MT lines and from there were taken to a new base at Djebel Abiod. For the moment the Headquarters Company remained forward.

At 15.15 on 3 March, Colonel Ware sent a small party to defend the little Arab village north of Sedjenane, to use it as an outpost to help break up any German attacks from the north. Among them was James Drake, who had already excelled himself in the recent fighting. He would play a key part in the defence of the village.

> We formed this group – Captain Balance and Lieutenant Lax, Sergeant Dunn, Sergeant Aitcheson and Sergeant Walton, myself and various other ranks – making a complement of twenty. We were to defend between Sedjenane and the hills. The colonel was there to give us all our instructions and he announced that I would be in charge of the operation, 'Had anybody any objections?' I think he had a bit of confidence in me! There was no objections. I said, 'Right then, we'll follow the river route down to a few huts on the right-hand side of the river, we'll [go] from the river-bank to this clearing, a few stone buildings with thatched roofs, surrounded by cactus trees!'[24]
>
> Lance Sergeant James Drake, Carrier Platoon

As they prepared the village for defence, Drake was aware that his every move could be seen from the hills to the north.

> We were going backwards and forwards for about an hour! I knew Jerry was in the hills and he'd be watching us! So he wouldn't know how many were in there and how many wasn't! We dug slit trenches just in front of the cactus trees. Everything was very quiet. Nothing happening. We all got in the slit trenches.[25]
>
> Lance Sergeant James Drake, Carrier Platoon

The officers had located several boxes of .303 ammunition abandoned by one of the companies in one of the huts, which now came as a blessing. Drake got all his men filling the rifle clips, and Bren gun drum magazines fast as they could, ready for the German attack which he sensed was brewing.

> We started being shelled. Everybody was down in our slit trenches. They then started with the mortars; mortar bombs flying about all over the place. There was a lull then. I knew what was happening – they were going to come forward. I

put one Bren on our left flank; one on the right flank; so they could cover all in front of them with crossfire. I gave strict instructions that nobody must fire a shot until I said so. I had a couple round the back of a small haystack on our right, with rifles, just in case they tried to filter round that side. We waited – and we waited – and we waited. Sure enough they came. They had to come over ground and I knew they were in for a hammering – we were all loaded up ready. They stood up and walked towards us, as if they thought we must all be dead! I waited while they got within 100 yards before I gave a fire order, 'Right, lads; FIRE!' Both the Brens started – and we simply mowed them down. They all fell flat. We got very little fire back from them. I said, 'If you see any movement at all in anyone – put a bullet in them!' Sergeant Dunn counted to twenty-eight that he's seen off by his own rifle. I shouted to him, 'Stop counting Dunny! Just keep knocking them down!'[26]

Lance Sergeant James Drake, Carrier Platoon

They seemed to be holding, but then one of the men in the haystack spotted some Germans creeping round to outflank them on that side. Drake sprang into determined action.

There was a little mound which obscured the view, so I shouted to Sergeant Aitcheson to take the Bren to creep up forward to this mound. He was in his trench and a few bullets were flying by – he said he couldn't. 'There's too much fire coming round!' Without any hesitation, I grabbed the Bren myself and ran it up. I got the gun just over the mound. Sure enough, there was plenty to fire at. I ripped one or two magazines off. Then I shouted for Lance Corporal Gipson to bring some ammunition – I wanted more ammunition. He brought some more magazines. I put him behind the gun then I went back. We carried on until we'd used more or less all the ammunition. The two Bren guns – both their barrels were bent – they were no good at all. There's two barrels for each gun and for every ten magazines you change them over so that one can cool off.

But we'd been firing them that much that when I looked down the barrels they were kaput![27]

Lance Sergeant James Drake, Carrier Platoon

As night began to fall, their situation became untenable.

We kept that up until daylight was fading. With it getting dark, he started with tracer bullets, and they set fire to the thatched roofs. So the buildings started blazing then. It did us a good turn because we could see what we were doing! We put what grenades we had on the ground in front of us. I said, 'They'll be sending patrols up!' I went to the cactus trees – and sure enough a patrol was coming up. I let them get close and let off my two grenades. Once all the grenades had been used up that was it as far as we were concerned. We'd no more firepower. I said, 'Right!' I sent them off in fours. I said, 'Go in different directions and probably, hopefully, some will get back and be able to report what's happened!' Two had got wounded, one in the feet, one in the arm, so I put men each side of them.[28]

Lance Sergeant James Drake, Carrier Platoon, Headquarters Company

By this time, Drake and all his men were exhausted, but they crawled back, dragging the wounded with them. Fortune was with them and most managed to evade German patrols. James Drake was recommended for the Military Medal. When he was interviewed, he still had the notification. Long afterwards, when he was back in the UK, he received his medal from the George VI himself.

At Sedjenane, a further counterattack was organised for first light next day. This would be carried out by the 6th Lincolnshires supported by some eight Churchill tanks of the North Irish Horse. Drake decided to go with them.

I said, 'I'm going to go up behind the tanks, because I know where there is a German big gun emplaced, just north of the town. He's in the bushes there – so I can guide the tank commander to know just exactly where he is!'[29]

Lance Sergeant James Drake, Carrier Platoon

Drake accompanied the tanks towards the Arab village.

> I informed the tank commander to just go to the corner – there was a slight bend in the road, and I said, 'Whatever you do, stop this side of the corner, then lower your turret, because he's right bang in front of you on the right-hand side of the road in the bushes!' He got back into the tank and the tank moved forward. I went up with the first tank, a couple of fellows with me. I was walking on the right-hand side, the driver's side. He stopped, but a little too far round the corner. The only thing I saw was the front lift up – and the driver's head popped up. As it popped up a shell hit it. It took his head clean off, splattered all his brains all the way round the side of the tank. I could see them twitching on the side of the tank. What a sight! Terrible! Somebody lifted him out of the tank and threw him on the side of the road and reversed the tank back. They knew exactly then what to do. They came forward again and I heard one blast.[30]
>
> Lance Sergeant James Drake, Carrier Platoon

It was the sound of the destruction of the German gun. Drake then decided to return to the railway tunnel area. Major Welch was in command of the tanks but had only about a platoon of infantry with them. Sadly, the vital importance of tanks, infantry and artillery all working together in harmony had not yet been properly appreciated. Or perhaps these were just desperate times with no time for tactical niceties.

> The tanks then shot up the village and the Germans retired except for snipers. I tried to get infantry support into the village but could only get one platoon. The Germans, as soon as they realised that there was no infantry with us, started to infiltrate back and to snipe. Our infantry was unable to cope with this. My tanks remained in their positions without support until I made contact with OC Lincolns, who had received orders to retire. He arranged to meet me again at 16.00 hours. During all this time heavy mortar and artillery fire was put down on the tanks, with several casualties, including the forward observation

officer. One tank of No. 1 troop, in trying to pull out some other guns, was bogged [down] and had to be destroyed.[31]

Major Welch, 'C' Squadron, North Irish Horse

If the counterattacks were failing, it was also true that the Germans were not making much progress around Sedjenane. But then there was a seismic tactical shift. To the north, the Free French positions in the town of Medjez were threatened with encirclement when Axis forces took control of the dominating high ground. The French withdrew, which left the 139 Brigade in a rather precarious salient. On 4 March, a general retreat was ordered from Sedjenane toward Djebel Abiod. Here the line would be held. But by then the 16th DLI had almost ceased to exist; it had been a cruel introduction to the horrors of war.

5

ADVANCE TO TUNIS

> You could tell them when they came in, 'Wait till I get out to them Germans, I'll show you what I'll do to them!' I says, 'Another bomb happy case!' Mind I was right – I always was. The ones that came out saying what they were going to do and what they weren't – they were trying to make themselves confident. But they were the first ones to go[1]
>
> Private James Corr, 'B' Company

THE REMNANTS OF THE 16TH DLI were brought together at the Tabarka Woods. They were part of a general retreat in the Sedjenane sector in the face of probing German attacks, which continually outflanked, or threatened to outflank, the successive defensive positions that had been hurriedly taken up by the increasingly disorganised Allied forces. The Durhams were suffering the bitter aftertaste of defeat. A sense of desolation caused by the loss of so many comrades, mingled with very real fears for their own personal survival. Tom Lister remembered the prevailing 'jumpiness' among the men in the woods.

> It was later when we got there; it was getting dark, and it was raining. I was to share a two-man bivvie – that meant three in a two-man bivvie. Stuck on a hillside in the woods. I got in with a lance corporal – he was in a terrible nervous state – he would never have made a soldier if he'd lived to be ninety! The slightest thing was upsetting him. And there was a Corporal Oliver; he was more of a friend of mine! It was cramped

enough with two, but to get a third one in – and it was pretty wet. You can be the best friends in the world but they're not too glad to see you. There was a little miniature hurricane lamp. It wasn't lit; I had to move it so I could get my head down on my pack. They were partially stripped – I was fully dressed – I just flopped down in between them with a blanket. We settled down and all was peace. Then there was a rustling sound and Oliver, says, 'Got a match?' Took a match and lit the little hurricane lamp and held it up, half raised. He says, 'It's a snake!' And the lance corporal jumped up – full height – and took the tent with him. And the rain was coming down in torrents outside. Oh God! The whole area was in an uproar – there was shouting and bawling! And I never saw any damned snake! I grabbed my gear and withdrew. Found a truck, crawled underneath, and settled down there for the night!²

Private Tom Lister, MT Section, Headquarters Company

With the 16th DLI effectively out of action, the fighting continued to rage. The Coldstream Guards had established a defensive line across the road and cork forests north of Tamara, but this too was under pressure as there were not enough troops to cover the ground. On 6 March, the Coldstream Guards were relieved by the 1 Parachute Brigade, while the 139 Brigade was made responsible for the Djebel Abiod sector. A German attack on 8 March was just about held, but the line was being forced back ever closer to Djebel Abiod.

But what of the Durhams? They had begun the slow process of rebuilding, almost from scratch. On 11 March, in the aftershocks of Sedjenane, Lieutenant Colonel Richard Ware was peremptorily replaced by Lieutenant Colonel Johnny Preston, a plain-spoken Yorkshireman who had been second in command of the 2/4th King's Own Yorkshire Light Infantry (KOYLI). Preston was not particularly military in his personal appearance, being neither tall not straight-backed. Approachable and friendly in his manner, he certainly liked a drink but confined such indulgences to opportunities out of the line. His men appreciated the interest he took in their welfare, but most of all they liked his tactical abilities, which he would deploy on numerous occasions to reduce casualties. Just a short time before, Major Dennis Worrall had joined the battalion. In peacetime, a gentleman farmer from Dorset, he had been originally commissioned into the Dorsetshire Regiment. A well-built jolly chap, he would become the battalion's second in command.

Another new officer was Captain Arthur Vizard. He was born in Stroud Green, London, but suffered the early loss of his father who was killed serving with the 9th Australian Battalion in October 1918. After an education at the Royal British Orphan School, he worked as an office boy and then as an internal auditor for a hotel firm. He was recruited and trained as a territorial on the Vickers machine gun with the 8th Middlesex Regiment at Northolt Drill Hall from 1936–9. His qualities were recognised and after gaining early promotion to company quartermaster sergeant he was commissioned and posted to the 7th Machine Gun Battalion, Middlesex Regiment, in Northern Ireland in 1941. Here he distinguished himself by misreading a map and accidentally crossing neutral Eire border with his three machine guns sections. They were taken to the local police station and detained for three days before being released. He was thus rather under a cloud when he was posted away to the 70th (Young Soldiers) DLI which was acting as a demonstration battalion at Westwick Camp. Finally, Vizard was sent with a large draft out to join the 16th DLI in early March 1943.

> I had to take speech training – I took it in Darlington before I left the UK! 'Why aye, bonny lad!' I learned myself proper Geordie! I had to! For the first six months they didn't know what I was talking about – and I didn't know what they were talking about! You had to know their culture. If you could sing some of the Geordie songs – it was very popular in the evening when things were quiet. It took a little while to become fully accepted.[3]
>
> Captain Arthur Vizard, 'E' Company

Vizard would prove to be a competent and popular officer.

The scale of the disaster at Sedjenane was such that the

survivors were merged into two composite companies. Chaos reigned and few men had a coherent picture of what was happening – even the battalion history is sketchy. One company was placed under the command of Major Dennis Worrall, and it was soon in action close by the railway viaduct at Tamara. Here Charlie Palmer had a close escape when pressed into service on an ammunition carrying party.

> Regimental Sergeant Major Thomasson asked for someone to collect ammunition. We were handy! 'I want some volunteers! You and you!' We moved out and we were shelled moving up this little stream valley. Obviously in full view of the enemy. The shelling went on and I knew that it was getting pretty near. You can always tell because you could hear the whistle, that's when you got down! This chap with me had just joined the section, he was behind me. I said, 'Drop!' He did drop – right on top of me – I was knocked flat! I was three-quarters down already! The shell had hit him, a big piece of shrapnel, because he was dead – he'd had his head blown off. That was my first experience of being with somebody when they were killed. It affected me very much indeed. I still remember it vividly and it's not something I can push out of my mind. It's still there. That night we went up and we had to bury him there and then. We dug a slit trench, you put the body in, and you put some kind of cross there. That had to be recorded – the map reference had to be given, so when it was possible those bodies could be removed and given a proper burial.[4]
>
> Private Charles Palmer, Intelligence Section, Headquarters Company

The other composite company was originally in 'The Mine', 4 miles south of Djebel Abiod. They then moved up to the Tamara viaduct, taking up positions behind Worrall's command, with the 1st Parachute Brigade on their left.

Captain Arthur Vizard and the new 'E' Company were not allowed long to settle down but were sent into action in support of the paratroopers.

> We took over these positions to take over from the Paras up on the Jebuls. Very rocky and filled with 7-foot-high cactus! Reverse slope, which became the bible in those days. So the only way they could hit you was by mortars and you were free from small arms fire or artillery. Lookouts on the crest.[5]
>
> Captain Arthur Vizard, 'E' Company

At 08.00 on 17 March, the Germans launched another attack on the French and British positions north of Tamara station. They managed to penetrate the lines held by 2/5th Sherwood Foresters, were pushed back by a counterattack, but then succeeded in smashing their way through by late afternoon. The 16th DLI was deployed only as company reinforcements attached to the frontline battalions. Vizard found himself sent forward to help extract the remnants of the Foresters.

> I got sent off from one set of hills to another set of hills! The 2/5th Foresters had got into some trouble; they'd had a bad time with mortaring, and they'd sustained a lot of casualties. Most of the casualties were holed up in a place called Maison Blanche – the White House – and I was told to go and get them out. I waited until nightfall and moved up. I had a bit of trouble with one sergeant, which was a tragic situation. He said it was suicide to go forward any further towards this white house. I said, 'Well, we've got our orders!' He said, 'Well, I'm not going!' I had to send him back to 'B' Echelon. He was a very popular sergeant, much respected by his chaps. If he had gone around saying that what we were doing was suicide, they would probably believe him and not me! His views would have influenced all his men – they trusted him – as they should. But he was a fine fellow, he was KOYLI, got an MM and was killed later on. We moved forward. It wasn't easy – small arms fire from Jerry we could see up on the hill. We'd gone through the village of Tamara and we came under quite a bit of fire there and I lost three men – it was a shock to me. Training had been useful, because I'd got used to bullets whistling by me and over my head! What I wasn't used to was bullets hitting people! That was new to me! It was a shock always to see your

comrades drop down, but it is one of those things you have to get used to. We crept into this white house and there were a lot of badly wounded men there. I had stretcher bearers with me. It was nightfall. The colonel was there, his headquarters was still there. I said to him, 'Well we're going out, Sir! What about your wounded?' He said, 'We'll bring as many as we can, but I think there will be some that we can't take – we'll have to leave them!' And we did. We could watch Jerry digging in – I could see the moon shining on the entrenchment tools up there on the hill! But we got out fifty or sixty. The majority of them were walking wounded, but some of them we carried out.[6]

Captain Arthur Vizard, 'E' Company

He would spend several days attached to 2/5th Sherwood Foresters. By this time, he had learnt a key lesson for any officer – don't attract too much attention from the Germans.

> I always took off my 'pips' and I carried a rifle. I didn't see any point in making myself a target. You single yourself out. If I was shot it wouldn't do any good to the company! You do take the same chance as other people.[7]

Captain Arthur Vizard, 'E' Company

He had also got to know his officer's batman – the man who had to look after him while he carried out his prime function as an officer and made sure his men were cared for.

> John Macdonald from South Shields. He was a great fellow. A simple fellow but very loyal and he did the job fairly well. If he saw anything he'd tell you. I called him 'Mac'. The word 'batman' or 'servant' is totally inappropriate. They were the chaps who watched your back! The chap who selected somewhere where you could sleep. A two-man slit trench. That way you had two gas capes to line it; two greatcoats over the top and you had a groundsheet to keep the rain out! Two fellows with some mutual warmth back-to-back. He was the man who went and got your grub for you in the mess tin and brought it to you! They didn't clean anything![8]

Captain Arthur Vizard, 'E' Company

The German advance forced the overall Allied line back toward the Djebel Abiod area. Here the situation at last seemed to stabilise, with the Germans having made a 20-mile advance from their original Green Hills positions. In all it had been a successful 'spoiling' attack, seizing important roads, securing good hilltop defensive positions and taking a large number of prisoners – including many Durhams. But the tide was turning as the 1st Division was moving forward to reinforce the line on the First Army front; while to the east, Montgomery's Eighth Army had broken through the Mareth Line.

On the night of 21/22 March, the 16th DLI relieved the 6th Lincolnshires at Djebel Bou Lahia, holding the line in what proved to be a relatively quiet period before the 46th Division launched a major counterattack late on 27 March. At 15.30 next day, there were signs of success as a party of 103 Italians from the 10th Bersaglieri Regiment came into the Durhams' lines to surrender. Soon after, they returned to the Djebel Abiod mine to reorganise, as the battalion was still not really in a fit state for active service.

Following the Battle of Sedjenane, several reinforcement drafts had arrived from various other light infantry regiments. This was meant to be a temporary measure, but they were all ultimately absorbed into the 16th DLI. Arthur Vizard was rewarded for his good early showing by promotion to major and command of 'A' Company. On 4 April, the 16th DLI were 'loaned' to the 78th Division, under the command of the 38th (Irish) Brigade. They would be part of a major new offensive to remove the Axis forces from the hills north of and overlooking the road stretching from Medjez el Bab to Tunis.

The 78th Division attack went in at 04.00 on 6 April, with the 16th DLI following up in reserve. After a brief attachment to the 12 Brigade of the 4th Division, on the night of 13/14 April, the 16th DLI were relieved and transferred to the command of 10 Brigade. This time they were to provide a firm base for the 1/6th East Surrey Regiment as they pushed on to Djebel Grembil which overlooked Sidi Nsir station. Once the front had stabilised, the 16th DLI were transferred back to the 139 Brigade, supposedly for a rest, but was then immediately farmed out to the 3 Brigade, 1st Division, taking up defensive positions at Bou Arada, where they found themselves facing the Hermann Goering Panzer Division, a formation that would become familiar to them over the next year.

> Johnny Preston used to make a joke about it, because he'd taken over what was really the remnants of the battalion. After Sedjenane, the battalion became, not ineffective, but unable to fight battles on its own. We spent our time coming to the assistance of other units who were threatened. He used to say, 'Is your base secure? If not send for 16th DLI!' He was more or less farming out companies to support.[9]
>
> Major Arthur Vizard, 'A' Company

Finally, they were attached to 128 (Hampshire) Brigade to take part in a planned attack by 46th Division. This time the 16th DLI would really be in the thick of it.

At 03.00 on 22 April 1943, the 46th Division would push forward on an 8-mile-wide front, with seven battalions leading the way, supported by an impressive artillery bombardment designed to crush all opposition. They were to break through the hills in front of the Gubalart Plain to allow armour through to Koursia. The 16th DLI would be attacking a strong well-defended position on the Sidi Barka Hill in the right of the attack. The two forward companies crossed the start line and at 03.40 a thunderous barrage came down on the German positions. Among them was Tony Sacco, born of Italian origins in Durham, who worked in the family ice cream shop in Langley Moor, before he was called up and trained as a signaller.

> We prepared for the attack and marched to a position. The Intelligence Section came with a long white tape. 'Right, get behind this tape!' We were told to line up in a great long line. I thought this was really funny. Then the bombardment started – our artillery! They started shelling the Jebul Barka. Plastering it, the shells were screaming over! Well, I thought, 'This is great! There'll be nobody left alive on that mountain!' Then we got

the orders to advance. I suppose it was something like the First World War. I felt great somehow – I didn't feel frightened.[10]

Private Tony Sacco, 'D' Company

At first all went well.

> When we got to the foot of the Jebul Barka, Sergeant Major Wales said, 'Well, we're not finished yet! We've got to go up to the top of it and then swing right!' Everybody got into positions, and we swung right leading on to a kind of plateau. We got there and these Spandaus opened up. They got quite a few with the first burst. We were completely pinned down. Absolutely couldn't move. Then he started with the mortars on us! We were pressed to the ground. Sergeant Major Wales was dying, he was maybe 4 yards from me. In the end he was crying for his mother. It was terrible. He died of his wounds.[11]

Private Tony Sacco, 'D' Company

After the battle, Jimmy James would find the corpse of Sergeant Major Wilson Wales.[12] It was a macabre sight that affected him deeply

> I found Sergeant Major Wales in the long grass. A mortar bomb had exploded right at the side of him and took half his back away. I'd seen him often in the sergeants' mess in England, asleep in a chair with his head in the palm of his hand. But then I found him like that on the battlefield dead – with his head in the palm of his hand – resigned to dying having taken off his battledress top tunic to look at his back. There was an enormous hole in his back – scarab beetles by the hundred marched out when I disturbed his body. I've never forgotten that.[13]

Company Quartermaster Sergeant Jimmy James, 'D' Company

The Sidi Barka had a false crest, so as 'D' Company breasted the ridge they came under heavy fire from German positions above them and half concealed by the cactus. Tony Sacco was in real trouble.

> You were completely pinned down. I was praying to Saint Jude! A prayer my sister gave to me! You couldn't do a thing; you were just lying flat. We must have been there for about two or three hours – I might be exaggerating. Every time we made a move, the Spandaus would open up! We were really in a terrible position. One of the stretcher bearers was shouting, 'It's another Sedjenane! It's another Sedjenane!' The Germans were on an 8-foot kind of ridge; they had complete command. We had no chance at all of getting it.[14]
>
> Private Tony Sacco, Headquarters, 'D' Company

As it got light, the German fire gained in accuracy. To make matters worse, on the 'B' Company front they encountered a ring of deadly anti-personnel 'S' mines. All along that ridge the Durhams were in a desperate situation; something had to be done; but what? Major Arthur Martin[15] and Private Frank Chambers[16] were both killed as they tried to crawl forward to get within grenade range of the Germans. The forward troops were too near the German positions for an effective artillery shoot and the promised tank support had been delayed by mines.

> Then Major Duffy eventually got on to the colonel. The order was, 'At the count of "Three", everybody up on their feet and make back to a gully about 60 to 100 yards down'. We got to 'Three', and we all leapt up! Then we started floundering. There was me, Gaffney and a chap called Thompson, I was carrying the [wireless] set, I'd lost the toss! Whoever lost the toss had to carry the set! Thompson on my right, he got shot in the legs, but he managed to keep going and we got to this gully.[17]
>
> Private Tony Sacco, Headquarters, 'D' Company

At 08.00, Preston despatched Arthur Vizard and 'A' Company to feel round the right flank of the hill. Using a lot of smoke from the mortars, Vizard pressed forward.

> I was making for a sort of cleft in the hills, I was making for that. When I got there, it was strongly held on either flank. I

> said to my second in command, Tom Logan, 'You take that side; I'll take this side!' I called up and asked for some mortar fire on my side. We went in and attacked – it was pretty rough! We overpowered them – we got into these dugouts. There were fellows still there, one jabbed at me [with his bayonet] – it opened up a large gash in my right thigh – before I shot him in the leg with my rifle, I never shot anyone to kill them deliberately that I could have saved their lives. Unless they were likely to shoot me! I didn't see the point of it. You disabled them, took them prisoner. I wasn't angry, you see.[18]
>
> Major Arthur Vizard, 'A' Company

That night the Germans had withdrawn and the whole of Sidi Barka was under control. George Lyons, who had only recently been posted in from the KOYLI, found his first experience of battle a harrowing experience.

> I went back and helped with some of the wounded. At the end of the gully, I met a young lad of my age who was badly wounded, with half of his behind blown off by shrapnel. His name was Crosby,[19] and I knew he was dying as he was losing so much blood. I tried to comfort him, and his last words were, 'Please, George, give me a drink of water!' Which I gladly did and held his head up to drink, but he passed away as I held him and bled to death. We dug a grave for him there and buried him there on the mountain. We placed his rifle with the bayonet attached and stuck it in the ground beside him so the follow-up troops would know that he was there.[20]
>
> Private George Lyons

One of the small patrols sent out that night was led by Sergeant Stoll. With him was a somewhat nervous James Corr.

> I was back in the wadi, and he came and said, 'You're going on a patrol! You, Corporal Green and me! We think he's moving out!' The Germans had moved out, but before they moved out, they had thrown everything they had at the battalion – all their ammunition. When I get to the top, he says, 'Now don't touch

anything! No matter what you see, and you "fancy" don't touch it!' All booby-trapped it was. They had binoculars on trees, just hanging. There was even two prisoners, two brothers, two of our lads, lying in a trench – booby-trapped. We called the pioneers up, mining experts, they felt round them, cut all the wires. We had no casualties, but then he called the Bren carriers up. Coming up they were running on these mines which we had walked between – and we got two carriers blown up.[21]

Private James Corr, 'B' Company

There was the usual aftermath of battle as the stretcher bearers moved forward. With mines still scattered about this was by no means an easy task. Charles Palmer watched as one lost his nerve.

The stretcher bearers were bringing in their wounded; they had quite a few of these. One of them had a mild attack of shell shock – in other words he panicked. We were standing by. It shook me rigid because the sergeant of the stretcher bearers, who was a very fine sergeant – took this fellow and he smacked his face on either side and said, 'That's it!' Do you know that actually worked! It was panic as much as anything else.[22]

Private Charles Palmer, Intelligence Section, Headquarters Company

After a period of rest while still on the Sidi Barka, on 25 April the 16th DLI reverted to 139 Brigade moving to join them at Djebel Bessioud. Then on 31 April, the brigade moved up to take up positions near the Salt Lake and facing the Djebel Bou Kournine, a prominent feature bequeathed the name of 'Twin Tits' by the soldiery. This dominating mountain had disrupted and thwarted plans for a rapid advance by the 1st and 6th Armoured Divisions. The whole of 139 Brigade was placed under the command of 1st Armoured Division and the main excitement came from countering German patrols probing their positions. On the night of 6 May, the Durhams could hear the roar of the barrage as an attack was put in to Medjez el Bab. Next day came a surprise for James Corr, who had been sent out with an ambush platoon.

> It would be about four o'clock in the afternoon and I saw shadows coming towards me. Well, you couldn't move – you were right underneath these 'Twin Tits'. I peered over the top and there were two engineers. We shouted, 'For Christ's sake, get yourself down!' And they started to laugh! He says, 'It's over!' We were lying there, and the North African campaign was over! All the battalion was back where we had left and enjoying themselves. Nobody had thought to come and tell us it was all over![23]
>
> Private James Corr, 'B' Company

The Allies had broken through and captured Tunis and Bizerta. With all hope gone, the Axis forces surrendered over the next few days.

With the North African campaign over, the battalion stayed in situ for a couple of days, before moving on 10 May to a rest area at the village of Oued Zarga. Here the medical officer, Captain Huw Jones, reflected on the evidence of German defeat before him.

> I recollect standing on a small knoll, looking back at the road to Tunis. The road was long and straight, and as far as one could see either way there were long lines of prisoners. This was May 1943, and I thought the Germans had seen nothing but victories and long lines of prisoners over the past three years. Now the boot was on the other foot and the position was reversed. It must have occurred to them that things would gradually get worse for them.[24]
>
> Captain Huw Jones, Royal Army Medical Corps

On 20 May, the Durhams were called upon to provide a squad for the Tunis Victory Parade, where many were delighted to cause the usual chaos through their light infantry marching speed.

> I was detailed to be 'right marker'; there must have been at least forty. The night before we went with our detachment to the scrublands, just outside the city. Each of us was given a one-man bivvy, a ground sheet and a blanket. We had a smart

new khaki drill uniforms to wear for the parade. We knew
the parade was going to be on the news – Pathé Gazette – we
saw the cameras along the route. It was a vast, tremendous,
wonderful parade – where they all came from, I don't know!
We were marching at 140 paces to the minute as DLI – at the
trail! We were behind the Guards; they had their own music
and they were strictly ninety paces to the minute. We were
marking time for a long time, allowing them to go on, before
we marched again at 140 paces per minute – drawing applause
from the crowds. We were the Durhams![25]

Company Quartermaster Sergeant Jimmy James, 'D' Company

By this time, German prisoners were reported to be driving themselves back into captivity, often in their own transport and without organised guards. Gradually the Allies got a grip on the situation and on 22 May, the 16th DLI moved to a new POW camp established at Ghardimaou and three days later some the first batches of prisoners began to arrive. They would not stay there long. Arthur Vizard was one of several officers detached to escort POW trains all the way back to Casablanca.

> The place was running 'hot and cold' with POWs – there
> must have been a quarter of a million of them. I and other
> officers, each with their own small cadre, took trainloads of
> POWs down to Casablanca. It took three weeks. You'd load
> these chaps on; the majority of those on my train were Afrika
> Corps. Bronzed, young, fair-haired, blue-eyed, vigorous, well-
> disciplined, well-behaved – not all with their spirit broken. They
> were under the charge of a feldwebel, and all orders were given
> through him. His English was excellent. I had picked up enough
> German to manage. These trains were operated by the French
> – they didn't understand English or German! My French was
> limited. The drivers used to say, 'Nous sommes partirons à huit
> heures!' We used to say, 'Ok, all ready for eight o'clock!' In fact,
> they would start the engine up, with all the hissing and roaring
> of steam, at about half past seven. A lot of the prisoners were
> suffering from diarrhoea; it was quite serious dysentery. Some
> of ours too! The chaps would get out of the train, go away a

few hundred yards or so and relieve themselves. Everybody got out, somebody 'brewed up'. Then suddenly there would be a great clanking in the train. Everybody thought, 'Oh, my God! It's going again!' They'd drag all their gear up and running by the side of the train, they'd put it in; they'd have time because it moved so slowly![26]

Major Arthur Vizard, 'A' Company

On 1 June, the 16th DLI began a well-earned rest period at Hammam Lif, a seaside town some 10 miles from Tunis. By then Johnny Preston had begun to make his mark. Preston was not just a brilliant tactical soldier and leader of men, he also had the knack of maintaining morale, sometimes using unorthodox methods to raise a smile.

Colonel Johnny Preston kept our spirits alive – he was a cheerful man. When we paused for two days he gathered Arab children – there were a lot still around – he gathered a group of about twenty and he taught them to sing, 'You are my sunshine'! They had no idea what these words meant; they copied the sounds. He was very proud, and he stood there and conducted 'You are my sunshine'! That whimsical smile and those twinkling blue eyes – he was a great character. The troops loved it – thought it was magnificent! They had all these Arab kids on their laps. Chocolate was given to them![27]

Major Arthur Vizard, 'A' Company

On 2 June, Churchill, accompanied by the Foreign Secretary Anthony Eden, paid a visit to Hammam Lif. Heaven and earth were moved to ensure that there were thousands of troops drawn up to line the road as Churchill and his retinue drove up. Sadly, the planned show of loyalty did not go quite as anticipated. The men had been – in true military fashion – left standing broiling in the blazing heat for hours on end. The result could be predicted.

They took us out in trucks, early morning, thousands of blooming troops from all over the place and we lined up each side of the road just outside of the town. We were told that when Churchill and his retinue came along, 'We want you all to cheer and throw your hats in the air!' Well, we stood! And we stood. It was getting hotter and hotter and hotter and bloody hotter! By gum, it was roasting! There we were stood on that flaming road, no shelter! It was eleven o'clock when he came, and we'd been there from eight o'clock in the morning! They just drove slowly along in their bloody big limousine! The only people that cheered and threw their hats in the air were the officers! The word had gone along the line, 'We're not cheering! After treating us like this! Bugger Churchill! They couldn't arrest us all.'[28]

Private Gordon Gent, MT Section, 'A' Company

★

ON 14TH JUNE, THE DLI BEGAN THE PROCESS OF LONG-TERM REBUILDING with a move all the way back to Blida in Algeria. Plentiful drafts of fresh young men arrived from the UK, with keen young NCOs and officers to lead them. One of the youngest and keenest was Russell Collins, who had just turned twenty. He was the son of a farmstead owner from Truro. His family wasn't that well off, but he was bright and after attending Bodmin County Grammar School, he studied the sciences at Exeter University from 1940–42. Here he was distracted and preoccupied with service in the Officers' Training Corps and local Home Guard. In August 1942, he was called up to Bodmin Barracks, where he was soon identified as prospective officer and eventually commissioned into the Duke of Cornwall's Light Infantry. After more training he was sent off with a draft aboard the *Britannic* to Algiers in June 1943. From there he was despatched to command the Machine Gun Section, Support Company with the 16th DLI. Collins was conscious that he was a boy in a man's army.

> I looked very young in those days – I was just barely twenty and rather small of stature. I was told subsequently that one of the sergeant majors said to his company commander, 'Gawd, Sir, they're sending boys out to us now!' When I was put in charge of the Vickers, that's a heavy piece of equipment, even when it's stripped down into its elements, the tripod and the barrel they weight something like, 60, 70, 80 pounds each! We had to go out on exercise, and they had to be carried up into the fire positions, up over the jebuls. A bit of bravado really, setting off, leading the way, carrying one of these bits and there was a certain amount of smirking behind me – that I was going to crumble under this load. In fact, I kept up very well – I managed it!²⁹

2nd Lieutenant Russell Collins, Support Company

Collins would demonstrate this kind of gritty determination throughout his time with the Durhams.

The miscellaneous drafts were gradually arriving, one of them being William Virr, the son of a stonemason from Bradford. After leaving school at fourteen, he worked on various jobs, unable to settle before starting as an engine cleaner and reserve engine fireman at the Aston Loco plant in Birmingham. Despite his reserved occupation status, he was keen to enlist and obtained permission in August 1941 to volunteer to join the KOYLI. After training, he was sent on a draft to Algiers and posted as lance corporal in charge of Bren gun team with 12 Platoon, 'B' Company. Another new arrival was Robert Ellison, the son of a colliery worker from Birtley. Pre-war he had worked as a grocer's delivery boy and then a van driver on the railways. In September 1942, he was called up and did his basic training with the Cheshire Regiment at Dale Barracks in Chester before continuation training at the DLI Depot at Brancepeth Castle. He passed out as a qualified driver on 15cwt lorries after which he was posted to the 14th DLI at Hornsea in January 1943. Here he did advanced training on the Bren gun before he was drafted out to join the 18 Platoon of 'D' Company 16th DLI at Blida. Another notable character was Ken Lovell who came from a working-class background in Wanstead, although his father had served with the DLI in the Great War. He was a bright lad and got a grammar school education before volunteering at just sixteen for the army in April 1941. During his basic training with the 70th (Young Soldiers) Middlesex Regiment he was deeply unhappy at the bullying discipline he encountered in what he felt was a badly run unit. From there he was posted to a large draft of the 70th (Young Soldiers) DLI at School Aycliffe, and Barnard Castle in April 1942. By then he was utterly fed up, so after being charged for being late on parade he deserted, with the result he was soon arrested, court martialled and served a sentence at Chorley Detention Barracks. On his release he was posted to the 14th DLI at Hornsea in October 1942. Here he was far happier and settled into military life. He was included in a draft that was sent to join the 16th DLI at Blida. After a brief period in the Intelligence Section, he was posted to 'D' Company.

Ronald Sherlaw was the son of a brick manufacturer from Morpeth. He got a scholarship to King Edward VI Grammar School and underwent OTC training, before starting work as a wages clerk while training in accountancy. In 1940 he was called up and spent a year as a private with the Royal Army Pay Corps before being posted for basic infantry training at the DLI Depot at Brancepeth Castle in January 1941. From here he was sent to 14th DLI at Shorncliffe Barracks, Folkestone, where he was approved for training as an officer and commissioned in December 1942. He served as a platoon commander with 14th DLI, before being sent with a large draft to North Africa, where he was posted to 'C' Company. Although he had considerable experience in training back in England, he knew he still had much to learn.

> I think that's the first thing you feel when you come 'dry' into a fighting regiment. There are people there who know a bit more about 'the game' than you do! I certainly had to rely considerably on my sergeant and some of the other NCOs.[30]
>
> Lieutenant Ronnie Sherlaw, 'C' Company

He would be one of the pivotal characters of the 'new' battalion.

Another notable officer to join the 16th DLI 'cast' was Gerry Barnett, who was the son of a cotton mill 'finisher'. He won a scholarship to the grammar school in Leyland before studying at the School of Architecture in Liverpool in 1940. Active in both the Senior Training Corps and the Leyland Home Guard, he enlisted in Royal Fusiliers, before being commissioned and posted to the 14th DLI in Paignton in January 1943. From there he was posted on a draft to the 16th DLI.

> For the first time I had a platoon – a real platoon! I had charge of 13 Platoon in 'C' Company. I tried to do the right thing. I wrote all their names in the book, talked to them all individually and wrote down notes about what they were in peacetime. They were not all from Durham by any means. Some were from South Wales and Yorkshire. A lot of them were miners or in similar jobs in peacetime. Some were hardly into jobs as they were all of a very young age. They were all good chaps! The sergeant and I were mates really! There was no social distinction, except in the unit, where they called you, 'Sir!' We were all in the same boat. I called him, 'Sergeant!'[31]
>
> Lieutenant Gerry Barnett, 'C' Company

The new arrivals had to be bedded into the battalion, so once again the old training routine began. Basic fitness had to be achieved, so daily drill sessions and route marches began while the specialists were busy learning their trades.

This was all building up to a series of arduous tactical exercises in the Atlas Mountains. It involved lots of marching, during which they had to maintain a strict water discipline.

> You'd fill your water bottles, but you hadn't to drink any! They'd check them to make sure you hadn't drunk any! Making sure that you got to where you were going with a full water bottle! Right at the top there was an ice-cold lake – absolutely sparklingly clear – and the Arabs had channelled it down. The water was running down, and you were walking past this cool water – and you weren't allowed to have a drink![32]
>
> Lance Corporal William Virr, 12 Platoon, 'B' Company

The Durhams went out on several exercises similar in character to modern-day orienteering. To encourage everyone to ever greater efforts, there was a very enticing prize for the thirsty soldiers.

> Each fortnight we used to have a map-reading race – and the prize was a bloody great barrel of wine for the winning company! We would go up into the foothills of the Atlas Mountains by truck and then set out from there. Fairly rugged. Eight in the team and anything between 5 and 10 miles. I was put in charge of the orienteering team and during the whole of the time we ran these contests my company never lost it! So, I became very popular in 'D' Company.[33]
>
> Private Ken Lovell, 'D' Company

The tented camp at Blida was not conducive to good health and the men suffered from a variety of unpleasant complaints. One was certainly not unusual for British soldiers in the Middle East.

> There was dysentery flying about. Flies – it wasn't very pleasant going to the latrines at all. You were tickled to death – I'll tell you! The latrines there were just a row of boxes with lids on and a canvas screen round. Every three or so, there would be a flytrap. Which was like a cone of gauze with a piece of watermelon or something like that. The flies would fly out of the latrine and fly up into this trap – and couldn't get out. They used to be full of flies![34]
>
> Lance Corporal William Virr, 'B' Company

There was also the scourge of desert sores, great carbuncles that seemed to gnaw into their flesh, leaving terrible long-lasting scars.

> Most people got those. They'd start off as blister and then it seems to eat in – like an ulcer really. The flies wouldn't leave it alone, you had to get it bandaged up and dressed. They used to dose it with gentian violet. I've still got scars now![35]
>
> Lance Corporal William Virr, 'B' Company

Another common ailment was classed as a disciplinary offence – cases of bad sunburn. They knew what they should and shouldn't do, but in that blazing hot sun it was easy to miscalculate.

> Once or twice, I was caught with sunburn. I used to keep my shirt on as much as possible. We didn't often go out without shirts on. Some lads went without shirts all the time – it didn't bother them at all, they'd get brown and that was it. I don't seem to get brown – I just burn![36]
>
> Lance Corporal William Virr, 'B' Company

The conditions of service were tough, but one panacea was that traditional obsession of the British soldier – tea.

> Tea was an absolute vital nectar. It was during the hottest part of the summer, we were at Blida, which was just a dusty plain, with no shade from any trees whatsoever. Under canvas. So, tea became essential. We used to go into the big marquees where all the officers sat at a long table at teatime – the centre of which was covered with a mosquito net to keep the flies off the buns and cakes! We used to wrap a handkerchief or neckerchief around our necks, because we knew we were going to perspire drinking hot tea in as large quantities as we could manage! There we sat: perspiring and dribbling into our neckerchiefs, snatching our buns from under the net and eating them before the flies got on them![37]
>
> Lieutenant Gerry Barnett, 'C' Company

Many of their men sought more basic pleasures during their time at Blida.

> The company used to go into Algiers. The trucks would take us in – they'd park outside the brothel known as 'The Black Cat'. It would be straight off the trucks, into the bar of the brothel! For a beer to get the dust of the road out of our throats. Then of course some of the lads used to sample the other 'wares'. We had lots and lots of ladies giving us the 'come on' – some of them were very, very attractive. Mainly French, or French North African girls, some Spanish, no Arab girls. One girl,

Janine, was probably the most beautiful girl I've ever seen in my life. A red-haired girl. She really was beautiful. I sometimes used to chat to her; she was engaged to a sailor in the French Navy, and this was how she was earning her dowry. Sometimes they were so busy that there would be a queue up the stairs. How blokes could fancy a 'screw' after dozens of other blokes I have never been able to comprehend.[38]

Private Ken Lovell, 'D' Company

*

AFTER REBUILDING, the battalion was once again considered ready for action. On 11 August, the 16th DLI and the rest of 139 Brigade were transported aboard the *Banfora* from Algiers to Bizerta. It proved to be a very unpleasant journey.

> The whole brigade was on this boat and very quickly everybody seemed to get dysentery or similar types of things. If they weren't being sick, they were galloping at the other end! At the bow of the ship was where the toilets were – and that was absolutely awash! I don't think the toilets had been working for donkey's years. They couldn't flush anything away! Guess who's platoon was given the job of cleaning that up before we got off the boat – No. 18 Platoon! We were bailing that out and putting it out through the porthole. We got the task done eventually, but it was terrible.[39]

Private Robert Ellison, 'D' Company

As this 'hell ship' arrived at Bizerta, there was plentiful evidence of the German bombing campaign.

> You could not get right into the harbour because Bizerta had been obliterated. We were offshore a little bit and they took everybody over to the shore in a landing craft. The kitbags were being lowered down and hoist into a landing craft. As the majority of troops had left the boat, the few that were left said, 'Oh, blow this!' And they just started throwing the kitbags out.

> The boat moved round – and a load of the kitbags went into the sea – including mine!⁴⁰
>
> Private Robert Ellison, 'D' Company

The battalion was moved to a tented camp in an olive grove behind the port. They soon found that the German air raids would be a regular feature of life at Bizerta.

> When the Jerry planes came over, we went up to the top of the hill to watch the fireworks. The bombs were dropping and the anti-aircraft fire from the ships. These planes used to come over and the sky was lit with the searchlights from all the ships. When they got on to him – there was beams going on from every which way and they never got out of it. Down they would come in flames. Poor devils. Then we heard a whacking great thud – very near! We thought, 'To hell with this – we'd better get shelter!'⁴¹
>
> Private Gordon Gent, MT Section, 'A' Company

Even without the best efforts of the Germans the British soldier could often be a danger to himself and those around him! This was demonstrated in truly spectacular fashion by Ken Lovell while attempting to keep the germs down in the primitive latrines. The chosen method was to throw in petrol and light it.

> There was a hell of a 'WHHOOSSHHH!' and a bloody great sheet of flame shot up towards me! I thought the most sensible thing would be to jump through it, because the wind was blowing the flames towards me. I jumped, but instead of landing right on the top of one of the drums, I landed on the reverse slope. With my steel-shod boots, I didn't have much chance, and despite all my efforts, I fell back and with a splash landed in the shit! They say the more you stir it, the more it stinks! I can assure you that's true! Fortunately, I went in with such a thump that it spread the burning petrol away from me and one of my lads grabbed my hand and pulled me out. I wasn't burnt but my hair was singed a bit. I walked the few hundred yards to the sea, and I just laid down in the sea

for about two hours, till I was cleansed! I did have to have a complete new set of khaki drill![42]

Private Ken Lovell, 'D' Company

★

ON A MORE SERIOUS NOTE, the 16th DLI were getting ready for the next major operation, which it soon became apparent would involve an opposed landing – and it was not difficult to work out where that might be!

> We began some fairly hard training. The officers and warrant officers were given an idea of their future target by being taken to a geographical formation the silhouette of which resembled what we ultimately found when we got ashore. We were told that this was such and such a place and the outline of what we were expected to do. Nobody told us where it was, but everybody had guessed that it would be Italy. Two weeks of fairly intensive preparation for the tasks that were to be set us. In the meantime, the rifle companies carried on some pretty hard work. We'd never been as well equipped since we'd come abroad. We were really given everything that we could possibly have asked for in the way of clothing; boots with a warning from the colonel that if we got the boots wet we should not get any further boots for three weeks after arrival! The weapons and armaments that had become depleted during the African fighting were all replaced.[43]

Major Arthur Vizard, 'A' Company

As the time drew nigh, there was also a briefing for the key personnel of 46th Division from a naval officer.

> The officers, warrant officers and senior NCOs of the leading companies went to the cinema. Big cinema it was and there must have been 800 fellows in there. He gave an address, and he had some maps. They weren't very detailed maps, but we were destined for what was known as Green Beach. He went through what they intended to do, and he was an amusing fellow – he

wound up the speech by saying, 'Well gentlemen, that's about all, there are too many of you to take questions. I'm not going to guarantee that my buddies will actually land you on Green Beach, but sure as hell I can guarantee that we will land you in the right country!'[44]

Major Arthur Vizard, 'A' Company

They commenced landing craft training, to ensure that no time was wasted in getting off when they could be under heavy fire.

We had to learn the best way to get off the landing craft. It was a long slender boat, with the two ramps, down the side going down. There was a series of steps. We had to go up and down those damn things; we spent nearly all day there. Up and down, up and down! You had to get used to the depth of the steps, that was vitally important, because once you slipped – that was it – you couldn't afford to slip. You had your two hands holding the rifle above your head. You stepped off the last step and you were on the edge of the sea – ankle deep water![45]

Corporal John Lewindon, 18 Platoon, 'D' Company

The vehicles would be loaded aboard, but they were often carrying far more equipment than was officially intended.

There were certain things laid down as to what had to be taken – and what was not allowed to be taken. The drivers were very ingenious about how much they seemed to squeeze into their trucks. There was a 15cwt truck which had about 30cwt of stores stacked into it! It was a question of getting on everything you possibly could, but only in such a way that the vehicle would still actually drive on to the landing craft and drive off again at the other end.[46]

2nd Lieutenant Russell Collins, Support Company

In the final stages of the preparations, Russell Collins made a foolish error. Like everyone else he was meant to take anti-malaria tablets, which was essential given the high rates of infected mosquitos in both North Africa and Italy. The medical officer, Captain Huw Jones, had early on realised the threat.

> It was quite an experience to see the 'shivering' and 'chattering' of the teeth, the rise in temperature and the sweating. We decided to make a demonstration of malaria. We collected mosquito larvae from the pools in the hills every day for ten days. We put each specimen in a jar. The oldest, ten days, was sizzling with mosquitos and the most recent contained the larvae.[47]
>
> Captain Huw Jones, Royal Army Medical Corps

Collins was one of the officers Bill Virr remembered being on duty, ensuring that every man had taken the required dosage of mepacrine.

> You couldn't get out of that! When you went for your dinner to the cookhouse with your mess tins, there would be an officer there, he'd throw your mepacrine in. There was no use spitting out, because the damage was done – it was that bitter that if you'd spat it out you still tasted it. You had to have one of those regularly. If you did catch malaria, you'd be on a charge for neglect.[48]
>
> Lance Corporal William Virr, 12 Platoon, 'B' Company

Sadly, Collins sometimes failed to take his own medicine!

> By the time I got into the officers' tent to have my own meal, I occasionally slipped up and didn't take my own tablet. So shortly before the invasion, I went down with a mild attack of malaria – I didn't get many brownie points for that! George Ballance gave me a pretty severe ticking off. Very well deserved really because that's the sort of thing officers shouldn't do. But it was only a very mild attack, I've never had a recurrence and it didn't keep me out of action for very long. But it did mean I missed the first phase of the battalion landing.[49]
>
> 2nd Lieutenant Russell Collins, Support Company

On the last nights before leaving, they had a splendid party to 'dispose' of all the alcohol that they couldn't take with them. It was quite a 'do'.

> We had to drink up the floating ration of whisky and beer that we couldn't take with us. So, we had rather drunken party. We played drinking games – 'Cardinal Puff' was a popular one. You have to say a funny rhyme, 'I drink to the health of Cardinal Puff' and if you get it wrong you have to empty your glass. At the same time. you have to tap on the table. You're bound to forget something, so they have to drink their glass and start again. Eventually chaps fell off their chairs – dead drunk![50]
>
> Lieutenant Gerry Barnett, 'C' Company

One thought was uppermost in the minds of men like Gerry Barnett who were going into action for the first time: would they be able to cope?

> There was apprehension; dread really is a better word. The prospect of going into action. I think you get through it mainly by being too ashamed to show that you couldn't get through it! I think that's the only thing that holds you together. You dare not, for your own self-respect, give way to the fear. We'd been brought up between the two wars with knowledge of war, really in a sort of Boy's Own Paper context of bravery, heroism and leadership. The kind of attitude that: 'You don't send a man where you daren't go yourself!' For a while that is the only sort of moral code you use. It's not bravery it's just doing what you're expected to do. It's a ridiculous experience to have to face – every instinct you have is to either hide in your hole and not come out of it even to look, or to run away! That's what any sensible person would do! But of course, you can't! It's your duty to your comrades.[51]
>
> Lieutenant Gerry Barnett, 'C' Company

They would soon know.

6

LANDING AT SALERNO

The natural reaction is not to do what you're doing! The natural reaction is to turn and get out of it! Find somewhere safe. You walk across a field that is being shelled – who would do that if they had any choice? They wouldn't, would they? But it's just discipline; you do it because it's been instilled in you that you do as you're told. If you're given an order, you obey it! That's what you've been trained to do.[1]

Lance Corporal William Virr, 'B' Company

THE INVASION OF ITALY WAS A DANGEROUS UNDERTAKING. Despite American misgivings, the decision had been made to strike at Sicily, with Operation Husky launched on 10 July 1943. The Allies had to be seen to do 'something' to support the Soviets who were facing the full might of the German Army. The invasion of Italy would prevent Axis forces from deploying from the Mediterranean area to the Eastern Front. It would also take advantage of the growing opposition to Mussolini's fascist regime. But the Americans feared a distraction from the 'main event' of the invasion of Europe if a 'slogging match' developed. They begrudged every military resource deployed on a 'sideshow' away from the main front. But their argument was weakened by the reality that the invasion of Normandy would not be a realistic proposition until the summer of 1944. In the end the British had their way.

After overrunning Sicily, an immediate follow up landing was planned and executed. On 3 September, Operation Baytown began when Montgomery's Eighth Army landed on the 'toe' of Italy at Reggio in the Calabria area. The intention was to clear the Straits of Messina for naval passage, but they were also to draw in Axis forces with a view to easing a second landing planned for a few days later at Salerno. The Reggio landings were a success, but the German commander, Field Marshal Albert Kesselring, had divined the British intentions and ordered most of his German troops to fall back, evading combat, relying on the inhospitable terrain and demolitions to delay Montgomery's advance.

Salerno was chosen as the site for the main Operation Avalanche landings to be made on 9 September by the US Fifth Army (US VI Corps, the British X Corps and the US 82nd Airborne Division) commanded by Lieutenant General Mark Clark. The intended beaches were some 20 miles wide and the approaches suitable for landing craft. The initial objectives were to secure the port of Naples and capture the local airfields. In an attempt to secure surprise, they would land without any prior naval bombardment or air attacks, but in this they would be thwarted, as Kesselring guessed where the Allies would land. Meanwhile, under Operation Bedlam, the British 1st (Airborne) Division was ordered to seize the crucial port of Taranto.

The 46th Division (commanded since August by Major General John Hawkesworth) was part of the British X Corps (commanded by Lieutenant General Richard McCreery). Colonel Johnny Preston and his adjutant Captain Waylen were briefed alongside all the other unit COs at a special conference. The initial 46th Division landings would be carried out by 128 Brigade in the Antiferro sector, just to the south of the coastal town of Salerno. To their right, landings would be made by the 169 and 167 Brigades of 56th Division. The Americans VI Corps would land some 9 miles further south facing Paestum. The German forces facing them in southern Italy consisted of the XIV Panzer Corps (15th Panzer Grenadier Division, Herman Goering Division and 16th Panzer Division). All were placed on maximum alert on 8 September, but it was to be the 16th Panzer Division that faced the initial Allied assault.

The 16th DLI would be landing in the second wave on Green Beach, following up behind the 128 Brigade (2nd, 1/4th and 5th Hampshire Regiment). In immediate support they would have a squadron of the 40th Royal Tank Regiment. At the start of the operation, the strength of the Durhams was assessed as some 681 officers, NCOs and men. On 30 August, the various lorries, Bren carriers and jeeps loaded aboard a series of Landing Ship Tanks (LST) at La Pecherie docks in Bizerta harbour. Next day, the men began to board three Landing Craft Infantry (LCI). The embarkation was completed by 5 August, at which point the LCIs set sail in a separate convoy heading for Sicily, where the Durhams would spend a couple of days marching to harden their feet. It was not a comfortable voyage for the men, or anyone else.

> There was a good deal of grumbling, but nobody was any better off than anybody else. It was very democratic: the troops were cramped, the warrant officers were cramped, the NCOs were cramped, the officers were cramped. There was a tiny wardroom topsides in the conning tower section which accommodated the skipper, his No. 1, myself and Tom Reynolds. Tiny![2]
>
> Major Arthur Vizard, 'A' Company

There were also the usual problems with seasickness for all but a few.

> With the LCIs being pretty shallow draft and flat-bottomed, it felt twice as bad as on a normal sort of boat. I was fortunate, I'm a good sailor, I wasn't seasick – there were very, very few others who weren't seasick. Every officer on board was seasick, half the crew were seasick, and the mess decks were absolutely awash with vomit. If we had been going straight into Salerno, the men just wouldn't have been able to break through the skin of a rice pudding, let alone the German defences. I think they'd have just gone ashore and put their hands up they were in such a terrible state. Next morning, I went up on deck about five o'clock and it had calmed considerably, and the sun was coming

up. Then we anchored waiting for the rest of the invasion fleet to gather. All troops were ordered topside, the crew of the ship hosed the mess-decks out, and men were given permission to go swimming in the sea. Those who had soiled their clothes just emptied their pockets, took off their boots, and went in fully clothed. After swimming around for a little while they came back, took off their clothes, laid starkers, hung their clothes out to dry and got themselves respectable again.[3]

Private Ken Lovell, 'D' Company

Then came a piece of news that gave many of the men some hope that the coming ordeal of a contested landing across an open beach might yet be avoided.

Suddenly the hatch doors opened, and the sun's rays stabbed down – and we saw the padre, the Reverend Meek. He said, 'Come on deck, lads, we'll have a little service, let's praise the Lord – Italy has capitulated! We shall have no bloodshed tomorrow morning! Thank God! All those lives saved!' Italy had jacked it in! The 'sages', the wise chaps amongst us said, 'Do you think that Jerry is going let them do that? Jerry will probably kick them in the balls and take over the country' – and he did! I was one of them, 'Praise the Lord! We'll be lucky! They'll be there tomorrow morning and we shall see the bloody lot!'[4]

Company Sergeant Jimmy James, 'C' Company

By this time, James was an experienced NCO, and he was well aware that things were rarely that simple. Officers and NCOs had to control the optimistic expectations of their men as false hopes could be disastrous for morale in the face of a vigorous German opposition.

Nothing would satisfy the padre but that he had a drumhead service of thanksgiving. I took him aside and I said, 'Now look, if you do this, you're going to put the wrong sort of emphasis into troops' minds. They think there's going to be the local mayor and a brass band ready to receive them, the Italians having surrendered. The chances are the Germans will have foreseen that the Italians were getting ready to "jack it in" and will have plenty of their own forces in reserve to take over.' 'No, No!' he said, 'It was a gift of God!'⁵

Major Arthur Vizard, 'A' Company

The grim reality was that the Germans had expected an Italian surrender and had already taken over the defence of Italy. The Durhams had to steel themselves once again. They would in a few hours be landing under fire. Surrounded by their mates, but at the same time somehow alone with their feelings, the men pondered their fate.

> A lot of us were going into action for the first time. I certainly became a little more pensive than I was normally – a lot of men became rather quieter. Some of the men became much more chatty! I wondered what it was going to be like. I wondered what my reaction would be, whether I'd be able to stand up to it. I prayed that if anything happened to me, I'd rather be killed than lose my limbs, or sight; death was preferable to being maimed for life. I wondered what it would be like to have people shooting real bullets at me. It's funny how looking back now, that faced with the prospect of death in a few hours, I was extremely calm. I think most of the lads were too. The married men in the platoon were a little bit more concerned, obviously, they had responsibilities, they thought about their children and there were a lot of family photographs brought out, passed round and commented on. I think we were kinder to each other than perhaps we would normally have been. Just before the landing, we paraded, and Woodlands, our platoon commander, had a weapons inspection. Then he suggested it would be a good idea if we commended ourselves to God and asked his protection. We said the Lord's Prayer together. I don't think I've ever in my life heard it said so fervently as it was on that occasion! We were called up on deck and saw this vast invasion fleet. Just to our left, there was the *Warspite* blasting away with its 15-inch guns, the shells going through the air making the

sound of railway porter running with his [trolley] along the platform.[6]

Private Ken Lovell, 'D' Company

As the LCIs moved towards the shore they came under an increasing amount of fire from German guns.

> I could see splashes when we were still quarter of a mile off. The skipper was very good – it would have taken all his time to be twenty-one – but he was very competent. He knew where he was aiming for. We had this profile of the hills – I could see it quite clearly. The training had been good, the profile was there, except that all the angles were much steeper! They'd warned us about that. I knew where we were going to, I could see the town of Salerno on my left, and we were pretty much on Green Beach. As we got closer, I could make out Positano not far down the coast.[7]

Major Arthur Vizard, 'A' Company

As they approached, there was some desultory fire from a heavy calibre German gun, yet the real fear was of a concerted German air attack. But the RAF and USAAF had done their work and they were mostly undisturbed.

> This sole German plane came across – one plane! We all said, 'It's going for the cruiser!' I said, 'Where's the ack-ack? It's going to sink the cruiser!' There was no ack-ack coming. When it got maybe about 10 yards from the cruiser – that's the way it looked to us – it just disintegrated. Every shell must have hit that flaming aircraft and it came down smashed in bits. Marvellous shooting![8]

Private Tony Sacco, Headquarters Company

This was the harvested benefit of Allied naval and air supremacy.

The landings were timed to begin at 03.30. The Hampshires would make the initial assault, with the 2nd Hampshires intended to land just north of the mouth of the Asa river, with the 1/4th Hampshire to the south, while the 5th Hampshires were in support. There was considerable confusion in the 2nd Hampshires landing, as they were put ashore on either side of the river, although the company landed to the north still managed to exploit inland to take Pontecagnano. The American forces had also managed to get ashore and pushed inland to take Paestum and the high ground beyond the coastal plain.

The 139 Brigade would only start to land much later in the day. Most of the 16th DLI were kept below decks as the LCIs made the final approach to Green Beach. The tension was excruciating, but they had to grin and bear it.

> We heard the gunfire. We heard the American commander of the LCI saying, 'I've got the signal! We're going in!' I can hear him now, a dramatic announcement! He got the signal from the beach master by torchlight! 'It's your turn!' The engines started up and revved, BBRRRRRMMMM! BBRRRRRMMMM! We were all standing to. Bloody bells ringing and blue lights flashing! All standing ready at the bottom of the wooden steps. Suddenly, 'WHUMMFFF!' we felt it shudder! We heard the chains, 'RRRRRRRRR!' The ramps go forward! The hatch door opens.[9]
>
> Company Sergeant Major Jimmy James, 'C' Company

'A' and 'C' Companies would be the first ashore. Led by their officers, they burst out of the landing craft, went running down the ramps and on to the beach. It was immediately obvious that things were not going according to plan. They were faced with a scene of utter chaos.

> I was the lead man off. There were two ramps. Tom Logan took one and I took the other. Then we had two subalterns; they were standing behind and we organised ourselves into three platoons. No. 1 Platoon moved off to its right, rushed up the beach, No. 2 rushed off, moving to the centre and No. 3 to the left. As they came off, they went in their different directions. The sergeant major had organised the disembarkation so that, fairly roughly, you got a fellow moving that way, a fellow moving that way and a fellow moving this way. Which

dispersed them, there were no solid targets on the beach at all. We all got ashore and ran like hell up the sand. There was a lot of small arms fire, some mortar fire, and a good deal of shelling. The sand was constantly being thrown up by quite large calibre shells. I think they were the 88s firing from the sand dunes. It was general fire, but I think they were principally aiming at the vessels because there were quite a few LCIs coming in, they were all along the coast. There were seven casualties on the move up the beach, but I don't remember anybody being killed.[10]

Major Arthur Vizard, 'A' Company

Not far away was Ronnie Sherlaw of 'C' Company.

I seem to remember doing the whole thing in a slight daze. I think I was in the first platoon off the ship. We went straight across the beach. We knew there was a possibility of mines on the beach, but we just had to go – there was no messing about. There was a fair amount of both shelling and indirect firing coming across and this to some extent surprised us as we had been told that the Italians had packed in – and we didn't know that the Germans had pushed their way in and were waiting for us – a certain amount of ammunition flying about![11]

Lieutenant Ronnie Sherlaw, 'C' Company

The priority was to get off the beach, a natural focus for German fire. The Durhams moved inland and established a line of defensive positions a few hundred yards inland.

We moved as far inland as we could get. We spent a very fretful night; I don't think anybody slept at all. In fact, I don't believe anybody slept for three days. It can be done when you're that age. It dulls your senses a bit but when your senses are being stretched like violin strings – it's the aftermath rather than at the time.[12]

Major Arthur Vizard, 'A' Company

On 10 September, the rest of the battalion landed. Not all of them were lucky enough to make a 'dry' landing and the beach area was still under fire. To make matters worse, in a few places the mines had still not been cleared.

> We came down the ramp and spread out, got down on the sands. The first thing you saw was lines of stretchers, the wounded men along the beach, waiting to be loaded back on to the ships. Some 20 yards from the edge of the water, there was a low wall, about 5 foot high. Loads of troops from the Hampshires crouching down behind the wall. Various ones were obviously dead. Mr Coutts was our platoon commander. Our corporal – he just lost it – he went to pieces, he couldn't move, he said, 'No, I can't!' Mr Coutts ordered him back on the boat – he was court martialled later on I suppose. I had to take over the section. I don't know what action he'd seen previously, but it did happen to people who'd seen quite a bit of action; I wouldn't blame anybody for it – a man has a breaking point and when you get to that – that's it. Nothing you can do about it. Another time it could be you![13]
>
> Lance Corporal William Virr, 'B' Company

Robert Ellison soon became aware of a problem with mines on the beach.

> We didn't quite hit the beach, we were waist high in water going in, having to keep all our equipment up above. As we were coming off the boat, there was people trying to get back on because they'd been wounded. One was our sergeant major. They'd got off and ran up the beach and they'd hit land mines. Maybe four or five were killed at that point and six or seven wounded were coming back on the boat with blood pouring off them. That was a bit of a shambles. They were trying to get up the planks as we were going down, which was totally wrong – but what could you do.[14]
>
> Private Robert Ellison, 'D' Company

Clearly some of the mines had been missed, perhaps understandably with the beach still under heavy fire.

> We were told to go to the left as we got off the beach and not to go forward because of the mines. Obviously, we'd landed somewhere that hadn't been cleared. Lying on the beach there was a lot of flak coming over, but it was landing in the sea. Our ships were firing back in – the noise was horrendous from both the Germans and us. There were bodies everywhere and at the far side somebody had piled up a lot of these Hampshires up on top of each other. They'd had a right hiding; they lost a tremendous amount of people there. The next call was the engineer who'd gone forward and put a couple of white lines up so we could get off the beach. We went up through the white tapes off the beach.[15]
>
> Private Robert Ellison, 'D' Company

The battalion was reunited a few hundred lines from the sea and began to move forward, preceded by the Carrier Platoon. Colonel Preston had not yet come ashore, so in the interim they fell under the command of Colonel Aubrey Miller of the 6th York and Lancashire Regiment.

> On the second day, it was easier, we reached the road between Positano and Salerno that we had been given as our immediate target. Working with the York and Lancs we advanced on towards Salerno town – surrounded it completely. It wasn't 'hostile'; the Italians had surrendered. The Germans had withdrawn what forces they had; they weren't very interested in holding a small, isolated fishing town.[16]
>
> Major Arthur Vizard, 'A' Company

When Colonel Preston arrived in Salerno, he organised an 'O' Group of his senior officers to take control of the situation.

> We were under fire! We had a shell on the roof, and I think Harry Mynheer had a nasty flesh wound – he was Support Company. It doesn't do to have too many people together in one group when you're in a forward area like that! The colonel gave us his instruction and 'D' Company and 'C' Company were moving towards the tobacco factory; that was their target.

The Guards were in that area too. My particular task, with 'A' Company, was to go up Hospital Hill.[17]

Major Arthur Vizard, 'A' Company

In the end, the whole battalion was ordered to relieve the men of the 6th York and Lancs on Hospital Hill, just to the north-west, which dominated the town and would be crucial to its defence in the event of any German counterattack. It gained its name through the presence of the La Mennola Mental Sanatorium which lay on a saddle of high ground with 'The Pimple' on the left and 'The Fort' on the right. As they moved forward, Ken Lovell had his first real experience of the horrors of war.

It was on the way up I came across my first dead German. I climbed over a wall and just in front there was a bush. Suddenly, a huge cloud of flies came up and there was a terrible stink. A sweet, sickly smell, something I had never smelt before. As I went past the bush there was a German halftrack that had received a direct hit from a shell. The whole lot, nine or ten men, had been killed, all sprawled in grotesque attitudes, many of them black from burns. I spewed my heart up, it really made me sick, the smell, the stench and the sight of seeing men so violently killed.[18]

Private Ken Lovell, 'D' Company

The relief of the front line – and all its horrors – was completed by 20.00 on 11 September: 'D' Company was around the hospital; 'C' Company was on their left occupying the Pimple; while 'A' and 'B' Companies were initially in reserve on either side of the hospital road in amid the vineyards. A section of Bren carriers and an anti-tanks gun had blocked the secondary road that ran back into Salerno, while the 2/5th Sherwood Foresters were holding the main road between Salerno and Avellino. To the left of the 16th DLI was an area of rough mountainous ground which was held by Commandos on Castle Hill which was to the north-west of the Durhams. Almost immediately, the 16th DLI were called into action. At 21.00, 'B' Company was called forward and ordered to advance through the Bren carrier roadblock and up the secondary road towards the Parato Hill. This move was stymied before it began as the carriers came under attack and 'B' Company were only able to take up positions in the vineyards, just a little forward of a line between the hospital and the road.

Lieutenant Colonel Johnny Preston went forward to inspect the 'C' Company positions at the Pimple although, in the circumstances prevailing, he was not always as welcome as he might have hoped.

> Our positions were just on the upper side of the seminary wall, a stone wall just behind us, about 6 feet high. Looking uphill I saw a big shell coming towards us – you could see big shells sometimes from big guns; they used to travel slow enough. Bouncing down this hillside – we could hear and see it coming! I just hoped it was going to clear the wall behind us before it went off! Which it did, fortunately! Colonel Preston came and stood on the edge of my hole, having a chat looking down on me, with his forked stick! I thought, 'I wish you hadn't come – making our position as obvious by standing in front of it!'[19]
>
> Lieutenant Gerry Barnett, 'C' Company

The company and platoon commanders soon organised their men to provide a continuous system of defence across Hospital Hill.

> The hill was fairly dotted with slit trenches, covered with low scrub on most of its slopes, there were some trees in gullies. Vineyards on terraces on the south-facing slope. The idea is that an infantry platoon has three sections – during daylight you want to keep a few men, perhaps a section, on the forward slope of a hill, where they can observe any impending attack. The other two sections stay on the rear slope of the hill, out of direct line of fire. At night the reverse happens – all three sections move on to the forward slope because you can't be seen, because it's dark, but you do want to have your troops ready for a night attack or at dawn. One of my jobs was to keep going round visiting the platoon trenches and the men in the forward positions. It was the only way of knowing what

was going on! Whether they'd seen anything? Any signs of a German attack. Were they all right? Any casualties? I usually moved flat on my stomach when firing was taking place – you get very good at it – like snakes you can squirm across the ground.[20]

Lieutenant Gerry Barnett, 'C' Company

The anticipated German counterattack did not come straight away. Instead, the hill was remotely harassed by heavy mortar fire. The Germans had developed great expertise with their mortars and multi-barrelled Nebelwerfer rocket launchers.

Mortar fire all the time! Awful! Really terrifying! We could hear them start off, they used to be fired electrically from six-barrelled mortars – we used to call them 'Wurlitzers', because they had a note as the barrels fired in rotation. Then you knew you had about twenty seconds before the bombs arrived. Terrifying it was. You used to lie at the bottom of this hole, looking at a beetle or something and wishing you were somewhere else! The mortar bombs were coming straight down.[21]

Lieutenant Gerry Barnett, 'C' Company

The idea that a mortar shell could crash down beside you in your slit trench, with little or no warning, leaving you with no protection and no hope of survival was a terrible strain. It also seemed to have a cumulative effect, gradually eroding a man's stock of courage.

It was my first experience of being shelled in that way. I was surprised to find that quite a number of the younger soldiers, who had already been in action, took very badly with it. I suppose they'd seen more of what happened when you were shelled than we who hadn't been in action before. I remember one young fellow started screaming and I had to guess how to handle it. I just gave him a good clout in the face, and he stopped screaming. We eventually had to get him out of the line. I was – and am – a great fatalist and I have a very strong

> faith too. I'm not saying that I wasn't frightened – I had the same sort of fears and apprehensions as anybody does, but I refused to let it worry me. I think it was just sort of ingrained in me – my mother always used to say, 'You can't help being frightened, but never show it!' And I didn't![22]
>
> Lieutenant Ronnie Sherlaw, 'C' Company

Strangely, artillery fire, although by its very nature involving larger and far more devastating shells, seemed to be less frightening, mainly because the men learnt to interpret from the sound where the shells would fall.

> An interesting thing happens particularly with artillery fire – you can hear shells coming and bigger shells make lower-pitched noises than smaller shells – but after quite a short time of two or three days, you can tell which ones are coming your way. Newcomers are laughed at when they duck for every shell, when the rest of you know it isn't on your position. I've never been able to describe what it is – how you can tell the difference – but you can![23]
>
> Lieutenant Gerry Barnett, 'C' Company

The Durhams had access to their own heavy support fire from the Royal Navy ships out in the bay. In the right circumstances naval guns could be devastating, as Tom Lister recalled.

> There was a Royal Navy monitor arrived offshore to try and counter this 210mm gun. There was obviously only the one 210 and they had an idea where it was, but they weren't too sure. They sent this young lieutenant, a petty officer, and another bloke, three of them. He was a gunnery officer and he wanted to go up as high as he possibly could to get, to look across the valley and observe. I took him up this place. We stayed there about three hours and there was no sign of any activity at all. He was quite a nice young fellow, and he was advisedly supplied with rum, so we got a nip of rum now and again! Plenty of cigarettes! It emerged – I didn't see it, he did – from a railway tunnel, just about the extreme range of his glasses – and they

were good ones. 'Now,' he says, 'I've got the bastards!' He had the radio, and he directed the fire from the monitor. They were 12-inch guns I think, and they were firing – and honestly you could see the shells sailing through the air. He overshot the first lot and gave some fresh directions – they just blew the entrance to this tunnel to bits – it just disintegrated – you could see it all collapse. He let me see it. He said, 'Well that'll do! I don't know whether I got the gun, but that'll keep them quiet for a day or two!' Which it did![24]

Private Tom Lister, MT Section, Headquarters Company

Unfortunately, the flat trajectory fire from the naval guns meant that not every identifiable target could be hit in the hilly terrain.

The company quartermasters made sure that every man had a full day's rations; it was not particularly palatable, but it had the calories and vitamins they needed to survive. The men located an unusual source of extra water for their tea in the nearby hospital.

There was this peculiar seminary on it, which was a Roman Catholic home for mentally retarded people. This was in the middle of the battle. It had both Germans and our own cooks visiting it for water! The priest in charge was trying to keep his buildings and his people from being involved in the battle, trying to keep in well with both sides to keep it as a peaceful 'island' as it were! Oddly enough, it was honoured by both sides – it wasn't hit.[25]

Lieutenant Gerry Barnett, 'C' Company

Ken Lovell was one of those sent into the hospital – and he actually bumped into the Germans.

We went into the basement of the hospital, a huge place, you could have driven a 15cwt truck along the passages! We found a sluice room and filled our cans up. We came out, got to the intersection of one block, were just about to turn left, and I saw four bloody Germans, also with their buckets of water coming towards us! I said, 'Hey! Fucking Germans! Get out of it!' So, we nipped back a bit sharpish.[26]

Private Ken Lovell, 'D' Company

Doubtless the Germans were equally startled at this brief encounter.

By the 12 September, significant German reinforcements had reached the front and began a series of counterattacks. They arrived faster than the Allies could manage to get their units ashore, who were then further hampered by the difficulties of manoeuvring in the shallow constricted beachhead. The initial concentration was against the American sector, who were forced back from the high ground, as the Germans launched a determined effort to drive a wedge right through to the beach, getting to within 2 miles of the sea. The level of fighting ratcheted up and Salerno became a real soldiers' battle, where tactical objectives had to be seized and held at all costs. Soon it would be the turn of the British to face counterattacks.

On the morning of 13 September, Major Arthur Vizard was ordered to lead 'A' Company as they infiltrated up on to the fort feature to the right of Hospital Hill in conjunction with a Guards attack. Vizard was a competent officer who organised his platoons to the best of his abilities.

> I had No. 1 Platoon[27] on the left, No. 3 platoon on the right and I was in the middle with the reserve platoon, moving up this heavily wooded hill. We really began to come under quite strong sustained fire. A lot of mortar fire. In fact at one stage I rang on my 18 [wireless] set and spoke to the colonel and said, 'Are you quite sure that we aren't too far forward and that we're not running into our own mortar fire?' 'No', he said, 'What you're getting is from Jerry!' And we were getting a lot! We moved on further up through these wooded pines, spreading out as far as possible. I could see defended positions, they were sort of dugouts, but the troops had gone. The Germans were mostly up and around the hospital up at the top of the hill. I think we may have moved slightly further forward than the Guards on the right towards the tobacco factory – I

think they were having a hard time and I could understand that. But we were moving forward, and as a result we were getting not only opposition from the front, but we were getting it strongly from the right flank. We were moving through this gully and there was tremendous burst of Schmeisser machine pistol fire from, it couldn't have been more than 300 yards away on the right hand side. Simultaneously Sergeant Major 'Nutty' Wilson, I and Tom Logan jumped. Unfortunately, poor Tom, he jumped a bit too late. I landed on top of the sergeant major, and Tom landed on top of me, but he'd been wounded badly through the stomach. We got him dressed as best we could, got him onto a stretcher and evacuated. But he died.[28] I always felt very badly about this, because I thought it was my job to jump last. It should have been me: I should have pushed Tom in and gone afterwards. But its instinctive when you've a Schmeisser firing at 800 rounds per minute – you jump![29]

Major Arthur Vizard, 'A' Company

They returned fire as best they could, but they were being drowned out by the German mortars and overwhelmed by a rash of small arms fire.

We were firing our small 2-inch mortars. I called up the colonel and asked him for the Mortar Platoon to lay [support fire] on to the right flank, and he said, 'I've got it on there already!' But it didn't stop whatever was happening over there! After Tom had been carted off, we pressed on up the hill. I left the No. 1 Platoon under Miller, and I half swung it off its axis up the hill, slightly to face the right hand side. I moved No. 3 forward – and we half veered towards the right – so we were facing where the trouble was coming from. It was quite clear that this was where Jerry was putting in one of his principle retaliatory attacks to try and force people back to the beach. We had some nice reasonably well protected situations – in these gullies with gnarled roots of these pine trees. We were able to lie in there and give them everything we'd got. We'd only got twelve Bren guns, but you can do quite a lot of harm with twelve Bren guns. We caused them to pull back and we were able to resume our move up the hill having at least quietened down if not silenced this flank attack from Jerry.[30]

Major Arthur Vizard, 'A' Company

As they resumed their advance the Germans retaliated with a further barrage of intensive mortar fire from the other side of the main hospital buildings.

> I sent Miller's No. 1 Platoon back over to the left, then Nos. 2 and 3 moved forward. We no longer had a reserve platoon; we were moving on a company front. The mortar fire became much more intense, and we began to sustain quite a lot of casualties. The stretcher bearers were at work – it was mostly shrapnel splinters, I don't remember anyone getting a direct hit, but it still does a lot of harm. It was quite clear that they had switched from the flank – they were now coming over the top of the hospital. The poor old nuns inside must have had a rotten time of it. This continued until about twelve o'clock. I was crouched and one of these mortar bombs landed to the right of me, a splinter zipped through and got me at the bottom of the back. It wasn't particularly painful at first, it was very largely a flesh wound, but it had damaged the spine a bit. It was difficult to walk. I got patched up and continued moving forward. But the medical sergeant who was with me said, 'You ought to jack it in, you're losing blood!' I said, 'Well, no, it's all right!' Tom Logan had gone you see. If Tom had been there, it would have been a different matter. We pressed on and in the end the sergeant was right because I passed out from loss of blood. Nothing I could do about it.[31]

Major Arthur Vizard, 'A' Company

He had refused morphia, keen to remain sharp, but now the unconscious Vizard was evacuated by stretcher for medical treatment.

> I got ninety-six stitches in the back, and I got clips put in which halted most of the bleeding. The trouble was the spine was chipped. All regimental aid posts and dressing stations were very gory places. Like a butcher's abattoir. It was shocking!

> Fellows covered in blood from head to foot. All over their hair and faces and everything else. Because they were really at the sharp end. Blokes coming in and they only had a matter of minutes to save a life. Amputations were carried out with incredible speed. I saw one fellow have his leg taken off and it didn't take more than a minute and a half. Away it went. They did a hard, a very good job.[32]
>
> Major Arthur Vizard, 'A' Company

He was evacuated aboard a hospital ship to Tripoli. Before he left, he made a generous gesture, which ensured he maintained his popularity among his men, as Gordon Gent, a lorry driver back at the 'B' Echelon could testify.

> The officers had an ammunition box for their private possessions on the corporal's truck. Vizard and his second in command, Captain Logan, were wounded – Logan died on his way to base hospital. Vizard sent word down with the quartermaster to open these boxes up and get out all the cigarettes – the officers always had a good supply of cigarettes! Vizard ordered us to pass on all these cigarettes to dish out amongst the lads – which was a fine thoughtful gesture really![33]
>
> Private Gordon Gent, MT Section, 'A' Company

Vizard loved telling a story of the insouciance of two wounded Guards officers he encountered on the hospital ship.

> There were a lot of guardsmen there. I remember two particularly: a company commander and a subaltern. Each had lost an arm. The company commander said, 'Well, it's all right George, you can pick my nose and I'll pick yours!' That's good Guards spirit![34]
>
> Major Arthur Vizard, 'A' Company

Vizard was not out of the woods himself and he had a further operation on his back while still at sea. Then a course of the new experimental penicillin treatment had amazing results, restoring him to health while in the South African General Hospital in Tripoli. At which point he promptly caught hepatitis which extended his convalescence period. Throughout, this 'born and bred' Londoner was keen to rejoin the 16th DLI and turned down all alternative postings. He eventually 'deserted' and unofficially caught up with them in Syria in March 1944.

Meanwhile, Lieutenant W. A. Miller and Company Sergeant Major S. A. Wilson took control of 'A' Company, but it soon became apparent that any further advance on the fort was hopeless, so they fell back under the cover of 3-inch smoke shells from the Support Company. Next day, 'A' Company was pulled back into reserve. At the same time the Hospital Hill defences were effectively doubled as the 2/4th KOYLI moved up into the line on the right and around the hospital itself. The Germans made several harassing attacks, but on the night of 15/16 September there were two serious incursions. The first was an attack at dusk by a company of Panzergrenadiers of the 16th Panzer Division on the 'D' Company positions, which were then to the left of the hospital. Whoever had been on duty in the forward outposts had either been dozing or had been silently despatched before they knew what was happening.

> They came up the hill, they spread themselves out, but there were quite a lot of them. A lot of them had Schmeissers and there were one or two who had the heavier machine gun – similar to the Bren. It was dark, but somebody in 16 Platoon on the right saw them and opened fire. Once they opened up, everyone else did. We didn't see that we'd hit that many of them, but there still seemed to be plenty of them.[35]
>
> Corporal John Lewindon, 'D' Company

Robert Ellison was one of those who were taken by surprise. It was a real shock.

> Jerry got right up on top of the hill – on top of us! The first thing we knew he was starting to fire down. I put my hand out to get a hold of my rifle and the bullets smashed it – the butt was blown to bits! There was no question then of getting the rifle, it was just a matter of trying to keep down. I was lying

there flat down, and some shrapnel went right down the side of my boot and practically severed the sole, the sole was hanging off. I was lucky! I might have lost my foot! There were men hit and they were screaming and yelling. We had a couple of grenades and we lobbed them back. One bloke grabbed the Bren – he'd only just got word in a letter that morning that his brother had been killed somewhere on another front. You can imagine the state he was in. He saw these Germans and he just went berserk – he killed a few of them with the Bren gun, firing from the hip. When he jumped up firing, we were able to get out of the hole and take part in the firing as well – and get under cover properly.[36]

Private Robert Ellison, 'D' Company

Their situation was still desperate and many of the men believed that without the support of their mortars, they would have been doomed.

> Frank Duffy and the company headquarters were just behind us – we could look round and see them, but they were some little way down the hill. They had a detachment of mortars there – it was a good job that they did! The mortars under Sergeant Joe Kellet were firing almost vertically, because the range was next to nothing! He had to be careful that his bombs weren't coming down and going off round 17 Platoon. Because Joe couldn't see anything, Frank Duffy only gave him a rough range. That broke the Germans up and they scattered a bit. Some of them turned around and started to retreat. Which made it a little bit easier for us; we were able to 'get on with it' more. They got quite close – within a 100 yards easily. I think we'd have been overrun if that detachment of mortars hadn't been there. Then Duffy did the only thing that he could think of – and the order went out to 'Fix bayonets!' I suppose it was a psychological thing. They didn't like bayonets any more than we did![37]

Corporal John Lewindon, 'D' Company

At the heart of the fighting was Lieutenant Woodlands as he led his men up the hill.

> Suddenly, Lieutenant Woodlands came galloping up and said, 'Right, fix bayonets, we're going to go into a bayonet charge!' He led us, at the front, up the hill, over the slope and into the Germans. We really ran as fast as we could, Lieutenant Woodlands called out, 'CHARGE!' and we charged! Now the Germans were virtually amongst the positions of 16 and 18 Platoons. We got stuck into the Germans. I hadn't got my Bren gun because it was still in pieces, but I'd got a Tommy gun, I think Mr Woodlands gave it to me. As we were going, I was firing from the hip. I suddenly saw a German lying down behind a MG 42. He looked at me and I looked at him – I pulled the trigger and nothing happened, so I just swung the Tommy gun round, grabbed it by the barrel and smashed him over the head. I didn't know whether I'd killed him, or whether he was unconscious, or what. I went on. I think they were taken by surprise. There's a lot of stories that the Germans don't like cold steel, but I don't think anybody does come to that! I think if some bugger had come at me with a bloody bayonet, I might have done a sidestep or something. The Germans fled into a box barrage that our mortars had put down behind them. We took quite a number of prisoners, killed quite a few. I went back and saw this German that I'd slammed. I really was sick. I don't think it was the fact that his head was stove in, but just the fact that I had actually killed a human being, which shook me. All right, he'd have killed me if he'd got the chance, but nevertheless I was physically sick. I vomited.[38]
>
> Private Ken Lovell, 'D' Company

Caught cold, before they could organise a coherent defensive position with allotted fire plans from their own mortars and artillery, the Germans were soon demoralised and either surrendered or faded back into the night.

> We took fifteen to twenty prisoners there. They got to the top of the hill, they were quite close and they realised that the bayonets were out and they weren't going to get very much further. We got round them – any arms that they had were taken from them. They were standing there with just the

clothes that they were wearing. We managed to take an officer prisoner – he was arrogant. We took them down to Frank Duffy. He passed this German officer, who had his hands on his head, but he was shouting giving vent to his feelings. Nobody took any notice, of him! Duffy reached up, unstrapped his watch and took it! That made him shout even more![39]

Corporal John Lewindon, 'D' Company

The prisoners were sent on to battalion headquarters back in the vineyards.

But the Germans were not done yet. Later the same evening there was another serious attack, this time on the 'C' Company positions on the Pimple. Once again, the Durhams were caught napping.

Major George Jobey had his company headquarters on the rear slope in a tiny gardener's hut used by the Italians in the vineyards. It was on one of the terraces where there were these few vines. At dusk, he sent for us, the three platoon commanders, for an 'O' Group. We all gathered in this tiny hut, but we never got round to getting the orders, because there were sounds of firing from outside the hut. Someone flung open the door and said, 'We're under attack!' Sure enough, the Germans were coming down the terraces, throwing grenades and firing with Schmeissers. It was a great mistake to call us away from our platoons at dusk because they are the critical times: dusk and dawn. They were right through our positions. We were at the rear of our company positions and the Germans were round the hut virtually. The sergeants must have been with us.[40]

Lieutenant Gerry Barnett, 'C' Company

This was a disastrous state of affairs. Whatever they wanted to do, the Durham officers would have to do it themselves, organised 'on the hoof' as there was no time to prepare a proper counterattack.

There was a box of grenades in George's hut, so we all grabbed a handful of grenades. That brings me to a little

> criticism of army uniform in that there is nowhere on a British infantryman's uniform to carry grenades. So, you stuff them down your shirt and hope your belt's tight enough to hold them up. We grabbed some grenades and ran out. There was no sort of orders or directions, we just started attacking back up the hill. It's just an instinct really – when you see Germans in the flesh to attack – there's nothing else you can do, you can't run away. We didn't know how to, it never occurred to us. Sort of unwilling – but duty bound.[41]
>
> Lieutenant Gerry Barnett, 'C' Company

As the officers charged up the hill, they were gradually reinforced as some of their men saw what was happening and joined in the attack.

> The Germans retreated and we slowly collected 'odd bods' from our trenches where they'd been overrun and not observed; that increased our strength a bit. But really it was an officers' and sergeants' attack! We used grenades and I had my Tommy gun. Darkness came as we moved up the hill, until we reached the little saddle below the final 'Pimple'. By that time, it was dark but bright moonlight.[42]
>
> Lieutenant Gerry Barnett, 'C' Company

Here they paused to consider the situation. At this point Ronnie Sherlaw made what could have been a fatal mistake, reflecting the continued confusion as to what was happening.

> The Germans were obviously on and around the final 'Pimple' because I could hear them talking in loud voices as they seemed to be digging in, while they used a machine gun to fire at us. Ronnie Sherlaw for some reason thought they were some other company's troops and he stood up in bright moonlight in his fairly light-coloured khaki drill uniform – you could see him for miles, stood up and shouted, 'Stop firing, you bloody fools, this is 'C' Company!' I said, 'It's the Bosche, Ronnie!' On which he dropped down smartly under cover![43]
>
> Lieutenant Gerry Barnett, 'C' Company

Total chaos reigned. No one knew what was happening.

> Complete confusion – the whole battle had been confused but this was very confused. We got to the top of this 'Pimple', it was a small summit sloping away on all sides and there must have been a group of Germans about 20 feet away. They were within grenade-throwing range. We could see the flashes coming from their Schmeissers as they fired at us. There were about five of us at the most on our side at the top – there wasn't room for any more anyway! We were firing at them and throwing our grenades; they were firing back and throwing grenades. I was lying down between bursts of fire, then kneeling up so I could see just over the crown of the hill, see their flashes and then firing back with my Tommy gun – when it worked. The first time I pressed the trigger and there was just a rough grating noise as the bolt slid forward because the dust was slowing the action. I got back, lay down again, pulled the oil bottle out of the butt, oiled the bolt and like a good soldier put the oil bottle back in the butt. I got back up and it worked, fortunately, it fired then. It's a very heavy weapon of course, a .45 round, a most dreadful thing really to use in action, a very slow rate of fire – it goes 'Bop! Bop! Bop!' whereas a Schmeisser is more like a 'raspberry'. It has a safety catch with three places: safe, which means you can't fire; single shot, which means that every time you pull the trigger you fire one shot, but the bolt re-cocks itself; or rapid fire. You always kept it on rapid fire because it was such a slow action that you could actually fire single shots – you had time to let the trigger go in between shots. That's how we used it – every shot was re-aimed. [44]
>
> Lieutenant Gerry Barnett, 'C' Company

Ronnie Sherlaw had even less confidence in his personal weapon that night – a Webley pistol. It was notoriously inaccurate in unpractised hands and few officers could hit the proverbial barn door. Many officers joked they would be better off throwing it rather firing it at any German they encountered. But Sherlaw was lucky.

> I was going forward with a .38 pistol in my hand – which is a useless implement! As I crawled up a slit trench, I put my head over it – and there was a German helmet came up – and I immediately pulled the trigger – and I shot him. Not very straight, but I hit him! I had a horrible feeling of dismay. That was the first time I'd ever been face to face – and it was fortunate I'd shot him – because if I hadn't, he'd have shot me![45]
>
> Lieutenant Ronnie Sherlaw, 'C' Company

Close by, Gerry Barnett was still firing his Tommy gun. Then he seemed to have a close escape from what appeared to be near certain death.

> Then I heard a little noise to my left, and glanced, just as a grenade went off about 2 feet away, just alongside my face. Nothing seemed to be wrong, so I carried on firing – and then I noticed that my Tommy gun was getting very slippy. We were in moonlight, and you can't see colours. When I relaxed again, I could feel the warm blood coming on to the weapon, felt around and found that it was coming from my chin, I had a flap hanging down, an artery had gone, and it was spurting out. All in the midst of this mess we were in. I bandaged myself up, put my chin back on and wrapped my field dressing round it because I'd heard it said that if you put the flesh back it seals. Wrapped my field dressing round my head and put my tin hat back on to hold it on. I carried on and the action finished very shortly after that. We captured two prisoners, one wounded, the rest had gone. I said to Ronnie, 'Well, I'll take these down because I'll have to go and get this chin sealed up – I can't stop it bleeding!' It was dripping you see. I walked down the hill with these two Germans. There was always a sort of strange friendship immediately prisoners were taken – I suppose we were all in the same boat because we were all relieved to be out of it.[46]
>
> Lieutenant Gerry Barnett, 'C' Company

Barnett had his rather badly cut chin and broken jaw bandaged up by Captain Jones. By then the combination of fatigue and loss of blood caused him to fall unconscious on his stretcher. He would sleep for some forty-eight hours as he was being evacuated by hospital ship. After periods in hospital, convalescent and transit camps in North Africa he would rejoin the 16th DLI in Italy in December 1943.

Back on the 'Pimple', Ronnie Sherlaw was once again master of all he surveyed. This was particularly apposite as he now had the assistance of a FOO from the Royal Artillery.

> We could see on the other side, running up from the Avellino Road, a road running straight up the mountain. We saw German vehicles travelling up the road; a big convoy of them, an awful lot. I had with me a chap from the gunners called Mike Frewer, a FOO from 149 Battery, 70th Field Regiment. We called on him to do what he could to do something about this. He brought in his own field regiment of course! He brought the navy in! He brought in AGRA – the Army Group Royal Artillery 5.5-inch guns! After he got all that on – he had a bit of RAF! We really did them an awful lot of damage. That was my first experience of using the FOO. It was very spectacular, and it gave me an insight into what could be done by the Royal Artillery by just having a FOO with you![47]
>
> Lieutenant Ronnie Sherlaw, 'C' Company

The correct use of concentrated artillery was one of the great lessons of the Great War, one that it had taken far too long to relearn.

They little knew it, but these were the last German attempts to disrupt the Salerno positions. On 16 September, Montgomery's Eighth Army had begun to arrive from the south, more Allied troops had been brought ashore, and it was evident that the Allies could not be driven into the sea. Reluctantly accepting this, Kesselring began to withdraw his forces to the north. As if by magic, the German troops in front of the 16th DLI up on Hospital Hill seemed to disappear.

On 18 September, Russell Collins, who had recently rejoined the unit following his misfortune in catching a mild dose of malaria, was ordered by Colonel Johnny Preston to carry out a fighting patrol with his men of 9 Platoon, 'A' Company, now commanded by Captain Pritchard replacing the wounded Vizard.

> I was briefed by the CO that the enemy were believed to be withdrawing from around Salerno to a range of hills further behind. It was just a question of me taking my platoon and going forward to find out how far they had gone, and whether the ground in front of us was clear. It was a fighting patrol – I was to take my whole platoon. We'd had these simulated situations innumerable times on training and I was well able to cope with them with distinction, although I say it myself. But here I felt totally confused, totally unequal to the situation. The CO was going on about covering fire from the ships in the bay, and there were American troops nearby, and so on and so forth. All would be well – and off I was to go! The radio communications were not very good.[48]
>
> 2nd Lieutenant Russell Collins, 'A' Company

At this point in his career, Collins was not yet ready for this kind of responsibility. As he was new to the locality, he was also not confident that he understood the situation he was facing. Nevertheless, nothing daunted, he led his men forward.

> I hadn't gone I don't suppose more than 100 yards, at the very most 200 yards, before we were fired on from a position beside the hospital which was about 150 yards down on the right. There was a light mortar detachment there and they were firing 2-inch mortars in our direction. We were on a slope leading down towards the hospital and machine guns were being fired at us. I was on this bank, completely exposed to fire, although a little bit concealed from view, and I could see the bullets hitting the bank either side of me. I thought, 'Well, this isn't on!' I was weighing up in my mind what do I do about these people: do I ignore them and go on? I hadn't really positively identified them. I decided that really they were too close on my line of attack and that I couldn't go on.[49]
>
> 2nd Lieutenant Russell Collins, 'A' Company

Baffled by the situation, which seemed to bear no resemblance to his briefing, he tried to get through to Pritchard on his portable 88 wireless set. He was doomed to disappointment.

> The wretched thing was totally unreliable, and it didn't have a range very often of more than a 100 yards. So I sent an orderly to run back to the company headquarters, with a written message to say what the situation was, and say what I was proposing to do: namely, trying to sort out this irritation on the right flank and then continue to advance. About ten minutes later the orderly came back a gibbering wreck, telling me he'd run into some Germans between where we were and the company headquarters, which as I say wasn't more than a very few hundred yards back, so that seemed pretty drastic. Certainly, there were Germans in very close proximity to us and as far as I was aware there were or could have been Americans as well. Their steel helmets are very similar in shape, particularly in poor light, or when partly concealed and camouflaged. Well, they could have been, or he could have just seen an apparition, but he was pretty frightened by something! I just had to assume or infer that they were Germans.[50]
>
> 2nd Lieutenant Russell Collins, 'A' Company

Left on his own, facing a situation that was foreign to him, Collins made what seemed to him to be the only rational decision.

> Far from the enemy having withdrawn, they were very much on the doorstep! I determined to make some sort of attack on this post that was firing on us, going around the right flank, which took me to the right – back towards the hospital wall below our position. As we approached the hospital wall, all hell was let loose, and our own battalion mortar platoon brought down the defensive fire slap on top of my platoon. Well, it was the first time for me. It wasn't the last time! I mean one is just cringing, there is nothing you can do. It's no good running, because if you run you're bound to be caught in the blast, or shrapnel. The only thing you can do is to hug the ground as

> closely as possible and just hope and pray that the next one isn't going to land on top of you.⁵¹
>
> 2nd Lieutenant Russell Collins, 'A' Company

Then the situation veered even further out of control when Pritchard, sighting 'unknown' troops moving about to his right, decided they were Germans and launched an attack on them.

> Our own company followed up the concentration with an assault with bullets and bayonets. I was screaming mad with them really! I'd been slightly hit myself in the hand – a tiny bit of shrapnel through the knuckle. I just stood up in front of this onslaught of bullets and bayonets with these chaps charging and waved my arms and said, 'You bloody idiots, can't you see it's us!' Then everybody was very crestfallen and then we tried to see to the wounded and pick up the pieces of those who had been blown to bits. I think we were about twenty-nine people and only five survived it. That was a rather nasty baptism of fire.⁵²
>
> 2nd Lieutenant Russell Collins, 'A' Company

His platoon, his first real command, had been almost destroyed. It was an inauspicious beginning for the young officer. But, what else could he have done? Collins was inexperienced, but it had been a terrible initiation.

> I had the time over again; I don't see what else I could have done. If I was more experienced, I might have played it differently, but I'm not quite sure how. To have gone on with, as I understood it, enemy troops around and behind me, would have been even more foolhardy. I would have just walked straight into the bag, so there was no point in doing that and I couldn't get through to the company commander. I'd only just arrived on the scene not more than thirty-six hours earlier. I was new in that company, I really hadn't got my bearings, and the communications were poor – the whole thing was what we also call an 'MFU'. If you don't know what that is, it's a 'Military Fuck Up'!⁵³
>
> 2nd Lieutenant Russell Collins, 'A' Company

Then to add insult to the very minor injury he had suffered with a 'chipped' knuckle, Collins found he was to be evacuated as wounded. To him this was nonsensical.

> I was very shaken, but I felt with a few deep breaths that I would be all right again. But I was made to go back to the regimental aid post for a check-up. Then I had to go and tell the CO Johnny Preston what had happened. He was very sympathetic and understanding, he said, 'Well OK, don't worry about it now!' Then, to my astonishment, the medical officer decided I was to lie down with the casualties who were going to be evacuated further back. I said, 'Well, wait a minute, there's some mistake here, I've only got this little bit of a nick through my knuckle.' They may have thought it was going to sever, or partially sever that tendon. The medical policy then was that it was impossible to treat people in the forward defended locality. You got them back. I wasn't given a choice![54]
>
> 2nd Lieutenant Russell Collins, 'A' Company

One suspects he was evacuated to give him a chance to settle down after his ordeal. Such a view is given credence by the reception he was given when he rejoined the 16th DLI in October.

> I was sent for by the CO, Johnny Preston. Then there was another psychological shock for me in a way. When he saw me he said, 'Well, I'm glad to see you, I had asked for you back!' That absolutely took the wind out of my sails – it hadn't dawned on me before then that of course he might have decided that under no circumstances did he want this officer back! It was nice of him to try to put me at my ease like that![55]
>
> 2nd Lieutenant Russell Collins, 'A' Company

He would prove to be one of the very best officers ever to serve with the battalion, but everyone must start somewhere.

On the night of 19/20 September, the 16th DLI were at last withdrawn from Hospital Hill and moved to San Leonardo which was the 139 Brigade rest area. It had been an exhausting ten days since they landed; days that seemed like weeks.

> I was absolutely shattered from lack of sleep. When they brought us off to go along to the far end of Salerno for a rest, we marched so far and stopped on the road – and I just went dead in the gutter, the ditch. The first thing I knew was my friend shaking me and saying, 'Come on, we're moving again!' Absolutely fatigued.[56]
>
> Private Robert Ellison, 18 Platoon, 'D' Company

For some it proved too much. One such was Albert Scriven who was evacuated from Salerno suffering from serious shell shock (Post Traumatic Stress Disorder or PTSD).

> They were really frightened of everything; they were living on edge. Their nerves had more or less given way. You tried to cheer them up and get them calmed down. I was with 'Ernie' Scriven when his [breakdown] happened. Ernie was bad then; he was really on edge. I think he went back. He wasn't the only one, there was quite a lot of them. There was not a lot you could do! They were just frightened to death. They've got to go back otherwise it upsets the other chaps.[57]
>
> Private Alexander Gray, Headquarters Company

One distinguished figure who left the battalion as they pulled out was Company Sergeant Major Jimmy James. He had suffered severe ear damage early in the fighting but had stuck it out until the end.

> One mortar bomb dropped very, very close to me. The blast made my ear suppurate. I was discharging from the ear. It was pouring out like custard! It got worse and worse! Pouring out of my ear down my neck. I didn't tell the company commander, but he must have been able to see! The adjutant came around and said, 'We're pulling out in half an hour! What the hell is the matter with your ear? You must be in agony!' I said, 'Aye, I know, I am!' He said, 'You go now, down to the Casualty Clearing Station, down that road and you'll be on that hospital ship!' I said, 'I don't want to go, Sir! I've seen that hospital ship being bloody dive-bombed! I'd rather stay here with the lads!'

He said, 'There's no hospitals, no treatment here, we can't do anything for you! I'm giving you orders now to go down to the CCS!'[58]

Company Sergeant Major Jimmy James, 'C' Company

He reported back to a casualty clearing station where he was diagnosed with a perforated ear drum and evacuated by hospital ship to Bizerta. He was medically downgraded due to permanent loss of hearing and ended up in various administrative capacities rising to being a RSM. He never returned to the 16th DLI. He would be missed.

During their brief rest period, the 16th DLI had their losses made up. One new arrival had an intimate knowledge of many of the key officers. William Cowans was born in Gateshead in 1919, but his father's early death meant that he had a very straitened upbringing with his mother working as a cleaner to keep her three children as best she could. On leaving school at fourteen he had various jobs before working in a boiler house at a coke works. After his call up in 1939 he proved an excellent soldier and was singled out for rapid promotion. He oversaw training squads at Brancepeth Castle, before being posted to 14th DLI on its formation in Edinburgh in 1940. Here he would train both Ronnie Sherlaw and Pat Casey as raw recruits. After promotion to sergeant, he was posted to serve with the 18th (Beach Brick Battalion) DLI in Syria, Tunisia and Sicily, before landing to carry out work in the Salerno harbour and docks. When that battalion was broken up, he was posted with draft to 'C' Company.

> RSM Thomasson said, to me, 'Hello, Cowans!' He took me to the camp, out of the line. He said, 'Well, I'm going to put you in "C" Company, you'll have a surprise when you get there!' I said, 'What do you mean? I hope it's a good 'un!' He dropped me at 'C' Company, and I went to knock at the company office. The first man that opened the door, I looked at him, it was Captain Sherlaw! The lad that was in my platoon for six weeks in Scotland! Next to him was Captain Casey! My old corporal from joining up in Brancepeth. They were both captains! Sherlaw was

company commander – he was good, very good! He was made a major before the next battle. Casey was assistant company commander. I remembered Casey – he came to see me before he went from Folkestone. He said, 'I'm leaving, Bill!' I said, 'Where you going?' 'Officer Cadet Training Unit!' I said, 'You'll never make an officer!'[59]

Sergeant William Cowans, 'C' Company

Now was the time to eat his words! But he was able to forge a decent working relationship with both Sherlaw and Casey. At the same time one young – nameless – officer joined the unit who seemed to have no idea of the realities of active service – or the exhausted state of the battalion.

We got an officer there who'd come straight from England. He arrived in semi-darkness one evening and he wanted to know where his batman was! He buttonholed a bloke and said, 'Bring my tea and shaving water in the morning!' The bloke said, 'You can get your own bloody tea, mate!' That attitude! He said, 'You're talking to an officer!' He said, 'Well, I'm not a batman either, I'm a corporal – and I've got my own job to do – I'm not running about after you! We don't do that in this battalion!' The officer was going berserk and, by pure coincidence, the second in command was having a 'decko' across the valley with some binoculars just above our heads. He came down and introduced himself and said, 'We'll just have a little word!' He told him that a quite a lot of them didn't have permanent batmen and he was getting off on the wrong foot![60]

Private Tom Lister, MT Section, Headquarters Company

One wonders how well that officer settled into the Durhams.

While at rest, the 16th DLI became embroiled indirectly in what is sometimes portrayed as a rather shameful episode in British military history. This had its origins in the insensitivity and duplicity of elements within the British high command. Some 1,500 previously wounded soldiers of the 50th and 51st Divisions had been embarked aboard transports from their camp in Tripoli. As far as these men knew, they were to rejoin their parent units in Sicily and indeed were soon to return to Britain to prepare for the invasion of Normandy.

One of them was Ronald Elliott, who had been serving as a signaller in a Holding Battalion before being drafted out and posted to the 9th DLI. Elliott, the son of a coal miner, was born on 19 February 1923 in South Shields. This meant that he was sixteen in 1939 and one way or another his date of birth meant that he was destined to take part in the Second World War. At the time he was working as a clerk at the borough treasurer's department at South Shields town hall. First, he joined the Home Guard, then tried to join the RAF, only to be thwarted by his myopic eyesight. Thus in September 1942, he was called up and the army began to 'make him a soldier'. He was obviously bright, but he failed the assessment for a possible commission as he was not considered practical enough to be an officer – a strange judgement. He had just been badly smashed up at the Battle of Primosole Bridge in Sicily in mid July 1943.

As they advanced beyond Catania, Elliott was wounded by German mortar fire and evacuated to 3rd New Zealand general hospital near Tripoli. After treatment he was sent to a transit camp on the beach at Tripoli.

> On September 15th, we were all dragged out, early morning. We all had our full kit with us. We were paraded at night; I think about 2,000 men. We were taken down to the harbour and embarked on three cruisers utilised in transporting this detachment from North Africa to Salerno. We were on the *Charybdis*; there were also the *Scylla* and the *Aurora*. The cruisers were all jam-packed – there weren't any proper facilities for troops – so we just slept where we could.[61]
>
> Private Ronald Elliott

When they were already aboard the ship, they were told that they were to be landed at Salerno and would be dispersed to units of the 46th Division – including the 16th DLI. They were to replace the casualties suffered in the recent fighting when the beachhead had appeared in real danger – as indeed was illustrated by the German night attacks on Hospital Hill.

The Salerno bridgehead was at a critical point – and someone panicked – they just grabbed for some convenient reinforcements. It could have been a debacle, a tremendous defeat, if we had to pull out of Salerno. However, we were not aware where we were bound for. It was all against the backdrop of the fact that 'Monty' had promised these divisions of the desert Eighth Army that they would be returning to England – and the people that were on that draft, were by and large, all ex-members of either the Scottish 51st Division or Durhams from the 50th Division. We were unaware of where we were going until the captain who had sealed orders read them out and told us we were going to Salerno. That was the beginning of a fair bit of feeling. There wasn't much else to do, people were talking about the situation – a lot of discussions going on and barrack room lawyers. The Scottish lads were very unhappy about going into Salerno. All they knew was that they had been promised by Monty that they would go home and, had it not been for being wounded in Sicily, that they would be with their battalion to go home. The people in the Salerno bridgehead were not 'Jock' battalions and therefore they didn't see themselves as being involved. This was just talk. At that point in time, the Durhams were just listening to them and talking amongst ourselves, saying, 'It was a dirty trick!' Instead of going home they were going into a whole new ballgame, a new area of war, with no finite end to it. I don't think I was terribly keen to be going back into action – I suppose that was my main preoccupation, really. Part of it was they still had some sort of respect and affection for 'Monty', but it wasn't with 'Monty', it was with an American general! There were any number of different strands of reasons people used either deliberately or unconsciously, to argue why they shouldn't be going into Salerno.[62]

Private Ronald Elliott

However, by the time they got to Salerno, the real danger was over, and the Germans had started to pull back. This did not help the overall mood. On landing, the draft was left to mill about in a field transit area.

> We were in this field with nothing else to do, but just talk amongst ourselves about the situation. The Jocks said that they weren't going to go and fight – they would definitely refuse to go! They had this sort of tribal feeling about it in terms of their argument that they were Scottish soldiers, so they should be in a Scottish division. It was a nationalistic thing from their point of view as much as everything else. For the Durhams it was more like trade union solidarity than anything else. 'Oh, we'll all stick together lads and they can't do anything to us!' I was in two minds. I thought, perhaps I ought to help them, but on the other hand, I really had only been in the 9th DLI about three weeks. I went to this tall redheaded Geordie sergeant and said, 'What should I do?' He said, 'Ah lad, you should support the Jocks, and the Durhams have been treated badly! If we all stick together, we'll be all right – you stick with me!' 'Oh, fair enough!'[63]
>
> Private Ronald Elliott

For a while nothing seemed to have changed as they remained in the transit camp. But the military wheels were moving behind the scenes.

> They provided us with compo rations, and there was this large area of tomatoes growing quite close by. So, we had tomatoes with everything! We stripped this fellow's field of tomatoes. We lived quite well. We cleaned our weapons and talked about the situation. It was quite a pleasant two days! It really didn't crystallise until they brought up all our kit. Until we had everything, which included kit bags, and so forth, they're kept in the ship's hold. When you get your kit bags, and your big pack – that means you're complete, then you can move. The kit came up one morning. After that point in time, we really didn't have any excuse for not going anywhere! Before that we couldn't have gone anywhere because we weren't fully accoutred as it were. But once we got our kit up, we were in a mutiny situation.[64]
>
> Private Ronald Elliott

The first step was a sympathetic 'pep' talk, but there was a touch of menacing steel behind it.

> Then we were all paraded and this chap, I think he was a major, he said in effect, that there had been mistakes made, they were sorry that it had happened the way that it did, and that every effort would be made to try and get people back into their proper formations. But for the moment we really didn't have any option but to obey orders and report for duty. We would be posted to appropriate battalions within the Fifth Army. Then the riot act was read out. Having that read out to you, you appreciate the enormity of what you're into. You were disobeying lawful orders and could be shot, or whatever! It brings a chill to anybody's mind.[65]
>
> Private Ronald Elliott

It was at this point that common sense came to Elliott's rescue. He had no real case to refuse a posting as he had only been in action a few days and had been very lightly wounded.

> The order was then given that all of those who wished now to obey the lawful orders were to centralise with all of their kit in the centre of this field, I thought to myself, 'I'm a bloody fool, what have I got that I can say is any sort of an excuse for what I'm doing?' I wandered off in the centre with my kit and lo and behold, there was my friend, the redheaded sergeant organising the collection together of the kit. I said, 'I thought you said if we all stayed together, we'd be alright! He says, 'Oh, lad, you have to obey orders at the end of the bloody day! You can't beat the army!' Quite a number of people, a good half, collected themselves together, were marched off and ended up with the 16th DLI![66]
>
> Private Ronald Elliott

But some of the men still refused to budge. During this period, Colonel Johnny Preston drove down to the transit camp to see what he could do. Nobody wanted to prosecute these men; persuasion was the order of the day. James Corr was also a witness to Preston's speech to the men.

> Johnny Preston was making a speech to them. About how we needed them, how the 16th Durhams were desperate for them! They were Durhams; they were in a battalion of Durhams! He didn't know what they were worried about, because they would just have been going to train for another landing – and we had made a landing for them! This was his speech, his sort of style. He finished up and he says, 'I give you my firm promise as an officer, and Johnny Preston always keeps his word, that as soon as the situation here resolves, you will go back to your own battalions – you've got my firm word on that!' Well, all but a few then decided to come to us. Just a handful stayed.[67]
>
> Private James Corr, Headquarters Company

A few more gave it up at this point. But some remained adamant and eventually gloves were off.

> Ultimately, they were left with a hardcore who did apparently finish up court martialled. But those that were left had certainly had opportunity for reconsideration. There were one or two who had gone the whole hog and finished up in prison and had quite a rough time. The army establishment behaved remarkably well under the circumstances, because, rightly or wrongly, they were fearful of some military problem. They took the advantage of having whatever troops were supposedly available and intended to use them. And it was a natural, a proper military decision. Anyone who didn't obey orders was in fact, in a mutinous state. No army would have accepted that situation. A month or so later, there was a signal came along from headquarters to the effect that anyone who had transferred from the 50th Division or 51st Division could apply to return to their own formations if they wanted to. In the event, I don't think many people did! Some were like me and thought that though it would be very nice to go back, one was going back to the Second Front, which was going to be no pushover. That was likely to be a very dangerous and deadly battle. On the whole, we felt that we were probably rather better off in Italy than on the Second Front – so we stayed where we were![68]
>
> Private Ronald Elliott

Ronald Elliott was posted to the Signals Section, Headquarters Company, but was then attached to 'D' Company. In the end some 192 recalcitrants were shipped off to Algeria where they were all charged with mutiny, a number unprecedented in British military history. They were all found guilty, and indeed three sergeants were sentenced to death, subsequently commuted to forced labour and then suspended.

> I don't think many of us had much sympathy for them, because we accepted that they'd had a pretty hard time, a lot of them had been wounded and they were cheesed off, but you're in the army and you do what you're told – or suffer the consequences – that's the point. It seemed rather stupid![69]
>
> Private Tom Lister, MT Section, Headquarters Company

7

NAPLES AND RIVER CROSSINGS

> I don't ever remember anybody saying, 'I won't go!' But it got to the stage where you were saying to a platoon commander, 'I think you'll have to take a couple of your sections this time!' And he would say, 'Oh God no! I've been out so many times!' You'd have a long job persuading them. It was better doing it that way than it ever was saying, 'Never mind what you think – you're going!' If you could get them to say, 'Oh well all right, it's my turn – I'll go!' It's much better. By and large I was always able to do that.[1]
>
> Lieutenant Ronnie Sherlaw, 'C' Company

SEE NAPLES AND DIE may have been a worrying slogan, but the capture of that major port loomed large in the minds of the Allied commanders. For obvious logistical reasons it was essential. On 23 September, the 46th Division was ordered to clear a way through the passes to the north of Salerno to allow the 7th Armoured Division to break through the hills and on to the Naples plain. As part of these operations, the 16th DLI were placed under the temporary control of 138 Brigade and ordered to help clear the road through the Vietri valley. The 16th DLI and the 6th Yorks and Lancs were to move through the hills to the left of the road, while the 2/4th KOYLI and the 6th Lincolnshires secured those on the right. The specific responsibility of the Durhams was to take and hold the heights of the La Crocella hill at over 1,900 feet; while patrols from the Yorks and Lancs cleared the way by taking first the small village of Dragonea not far from the front of the existing British lines, then the low hill of Monti di Amici, and finally the village of Corpo di Cava at the foot of La Crocella.

Colonel Johnny Preston issued his orders at 12.00 on 22 September: 'B' Company would push up on to La Crocella and 'D' Company would take the spur stretching down to the road. The rest of the battalion would follow up in reserve to Dragonea. It would be a night approach march, and to try to maximise the element of surprise, would be without artillery support. They took a convoluted route across hilly wooded terrain before plunging into an intimidatingly dark ravine.

> We were all in single file. It was that dark we had to hold each other's bayonet scabbards. Like elephants holding each other's tails! We passed a shell that must have been from one of the ships – it looked like a 15-inch shell – it was just laid on the top of the ground as though it had bounced and not exploded. It was pitch black. There couldn't have been a moon. There were frequent stops, as though whoever was leading us wasn't quite sure if we were in the right direction. Each time we stopped, everybody seemed to go straight to sleep; everybody was that worn out with the previous week of constant living on your nerve. Every halt you had to more or less kick them awake![2]
>
> Lance Corporal William Virr, 'B' Company

In the event they met no opposition on either La Crocella or the spur stretching down to Corpo di Cava, so both were secured by 06.30 on 23 September. However, Robert Ellison had a brief encounter that could have gone very badly for him.

> My rifle got dirty climbing round the hill, and I had it all to bits cleaning it – and here's a Jerry officer coming down! What do you do – stick him up with a rifle with no bolt in? Jack was doing his rifle as well! We learned a lesson there – never both be doing it together! The Jerry officer gave up, said, 'I've had enough!' He put his hands up in the air and he handed his Luger over. He'd seen the situation and he wasn't going to get

killed! One of the other chaps took him back to the base as a prisoner.³

Private Robert Ellison, 'D' Company

Meanwhile, a platoon of the 6th Yorks and Lancs had taken Corpo di Cava but was embroiled in fighting with a German anti-tank gun and a small party of infantry. However, on the other side of the valley, the attack by the 2/4th KOYLI and the 6th Lincolns had stalled as they met heavy opposition, and even calling in artillery support had not helped them achieve their objectives. This left the Durhams rather out on a limb, as the road through to Corpo di Cava was still not passable. It was decided to send forward a small fighting patrol, contour chasing around the ridges above the valley.

> I was required to get a forward observation officer up to 'B' Company on this hill, La Crocella. I had to find a route through to Corpo di Cava, which was a small village at the foot of the hill. I took twelve people with me, and a FOO called Len Garland, who was a captain with 449 Battery of the 70th Field Regiment. We kept a good 3 or 4 yards apart, each man; we had a couple of 'points' who looked forward, generally a corporal or lance corporal for that sort of job. I led behind the points. We went as fast as ever we could go. There was an urgency in getting the FOO to the top and to some extent the faster you went the less likely you were to be hit anyway. We had a few skirmishes. As we were walking up there were little attacks from our right where the Germans were. On the left was woodland. We were above the valley; we walked above it and looked down to it. There were Germans all the way along on the right in little patches. As we were going along they would have a go at us – and we would stop and have a go at them. Then we would move on. When we got about halfway along, some of the chaps got so fed up that they left – they just disappeared – half a dozen of them! They would say that they got lost. To some extent, you had to sympathise with the ones that couldn't stand being shot at all the time, and as long as you could carry out your mission, you wouldn't make too much of

an issue of it – unless it was affecting everybody. These fellows turned up eventually at the village. I had to accept that they had got lost, although my own view is that they went and hid themselves out of the road in the woods until it was safe to go on. Well, half a dozen of us and the FOO struggled on until we got there![4]

Lieutenant Ronnie Sherlaw, 'C' Company

At around the same time, 'B' Company sent out a patrol to see what was happening in the village. This was commanded by Lieutenant Fred Strothart, accompanied by the newly promoted Corporal Tom Turnbull.

Lieutenant Strothart said, 'You go in that direction so far, to see if you can find the cross-roads, and we'll go in this direction!' We went down and we grabbed an Italian coming up the road and by using a stick in dust made a map to direct us back to where the crossroads was. When we got towards it there was an abandoned German anti-tank gun in a sunken road where the fields were higher than the road. The anti-tank gun was facing down to Corpo di Cava. As we were walking past, one of the lads comes flying down, 'You've got to come back,' he says. 'Lieutenant Strothart has seen some Jerries going into a house and they're going to get as near as possible! He's gone forward with Corporal Smith and another one of the chaps. He says you've got to lie up here till he comes back!' So, we get on this bank side with our legs facing towards the road. The chap next to me said, 'Tom, there's a tank or something coming up the road behind us!' I said, 'Get away man! That'll be the carriers coming up with the rations!' I'd no sooner said that then, 'BRRRRWWRRR!' The tank opened out at us, killed the bloke alongside of me and scattered us with the machine gun fire.[5]

Corporal Tom Turnbull, 'B' Company

The unwelcome newcomer was one of three German tanks accompanied by supporting infantry that had arrived at 17.00. By then, Ronnie Sherlaw had got to Corpo di Cava, where he got in touch with a sergeant commanding the small detachment of York and Lancs.

> They were in trouble with tanks, which couldn't actually get into Corpo di Cava, because they couldn't get across the bridge – it was too narrow for tanks. But they could shoot at us quite easily! What we did until it was dark was just lobbed 2-inch mortars at them which didn't worry the tanks, but it stopped the infantry coming across. They didn't like being shelled. Once it was dark, there wasn't much they could do.[6]
>
> Lieutenant Ronnie Sherlaw, 'C' Company

The FOO, Captain Garland, who was up on La Crocella, used his wireless to bring down artillery fire on the tanks. But they were incredibly close to the 'D' Company positions of La Crocella spur and thus everyone was ordered to take cover in their slit trenches. Ken Lovell was not amused.

> We were dug in only about 100 yards from the tanks. We got a fearful stonking from our own 25-pounders. Frank Duffy had been out somewhere and during a lull in the bombardment he went to dash over to company headquarters. The bombardment opened again, and he dived into my slit trench – and I noticed he'd only got half of a revolver – a shell fragment had evidently cut it in two – he'd lost the barrel. He went a bit white when I told him. There was another little lull and he got back to company headquarters, got back on the radio again and they dropped the guns. They never hit the tanks.[7]
>
> Lance Corporal Ken Lovell, 17 Platoon, 'D' Company

The barrage also landed close to the men of Turnbull's patrol.

> We had the artillery spotter on this hill with us and he brought artillery fire down. You can quite imagine, us on the patrol, we were in the middle of it! We had to scatter back up the hill! You've never seen anybody go up a hill as fast as what we did![8]
>
> Corporal Tom Turnbull, 'B' Company

Even the regimental history mentions that the men of 'D'

Company considered it an absolute fact that they and not the tanks were the main point of impact of the 25-pounder shells. However, it also points out that there were no casualties from the 'friendly fire' and in contrast to Lovell's pessimistic belief, one of the German tanks was disabled and the other two fled the scene. Garland was awarded the Military Cross (MC) for his valuable work that day. However, the road was still not open, which meant 'B' and 'D' Companies were beginning to run out of food, having exhausted all they could carry. Something had to be done, and that night, the second in command, Major Dennis Worrall, led a ration party in several jeeps and accompanied by a platoon, that managed to force their way through. By this time jeeps were highly valued, reasonably fast, easy to drive, with two gear boxes to enable them to get across rough ground. They were perfect for carrying heavy rations, ammunition or even support weapons like mortars. In the aftermath, Worrall too would be awarded the MC. In addition, Lieutenant Colonel Johnny Preston was awarded the Distinguished Service Order (DSO) for his tactical expertise, while Ronnie Sherlaw was awarded an MC.

> I was very surprised! The biggest trouble with winning anything like that in a war is that people always then expect more of you. You have an awful job keeping up with your reputation. After that patrol I tended to become the bloke they sent out on patrol. It's a lot of rubbish really, because you really aren't any better than anybody else at it – although the more you do you do get better at it. But because you happened to have one good patrol doesn't mean you became an expert; you had one good patrol probably because you're born lucky![9]
>
> Lieutenant Ronnie Sherlaw, 'C' Company

His grounded realism meant the award never went to his head.

The fraught situation had still not yet been resolved, but on 24 September, 'A' Company moved forward from reserve and pushed out from the 'D' Company positions of La Crocella spur to take the village of Santarcangelo. The 6th Yorks and Lancs also got moving and pushed down the main road, taking a substantial number of prisoners. Then, at last, on the night of 25 September, the 128 Brigade managed to overcome the German defences on the other side of the Vietri defile. The divisional commander seemed pleased.

> Not only have we opened the door, but we have torn it off its bloody hinges![10]
>
> Major General John Hawkesworth, Headquarters, 46th Division

Their efforts allowed the tanks and lorried infantry of the 7th Armoured Division to be launched forward to break through on to the Naples plain on 28 September. The operations had been a demonstration that modern warfare demanded an all-arms approach: the artillery, armour and infantry all had vital roles to play if success was to be achieved.

The 16th DLI then had a period in a rest camp out of the line, where Ronald Elliott noticed an amusing phenomenon.

> If you were in a permanent position you have to make provision for latrines, generally dug out of the soil to a depth of about 2 yards and about a yard wide. They had a trestle with a big telegraph pole – and you squatted on the telegraph pole and did your business. These holes were filled with lime. There was a story that our signals officer fell in to one of these latrine pits! But the funniest thing was we were there at the time that the grapes were just about ready. People were gulping grapes down out of these vineyards as fast and were getting dysentery on that account. We had one of these latrine pits in a vineyard, so people could sit on the pole, and just pick handfuls of grapes from the vines that were just above their head, while sitting on the pole. We reckoned that was the nearest one could get to perpetual motion as you were likely to see in this world![11]
>
> Private Ronald Elliott, 'D' Company

On 6 October, after this period of well-deserved rest, the 16th DLI were transported through Naples. The streets were lined with cheering Italian civilians, but here again there was a humorous element to the Durhams' 'triumphal' procession.

> The battalion went through Naples on the lorries and the inhabitants came out and cheered us. It was quite funny. They pelted us with apples, because they were just collecting them at the end of the season. But apples are quite hard, and people were getting hurt by them! So, we threw them back again. Before we got to the end of the run through Naples, there was a battle going on with people firing apples back at the civilians. It finished up quite a conflict, truth be told.[12]

Private Ronald Elliott, 'D' Company

★

THE ITALIAN CAMPAIGN WAS NOT SUPPOSED to be a long drawn-out affair. The Allies wanted, needed and expected a relatively quick victory once Italy had dropped out of the war. But the Germans had other ideas. Kesselring knew that Italy was no 'soft underbelly' but a potential nightmare for the Allies. He planned to make best use of the Italian geography to fight them every step of the way. A spine of mountains ran down the middle of Italy with a series of jagged ridges running off to left and right, with deep rivers in the valleys in between. Communications were tortuous, with bridges demolished and few viable roads. Any advance would be faced with a series of difficult river crossings, followed by uphill struggles over mountainous ridges. Kesselring's main defensive position was the Gustav Line, which ran right across Italy from Minturno to Ortono. The bedrock of the line was the imposing 1,700-foot Monte Cassino, which overlooked – and dominated – the Garigliano and Sangro rivers which lay in front. Machine gun posts and artillery positions had been carved from the rock, while every village and town seemed to have been turned into a miniature fortress. The German lines could in theory be 'turned' by further naval landings to the north, but the shortage of troops and military resources caused by the conflicting demands of the Normandy landings meant that this was a difficult and risky option – as was discovered in the Anzio landings of January 1944.

Naples and River Crossings

To give the Germans time to prepare these positions, Kesselring planned an additional series of defensive positions designed to delay and harass the Allies in their advance. The first of these was the Viktor line, which stretched from Termoli on the east coast to Castel Volturno in the west. The US Fifth Army sector on the western coastal plain was solidly based on the Volturno river. This would be the next challenge that faced the men of the 16th DLI.

*

THE 46TH DIVISION WOULD BE THE LEFT FLANK of the advance of the US Fifth Army towards and across the Volturno. It was a challenging assignment as they were advancing across a flat flood plain, under observation from German defensive positions. After the Vietri defile operations under the command of 138 Brigade, the Durhams had been returned to 139 Brigade. On 7 October, the battalion moved up from their rest positions to Villa Literno. By this time the men had become accustomed to the German scorched earth tactics employed whenever they were forced to retreat.

> The Germans used to kill everything, rather than leave it, because the Italians had packed in then. He wouldn't give them an inch. He used to kill the cattle as he went back. There was always that smell, sickly smell of death wherever you went.[13]
>
> Private George Bland, Carrier Platoon, Support Company

As they moved forward, Gordon Gent was forced to go sick. He didn't want to leave the battalion; he certainly didn't want to be parted from his mates of the last couple of years.

> I was feeling bloody awful. I wasn't well at all for days and days! These dammed mosquitos were worrying you all day – driving you mad! I was having a job to drag one foot in front of the other. Sergeant Major Wilson looks at me and he says, 'Are you all right, Gent?' I said, 'Well, I don't feel very good!' But I wasn't for giving up! I didn't suggest I was going to the medical

> inspection room. He says, 'Well you don't look all right, have you seen yourself?' I said, 'How the hell am I to see myself!' If we shaved, we only shaved by feel, I hadn't a mirror on the blooming truck – my two side-mirrors were both smashed. 'Well, let's get you along to the advanced dressing station and get yourself some attention! You look ill to me!'[14]
>
> Private Gordon Gent, MT Section, 'A' Company

He was diagnosed with a severe case of jaundice and evacuated by hospital ship from Naples to a base hospital in Tunisia. His weakened state of health took a while to improve, and he never managed to return to the 16th DLI.

On arrival at Villa Literno, the 16th DLI found they were to be the reserve battalion for the 139 Brigade, behind the 5th Sherwood Foresters and the 2/5th Leicesters, but they were also charged with carrying out patrols along the whole of the brigade front, exploring all the ground up to the Volturno. These patrols commenced on the night of 8/9 October. Next day there was a major incident when 'D' Company were ordered forward to the canal that lay just to the south of the Volturno. The Germans had destroyed the bridges, so the Royal Engineers moved forward to build a Bailey bridge. To screen the bridge construction, 17 and 18 Platoons of 'D' Company were ordered to cross the canal and set up covering defensive positions, with Ronald Elliott accompanying them to set up a wireless link back to battalion headquarters. On arrival, there was no sense of urgency as they jumped down from the lorries and unloaded their canvas assault boats.

> The engineers were just on their own, putting this Bailey bridge across. We went across in our canvas and wood assault boats – they took about six men. They had a wooden bottom, canvas sides with a wooden frame at the top. You sort of lifted them up, pushed two or three struts in position to keep them rigid, got in and paddled across the canal which was about 10 feet deep. My platoon came across and our platoon sergeant, Ray Sykes, said, 'As soon as you get over, get into those trenches and take up fire positions!'[15]
>
> Corporal Ken Lovell, 'D' Company

The crossing was not that easy, as few of the men had any familiarity with rowing.

> The boats were wooden canvas affairs; they have to be portable and transportable by hand, so they were light, but they were somewhat difficult to manoeuvre. I don't know that anybody was particularly adept at using them! We got into the boats and after the usual problems about going around in circles, which one tended to do, we were going up towards the southern bank. We all got across and they fanned out ahead of us with the platoons. We were in the company headquarters, which was close to the canal bank. We'd taken off the set and put it down and were establishing communications with the base and taking our kit off.[16]
>
> Private Ronald Elliott, 'D' Company

The two platoons began to set up firing positions across the road stretching forward towards the Volturno. All was still quiet, but there were a few disquieting signs that the Germans might be close by.

> In the distance, I observed a couple of Jerries running across the road carrying a machine gun. I passed word back to the corporal, and he just ignored it – he didn't want to know! We didn't know what we were talking about, we were blind! 'There's no Jerries there!' Whether they'd had false information previously, I don't know! I said, 'There is!' He wouldn't have it – he was back nearer the canal. It was his fault. I wish we'd taken it upon ourselves to fire our Bren gun along the road – and we might have saved the day – but we were so disciplined we daren't. At least we would have got the first shots in.[17]
>
> Private Robert Ellison, 'D' Company

For whatever reason the warning went unheeded. As a result, a German fighting patrol launched a terrible surprise attack – and they sprang it before the men had any chance to dig proper slit trench defences. The men were in the open as a storm of lead burst upon them.

> All hell broke loose. Machine guns opened up at us from every bloody quarter – from behind us, from our sides, from the front. The Germans had set up a beautiful ambush. Martin's platoon [18 Platoon] got cut up, he got badly wounded, that's when he started screaming his head off like a bloody baby. We had taken up fire positions: we opened up; we could see flashes. 'Brothel Baby', he was my Bren gunner, he was next to me, and he got a bullet through the wrist. After a while he said to me, 'Here, Corporal, give us a drink, will you?' I felt for my water bottle and found I'd had a burst of machine gun bullets go through it, I cut my hand quite badly as I felt for it, where the metal had been ripped to pieces. The Germans were just a few yards away. The buggers! We opened up and it was very, very dicey.[18]
>
> Corporal Ken Lovell, 'D' Company

They were in an extremely vulnerable position as the Germans held all the advantages.

> The Jerries set up the machine gun and started firing down the road at us, didn't they! There was quite a lot of Germans came down. We had to scarper back to the canal. Running back, they were lobbing these little stun grenades, and I got quite a few shrapnel wounds on my wrist and arm. You didn't know it had happened – just a flash at the side of you. But the other lads were getting bullets in them, but fortunately I didn't! We lost quite a lot of blokes there. It was completely flat, the whole area, like a playing field. The thing was to get back to the canal and take up a position on the canal. There wasn't enough cover just behind the embankment – the water was pretty high up – so we were stood in the canal up to the chest in water. Jerry came down and he was firing on them in the canal, as they were trying to get over the canal. Captain Whitehead,[19] our second in command, was killed there – he was trying to rescue blokes in the canal. They found his body down near the sea; it floated down the canal. Corporal Lewindon and Sergeant Sykes were at the parapet of the bridge lobbing grenades back on to the top. They killed quite a lot of Germans and saved the day. As

things quietened down, we got out of the canal on to the bank. Sergeant Ferrell[20] had been mortally wounded – I was told that he had about twenty-two bullets in him.[21]

Private Robert Ellison, 'D' Company

Many of the men were panicked, but a few still had the self-possession to realise that it was their duty to try and cover the retreat of their men, but also to protect the all-important bridging party. After all that was why they were there. Ray Sykes and John Lewindon were at the fore in trying to get close to the Germans positions to exact some revenge.

> We had to get as near as we could and try and get them out of there. I was quite close to Ray Sykes. The Germans couldn't see us. The only thing we could use was grenades. We managed it – we certainly moved them! The trouble was, we got to the point where we nearly ran out of grenades! Somebody had the presence of mind to go back over the other side of the canal, pick out some more grenades and brought them back to us. That was really Ray Syke's show; he thought of it, and I wouldn't take any credit for that – I just backed him up that's all. Ray was decorated for that – and rightly so![22]

Corporal John Lewindon, 'D' Company

Meanwhile, there is no doubt that Ronald Elliott was one of those panicking. Few would have the heart to blame him. These were genuinely terrifying circumstances.

> There was a rush back to the river. I got into the river or was pushed into the river. Some people got into a boat. I found myself in the [canal] and not being a good swimmer was in some danger of drowning. I got a hold of the boat which was floundering around and someone either deliberately or unconsciously waved a paddle around and knocked my glasses off. Whether he was trying to knock me off the boat, I don't know. But I had no intention of being knocked off the boat – I hung on grimly. Meanwhile pandemonium was still going on on the far bank. Some of the platoons were fighting back and

it wasn't a total retreat, but some small number had retreated, including me! Eventually, we got to the other side of the canal, I was soaking wet, without my glasses on, I didn't know where to go. Didn't know where the Germans were or anything! There was I – a pretty sorry sight, wandering around on the riverbank with the mosquitoes around, not able to see very far without my glasses, waving my Beretta in the air, prepared to defend myself, although quite how and in what way, wasn't very clear.[23]

Private Ronald Elliott, 'D' Company

The whole skirmish only took about ten minutes, after which the German patrol melted away. In the aftermath, Ray Sykes was awarded the Military Medal (MM) and John Lewindon was promoted to sergeant for their exemplary conduct. In all, there were some forty casualties.

That night, two more recce patrols were sent out to explore the ground south of the Volturno. One was under the command of 2nd Lieutenant Russell Collins. It was a challenging assignment, feeling their way across the floodplain, crisscrossed as it was by dykes, with what few roads there were raised up on embankments with drainage ditches on either side. Collins was still mortified by his previous misfortunes on Hospital Hill; this time he was determined to make no mistakes.

> We were provided with some very good aerial photographs of the approaches to the river and the crossing points. I spent hours poring over these things committing them absolutely to memory and I knew in my mind very clearly the whole of the area that was going to be our approach to the river. A reconnaissance patrol was very lightly equipped and armed. You might wear rubber shoes and no helmets, no equipment – just a personal weapon each – and perhaps a compass. The idea being to see and not be seen and to take evasive action if encountering any enemy. In single file, with me leading. The next chap behind keeps a sharp look out to the right, the chap behind that a sharp lookout to the left. The chap behind that keeps a sharp lookout behind. I went down the road, or in the ditch to the side. When I had completed my patrol to see where

it might be possible to launch boats, it was time to come back. I remembered one very important lesson in training for patrols. That was that you don't come back via the same way as you went out. I regret to say Ray Mitchell[24] didn't remember it! I struck another route across country. It turned out to be very propitious one, as we went right through a melon field – and they were all ripe. We were sitting in the middle of the field, eating these melons, when all hell broke loose on the road that we'd gone up by. Poor old Ray Mitchell's patrol had come back down that same road and the Germans were lying in wait, they put an ambush there. They had to fight. He got hit and one or two others. I felt very gratified that I'd remembered that lesson, 'You don't go back via the same route!'[25]

2nd Lieutenant Russell Collins, 'A' Company

Collins had done well and taken the first steps to establishing a glowing reputation.

Collectively, this series of patrols, checking and rechecking the ground where they were to make the Volturno crossing, had managed to identify the shallowest section where a crossing on foot was just about possible without the Germans noticing what was going on. Nevertheless, the Volturno was a fearsome obstacle; swollen by autumn rains it was fast flowing, around 4 foot 6 deep, and some 300 feet across. Clark planned for the VI US Corps to attack on a two-division front, pushing for the high ground across the river. The X Corps would cross the Lower Volturno, with the 56th Division attacking at Capua, the 7th Armoured Division at Grazzanise and the 46th Division between Cancello and Castel Volturno. After a 139 Brigade conference on 11 October, Colonel Johnny Preston briefed his company commanders and warned them to be ready to move forward from the debussing point at 17.00 on the night of 12/13 October. Russell Collins was given an important role.

> I was detailed to lead the battalion up to the river because I'd reconnoitred it. The outline brigade plan was that the unfortunate Foresters were to purport to be making the main assault – they were the decoy for us who were going to make

> the actual crossing a little bit further down the river. The Bofors light anti-aircraft gun fired tracer rounds and the scheme was that every five minutes they would fire a burst of five rounds along the axis of attack, so that everybody moving forward could keep their bearings. I was leading this entire battalion party and we were due to cross the river at 'H' hour. Now I don't know whether I performed particularly well there, because I was very cautious in leading the battalion up, because I had it very much in mind that our patrol had been ambushed only a night or two before and I didn't want the whole battalion to walk straight into an ambush – it was my responsibility to make sure we got safely through and there were undoubtedly Germans on our side of the river. So, I proceeded rather cautiously – to the point that we lost a bit of time. The adjutant, Captain Pritchard, came up to know why on earth I was being so slow. I said, 'Well, because there are Jerries around the place on this side of the river and I don't want to walk the battalion into them!' Anyway, we had to get a bit of a move on and in due course got to the river.[26]
>
> 2nd Lieutenant Russell Collins, 'A' Company

'A' and 'C' Companies would wade across the Volturno at the shallowest point and establish a firm base. They would be followed by the battalion headquarters; then 'B' and 'D' Companies, which were charged with pushing on to cut the main coast road. The men were dressed in battledress as the weather was too cold for khaki drill. Bill Virr remembered how they were loaded down – always a worry in a river crossing.

> Field service fighting order. Your pouches for ammunition. Your weapon. Your small pack with all your gear in – your shaving kit, your towel, soap, mess tins and your emergency rations. Your entrenching tool. Water bottle. Bayonet. Your heaviest thing was your ammunition – I had ten magazines of Tommy gun ammunition. They were fairly heavy. The lads also had Bren gun magazines. It all adds to your weight. They had the rifle; somebody had the Bren gun or the PIAT.[27]
>
> Corporal William Virr, 'B' Company

Having reached the river safely, 'A' Company (commanded by Major John Morant) had the grim prospect of crossing the swirling cold water. Collins was at the forefront.

> Then with my platoon leading we had to make the first crossing. We hoisted our packs up as high as we could on our shoulders, put our rifles in our outstretched arms above our heads – and the first few of us waded into the river. Ray Mitchell must have established the depth of it, but it was certainly up to my armpits, if not up to my shoulders, being a rather shorter chap! We had to take a rope across and secure the rope at the far end. Then the boats were brought up; people following on behind came in the boats. The whole company got across. While we were crossing, the Germans weren't aware of our presence; at least there were no signs that they were aware![28]
>
> 2nd Lieutenant Russell Collins, 'A' Company

They struggled to climb the steep bank, slipping and sliding, but at least there wasn't the dreaded rattle of machine gun bursts that could have swept them away in moments. Collins and his men then moved forward.

> We fanned out to some extent, controlled by word of mouth, and our first objective was a high dyke, 200 to 400 yards to the north of the river. It seemed like a mile because when we were about halfway across somebody [behind us] fell into the river and cried out – that alerted the Germans. Suddenly we found all along this dyke were machine gun posts – we came under machine gun fire as we were crossing the flat ground. One of my young soldiers – Anderson[29] – was badly hit. He felt he was dying, mortally wounded. I was kneeling beside him, and he was giving me a message to give to his girlfriend. We were still trying to get on; just making our way forward; we managed to get under the lee of the dyke. Sergeant Major Wilson was as cool as a cucumber – whenever he got an order he always said, 'Very good, sir!' Major John Morant was a bit laconic and he said, 'Sergeant Major!' 'Sir!' 'I've been hit!' 'Very good, sir!' We

were in such numbers that the enemy probably withdrew to a concentration area.[30]

2nd Lieutenant Russell Collins, 'A' Company

Tony Sacco was still in the water when the 'drowning soldier' panicked. The leading men had tied ropes to trees on either side of the river, which the men could cling on to.

> We were crossing, great, not making a sound! I was up to my neck, holding on to this rope. The slopes to get up on the top – you've never seen mud like it. It was shiny black, it looked like coal tar. Those who managed to get on the top had to pull you up – we were covered in this black slime. But we didn't make a sound crossing! Further up they were crossing in dinghies. Suddenly this lad started screaming – he was a Cockney lad – we got all sorts after Sedjenane! He was screaming, 'I'm drowning, I'm drowning; I'm drowning!' He must have woken the whole German Army up! Somebody was saying, 'Drown, you bugger, drown!'[31]

Signaller Tony Sacco, 'A' Company

Everyone heard the shouts, but it is nice to record that the man who lost his nerve would survive his terrifying experience; he would also overcome the initial scorn of his comrades. They knew what it was to be afraid.

> One of the Cockney lads from the 70th [DLI reinforcement drafts] he must have been terrified of water. Because the canvas boat capsized, and he started screaming for his mother. He woke the whole front up! The Jerries started blazing away. If it hadn't been for him, we'd have got over all right. But he must have been a brave lad, because he stood all the derision, he stuck with the battalion to the end.[32]

Corporal Edward Grey, 'D' Company

As Collins indicated, the shouting awoke the Germans from their slumbers and their machine guns opened rapid fire, although they were firing blind. Their nebelwerfers also opened up, but were firing on a prearranged targets which did not conform to the Durhams' positions.

Behind the leading companies came 'B' and 'D' Companies, who were meant to be carried in the boats.

> I had to get in the water and wade across. It says in the book [the Laurie Stringer Battalion History] that 'B' Company didn't wait for the boats – we had no other option – they took them off us, because they wanted them for the machine gun battalion. We got across and by God it was a cold night. You can quite imagine with the depth of water when it's nearly up to your shoulders and you're going across with your weapon above your head![33]
>
> Corporal Tom Turnbull, 'B' Company

Once across, they pushed out to the flanks of the bridgehead established by the two assault companies. By this time the Germans were beginning to realise exactly what was happening and the accuracy of the fire was ramped up considerably.

> We were getting hit right. left and centre with machine guns. Jerry was firing on fixed lines, sweeping this field. We were crawling in this open field. The lad next to me was behind a Bren and he inched his way up to stretch his back – with lying down all the time. As he stretched up a burst of tracer hit him. It seemed as if it was going in and dropping out at his back – the tracer – I'll never forget it. He went down. They started shouting for the stretcher bearers and when they crawled towards us, I said, 'It's no use, he's dead!' I heard him die, the rattle. A lad called Private Tuck.[34] The lads on the other flank, one of our sections, put the machine gun out of action with grenades, while our section gave them covering fire when they went in. We went over these fields, and we came to a dried-up canal. We always seemed to be bloody unlucky, our section of our platoon! We got sent on another patrol to find a road across the canal. Another patrol had been across and come back and said that there was nothing along there. So they sent us! We just got about 200 or 300 yards and a Jerry came over the bank side.

He says, 'Achtung!' He practically said, 'Share that amongst you!' We watched the grenades come over our heads and it hit three of the last lads in the patrol. One was wounded about the face, one of the corporals lost his heel and the other lad – it was his nineteenth birthday the day before – and it had shattered his arm. We got them and naturally we had to get back. We fixed them up and then we dug in till first light.[35]

Corporal Tom Turnbull, 'B' Company

Ken Lovell found himself dug on the reverse slope of a dyke bank and under harassing fire from an unknown number of German snipers. Not so far from him was his friend, Lance Corporal Bill Crummack from Leeds.

We came under a lot of sniper fire; we lost a few men killed and wounded. It was very difficult to say the number of snipers; because it could have been one or two moving about. However, many were sniping; they were good at their job. We never had a pinpoint which we could saturate with fire. One poor fellow, he went to answer the call of nature, had dropped his trousers, more or less finished his business, and he got a bullet right through both cheeks of his arse and fell back in his own mess. It was evidently a most painful wound as well! Ray Sykes, the platoon sergeant, had put two chaps in a slit trench on the forward slope of the bank. It must have been a very lonely position up there. My great pal, Bill Crummack, in whose section they were, went up to see they were all right. He went up over the top of the bank, about 4–5 feet wide, crawled down to them. Yes, they were all right! Instead of sliding down, he stood up on top of the bank. The next thing I heard was a single shot, Bill came down, clutching at his equipment, he'd obviously been hit. He virtually fell into my arms trying to undo his belt to take his equipment off. All he had time to say was, 'Mother! Mother!' And he was dead. Bill[36] was the chap who taught me never to stand on the skyline; I thought it was a shocking trick of fate that this had happened.[37]

Corporal Ken Lovell, 'D' Company

By about 04.00, the 16th DLI had gained some of their objectives, but they were still being severely harassed by German machine guns located on their right flank. Colonel Preston established his headquarters in some pink farm buildings and ordered Russell Collins to lead a fighting patrol to pinpoint and 'take out' the German strongpoints.

> There was a pocket of enemy some few hundred yards to the east, who were holding up progress. I was to go and try and sort it out. I got up on to a high vantage point, where I saw John Smith, who was the mortar officer. I quickly conferred with him, told him that I was going to have to attack, and I really didn't know what to expect! This tall dyke – 20 or 30 feet high – had ditches on either side. I quickly made a little plan that I would take a number of men, perhaps half my platoon, and go along the dry channel beside the dyke, which afforded cover from view. I said, 'Right, I'm going to move along the dyke. You put down six rounds rapid; just six – no more, no less – and then we'll go in!' I hadn't pinpointed the machine guns, but the mortar officer had seen them. I mean it was by guess and by the grace of God really! I just said, 'Right, fix bayonets!' Everybody lined up behind me and I set off.[38]
>
> 2nd Lieutenant Russell Collins, 'A' Company

This was more than dangerous! So many things could have gone wrong. Undaunted he and his patrol crept forwards.

> Down came these six bombs, 'One! Two! Three! Four! Five! Six!' And then we up and ran full tilt. About 100 yards on, there was a junction in the gullies, one going off at right angles in a northerly direction. Just as I arrived at that point, I saw the last German's backside disappearing into the bunker – they'd got bunkers dug into the walls of the end of the dyke. I'd got them absolutely like rats in a trap, they hadn't even time to turn around and look out of their foxholes. I was right upon them and in total command of where they were. I just called on them to come out, and of course they had no choice, because I was standing there with my weapon in the entrance.

> I 'winkled' them out one at a time – they came trooping out, officers, NCOs – it turned out to be the company headquarters. I quickly gave orders for these chaps to be disarmed and we just shunted them out, one by one, with their hands above their heads.[39]

2nd Lieutenant Russell Collins, 'A' Company

They captured three officers, three warrant officers, eleven other ranks, plus several machine guns and a large amount of ammunition that might otherwise have been fired at the Durhams. The debriefing interview with Johnny Preston was in sharp contrast with that which had followed the debacle he had suffered on Hospital Hill. But Collins was also aware of the part played by blind unreasoning chance.

> I think I must have shouted at some time, because I remember that when the CO interviewed me, not a quarter of an hour afterwards, I'd lost my voice; my voice was a bit husky. He was very pleased and recommended me to higher authorities for an immediate award. I was as lucky in that as I was unlucky at Salerno. There's a big element of luck in these things. I mean the bombs could have fallen on us, or I could have got there, and it might have been bomb proof, or they might have been just 50 yards further down waiting for us as we came round the corner. But it was a good plan, directly and confidently well executed – and it just happened to work absolutely like a dream.[40]

2nd Lieutenant Russell Collins, 'A' Company

His success would bequeath him the nickname of 'Winkler' because of his success in 'winkling' out Germans from strongpoints. But at the time he was overcome with exhaustion and the sheer stress of it all.

> When we eventually got into one of these farm buildings, we were given very, very strict orders that we were not allowed to light any fires. There was a fear that the smoke would give away our locality. We hadn't had any hot food and we'd been

wet through – we were getting at a pretty low ebb by this time. There were some straw paillasses. I had some cigarettes I'd managed to keep them dry, and I was so dog-tired that I got down on this bed smoking a cigarette. I woke up with the mattress burning and I was so tired that I went to sleep again without putting out the fire! I was absolutely knackered, as they say these days.[41]

2nd Lieutenant Russell Collins, 'A' Company

The 'boy' had come of age.

Overall, X Corps had mixed success in the Volturno crossings, but the success of the American attacks further east meant that the Germans had little option but to fall back. The 16th DLI had a period holding the line they had taken, patrolling ahead and to the flanks. When the rest of the division had 'caught up', the battalion was pulled back for a period of rest at Casaluce.

> The lads had the time of their lives. The ladies of the town started off at 5 lira – and a bottle of wine was a couple of lira! The boys were having a high old time for about a week in the time we were out of the line – until the Yanks came in and the prices went up suddenly! They were much higher paid than we were. This did cause some resentment! Whilst we were here, we were taken by companies and compelled to see a photographic exhibition showing the ravages of venereal disease! They were pretty ghastly photographs – not the sort of thing you wanted to see immediately before lunch! I think the infantryman's view is very much, 'Well sod it! I may get killed tomorrow, so why not!' But it put a lot of the lads off their 'nookie' for quite some time – they no longer rode 'bare back'![42]

Corporal Ken Lovell, 'D' Company

The ambitions and concerns of young men in the midst of war may be slightly basic, but death was stalking them all, indeed many would be dead within the year.

★

THE NEXT RIVER THAT BARRED THE WAY TO ROME was the Teano river, a tributary of the Volturno. On 25 October, the 16th DLI moved forward to take up positions around Francolise, about 10 miles to the north-west of Capua where the Americans had stormed across the Volturna. This time there was far less chance to thoroughly patrol the approaches to the riverbanks. The only effective recce patrol was conducted on 27 October by Ronnie Sherlaw, now, as he had feared, an automatic choice for this kind of task after his successful patrol to Corpo di Cava. He recalled the briefings he had from Colonel Johnny Preston and the preparations that followed.

> He might have some aerial photos; if he didn't he would have the maps out. He was quite specific about how far he wanted you to go. What he couldn't be sure about was what obstacles were in the way, so he had to give you a certain amount of leeway about the direction you took. But he would always want to know what was there between Point 'A' and Point 'B'. If he knew anything about the area, he would tell you. We'd usually travel as lightly as we could because we were not going to take anybody on, or very rarely anyway. I wouldn't bother with a small pack. I'd have a water bottle, Tommy gun and plenty of ammunition. They'd all have one or two grenades in their pouches. You didn't bother with your steel helmet because it made a noise, and you were hoping you wouldn't need it. Maps if you needed them. You blacked your face with dirt, as long as it was something that didn't reflect. Wherever you had to go out or come back, they were normally told, and you usually had a password. If there were half a dozen of us, we'd take a 'V' formation – and point would be the patrol commander. You wouldn't let the Germans know you were there if you could help it, but the chances are that he knew – and that is how you found him! You found him because you came under fire! Your concern then was whether or not he was in strength, or whether it was just an isolated post. If it was a long way short of your ultimate objective, you had to find some way of getting past him and finding out what was beyond. That wasn't

always easy. If we could tell it was [just] a couple of fellers with a machine gun, then yes we would probably try and shift them. On the other hand, if we thought that by starting an attack we would alert a lot more, we would try and avoid it.[43]

Lieutenant Ronnie Sherlaw, 'C' Company

On this occasion everything went relatively smoothly and Sherlaw decided to probe even further when they got to the river.

We actually crossed the Teano, just waded through it. It wasn't a very deep river at all, about 15–20 feet across, and we got to the other side. We were travelling down a big built-up hedge, and it was from there that we eventually got machine gun fire. There was a set of Spandaus and a certain amount of Schmeissers. It was haphazard – they didn't know where we were; they were just firing because they could hear somebody. I think if they'd have seen us, they'd probably have hit us! Of course, they would see us once we fired back. We guessed that it was a little pocket of probably half a dozen Germans – that meant, of course, that this was the outpost probably of a decent-sized company. We fired back and then moved; we had a couple of lads who were pretty good at this, they wriggled about to try to find out exactly where [the Germans] were. We fired again and we got fire from further up. We returned fire because we were hoping to get further, but in fact it became so heavy that we eventually abandoned it – and came back. We didn't see any point in launching in and getting half of us killed. We came back and I reported to the battalion intelligence officer, who asked you what you'd found, what you'd seen, what the terrain was like, if you could identify any particular hazards and obstacles. You told him as best you could and used the map, or an aerial photograph, to try and mark things on. If he felt you hadn't quite done the job he would tell you![44]

Lieutenant Ronnie Sherlaw, 'C' Company

At dusk on 29 October, the 56th Division would attack the town of Teano and then push east into the foothills leading up to the mountainous heights of Santa Croce. Meanwhile the 46th Division were on their left, with the 139 Brigade charged with carrying out the assault over the Teano. This would begin with the crossing of the 2/5th Leicesters on the left at 18.30; to be followed by the 16th DLI on the right at 19.00; both sites to be covered by fire from the 5th Sherwood Foresters.

Crossing a river is always intimidating, but 'C' Company led the way and were unmolested, before spreading out to form a defensive screen. All was still relatively quiet, although there were considerable problems with German booby traps. Indeed, Major George Jobey trod on one artfully laid trap, which proved a little too cunning as it failed to explode. He had been very lucky! 'D' Company was next across, and began to move forward on the right of 'C' Company. They too were plagued with the booby traps, but then 18 Platoon was hit by heavy bursts of machine gun fire as they pushed forward.

> We had reached this farmhouse and we were giving the instructions to cross this open ground. It was black dark, but you visualise a field with trees round the edge and the far side, three sides. We were to go over and get through the wood at the other side. We went forward in arrowhead formation under horrendous machine gun fire. I thought, 'Well, somebody's got to knock this out!' I went forward to lob grenades into this area where the machine gun was. The last I knew there was the sergeant was telling us to retreat back, because we were being overpowered. Then, 'BANG!' And I was out! I don't know whether it was a shell or mortar or whatever. I was not injured by shrapnel; it was blast more than anything. It blew me back towards a tree – that's where I hurt my back! They thought I was out – dead! Jack Clatworthy said I wasn't! He and I were always together right through the war. He got shot through his arm helping me out of this situation. He got us back to the farmhouse where the medics were.[45]
>
> Corporal Robert Ellison, 'D' Company

In a few moments one man was killed and eighteen more wounded. Ellison himself later woke up in an American hospital back in Tunisia. His wounds were such that he was medically downgraded to category B1 and never rejoined the 16th DLI.

Despite the German machine guns, the Durhams managed to get forward, reached and consolidated their objectives some 500 yards from the river. The German positions were overrun.

> Apparently, Jerry had hopped it. We jumped into his slit trenches. We were all hungry, our rations had given out again! In one of the weapon pits he'd left cold potato, cold slices of bacon and loaf of hard brown bread. The lads dove for it, and they were eating the potato and bacon – I grabbed the loaf! I cut it into two and I says to Jock Keddy, another corporal, 'Do you want a bit of this? 'Go on to hell, it might be poisoned!' I said, 'Well, I'm taking the chance!' So, I cut all the crust off and we had the bread! Two days after we pulled out for short rest and Jock Keddy went down with dysentery and he said, 'You and your bloody brown bread!' You laugh when you think about things like that![46]
>
> Corporal Tom Turnbull, 'B' Company

Behind them the sappers were working with bulldozers to allow some sixteen Sherman tanks to get across the river.

> This was the first time we had ever worked with tanks. The plan was that the tanks would go in first, and we would come up behind them. We discovered that being close to the tanks was the worst thing in the world; because in going for the tanks, the German shells found us. So, we let the tanks go over on one side and we went over the other side! We let the tanks soften the Germans up – and then we moved in separately from them.[47]
>
> Lieutenant Ronnie Sherlaw, 'C' Company

This was not an isolated opinion with the 16th DLI. Russell Collins was also very sceptical as to the realities of infantry–tank cooperations.

> What a racket they make – as a matter of fact I used not to like fighting with tanks because one relies so much on a

sort of sixth sense – you can just hear and feel if there is any movement, or any shells approaching, and you can take evasive action. Being in the close neighbourhood of a tank is very like being blind; you're deafened and so you just lose the capacity really to exercise that sixth sense. I always felt very vulnerable if I was anywhere near a tank.[48]

2nd Lieutenant Russell Collins, 'A' Company

During the advance that followed, there was an amusing exchange back at the Headquarters, 46th Division, which was overlooking the battleground from Francolise. Here Major General John Hawkesworth was monitoring the progress of the battle as light dawned on the morning of 30 October. The colonel of the Durhams took great pleasure in reporting what was said.

The divisional commander surveyed the battleground. There were the Sherman tanks. Where were the Durhams? 'Jones, can you see the Durhams?' Answer, 'No, Sir!' A pause of five minutes. 'Jones, can you see the Durhams?' Answer, 'No, Sir! They are probably making use of ground and cover!' Jones knew the Durhams well and had read some infantry textbooks. A pause of ten minutes. 'Jones, can't you see the Durhams yet?' Answer, 'No, Sir. Those tanks are very slow, aren't they?' An effort to divert attention from the Durhams – Jones was a very loyal officer! A five-minute pause. 'Jones, have a good look and see if you can see the Durhams!' Answer, 'No, Sir, they are probably on their objective – they generally get their objective!' Full marks for loyalty and devotion. A final pause and then, 'Jones, where are those WRETCHED Durhams?'[49]

Lieutenant Colonel Johnny Preston, Headquarters Company

It was not until March 1945, that Preston had the nerve to tell the irascible Hawkesworth that the battalion had taken great pride in being 'The Wretched Durhams'. The War Diary wryly noted in a section entitled 'Lessons to be learnt on crossing the Teano' that 'If you are to work with tanks, previous training should be given'.[50] However, the Durhams had taken their objectives and overall, the operation was a success. The crossing was soon consolidated, and the advance was resumed as the Germans fell back to their next line of defences. On 2 November, the forward elements of the 46th Division and the 7th Armoured Division reached the coastal plain where the flooded Garigliano river was a formidable obstacle, dominated as it was inland by the inhospitable mass of the Monte Camino range. Once again there was trouble in store for the men of the 16th DLI.

8

MONTE CAMINO

There were two Germans who had been blown to pieces – there was nothing except bits and pieces all over – which had to be gathered together and buried under the stones. That was all we could do. We found their pay books and photographs; these were sent back to the Red Cross. You think, 'Well, it could have been me; it could be anybody!' After all it doesn't matter how good a soldier you may be, if you come under fire from a distance, the enemy doesn't know who he's killed. It's not a personal battle.[1]

Lance Corporal Charles Palmer, Intelligence Section, Headquarters Company

ALL ROADS MIGHT LEAD TO ROME but from the perspective of the Fifth Army, these roads were firmly blocked by the Gustav Line. The outer defences – the Bernhardt Line – were built four-square on the heights of the Monte Camino massif, just inland of the flood plain of the Garigliano river. By this time the underlying flaws in the Allied strategic planning ought to have been apparent. As a diversion, to draw German strength from the Eastern Front, or from the site of the intended Anglo-American D-Day invasion of France, the operations in Italy were clearly not working. Although suffering heavy losses, the Germans were still providing a determined resistance with their existing forces in Italy. Furthermore, as D-Day became the prime concern, the Italian 'backwater' began to be starved of the resources necessary to secure a rapid success. Mission creep and Churchillian diplomacy had inveigled the Americans into first North Africa, then Sicily, and now lumbered them with a terrible battle for Italy, a country that had already surrendered. It was evident that the Italian campaign was sucking in landing craft and resources needed for D-Day. Yet the fighting went on.

On 5 November 1943, the American commander of Fifth Army, General Mark Clark, ordered his British 56th Division to storm the heights of Monte Camino which was held by elements of the 15th Panzer Grenadier Division – it was a truly challenging prospect. The 201 Guards Brigade was to capture the village of Calabritto, then ascend the evocatively named Bare Arse Ridge to attack the summits of Point 727 and Monastery Hill, while 168 Brigade were to take the Cocuruzzo village before advancing up the ridge on Point 530. Although some progress was made, the attack fell apart; there were simply not enough troops allotted to subdue the strong German resistance on such a huge dominant mountain fastness. However, failure was not considered acceptable and they were ordered to try again next day. More troops were fed in to the meat-grinder, with freezing temperatures, rain or sleet, high winds and pervading dank mists all adding to the overall misery. No matter what was tried, the Germans still seemed to be above them, controlling the peaks. At last, on 14 November, the 56th Division were allowed to withdraw, having suffered grievous casualties.

The Fifth Army would gird its metaphorical loins and try again on 2 December with Operation Raincoat. This time two British divisions would be deployed, backed by the copious artillery support of some 820 guns to help blast their way on to Monte Camino, while just to the north the Americans sought to capture Monte La Difensa. The 56th Division would once again take the direct route from Calabritto up Bare Arse Ridge, but this time it would be assisted by a preparatory attack the previous day by the 46th Division, whose 139 Brigade would capture the various spurs and foothills stretching down to the south from the main massif: Pillbox spur, Terrace Hill and Telegraph Hill. This would provide a threat on the Germans' right flank and hopefully distract them during the main assault.

At 22.00 on 1 December, the 5th Sherwood Foresters and 2/5th Leicesters moved forwards, while the 16th DLI was in reserve back at the village of La Murata. The Foresters were to move up onto Pillbox spur, which would act as a base. Then they would move along the ridge, pushing through the woods to take the village of Calabritto, after which it would be the turn of the Leicesters to advance on their left to take Terrace Hill. At first all went well, as Pillbox Hill was taken without any opposition, but when the Foresters attacked Calabritto, disaster struck. Deep mud, barbed wire, minefields, machine guns and heavy mortar fire from Terrace Ridge first caused a stumbling halt, and then a pell-mell retreat to their start line on Pillbox Hill. The Leicesters fared no better. Badly shelled as they passed through the village of San Clemente, they too ran into a minefield, before their attack on Telegraph Hill collapsed in a welter of casualties. With the attack stalled, as night fell on 2 December, 'B' Company was detached from 16th DLI and sent forward into action. Bill Virr had only just rejoined after a brief hospitalisation with jaundice, and he had celebrated a little unwisely.

> We had a right good night out. I drunk too much wine at a little wine shop in the village. The wine was 22 lira a bottle and at the time the lira was 400 to the pound! About threepence a bottle! We had a drop too much! Bill Holder was a good pianist, and there was a piano in this place where we were billeted. It was a right good singsong![2]
>
> Corporal William Virr, 'B' Company

Little did he know what lay in wait for him in just a few hours' time as they marched up towards Calabritto. They came under dreadful mortar fire and were forced to take cover in what remained of some former German slit trenches.

> It came on absolutely bucketing down with rain – terrible weather. It just churned it all to mud; the slit trenches were half full of water. You were just sat in them, trying to get a cigarette going, but you couldn't. Then they started mortaring us. Well of course they knew the exact range for these trenches, because

> they were the ones that they'd dug [before] they'd withdrawn higher up the valley! They were dropping these bombs all round and luckily half of them were dud – they weren't exploding because of the soft ground. A chap in the trench next to me, a bomb exploded and killed him. His mate with him was badly wounded. It was awful. I never did like mortar shelling, because they come straight down. You can be in a slit trench, but it can drop right in with you, whereas a shell at least comes down at an angle! You'd got the fragments from the mortar bomb, but also all the rock fragments as well, which doubled the effect of the shrapnel. Shattered rocks flying about will kill you just as well as a piece of metal if it hit you.[3]
>
> Corporal William Virr, 'B' Company

Casualties were high, with one shell killing Lieutenant Fred Strothart[4] and mortally wounding the popular company commander, Major George Ballance.[5] On a personal level, Bill Virr felt even more deeply the loss of Bill Holder,[6] the man who had led the jolly singsong playing the piano just the night before. Holder was hit in the head and his mates tried to help him back to safety, but he died in their arms. As the shells fell all around them, with death seemingly only a moment away, Virr felt he was on the edge of madness.

> If you're under a long bombardment, I think you'd go mad eventually – go off your rocker. Every man has a different breaking point, and some go before others. You could never point the finger at anyone because he'd reached his breaking point, yours might be just a little farther on – another half hour and it might be you. You tend to be on the brink, and it takes all your striving to prevent yourself from going to pieces, when you feel like letting everything go – gabbling and screaming, gibbering away – just letting go. You just curl up in a ball and hope nothing comes your way. I always lay on my left side and put my hands between my legs, my tin hat on the top and hoped for the best. I felt I was protecting myself a little bit! I probably wasn't! There was nothing you could do.[7]
>
> Corporal William Virr, 'B' Company

Their position being untenable, they fell back towards Pillbox Ridge.

In these operations, 139 Brigade had suffered a dreadful hammering from the 129th Panzer Grenadier Regiment holding the Calabritto basin sector, but it had done just enough to secure the flank of the 56th Division. The main attack went in on the night of 2/3 December, preceded by a withering bombardment. The 169 Brigade advanced up Razor Back Ridge towards Monastery Hill; while 167 Brigade slogged up Bare Arse Ridge towards Point 819. This time 56th Division stormed home, wrenching control Point 727 before attacking Point 819 itself. Meanwhile, the Americans had also captured the heights of Monte La Difensa. But still the Germans would not surrender Monte Camino. A gruelling phase of attacks and counterattacks followed, with both sides bringing up reinforcements to create a hell on earth on that blasted summit.

At this point, on 5 December, the 16th DLI were called upon to try and exploit the gains made by the 56th Division by taking the Cocuruzzo spur (Point 430 and 420). After a conference with the colonel of the 5th Sherwood Foresters, Colonel Johnny Preston came up with a plan to avoid having to make a frontal assault across Calabritto basin. Instead, Preston planned to attack from the north, more or less from the rear of the German positions. This involved a significant flanking march, starting at 11.00 from the base at La Murata, then tracking all the way round through the 56th Division area, climbing up Bare Arse Ridge, on to Monte Camino, then across to the Formelli position which had just been taken by the 201 (Guards) Brigade. It would be a hell of a climb, but if it offered the chance of tactical surprise, which might reduce the casualties, it was a chance worth taking.

> We were all concentrated at the bottom of this mountain, the battalion, the support company, ready to climb that mountain and get over the top. The night before I think there were 650 guns of our artillery fired on that mountain. Every gun was used. The whole lot were firing – the 7.2-inch, which are huge

guns, the 5.5-inch, the 25-pounders and the Bofors. It was like bonfire night – the shells landing on this mountain. And the next morning, we had to climb up.[8]

Company Sergeant Major Leslie Thornton, Support Company

Before they left, Leslie Thornton encountered a surprising but welcome visitor.

> We started and got to the bottom of the mountain to wend our way up. I had my company headquarters with me and the captain. I had my full kit on, and on top of my pack on my neck was a coil of barbed wire – sergeant majors had to do the work as well you see! Just a little way up this tall figure with a stick came bouncing down and says, 'Good morning, sergeant major!' 'Good morning, Sir!' I wondered what the hell he'd been doing up there – it was the corps commander, Lieutenant General Sir Richard McCreery – he'd been to have a look. Naturally he couldn't stay up there; you can't have generals being taken prisoner or killed.[9]

Company Sergeant Major Leslie Thornton, Support Company

There were no roads, just rough mountain paths, and there is no doubt that the men found it extremely hard going, laden down as they were.

> It was like scree – very rough and broken ground. There were very steep tracks, and of course we were carrying full battle order, forty-eight-hour rations, full water bottles and full load of ammunition. There was no possibility of any motor transport going up there, so we had pack mules which took the heavy stores up. Going up this winding track, all through the night, with periodic breaks of five or ten minutes each hour and so on. With the mules going along beside us, going up as quietly as we could, By the morning we got up on the high ground – unobserved – the enemy quite unaware, as far as I know.[10]

Lieutenant Russell Collins, 'A' Company

After an exhausting long march, they reached Point 683, the furthest point taken by the Guards, at 20.00. They then stayed out of sight, gathering their forces, and resting, concealed as they were from the Germans. The officers carefully carried out a recce to get the ground configuration in their heads. The attack on Point 430 would be made at first light on 6 December by 'C' Company. At this time, Ronnie Sherlaw had risen to be second in command – promotion was fast due to the frequency of casualties.

> Cocuruzzo spur ran out from the west side of Monte Camino. 'C' Company were the leading company. One or two casualties, but nothing serious. We consolidated Cocuruzzo spur – there was a similar spur about 300 yards away that the Germans held. It was this contingent that was making life difficult for us. Mainly small arms stuff. We'd done a little bit of digging, we had little sangars of piled up rock. During the course of the action, I was hit in the left shoulder by a sniper bullet. I was being stupid actually – I was pointing out the man that shot me! Pointing with my left arm! I was spun round. I was taken straight out of the line – the stretcher bearers were very good. They wrapped me up straight away and put a dressing on. Then took me out down to the regimental aid post.[11]
>
> Lieutenant Ronnie Sherlaw, 'C' Company

He was lucky. The bullet had chipped not shattered his shoulder bone, and after a brief period of hospitalisation and convalescence, he was soon back with the 16th DLI.

Major Ray Mitchell's 'A' Company was tasked with making the next push forward, leapfrogging through to take an intermediate small promontory given the codename 'Dick'. Among them was Russell Collins, once again leading from the front.

> As we were going across there we came under a lot of small arms and artillery fire. In fact, the artillery fire was extremely confusing; it was all so close to us that we were never very sure if it was German defensive fire, or our own barrage supporting us, because the shells seemed to be falling all around. But

the most conspicuous thing was the small-arms fire – and we suffered a lot of casualties, about eighteen men in 'A' Company were hit with bullets in the space of about half an hour. The medical officer did a tremendous job, because he had brought his regimental aid post forward and set up in a sort of crofter's hut down on the leeside of the mountain. These casualties were taken down to him.[12]

2nd Lieutenant Russell Collins, 'A' Company

'A' Company was forced to ground by the heavy small-arms fire. Collins and his men took cover behind boulders and a convenient low drystone wall. Here they were pinned down and any move they made was met with a storm of fire.

> I spotted where this fire was coming from, about 80 to 100 yards on our right, as we were going across. A lot of fire was coming from there – like a crofter's small farmstead. I was so incensed really, very angry that some of my chaps were being hit. One very nice lad, Private Jimmy Baglin,[13] was hit and died subsequently. Ray Mitchell was there, really wondering quite what to do I think! I said, 'Well look, I think I'd better go and sort it out; will you let me go?' He said 'Good Lord, if you want to – sooner you than me!' I said, 'I'll take a little assault party round to the right flank!' He said, 'Well, all right – good luck!' I set up a machine gun post to fire back at these people, to keep their heads down, while I moved with two or three chaps: my batman Phillips, Corporal Clayton was another of them – I handpicked about three or four men.[14]

2nd Lieutenant Russell Collins, 'A' Company

He would not delegate the task to an NCO as by this time Collins had realised that the real role of a subaltern like himself was to provide an inspirational example to his men.

> It depends so much on the individual. Some officers might make the plans: 'This is the plan, sergeant. I can do the covering fire from here, and you take the assault party round there!' That was not my way! Rightly or wrongly, I led from

the front whenever possible. I felt more confident that way. I felt it was my duty, to tell you the truth, I really felt I couldn't send somebody else there if I wasn't prepared to do it myself. I nearly always led from the front. In the war the dominant lesson I learnt was the crucial role of the junior officer, because it was quite clear to me that unless platoon commanders led their platoons, nothing happened.[15]

2nd Lieutenant Russell Collins, 'A' Company

Machine guns and rifles provided covering fire as Collins lunged off to the right towards the farm buildings. It was a desperate business,

We went around to the right flank. I wanted to get on with it. I went positively, you might say impetuously, but anyway straightforwardly. As I ran into the target area, on to which our machine gun was still firing rapid fire, the bullets were cracking over my head, but I think they saw us just in time. When I got round the side of the building, I saw that there was no ground entrance but there was an outside staircase. I rushed straight up the staircase and there was a door open at the top. I was aware of the danger of going into an open doorway, but somehow, I established that there was nobody in that upper room. Then I looked over the sort of parapet, where I was standing at the top of this stairway, and down behind was an extension to the farm building, a cowshed or something like that. It was clear then that the enemy were all in there. I was standing about 10 feet above them. I opened up with my Tommy gun down through slates or tiles of the roof and I ordered my other chaps around the side of the staircase to my left. There they were standing outside the door with their rifles at the ready – and I was standing up above, firing down. What came out through the door was a white flag on the end of a rifle bayonet, because there was absolutely nothing else they could do. We shouted at them to come out with their hands up. They came out, something like sixteen or eighteen of them. I'm afraid that when we lined those prisoners up, if any of them had any cameras or anything like that which we didn't want to fall into the hands of the people guarding the prisoner of war camps behind, we helped ourselves – we felt that we were more entitled to them than they were. Perhaps slightly reprehensible in some ways. Among them was a camera and I took some snaps there and then. Then we dug in, consolidated the position, and had a brew up![16]

2nd Lieutenant Russell Collins, 'A' Company

Thanks to the intrepid Collins and his men, the position was captured. Russell Collins would be awarded the MC for his performance that day.

> I don't think MCs came up very frequently for platoon commanders. They came up sometimes for company commanders who'd commanded a successful attack but hadn't done anything perhaps too personal. I think in general they were well merited. The thing that sticks in mind is that I did many things which in my mind were equally meritorious and some of them even more hazardous which just weren't recognised at all. But one doesn't complain about that, it's the luck of the draw. I was quite chuffed about mine![17]

2nd Lieutenant Russell Collins, 'A' Company

Tony Sacco could confirm that the men carried on the less than noble tradition of relieving prisoners of any valuables they might possess.

> We lined them all up – about thirty-five of them. As they were standing there, the lads were going and taking their weapons off them – and also stealing their watches! The German sergeant major, he spoke very good English, he said to Company Sergeant Major Wilson, 'I think your men are a bunch of recruits!' Wilson just grinned! I didn't believe in looting – I never did.[18]

Signaller Tony Sacco, 'A' Company

But worse was to follow. During the fighting, two stretcher bearers, Privates Clifford Millett[19] and Bernard Davenport,[20] had been killed by a German sniper. Major Ray Mitchell was incandescent with rage and resolved to have his revenge. It resulted in an ugly scene.

> Major Mitchell was going mad, 'Who's the sniper? Who's the sniper that had killed these stretcher bearers?' There was only one there with a camouflage suit on; he didn't look like a German at all, dark hair. Mitchell said, 'Right, you're the sniper, go to the side!' And he pointed to me, Webley and Mason, that was the other two signallers, 'You three – aim your guns!' I thought, 'We can't do this!' But this German was just standing up, not showing any fear at all, just standing, scowling, just glaring at us. Major Mitchell was looking for him to show fright and he wouldn't. I thought, 'Hey, I don't like this idea at all!' He said, 'Right, get back in – shoot the lot!' I thought, 'Oh God!' Everybody lined up with their guns. 'Right aim, when I tell you fire, fire, now aim!' They were all standing, nobody moved. Then suddenly this great big fat one, right at the front, he must have been about 18 stone, he started crying. He got down and started taking all his photographs out of his wife; he was looking at them. But the other Germans were looking at him as if he was dirt. He was crying. I don't think Mitchell would have shot them, but he wanted somebody to show fright. I think that's all he wanted in the end. He said, 'Right, march the lot away!'[21]
>
> Signaller Tony Sacco, 'A' Company

While 'A' Company was dealing with this flanking German strongpoint to the right of the 'Dick' position, 'D' Company was sent up to the left of 'C' Company who were still holding Point 430. Together they launched the final assault at 14.30 to take 'Dick' and Point 420 with the assistance of a heavy barrage supplied by the 25-pounders of the 70th Field Regiment and smoke shells fired by their own 3-inch mortars. After vigorous fighting the strongpoint was finally stormed and defensive positions established. Behind them the Support Company had been struggling up through the charnel house of a battlefield. It was a grim scene.

> We finally got to the top. The carnage – there was guardsmen hanging out of holes in the ground, there was Germans lying all over. There was still some rifle fire. They were disposed of, and we started our climb down to the valley. This barbed wire on my neck was bouncing up and down and it wasn't very comfortable at all, you believe me, especially going down. It wasn't so bad going up! Eventually we got to the bottom; it was getting light. On we went to where I had to put my company headquarters in the valley. We halted there and waited for orders. I saw two bodies lying on the ground – Sergeant Kennedy,[22] a friend of mine from Bishop Auckland – dead – and his corporal lying beside him – they'd been caught by German machine gunners – hit in the head. We buried them there, a shallow grave, took their discs, put their gas capes over them and marked it so that the padre would come along later on, see them and they'd be moved.[23]
>
> Company Sergeant Major Leslie Thornton, Support Company

During the fighting, Thornton's company commander had been injured and Thornton had been required to take over command of the Support Company. In the end they were up there for four days. He would later recall it was the longest time during which he never shaved in his whole adult life. But there were still more deadly dangers than stubble lurking on the Monte Camino wastelands.

> I heard a shot, and something went past me. Then this guardsman came over and I saw a bullet hit beside him. It was a sniper just on our left – up a tree! He was unlucky! The guardsmen saw him and blasted him – down he fell. That was the end of him! He could have got us – if it hadn't been for the fact he missed![24]
>
> Company Sergeant Major Leslie Thornton, Support Company

On 7 December, 'C' Company advanced to the left from Point 420, along the Cocuruzzo spur to take the village of Cocuruzzo, which was the battalion's final objective. By 12.00 the village was secured as the Germans had fallen back. The domination of the Calabritto basin had been achieved, which meant supplies and casualties could use the direct route to La Murata through the valley, rather than the terrible mountain trail. Thornton remembered the state of the village, blasted by artillery as he was marching back out of the line.

> We marched through the little village of Cocuruzzo, which was absolutely devastated. One poor Italian was hanging upside down on the side of the road where a shell had blown him. An old man, grey haired, the blast had just plastered him against the wall. The scene was terrible. The place was really wrecked.[25]
>
> Company Sergeant Major Leslie Thornton, Support Company

After such an ordeal the battalion was given a short period of rest. Leslie Thornton was delighted. His appearance as a company sergeant major was very important to him: part of his self-image; part of the pride that kept him going when others faltered. But that wasn't all. He was also just bloody knackered – and who could blame him or any of the men?

> To get out for a couple of days from the line was a treat. Just to clean yourself up really, because we were really filthy – not having a shave! You felt really scruffy! If you live with pigs, you live like a pig! Which you do! If you couldn't get a wash and shave, then you just don't care and you live that way! And to clean the weapons, they have to be cleaned, to make sure that they are in working order for when you want to use them again. No training or anything like that. It was a rest, and it had to be. The colour sergeant met me coming along and he saw we were absolutely shattered. He got hold of my arm and he said, 'Come on, Les, I've got some nice clean blankets for you! And a cup of tea!' I said, 'You what, clean blankets, lovely!' We went into this building for a rest – we were shattered. It was really nice to lie down, even although it was only on the floor, but those clean blankets were a luxury! Well – right outside the building opposite was a 7.2-inch artillery piece, that was the biggest gun we had. They started to fire – well our building

went up and down like that! I said, 'Who thought of this place for a rest!' My God, every time it fired the blast was terrific. But even with the artillery over the road I did sleep because we had had very little sleep for four days.[26]

Company Sergeant Major Leslie Thornton, Support Company

The men were all exhausted. They had been involved in a terrible battle, but it was one that has been largely forgotten; the memories dissipated by the horrors to come at Monte Cassino. Fortunately, that was one battle the 16th DLI would miss.

★

AFTER SUCH AN ORDEAL the men treasured any chance of a rest, to put their feet up for a while. And there was a lull in the storm. On 15 December, the 16th DLI moved into new billets at Campo. Here they were in reserve in case the Germans made an attack back on to Monte Camino, although there were calls for men to join working parties controlled by the Royal Engineers in constructing a viable road between Calabritto and Cocuruzzo. While at Campo, the battalion also received a draft of new officers to replace the steady drip-drip of casualties over the previous months. One who became prominent in the history of the 16th DLI was Lieutenant Alan Hay. He was slightly older than many officers, being born in 1912, the son of a master plumber in South Shields. On leaving school he worked in an accountant's office, but trained with the 1st Cadet Battalion, DLI at the local drill hall in the years leading up to the outbreak of war. He failed to get a TA commission, so he volunteered as a private with the DLI in November 1939. Identified early on as a potential officer, he was commissioned into the 13th DLI in 1940, moving to the 17th DLI at Folkestone. Since then, he had been mainly occupied on a training role, before the battalion was finally broken up to provide replacement drafts and he was finally posted to the 16th DLI as a platoon commander. Because of his lengthy service with the DLI, he found he knew many of the officers he encountered.

> Duffy was a well-built lad, a major, an MC, whom I had sent out as one of the draft officers [from the 17th DLI] some time ago. He was keen to get out and had been doing the Battle Schools and that was what he was best at – he was a bit wayward in other respects: getting into trouble over larking about and not having that sort of respect. He loved the Battle Schools and so he was a natural to get abroad. He was company commander and he said, 'What are you going to do, Alan?' I said, 'Well, I haven't been told yet!' He said, 'Would you like to come to my company?' I said, 'Certainly, yes – which company is that?' He said, '"D" Company – we'll look after you!' So, I went to 'D' Company. The men I'd brought, they mixed them in straight away. Because they'd had a lot of casualties they were well below strength, and they were ready for these men. I would certainly think the reinforcements formed about 40 per cent of what was needed.[27]
>
> Lieutenant Alan Hay, 'D' Company

The 16th DLI were then moved forward, replacing the 5th Hampshires in the front line in a mountainous area to the north-west of San Carlo.

> I just remember climbing, and climbing, and climbing; just following blindly in single file to get into this holding position in a dry riverbed, a fairly dried up stream – there was water coming through – but it afforded protection and shelter. Duffy said, 'Put your platoon there!' This was the first time I'd been in a position where I had to look after myself, look after the men. I said to the sergeant, 'Tell your chaps to look after the new men!' 'Oh, yes, they'll do that!' I went round and looked at them! With these rocks you couldn't dig; it was all rock; you just had to build the rocks up. You couldn't make an attack; you were just holding high ground; being present. Of course, you could hear guns firing. I learned how to use my gas cape to keep warm. It had been raining ever since I arrived and during the night there was roaring – and the water came gushing down the mountainside. It washed over everything – and us! That was my introduction to soldiering! This was for real![28]
>
> Lieutenant Alan Hay, 'D' Company

During this period, Gerry Barnett, who had been wounded at Salerno, arrived back at the unit. He was not happy at what he found.

> This was really the most horrible place I was ever in. We were on rock into which you could not dig. We had in the rear positions one or two clefts between rock which gave slightly better cover, but in the night positions on the forward slope we could only lie behind sangars – which are little piles of rocks in a circle which you try and take cover behind. We had to stay all night and we were shelled. These shells used to be dropping down and not penetrating into the earth at all – they used to go with a clang instead of a bang when they exploded – and the ground was littered with these huge pieces of jagged metal each morning. It was really a hell on earth.[29]
>
> Lieutenant Gerry Barnett, 'C' Company

There were no major operations underway in the sector, but recce patrols still went out on a regular basis, to make sure that the Germans were not up to anything untoward. The recently joined officers were soon called upon to lead patrols, but did they have the practical experience to make a success of it?

> Lieutenant Critchley, who came out with me, was going to take the patrol. I was curious and I said, 'Can I go down and see what the procedure is for them going out?' 'Oh, yes!' I went down and I saw Critchley and his men. I said, 'Don't worry! Good luck!' They walked into the Germans and Critchley was killed and one or two of our new men. Their first day 'out'. I wouldn't say we did much patrolling in our training at home. You moved about at night, but you weren't in any danger, you were just finding your way to a certain spot. Critchley[30] was just doing his normal thing; he'd walked straight into this – he hadn't the experience; it was his first time. I thought: All the time we've been wasting in England, why couldn't they have brought one or two of us out, just to be there to get the feel of things. Because it is a hell of a sight different, particularly in small patrols against a real enemy. Where you need to get this

'nous' about the thing, get the 'feel' and the 'smell' of the thing! To get more confidence.[31]

Lieutenant Alan Hay, 'D' Company

Then it was Alan Hay's turn. He had been an officer since 1941, but this was very different from exercises in England.

> 'Giff' Footer helped me with selecting the patrol. He gave me an experienced corporal and one or two other men, and three of our draft, newcomers. I was told where I was going, and I could see through the glasses – get an idea. I said, 'Has this been patrolled before?' 'Oh, yes!' I said to 'Giff' Footer, 'Look, I'm going out there, anything you can tell me?' He said, 'Oh, you'll get there all right, you're safe enough up to there, just be careful beyond that!' We were to find out whether the Germans had standing patrols, how far they'd come back. Not much happened on the first patrol. We just went out and this experienced corporal, said, 'I'll just go down here – I think there might be something!' He went away for it could have been twenty minutes to half an hour. Then came and said, 'No, they've been there, but they're not there anymore!' These chaps said you can smell the 'Tedeschis' [Germans] as they called them. There was a lot of old wives' tales told about that! I learnt not to rely on these soldiers who'd been out there a few months – they had their own way of going about things![32]

Lieutenant Alan Hay, 'D' Company

Hay believed his corporal had simply 'gone to earth' for a suitable period before returning to avoid having to move into dangerous ground. It was not long before he was required to take out another night patrol. Time spent in preparation is seldom wasted, so Hay spent the day making sure he was well briefed. He interrogated Lieutenant 'Giff' Footer, who had been out several times, as to what he might expect.

> I said, 'Did you find any difficulties?' 'No, there's no sign of anything!' 'Are there any pitfalls?' 'No! No!' I spent the day with my glasses, [binoculars] looking over the ground, memorising

it. I had the Tommy gun, we had one Bren gun, I had a couple of hand grenades. When the patrol boots come in a sack, you hand them out to the members of the patrol, who start wearing them so that they're used to it. They are felt and rubber. I had an experienced sergeant, and the other members were picked for me. There would only be eight of us. The idea was we had to go forward, not so much to get a prisoner, but to probe to see how far the enemy had come forward, what their forward positions were. When I bumped into them, I was to fire a red light from the signal pistol – and give myself five minutes to get out – this was the signal for the artillery to come down.[33]

Lieutenant Alan Hay, 'D' Company

Hay became aware that not everything was as it should be in 'D' Company. His unreliable corporal was not an isolated case. Morale was poor, with a curious mixture of experienced men, some of whom had quite frankly had enough, and new arrivals who had not mastered the basics of their trade.

> We were going along very slowly, I found they were straggling a bit and the man with the Bren gun who should have been ready to fire, he was lagging. I didn't think we'd want to use him, but I just wanted him to be there. Then we'd got beyond where my glasses had 'taken me' in daylight – and suddenly, confronting us were three or four Germans that seemed to be in a set position – about 20 yards away – we were almost on top of them! There were one or two shots, but what I was conscious of was I could see that they came up from the ground with these grenades in their hands! The ones with the handles! Which they threw and they exploded! I marvelled that nobody was hurt! I said to the Bren gunner, 'Get your gun going!' But he wasn't able to fire it for some reason. My Tommy gun fired two shots and then stopped! I got the shock of my life! I learnt to make sure your own weapon was working properly! And it was a little chaotic. I said to the man who had the pistol, 'Fire red!' He had a red one already in! He didn't get that off! The others had rather gone to ground and didn't use their weapons! So we withdrew! We were being fired on, but we didn't have

any casualties. Then I got the man to work the Very pistol and the red shot went up. Five minutes – and then the artillery came down.[34]

Lieutenant Alan Hay, 'D' Company

Later, Hay discovered that 'Giff' Footer had not reccied as far forward as he had implied, which was why he had not discovered the advanced Germans defensive post. It is fair to say that Hay was not amused! On 31 December, they pulled back into rest billets at La Vaglie. Here they had belated Christmas celebrations and approximately 450 Africa Star medal ribbons were issued to those entitled by their service to wear them. But the war was not finished with them yet. Not by a long chalk.

9

ACROSS THE GARIGLIANO

> I went to sleep with just one blanket, laying in amongst these rocks. I thought, 'It's raining!' and pulled my blanket over. When I woke up, I was covered in snow! The weather was atrocious. It makes you wonder how we really survived, really, nowadays you couldn't do it. But the weather was atrocious in Italy for that period. They did say that at the time that it hadn't been like that for years. Really bad![1]
>
> Corporal William Virr, 'B' Company

IT WAS ALL CHANGE for the Allies in Italy by January 1944. Firstly, Eisenhower had left to become the Supreme Commander, charged with carrying out the D-Day invasion of Europe. He was replaced by General Sir Henry Maitland Wilson who was designated commander of the 'rebadged' Allied Forces Mediterranean. General Sir Harold Alexander would continue to command the 15th Army Group (US Fifth Army and the British Eight Army), but Montgomery also left to assume command of the 21st Army Group who would launch Operation Overlord with the Normandy landings in just six months. Lieutenant General Sir Oliver Leese took over the Eighth Army. The draining effects of the Monte Camino operations and the intimidating strength of the Gustav Line founded on the 'rock' of Monte Cassino had brought a grim stalemate in the winter months. In response, an ambitious plan, Operation Shingle, was conceived to launch an assault landing at Anzio some 26 miles north of Rome, with the intention of threatening the rear communications of the Gustav

Line. This was controversial as it clearly involved landing craft coveted by the D-Day planners, but it was also vulnerable to counterattacks if Clark's Fifth Army could not batter their way forward. Overall, it was evident that the British were still keen to extend the Italian campaign, whether it was pessimism as to the prospects of Overlord, or just a more mundane desire to keep up the pressure on the Germans.

While the great and good pondered their actions, for the Durhams it seemed to be just more of the 'same old same old'. On 6 January, the 16th DLI relieved the 6th Yorks and Lancs on the lower slopes of Monte Maggiore. They were called into action almost immediately in support of the 5th Sherwood Foresters' night attack on Rocca Station, pushing towards Cedra on 7/8 January. Again 'B' Company was chosen to provide flank protection, and they moved forward, wading across the Peccia river, then followed a track to take up defensive positions in a small wood. So far so good. However, the Foresters' attack failed, a company had got into Cedra, but could not hold their positions in the face of heavy shellfire and German counterattacks. 'B' Company had some shelling to endure but held on until they were relieved by 'A' Company. On the night of 9 January, the rest of the battalion moved forward to relieve the Foresters, but as they were doing so, reports came in that Cedra had been abandoned by the Germans and in consequence an immediate night advance of some 1,000 yards was ordered.

> We had no maps of the terrain; they hadn't been prepared; the German retreat was too fast. We had gridded aerial photographs, with which we hoped to call for artillery fire if needed. We set off: first 'D' Company went a short distance into this flat valley bottom, arable land crisscrossed with ditches and hedges. Then 'C' Company set off, more or less in single file into this apparent wilderness. As soon as we left the road across a little river on a log bridge, one of my men dropped his rifle, and without a second's hesitation instantly jumped off into this river, which was about 5 feet deep and groped on the bottom for his rifle – and found it! We crossed on to a stretch of very

> soft ground which was pockmarked with shell holes – and we were being shelled. Then we moved out on this patrol. Single file, platoon after platoon following the company commander. It sounds ridiculous! Completely vulnerable to ambush! We moved to a collection of farm buildings, Cedra, this little mound in the valley bottom. I saw a big white cow in one of the byres there, deserted by the farmer. We put out sentries round the farm buildings and bedded down for the night. It was then the early hours of the morning. I found some German black bread which I ate for supper – it was still reasonably fresh.[2]
>
> Lieutenant Gerry Barnett, 'C' Company

At dawn, visibility was initially poor as there was a thick mountain mist hanging over the valley. A FOO from 449 Battery, 70th Field Regiment came forward and began to establish an observation post. Then as the mist lifted there was an alarm.

> One of the sentries had seen some German soldiers right outside the building. I rushed out, as I was, I didn't even pick up my Tommy gun. I had my pistol on my belt of course. I rushed straight out and there they were a few yards from the door – a group of six to eight German soldiers. There was then something like half a dozen of my men with me, including my sergeant – and we ran at them. Two dropped to the ground in the ensuing melee and the others scattered and ran. It was at that moment that this delightful sergeant of mine, a Yorkshireman with an unbelievably big moustache, danced round us waving his rifle and shouting, 'Try to take prisoners, try to take prisoners!' I can only say I felt absolutely delighted that such a humane action could take place at a time like that. But it didn't stop us of course – there wasn't time to do anything about it. Two of the Germans had thrown themselves to the ground and were taken prisoner; the others were still running, so I shouted to the men to fire, and emptied my pistol myself in their direction – I didn't hit anything of course – you can't with a pistol! I snatched a rifle from a man, had a go myself and then they were all in cover; they'd all gone down the slope.[3]
>
> Lieutenant Gerry Barnett, 'C' Company

Later, Barnett believed that they were not a raiding party or patrol, but perhaps a working party that had blundered into trouble, ignorant of their presence in the area.

> All this was very quick and took only a few seconds of time – a minute at the most. Almost immediately [after] they'd gone to ground a German machine gun opened fire on us. For some reason I thought it was on the higher ground on the left on the knoll. I set off with a few of the chaps following me along this partly made road to look for it, thinking I was having a little bit of cover from the revetment on the left of the road where it was dug into the hill. I'd gone only 50 yards when the machine gun hit me. I realised from the wound I received that I'd made a mistake and it was [located] on the right down on the lower ground. I was hit in the neck, and, because of my crouching position, the bullet went through the right of my neck and out through my left shoulder – taking a lot of my shoulder blade with it. The hole in the neck was very small, but the hole in my back was fairly large. I didn't know that then of course. It was a curious experience – I had time to reflect on it – I thought I was dead at first because all the consciousness of my body went. I could see and I could think – and that was about the limit of it. I knew I was folding up because I could see I was slowly falling to the ground; my body was collapsing. I thought, 'Well, this is yet another interesting experience to add to the list!' I folded on to the ground, and I was lying on my back with my knees sticking up. Then I found I could move my right arm. My first thought was to push my knees down because they could be fired at. Then slowly some feelings returned. I couldn't move my left arm, that was paralysed. For some reason I thought I'd been hit in the groin – Heaven knows why – I wasn't! I got with my right hand my field dressing out, but I couldn't open it, so I stuffed it inside my trousers thinking I was bleeding there. Then, very bravely, my runner, King, and the sergeant rushed out to me and dragged me back along this road to where they'd half constructed a drain. There was hole just under the bank at the higher side of the road into a culvert underneath –

and they threw me headfirst down this drain and ran for cover themselves to the ditch, crawled into the drain and dragged me through it and back to the buildings. I was just numb; I didn't feel any pain. The stretcher bearers got hold of me, took me into one of the farm buildings. I was wearing a new trench coat and a leather jerkin. Leather jerkins were issued in the winter, but they didn't have enough to go round, so we used to take it in turns to wear it – and it had been my turn that day! I asked the men cutting my clothing off to get a dressing on my back, to ease me out of the jerkin rather than cut it, because it was a precious garment! It probably had a hole in the back of course! Consciousness went then.[4]

Lieutenant Gerry Barnett, 'C' Company

Continuing harassing fire meant he could only be evacuated by the stretcher bearers the next night. After hospitalisation and convalescence back in the UK, Barnett was downgraded to the Medical 'C' Category and posting to the Green Howards, where he was restricted to a training role. He would never return to the 16th DLI.

The battalion was in the Cedra area for a while, engaged in patrolling and countering German patrol activities. After being relieved by the 5th Sherwood Foresters it was then withdrawn behind the Peccia for a period of rest. Then a move back to La Murata, where the Durhams learnt that they were to be attached under the command of 138 Brigade. On 25 January, they would cross the Garigliano river by pontoon bridge, before relieving the 6th Yorks and Lancs in the line in the Suja area at around 04.30 on 26 January. They were to be in reserve as a series of attacks was launched in the Monte Turlito sector. Once it was apparent that the 2/4th KOYLI had taken Ruffiano, the 6th Lincolnshires seized Monte Turlito, while the 6th York and Lancs captured the nearby Point 400, the 16th DLI was then ordered forward on 29 January to help secure the latter two gains. At 13.00, 'A' Company led the way, passing via Mass Valle di Suja, round the lower slopes of Monte Turlito, and across to Point 400 which they reached at 16.00. After a few hours rest, at 23.00

Russell Collins's platoon was selected to carry out a recce patrol, feeling round the north side of a spur and on to Monte Siola.

> It was quite a deep patrol and we got into this gully. Well, the Germans were in it, that was the trouble, they were covering it – machine guns certainly on one side and possibly on both sides. We were trying to make progress, but I realised that we had gone too far and were going to have difficulty in extricating ourselves. We came under fire – so we just had to get out of the gully as soon as we could. But poor old Mawson was hit – and he couldn't move. It was a question then of whether anybody could go down and recover him – or not. He was some 30 or 40 yards from me to my left. I agonised as to whether or not I should go – or send anybody to try and get him out – whether or not we should hazard more of us to try and get him out. You couldn't rely on the Germans; it wouldn't be any good taking a Red Cross flag or anything like that. If anybody else went down there they would have been fired on as well. He was just unlucky, but still, that was that – Private Mawson[5] died of his wounds and this caused us all great sadness. He was a splendid little man, totally reliable though he wouldn't say 'Boo!' to a goose.[6]
>
> 2nd Lieutenant Russell Collins, 'A' Company

At first light on 30 January, 'B' Company was ordered to attack Siola, leading the way through the gully, followed up by 'A' Company who would then attack on the right. It proved to be a fateful day for Tom Turnbull.

> It was daybreak, Sunday morning. We were going down this hill. We were told the Jerry was in front of us. Then we could see them moving about, so we got down and opened fire. The machine gun fire started coming back at us and it was coming from both sides! Sweeping all over the place – if there'd been a blade of grass you would have got behind it! All of a sudden, 'BOOOUF!' I thought my leg was away down the hillside – I'd got hit – a bullet in the foot. I got up and I gave the lad next to me my Tommy gun – and I started walking back up the hill. Another corporal came towards me – and he had a rifle in his

hand. Whoever was behind the German machine gun put a burst between us, because he had a weapon in his hand – and I politely told him where to go! I said, 'He's never touched me up to now!' He went away! Two lads, one had been hit in one shoulder, the other in the other shoulder! They put their good arms round me and helped me until we could get treatment at the Yorks and Lancs regimental aid post.[7]

Corporal Tom Turnbull, 'B' Company

The machine gun fire was emanating from Siola and Point 150. Coming up behind was Bill Virr.

We were the last of the three platoons going forward. As the first platoon got there, all hell let loose. They threw everything at us. We had to just scatter. There was a sangar, just one, built round this tree. The three of us dived into this sangar. There were rocks as well you could have got behind. But this looked handier! We all jumped in; a lad threw a Bren gun in with us. As soon as we got in we realised that they'd got a fixed line on it with a machine gun; so once we'd got in we couldn't get out! He was hitting the rock, gouging it! The other troops in front – quite a few were killed. Mr Coutt's batman, Jack Vile, he was hit. All the flares in his pouch for the Very pistol, all set alight and burnt. Sergeant Makepeace[8] he was killed and several others. One or two lads in front of us took their packs off and slid back. It wasn't a matter of running away; you were in a position where you couldn't do a thing about it. What could you do? The Germans had more or less done away with the first two platoons. If we'd got up and walked into it, we would have been wiped out as well. We thought we were all there was left of the company. Our platoon commander, he was a little bit of a windy bloke really, he got his head down as well. He should have been the one to tell us. You could kid him into going back if you wanted – he didn't take a lot of persuading! He said, 'Oh, I've been hit, I'll have to go back to the medical officer, you stay here!' A piece of rock had hit him, thrown up by a mortar bomb – it wasn't much.[9]

Corporal William Virr, 'B' Company

It is worth remembering that perceptions of the seriousness of a wound can differ.

The attack had broken down. Behind 'B' Company, 'A' Company was still stuck in the gully which had become somewhat of a bottleneck, with the German machine guns, augmented by mortar and shellfire, providing the 'stopper'. The two companies were withdrawn and soon German counterattacks developed as they sought to recapture Point 400. Neither side could dislodge the other and this proved to be the start of a period of static warfare in terrible conditions that gradually eroded the men's morale.

> The area was so stony, that one couldn't dig down. So you got stones and built up sangar fortifications which gave you a protection against shellfire. We were shelled almost all the time throughout the day and sporadically at night. It rained; it was miserable. We had lice. We spent a good part of our time killing lice on our shirts. They had a powder supplied to us for killing lice, which you had to rub into the seams of your shirt and your trousers. It got on your balls and it inflamed them – absolutely incredible. I also had a boil at the time – you can imagine the depths of unhappiness that there was. Morale was pretty low. One comes to the end of one's tether no matter how good one is. It's just a question of attrition.[10]
>
> Private Ronald Elliott, 'D' Company

In makeshift sangar trenches, at the mercy of atrociously wet and cold weather, with intermittent mortar and artillery fire, harassing machine gun fire and the threat of sniping for the unwary, this was one of the worst periods as remembered by many of the men. Yet there is no detail to their recollections; this was just a misery. The NCOs were not unaware of the change in mood among the men.

> It was cold, miserable. They were sick, they were fed up. Normally in a war you are fed up, but you could see the difference in the men. They were tired, they'd been up in those hills for three weeks, so they hadn't really had a rest. None of us

> had had a real rest, not what you'd call a rest – just a couple of days when you knew straight away you were going back in the line. Your mind didn't register it as a rest at all. The men were battle fatigued and war weary. Just fed up, they'd had enough, they'd been there too long. They'd been fighting since Salerno in September.[11]
>
> Company Sergeant Major Leslie Thornton, Support Company

If they were fed up, who could blame them?

At last, on 10 February, there came the welcome news that the 46th Division was to be withdrawn and reorganised. Then the weather began to improve; everything was coming up roses! On 14 February, they were relieved by the 2nd Hampshires and moved back across the Garigliano to La Vaglie. Never was a rest more needed.

> The 'B' Echelon moved and joined the battalion – which was never done. Then rumours started circulating around the battalion – people saying we were going home. And, of course, that wasn't true. But G10/98 stores, the heavy stuff, was being handed in. People said, 'What's happening?' Then we were told that the battalion would be out of the line for a longish period. Spirits went up![12]
>
> Company Sergeant Major Leslie Thornton, Support Company

A period of administrative reorganisation followed, with a new uniform issue and the gathering together of all heavy equipment, but ready for what? On 18 February, the corps commander, addressed a gathering of all officers, warrant officers and sergeants, where he expressed the hope that 46th Division would return in the future to fight alongside the rest of X Corps at some time in the future. But where were they going?

10

A MIDDLE EAST SOJOURN

It was a tented camp; the sergeants' mess was together in a tent. We had a table and tablecloths; we had knives and forks. We had grapefruit for breakfast every morning and we had food laid out for us. We got to know each other, the sergeants of other companies, because you never saw them – this is the first time we'd been together for months and months. It was a good thing![1]

Company Sergeant Major Leslie Thornton, Support Company

THE DESTINATION WAS REVEALED when on 21 February the 16th DLI embarked aboard the Polish tramp steamer *Sobieski* in Naples docks. One interesting point was that the skipper of the *Sobieski*, Captain Walter Schmidt, had been a German U-Boat commander in the Great War. In total he had sunk two merchant ships, a trawler, damaged one destroyer, and sunk a further two torpedo boats, for which services he had been awarded the Iron Cross (2nd Class). It was by no means a luxury passenger ship, but anything was luxury compared to living in a hole carved from rock on a bleak freezing mountainside. It was certainly better than participating in the grim battle to capture Monte Cassino.

It started to get warmer and warmer and warmer, of course all the spirits rose, the chaps were thinking, 'Ahhrr, great this!' On the 27th February we arrived at Port Said and the contrast to the weather – sun, warm, even at that time, warm lovely weather and spirits were very high.[2]

Company Sergeant Major Leslie Thornton, Support Company

Impromptu concert parties further improved the mood, while the officers held conferences to discuss the lessons that could be learnt from the recent fighting, and how they could be incorporated into future training programmes. They disembarked at Port Said and were whisked away by train to the El Quassasin camp where they were accommodated in tents, with bamboo bed frames issued to the men. Soon they had established sergeants' and officers' messes. But the most important priority was to get the men away off on local leave in Cairo.

Cairo was an eye-opener in many ways for the troops. The usual agenda of the soldier was much in evidence: excessive drinking or an unashamed hunt for sex. Most settled for the former.

> There was a big hotel called the Hotel des Roses and it was a warrant officers and sergeants' hotel. We made our way to this big hotel and in it was a heap of Americans. Well, they were pleased to see us! We got on well with them! The beer was on, but when it was gone, it's gone. You couldn't drink it all night. The Americans went to the bar and filled up these tables with beers. We had a terrific night with dancing – no women there. But we were dancing with this couple of Yanks about 6 foot 4 who had hold of me and we were dancing round with all my legs off the floor. We went off to our billet not quite sober – believe me![3]
>
> Company Sergeant Major Leslie Thornton, Support Company

As they careened around the streets of Cairo, many of the men ran into trouble with the military police, who did not seem inclined to 'let things go' or understand what horrors the Durhams had been through in the last few months.

> Four days leave in Cairo. First day, two hours after we got there, two sergeant majors were under arrest! I wasn't one of them! They went into a red-light district – out of bounds. Didn't know the area, hadn't been to Cairo before, [they] went into an out-of-bounds area and the military police picked them up and took them in. Well, after some phone calls, the adjutant had released them.[4]
>
> Company Sergeant Major Leslie Thornton, Support Company

Some of the troubles were not really of their own making. Luckily, Johnny Preston was an officer who believed in standing up for his men.

> Everybody got pinched for not having gaiters on! That was the dress out there, but we didn't have them! Johnny Preston got the whole battalion on parade, and he says, 'Now, everybody that has been charged with being improperly dressed – I've decided to hang fifteen of you and jail the rest of you for life!' He says, 'They're stupid bloody men; they've got some on a charge for fighting – I've trained them for fighting! Cases dismissed!'[5]
>
> Private James Corr, 'B' Company

Bill Virr well remembered his trip to Cairo. He and some chums hired a local guide, but they were soon aware that 'tourists' were easy game to the local Arab entrepreneurs.

> They picked us up in this biggish car. First of all, he took us to some bazaar, probably his brother-in-law's bazaar! Had us looking round there. Then to the Museum of Hygiene! That was showing you various models of people with syphilis – that was something we didn't want to see! Eventually we got to the Pyramids – you could have got the tram there actually! We got on these horses, we had a horse each, a lad with each one, and they led you round the Pyramids. We had our photograph taken. He gave us his card and said, 'Your photo will be ready tomorrow! You pick it up at Kasir el Nir Street – a shop there.' Next day we go to this shop. We came to a gharry, a horse and cart, asked him could he tell us where this place was? 'Yes, jump in!' He took us all round Cairo, finishing up back at the same place! 'It's just down there!'[6]
>
> Corporal William Virr, 12 Platoon, 'B' Company

Arthur Vizard also remembered the local Arab salesmen upsetting the padre.

> In Egypt there was a lot of pornographic literature circulating. 'Johnny Arab' would come round and shout, 'Horny books!'

And the troops would buy these books. The parson used to get very upset about it and I used to confiscate them when I came across them, but you couldn't do anything about it. There you were in the spring of '44 and the troops had been away since the December of '42. Better that probably than the brothels![7]

Major Arthur Vizard, Headquarters Company

Most of the battalion managed to get through the Cairo experience unscathed, although VD rates may have risen in the aftermath.

More welcome was the arrival of a new draft of officers, including Lieutenant Richard Hewlett. He had been born the son of a writer and concert party performer in Kensington in 1919. On leaving school he had worked in the motor trade, before joining an accounts department for a firm in Stroud. After being called up with the Royal Army Service Corps, he had risen to the rank of staff sergeant, serving in Egypt since 1940. He applied to join the infantry as he had decided his life was too 'cushy' and was commissioned into the Oxfordshire and Buckinghamshire Light Infantry. From there he was posted to join 'B' Company, 16th DLI, where he first encountered the acting company commander, Captain Jimmy Coutts.

> Jimmy Coutts often seemed to be very angry; he was angry with life! A good officer, very good for an infantryman – aggressive, hating the Germans and hating anyone who was around to be hated one felt! Very good company. He had painted on his bivouac in black paint, 'Base wallahs – hack 'em in the fork!' In big letters all across the thing. That summed up his outlook to base wallahs.[8]
>
> Lieutenant Richard Hewlett, 'B' Company

They weren't at El Quassasin long. On 13/14 March, the 16th DLI moved to Kefar Yona which was near Tel Aviv in Palestine.

> It was a new tented camp, everything was spic and span, eight-man tents. The camp was surrounded by an expanse of barbed wire and immediately behind the barbed wire were these very

> lush orange trees. But there were notices all round the barbed wire, 'Do not trespass beyond this point!' There was a supreme optimist at the entrance to the camp who had a pile of two or three tons of Jaffa oranges trying to sell them to the troops. I must say I don't think he sold any! The troops just went under the wire and everybody had a tent full of oranges![9]
>
> Captain Alan Hay, 'A' Company

They had not long settled in when, at 12.00 on 24 March, the whole battalion was put on one hour's notice that it was to move to Tel Aviv to aid the civil power, in this case the Palestine Police. There had long been tension between the Jewish and Arab communities, but the night before there had been a series of attacks attributed to Jewish settlers on British soldiers in Haifa, Jerusalem and Tel Aviv. It was felt a response was needed, and the companies were split up and despatched to various commandeered school billets. The recently promoted Captain Alan Hay, who was soon to replace Major Pat Casey in command of 'A' Company, recalled the situation as it seemed to him at the time.

> The Stern Gang started to put posters on the trees – an arm with a clenched fist clutching a rifle – with words to the effect of, 'We will conquer Palestine!' They were being plastered up during the night. Round about Tel Aviv the kibbutz were grossly overmanned. This was the 'hidden army'. These were fit men; they weren't growing things. You could see them; they were pretending to work. They were obviously building up something. We had to report this. Then there were attacks on the Palestine Police. My company was moved into Tel Aviv proper, and we were billeted on a school. Our job was to send patrols round with the police.[10]
>
> Captain Alan Hay, 'A' Company

As the overall tension grew it was decided to enforce a general night-time curfew stretching between 17.00 and 05.00. This was a difficult undertaking.

> You have got to imagine: Tel Aviv had this beautiful beach, it was very busy, a normal people not at war, no signs of any war. To shut this down at five o'clock when everyone had to get off the streets! They'd had plenty of warning, so we used to go round with these patrols. In one particular area, there was a leader. He wore a distinctive shirt; he was unmistakable. They were on their balconies; he would get in the middle of the street waiting for the truck coming. He was a right rabble rouser! Now we weren't allowed to go into any houses, so we devised a little scheme. We would send the truck round going slowly, attracting people's attention. It would get past this chap – and we came quietly behind with the jeep – but we didn't nab him – he got inside his house! We still went in and gave him a good what you call 'duffing up'. Of course, there were complaints about it! That was an isolated incident.[11]
>
> Captain Alan Hay, 'A' Company

One can imagine that the Jewish perception of such events would be very different. But this was a hotbed of emotions. The daytime patrols sometimes ran into trouble, with the various sides accusing the others of terrorism and brutality.

> We did patrols with pickaxe handles, supporting the Palestine Police. Usually, an NCO and six men in the back of an open 15cwt truck. Just went round and patrolled the streets. Looking down these side roads to see if there were any disturbances. There had been a meeting of Orthodox Jews, the ones with the beards and hats, young and old, in this cinema on the corner not far from the school billets. These sods waited until at least half of them got out and were congregating in this small courtyard – then drove past and threw a grenade or two in amongst them. Then they tried to blame us, but we had pickaxe handles – you can't blow anybody up with them![12]
>
> Private Tom Lister, MT Section, Headquarters Company

At 11.00 on 27 March, a warning was received by telephone at the District Commissioners Office and the Income Tax Office that the buildings should be evacuated as bombs had been planted and they would go off soon.

> They'd cleared the building; the employees were standing outside, being kept back by the police. I had taken a squad of men and the superintendent said, 'There's been a report of a bomb being planted in here!' I said, 'Why this building?' He said, 'Well, this is the government tax building – let's go in!' I had no option but to go in with him! Everything was just as the people had left it: there were cigarettes burning and you could see that people had come out in a hurry. He went round, kicking wastepaper baskets, looking. There were a lot of rooms, and we went round. After a while he said, 'I don't think there's anything here!' Well, it wasn't what I'd call a thorough search and I said, 'Do you want an organised search by one or two picked men of ours?' 'No, no, it's just one of these scares – they're starting to do this to disrupt life!' He didn't think there was a bomb.[13]
>
> Captain Alan Hay, 'A' Company

The tension and pressure meant that sadly attitudes towards the Jewish population began to worsen among the soldiers.

> If you went round on your own, you were a mug because these Jewish youths used to be waiting! If they got half the chance, they used to beat you up. At first, until I knew better, I was more sympathetic towards the Jews, but after I saw their behaviour of the various parties, I changed my mind and decided that the Arabs were getting a rough deal.[14]
>
> Private Tom Lister, MT Section, Headquarters Company

When the civil unrest finally died down, on 4 April, the battalion moved back to the Kefar Yona camp, then on to Er Rama camp set in an olive grove close to the Galilean hills, which provided good training opportunities. Battle training courses were being run for section and platoon commanders, brushing up on their tactics and leadership, but which also allowed newly arrived officers to 'bed down' into the unit. One such was Douglas Tiffin, the son of a dentist in Sunderland, who worked as a clerk in a marine insurance office. After volunteering as a gunner, he rose to the rank of sergeant, serving with various artillery units in the UK, Iraq and North Africa, before being commissioned and joining the 16th DLI in Palestine.

> They might assume that you hadn't any army experience. I had no difficulty there – if I had been a new officer coming in straight from 'Blighty' I would have perhaps been a bit apprehensive, but I'd been a sergeant – I was used to dealing with men! I wasn't going to have any nonsense.[15]
>
> 2nd Lieutenant Douglas Tiffin, 'A' Company

So the training went on: multiple courses, weapons firing on the Acre ranges, the temporary attachment of officers to the 70th Field Regiment, Royal Artillery – anything and everything to get them 'tuned up' and once again ready for war.

On 11 May, they moved for special training based at the J. Mezar camp in Syria – some 15 miles due west of Damascus. Here they began a series of tactical exercises. The battalion would move out of the camp and take up positions as if on active services. Patrols would feel their way forward and clear gaps through a minefield. The exercises expanded in scope to become full-scale brigade and even divisional exercises. Special attention was supposed to be paid to tank cooperation – something that early after-action reports had noted was lacking.

> We were to work with the tanks when we got back to Italy, because there was going to be a major attack. The commander of the tank regiment would get with the CO. The CO would say, 'Right, this is our task. We are going to attack this objective. What we propose to do is this, we don't know much about the enemy. How best can you support us?' We chatted over it and did one or two little exercises together. They used to work it out purely on the topography of the thing. It was no use putting tanks in minor lanes, they had to be in the open. Street fighting wasn't very good for tanks. In Syria it was more arid than it was going to be in Italy. I don't know that we learnt a

great deal, but we worked together, we got to know the chaps, how they worked, how they liked to do things.[16]

Captain Alan Hay, 'A' Company

At the start of June, the 16th DLI moved back to Kefar Yona, but the training continued unabated until they began the long journey back to El Quassasin camp, which they reached on 18 June. There was a real dichotomy between front line units who thought they were 'at the sharp end' and the people who had jobs – often important jobs – that kept them behind the line – and far from the fighting. For many of the 16th DLI this rankled.

> We weren't received very well by the people there – the lads called them 'base wallahs'. There were quite a few scuffles went on – the lads were let loose. There was a bar there, there was beer there, so even in the sergeants' mess there were quite a few arguments and scuffles with these chaps who thought that we shouldn't be there.[17]

Company Sergeant Major Leslie Thornton, Support Company

The officers did not help in these matters as they were pursuing their own somewhat rowdy pursuits.

> We weren't very popular, the Durham Light Infantry, at the Quassasin Officers' Club. It was mainly caused through drinking a drink which we christened 'Culloden Field'! This consisted of every drink of that [row of bottles] all in a pint glass. The base was a tomato juice and everything else went into it – it was a lethal concoction! We had everybody, including the padres, drinking it. This drink created games of rugger in the mess with cushions and things like that. Finally, we were banned for very unruly behaviour. They probably had good cushy jobs and were there for the duration of the war. They didn't really understand that for infantry officers, things were a bit different.[18]

Lieutenant Richard Hewlett, 12 Platoon, 'B' Company

On 24 June, they had a piece of really bad news as they found their popular colonel had been promoted away to become a senior staff officer with the headquarters of 78th Division.

Lieutenant Colonel Murray, Captain Ballance, Sergeant Henderson and Private Turner are here out in the country on an tactical exercise.

To be part of the invasion fleet was an awesome experience.

Typical scene on the Salerno landings on 9 September 1943.

The bridge blown up at Corpo di Cava, 24 September 1943.

British troops coming out of the linie from Monte Camino in December 1943. This gives an idea of the inhospitality of the mountainous terrain.

Photo from Cairo in March 1943. Back row left to right: Tony Sacco, L. Smith and Ronald Elliott. Front row: C. Grey and D. Jordan.

Lieutenant Russell Collins and his platoon in rest billets. Peering over Collins's left shoulder is Sergeant Joseph Jerrison, and over his left shoulder we see Private Arnold Mawson.

Bren gun carriers of the 16th DLI lined up ready to cross the Foglia river, 30 August 1944.

Ruins of Gemmano hammered by the guns of both sides in September 1944.

An example of the painful nature of street fighting in Athens, December 1945.

Major Laurie Stringer in front of the Parthenon.

'A' Company officers and sergeants in 1944.

The sergeants of Support Company in Phaleron, February 1945.

The Carrier Platoon then commanded by Lieutenant Russell Collins during a field training exercise in Greece early in 1945. Collins is on the left with binoculars.

The 'B' Company gondala at the VE Day celebrations, May 1945.

Lieutenants Russell Collins and Lionel Dodd in drag during the VE Day celebrations, May 1945.

Lieutenant Colonel
Dennis Worrall

Major Arthur Vizard

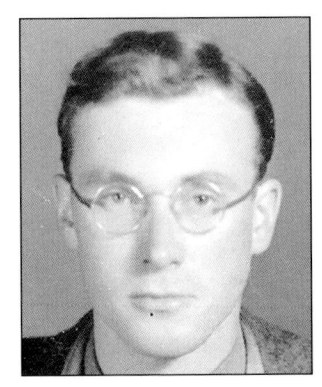

Ronald Elliott

Douglas Tiffin

Lance Corporal
William Virr

Richard Hewlett

Major Laurie Stringer

Major Ray Mitchell

Sam Cawdron

> Colonel Johnny Preston said goodbye to us. He was a great colonel – we all got on well. He brought out soldiering in us that we obviously didn't have. He was great. When he gave his orders, it wasn't in a profound military sense – he chatted to you. I know he was the same with other company commanders; when you had a particular job to do, he would say, 'Don't be suicidal, do what you can, you've got a few more battles to fight – don't make this one your last one!' He was encouraging in that way; he was very humane. He understood, 'No good dashing in to lose more troops than need be!'[19]
>
> Captain Alan Hay, 'A' Company

He was replaced by the promotion to lieutenant colonel of Major Dennis Worrall, who was Preston's second in command. Worrall had joined the 16th DLI in North Africa and won his MC for his courage in getting supplies through in the Corpo di Cava operations. He rather divided opinion among his officers and men: some admired him, recognised his personal courage and leadership qualities; others were sceptical and felt he couldn't see the difference between courage and foolishness. Tactically, he would prove to be not quite as adept as Johnny Preston, but nevertheless he proved a competent officer. Armed with their new leader, on 28 June 1944 the men of the 16th DLI set sail in the *Sobieski* again. Their destination? Back to Italy.

> We were expecting it, and it was quite a relief really to find that we were going back to Italy, rather than go and face the Second Front with new dimensions. New commanders, new chiefs, new everything! In soldiering, you get a comfortable feeling about something. It's not always pleasant, but you know the people about you, you know your commanders, you get to know the German habits – what to expect. We knew Italy and it wasn't bad fighting. If you're going to have to fight, you may as well go in knowing something about what to expect.[20]
>
> Captain Alan Hay, 'A' Company

Little did they know what lay ahead of them.

11

GOTHIC LINE HORRORS

Once the shelling started proper, you went as deep as you bloody could, as fast as you could. Two of you used to normally work together to dig a slit trench. Mostly it was cultivated ground, so it wasn't very difficult digging a hole. I'd been a pitman and I could use a bloody spade – and a shovel – and a pick! Some of the lads didn't know how! You carried an entrenching tool on your belt. It had a blade at one end, a point at the other end, and a handle.[1]

Corporal Tony Cameron. 'A' Company

AT LONG LAST THE ALLIED GREAT LEAP FORWARD in May 1944 broke the stranglehold of the Gustav Line. But the lure of Rome was too strong, and tempted General Mark Clark away from a concerted attempt to cut off the retreat of the German Tenth Army from the Monte Cassino area. Clark's dash for Rome allowed Kesselring to withdraw most of his troops before they could be encircled. In truth, the capture of Rome in early June made little real difference, as it did not really affect the main issues. The Italians had already capitulated, and for the Germans there were still plenty of easily defendable positions they could fall back on. On the west coast, the Allies had fought their way up to Florence, but on the east coast the Germans had occupied strong positions in the Apennine mountains which then bent across to the Adriatic providing a wall to further progress. During the static period, the Germans had spent a considerable amount of time and effort in augmenting the natural defences to form the Gothic Line, which would be a nightmare to break through. Yet this is where General Sir Harold Alexander planned to assault. He would secretly concentrate the Eighth Army (V Corps, X Corps, I Canadian Corps, II Polish Corps) on the Adriatic Coast and launch Operation Olive to smash through the Gothic Line.

The 16th DLI had been lucky to miss the Monte Cassino battles, but there would be no escape this time. On 3 July 1944, the battalion was disembarked from the *Sobieski* at Naples. They were then moved to San Secondino, near Capua, where they overhauled vehicles and weapons, before beginning a series of platoon and company field-firing exercises. On 17 July they moved to a tented camp at the village of Bastardo near the divisional concentration area around Assisi. Here they were inspected as they lined the route by George VI. As at Camberley, so many lifetimes ago, despite it being only in December 1942, the Durhams were less than impressed.

> We were taken down to Perugia, where we were to man the route because the King was paying a visit. We travelled nearly all day in these vehicles. Red hot it was! We lined this road in the midday sun. They came along with water carriers, sprinkling it on the road to keep the dust down – we would have been damn glad of having something to drink! The King came along – old George – he was dead white. He had these very white milky knees with a blanket over him – and it was red hot. The officers were saying, 'Hip, Hip, Hooray!' Everybody said, 'Hooraaaay!' The lack of enthusiasm must have been quite noticeable even to the King! We were right up to our noses in it by then – the thought having to go through all of that just to go and say, 'Hello!' to the King. That was supposed to be a morale booster! Nobody was at all charmed![2]
>
> Private Ronald Elliott, 'D' Company

Back at Bastardo, the training continued apace with a special emphasis on building up fitness with tactical exercises, route marches and river crossings. There was also some specialist training in street fighting, reflecting the changing nature of the terrain they were to face in the months ahead. Naturally, there was a great emphasis on playing sport, especially football, with tough competition to become the champion soccer company. On 8 August, their recreational needs were catered for when the battalion organised a 'village' fete with traditional stalls, a horse racing game, a treasure hunt, and another football knock-out competition. In the evening they were entertained by the divisional dance band and a film show courtesy of the mobile cinema. It was a good-humoured occasion enlivened by much cheery banter between the ranks.

Reinforcements were still feeding into the battalion, with many emanating from former anti-aircraft units which were being broken up.

> A lot of ack-ack gunners were being stood down because they didn't need them to the same extent – air superiority having been gained. A great many anti-aircraft gunners joined various infantry divisions. They weren't very pleased about being 'downgraded' to infantry. Oh yes, they felt that as part of the 'ubiquitous' artillery that they were superior – after all, artillery were the 'right of the line'. They didn't feel very happy about coming to infantry, and we had to make them feel at home as best we could. We did this by 'pep' talks and so forth. They couldn't understand what the Durhams were talking about for a long time. It was always that language problem, but little by little they settled in. After all, it was a question of survival, so you learn very quickly then.[3]
>
> Major Arthur Vizard, Headquarters Company

One such new arrival was Tony Cameron, the son of a coal miner from Crawcrook in the Tyne valley. Before his call up he had worked in a brickworks, then as a pony 'putter' at a local colliery. He didn't enjoy it and was keen to get away when he was called up as a gunner. He served with various anti-aircraft batteries, including active service at gun sites in the Middle East from 1943–44. By then an experienced NCO, Cameron was posted for infantry training in Egypt in June 1944.

> I was keen. I realised that the more you got to know, the better chance you had if you were going in the line, going into real action. There was a bloke there, King's Royal Rifle Corps, he had been with the 7th Armoured Division as an infantryman. He had a lot of pamphlets and things. I used to talk to him, especially on an evening. We used to sit and chat; he realised that I was wanting to know. He lent me quite a few small-arms pamphlets. I tried to get out of them what I could. It wasn't very satisfactory, but it was more than I knew before![4]
>
> Lance Sergeant Tony Cameron, 'A' Company

He then had a fortuitous encounter with Colonel Johnny Preston, who had just left the 16th DLI.

> There was a bloke coming towards us, he gets about 40 yards from me, and I could see he was a lieutenant colonel – and he had a Durham Light Infantry badge! Now I'm a Durham man. If I was going to be in the infantry, I fancied being in my county regiment. I stopped in front of him, slung a smart salute up, 'Excuse me, Sir! My name's Cameron and I'm a Durham county man. I'm training to transfer to the infantry. What chance is there of getting to the DLI?' He says, 'I'll see what I can do for you!' When it came to posting, me and another dozen NCOs – a lot of my mates from 295 Battery – all finished up posting to the 16th. I think I was to blame for that! I felt a bit guilty at times because half of them never came back.[5]
>
> Lance Sergeant Tony Cameron, No. 2 Infantry Reinforcement Training Depot, El Qassassin

Cameron was posted as a section leader to 'A' Company, but was reduced to his war substantive rank of corporal as he still lacked infantry experience. Cameron himself was aware of the problems he might face.

> It was a strange thing to us – they were infantrymen – and we were artillerymen. It's hard to explain. We knew that they knew what infantry was about and we didn't – we had to find out. I won't say we weren't made welcome, we mixed in fine with them, but for myself I always knew that I'd got a lot to learn. I

was never sure whether I was doing the right thing. That was a snag, being an NCO and learning, where they already knew.[6]

Corporal Tony Cameron, 'A' Company

He would find out what it was all about soon enough.

On 10 August, the 46th Division became part of V Corps (4th, 46th and 56th British Divisions, and 4th Indian Division) and thus part of Eighth Army. They were destined to take part in the assault on the Gothic Line fortress, which lay behind the line of the Foglia river. Five days later, they had a visit from the Eighth Army commander, Major General Oliver Leece, who briefed the officers as to how they would shatter the German defences and giving them the ultimate objective of Vienna. How they were to do it was not really detailed. A similar approach was taken by their divisional commander at another briefing before they began to move forward to Isola del Piano on 22 August.

> General Hawkesworth, he assembled everybody and said, 'The 46th Division will "bust" the Gothic Line!' That was about the extent of his divisional orders. He wanted no daylight movement; all movement was to be at night with lights restricted to the slit with the mauve bulbs. There weren't any roads to speak of – they were tracks really more than anything else. They were dusty and it was early August. The moment you started a vehicle going you got clouds of dust behind which was visible for miles. It took us two days to move into a forming up area. The whole thing was done with the utmost secrecy in order to have surprise. We didn't want anyone to know we were preparing an attack on the right-wing – the Adriatic wing – up towards the Gothic Line.[7]
>
> Major Arthur Vizard, Headquarters Company

There were some reasons for confidence: the D-Day invasion of Europe had begun, Paris had fallen, Operation Dragoon had landed a further invading force on the French south coast, while the Russians were advancing remorselessly on the Eastern Front. The Germans may have had well-conceived defence works, but they were short of troops to man them. The LXXVII Panzer

Corps facing the Eighth Army was just three divisions strong and they were short of tanks, artillery and air support, in sharp comparison to the Allies. But the defenders were determined; it would be wise not to underestimate them.

On the early morning of 25 August, Operation Olive began with the advance across the Metauro river and approach to the Foglia. The 46th Division was part of Leece's huge offensive, with the 4th Indian Division attacking on their left flank, and the I Canadian Corps on the right. Next to the Adriatic coast was the II Polish Corps. The 139 Brigade was on the left of the 46th Division front, with the Hampshires of 128 Brigade to the right. At first it all went rather well. The 5th Sherwood Foresters crossed the Metauro river and pushed up on to Monte Bianco and Monte Della Morte, after which the 5th Leicesters passed through them to take Tomba. Only at 17.00 on 27 August did the Durhams move forward, with one company moving to relieve the 5th Hampshire Regiment on Monte Grosso. On the 28 August, the rest of the 16th DLI were launched forward into an attack on the Petriano village, about a mile short of the Apsa river, accompanied by the tanks of 51st (Leeds Rifles) Royal Tank Regiment. Initially it appeared a gentle return to action.

> We had tanks with us. It was rather like these pictures which I always suspected were posed, pictures of people marching behind tanks with their bayonets fixed. However, that is what in fact we did! We were behind the tanks, and it all looked a bit like a posed picture. There wasn't any resistance in Petriano itself, but there must have been the odd sniper here or there, because as we were walking up behind these tanks; you could hear the odd whine and ricochet going off. We advanced cautiously into Petriano, taking the necessary steps, doing it all by the book – very carefully! It could have been heavily defended, as it turned out it wasn't! That was a great relief, a certain amount of euphoria and I think everybody was then a bit too relaxed.[8]

2nd Lieutenant Douglas Tiffin, 'A' Company

For about half an hour nothing much happened and the men

took shelter in the buildings. But the Germans had them in their sights.

> A lot of us, including my company commander, Frank Duffy, were in this stone house, very thick walls, cellars underneath. We weren't in the cellars – we were just relaxing. I was leaning against the wall; Frank Duffy was on my left. Further to his left there was a door which led into a bedroom. We were tired and we had our packs on, which we just rested up against the wall. In came this chap, who remarked to Frank Duffy and myself that there was a bed there, 'Why don't you go rest on that?' We both said, 'Oh, can't be bothered, we're all right where we are!' Three minutes later the room, the bed and everything else disappeared in a cloud of smoke – a direct hit by a shell. We were no more than a few yards from it! Frank Duffy simply got up, obviously dazed, shocked, muttered something and walked out of the door. He said, 'I'll have to go back.' He'd obviously taken more of the blast – I'd taken only a comparatively small amount. What struck me so forcibly was that if we'd laid on this bed, we would have been dead.[9]
>
> 2nd Lieutenant Douglas Tiffin, 'A' Company

Frank Duffy was clearly shell-shocked and had to be helped back to safety. Major Ronnie Sherlaw took over in command of 'D' Company. As a veritable barrage of shells fell all around them, the Durhams had a visit from Brigadier Allen Block, whose conduct proved inspirational to his young officers.

> At Petriano we got shelled quite considerably. It didn't seem to do a lot of damage, but it was noisy and frightening – as shelling always is! I was impressed with Brigadier Block, who simply ignored shells as though they were just flies. He didn't even go through the motions of brushing them away! He didn't have a tin hat on, he just strolled around doing good to people's morale. He was a brilliant brigadier.[10]
>
> Lieutenant Richard Hewlett, 'B' Company

During the shelling, Douglas Tiffin was faced with a call for assistance for some wounded men who were lying helplessly in the road, which was still being shelled.

> Somebody would have to go and pick them up! One of the chaps in my platoon – he was a little bugger, a very bad disciplinarian, but quite an intrepid follow in many ways. He said, 'All right, I'll go and pick them up! I'll get a jeep!' I thought, 'Well, I must do something about it! I'd better go with him!' We got in this jeep, which he drove very badly – and I subsequently learnt that he couldn't really drive! He drove it along this village road, which was being quite heavily shelled – a rather hair-raising experience – and we picked these fellows up who'd been badly hit by shrapnel.[11]
>
> 2nd Lieutenant Douglas Tiffin, 'A' Company

That night the 16th DLI moved forward, crossing the Apsa river and climbing up the next ridge where they were able to dig in. It was becoming apparent that the Germans had fallen back to the main defences of the Gothic Line along the ridges behind the Foglia. As they moved forward, Charley Palmer had a misfortune.

> This night we were moving forward, we had our jeep, and we hadn't gone a dozen yards, when the thing went up on an uncleared mine. One of the section was sitting on the bonnet and he was blown off. I was sitting next to the driver, but there were sandbags in the seats, so that lessened the impact to a large extent. But when I got out, I could hardly walk – I could hobble. They sent both Harry Senior and me back; we were the only two that were affected. I didn't know the extent of the damage. That night I couldn't sleep and was listening to Senior's groans. I was trying to shout out to him and give him a bit of comfort, but he had obviously got it badly, I think he'd got something through his 'middle'. He died[12] later that night.[13]
>
> Lance Corporal Charles Palmer, Intelligence Section, Headquarters Company

Palmer himself had suffered a broken foot – which was black

and blue, with severe bruising. He was evacuated and would spend the rest of the war with the Army Education Corps.

On 30 August, the battalion crossed the Foglia. The Durhams were ordered to relieve the 5th Sherwood Foresters from their positions just short of Monte Vecchio. As they went forward, some of the men found themselves marooned in a German minefield. For Bill Virr it was a nightmare.

> We came to a minefield. It was marked – just one strand of wire and these signs, skull and crossbones, with 'Achtung Minen!' It was obviously a minefield. The first section were wondering, 'What are we going to do now?' The Foresters were supposed to be sending a guide; they must have made their way through somewhere. He hadn't arrived, so the company commander said, 'Push on!' The first section ducked under the wire and gingerly walked through to the other side. The next section followed – and they hadn't gone 2 yards when one of them stepped on a mine. They were 'schu' mines, just a wooden box with pegs in which held the top half from dropping on to the bottom half. The weight of a man would break the pegs and allow the top half to go down, ignite the charge and blow your foot off. They stepped on one of these and a lad lost his foot. One was killed, something flew up and hit him in the throat, and another lad was wounded. We called for the stretcher bearers. Two of them came, ducked under the wire – and they stepped on a mine. So that was another lad – he had his foot off as well. We managed to get them back out and the company commander then called the first section back. Well, if you'd have seen chaps walking on eggs – you can imagine! This corporal, he didn't know where to put his feet; but the other lads knew where to put their feet – they put them wherever he had put his! They all came back and didn't set another mine off. Mines was one of the things I dreaded most – I'd rather have been killed than maimed. You couldn't see them – till you stepped on one! There were that many ingenious ways of setting them up. I dreaded 'S' mines especially. They were a shrapnel mine, if you stood on that it jumped about 5 feet in

the air and exploded with about 350 ball bearings inside which spread out. You'd really no chance, you stood on one of them and that was it. With a mine if you stood on it that was it – you'd lost your foot or lost your life.[14]

Corporal William Virr, 'B' Company

In all, one man was killed and five wounded by the mines. Snipers also took their toll, although a terrible retribution awaited them if they were caught.

> We were rather badly exposed to snipers. We were on a low piece of ground where there was no cover, and we were hit by snipers. There was a sniper – we caught him – he was up a tree. He didn't have any special camouflage; he was just up a fairly bare tree – fairly visible actually. A very young German and we had to fill him full of bullets before he'd give up – I think he probably had thirty bullets in him before he died. He was a really militant Nazi. They were very incensed at the damage he had done sniping at people.[15]

Lieutenant Richard Hewlett, 'B' Company

On 31 August, the 'A' Company were then ordered to attack a feature known as 'The Triangle' just to the north-west of the village of Mondaino as part of a general advance by the 16th DLI and the 2/5th Leicestershire Regiment on the town and the Monte Gridolfo Ridge that lay not far behind it. Alan Hay, the company commander, did not like the prospect one little bit.

> There was a huge hill which dominated our line of advance. We couldn't see what was behind that. Obviously, you were trying to pick out where the main German defences were. They were highly organised. They'd had a lot of time to prepare the Gothic Line. Their Todt organisation had built concrete emplacements, they had tanks that were sunk into these emplacements so that you couldn't really pick them up, they were nicely camouflaged. They had fields of fire for their small arms – and here we were in broad daylight marching up. We didn't seem to have a great

deal of supporting gunfire at that stage; and there were no signs of any tanks!¹⁶

Major Alan Hay, 'A' Company

He was not shy in making his views known to Colonel Dennis Worrall when he received his orders. From Hay's perspective, Worrall was clueless.

> I said, 'Well, what is the plan? Where are the tanks? What about the artillery fire?' He said, 'Oh, they'll be coming!' I said, 'Well, we'll wait till we get some support!' Then he went away. We advanced a bit further and we took some prisoners. We were then waiting for support. This was just after midday, and I got a message from the CO that we were to advance immediately. I said, 'Well, what about the support? I can't see any support!' He said, 'That will be coming!' We waited a while, nothing came! Then he ordered me, he said, 'The general said you must advance immediately!' I thought it was absolutely stupid, broad daylight! When we were looking at this target, the colonel said, 'Our friends the Leicesters are there!' I said, 'Colonel – they're Germans – look!' He said, 'No, they're our friends the Leicesters!' This was his first mistake; I thought, 'Dear me, we are in trouble here!' The Leicesters on our left had not taken their objective and they were still heavily engaged, plus one of our companies. The Hampshires on the right had taken their objective, our 'C' Company was too far away to give us any support and I wasn't in charge of them. So we all had to do this. I was threatened; I assumed I'd get court marshalled if I didn't. I said, 'Well, this is suicide!' He said, 'The general said you must – or you will be in trouble!'¹⁷

Major Alan Hay, 'A' Company

The chain of command stretched down unerringly from Major General John Hawkesworth, via Brigadier Allen Block, through to Colonel Dennis Worrall. It was part of the much larger operation to gain the Gridolfo Ridge; Worrall himself had no real choice, he had to do what he could to achieve the given objective. Alan Hay briefed his own company officers, perhaps unaware of the irony that he was now forming part of the selfsame chain of command.

> We were entirely on our own at this stage. I gave Lieutenant Marshall some buildings just short of Mondaino, and there were some old buildings on our right that I gave to Lieutenant Hood. I brought up the third platoon with my company headquarters. I discussed it with them and said, 'Well, this is it; we've got to go!'[18]
>
> Major Alan Hay, 'A' Company

With nothing left to say or do, they set off toward Mondaino. It is difficult to imagine what thoughts were passing through their minds. They soon began to come under heavy fire.

> We advanced over this open space knowing that these Germans could see us – and they just turned their machine guns on us. We hadn't got very far. They were going forward to these lower buildings, and they were immediately under machine gun fire coming from the left. Tim Marshall got quite a few of his platoon across the road to the first buildings. Hood got to the buildings on the right. I was following up. When I saw Marshall's platoon in trouble, I took my third platoon to support them. But the casualties were alarming. The Gothic Line had been prepared specially for this. They had their lines of fire, they had machine guns set and it was just chaos. I got forward, I said, 'Where's Mr Marshall?' They said, 'He's down here!' By the time I got to him he'd been killed.[19] I said, 'Get out to the right to the other buildings!' I got quite a few of them out. We rested up, counted the cost, tended the casualties. We'd lost almost a platoon. I looked at the situation: still no support, no sign of tanks. My wireless set had been knocked out by that stage, and I was almost glad not to have a word with the colonel. We reassembled, and I got Hood to go round to the right behind these buildings and we were going to attack them from the side. By that time, we were only one good platoon, which was the one I'd taken over. Just then two aircraft from the Desert Air Force came in quick succession and each dropped a bomb on the target

we were going for, but nobody had warned us, and we were almost on the target – and so we had casualties.[20]

Major Alan Hay, 'A' Company

William Hood's platoon had indeed been hit hard by the 'friendly fire' bombing, and they suffered several casualties, including Hood himself who was killed.[21] The various groups of survivors took shelter, but it was soon evident that their problems were by no means over.

We were in the first buildings where the first bomb had hit. There were still Germans in there, wounded, that we hadn't time to look at. This bomb had really done quite a lot of damage. We were still under fire from these machine guns on our left. The right was clear because the Hampshires had got that. 'C' Company, who were watching all this, had no orders, and when I saw Major Mitchell later, he said, 'We had orders to stay there, and we were far too far away to give you any small arms fire support – we had nothing else.' At that time, we had to count the cost. I had lost one platoon officer; I didn't know I'd lost the other one. I got the chaps in some sort of defensive position. Getting behind these brick walls in the ruins, just to protect ourselves from this machine gun fire. There was certainly more than one heavy machine gun. But they had us in their sights. We were near enough to the Germans for them to be shouting at us to give up, surrender. Morale amongst the men was very low at that time; we had chaps who'd been wounded and couldn't be attended to – the stretcher bearers were doing what they could. The sergeant major was extremely good; he was rallying them, taking command. I said to him, 'I must go round to the right, where I sent Hood's platoon to see how they are doing!' I found Hood had been killed and I am quite sure a lot of the casualties were caused by this bomb.[22]

Major Alan Hay, 'A' Company

In all, Hay estimated they had advanced about a mile and a half, but although they had made some progress, his company had been severely handled. For the rest of his life, Hay was bitter at the lack of support he had received.

> We were on the objective, this was the main attack, we weren't there alone. Generals must have seen what we were doing. You think you are alone; but all sorts of people are there watching the battle as it proceeds. This astonished me, that we were allowed to go on without support, not even our own carriers, not our own mortars. I said, 'Well, we'll just wait; they're obviously waiting until night-time to reinforce us!' I went round the men and eventually the count of fit men was twenty-seven. About ninety went in![23]
>
> Major Alan Hay, 'A' Company

Stuck in not so splendid isolation in a shattered building, his men were vulnerable to a German counterattack. Hay came to a somewhat rash but understandable decision.

> We'd come to expect if you got on to a place, the Germans were bound to counterattack. They know there are not many of us; they're going to counterattack. I said to the sergeant major, 'There's only one thing to do. Let's go for these machine guns. It's dark now, we know where they are!' I led this little composite platoon of twenty-seven. We were working under cover to get the machine gun. I had a grenade in my hand, when suddenly out of nowhere I saw the tracer fire coming from another position – I was so surprised – and I was hit on the temple. Germans always cover each other! My first thoughts were, 'Have I pulled the pin out of the grenade?' I think I was concussed, but I was still thinking, and I said to my runner, Wood, 'Are you all right?' 'Yes!' 'Well, I've been hit. I don't think I can carry on.' I was trying to get my first field dressing out and I couldn't get the plastic wrapping off it – obviously I couldn't see very well. I didn't know how bad my wound was, but I was still thinking! I saw the two Germans get up from the machine gun – it was only about 20 to 30 yards away. They were coming towards us. I said to Wood, 'Are the others near?' He said, 'I can't see anybody.' 'Well get up and run – I'll

follow you!' He got up and ran – and I ran – I don't know much about it after that. I remember meeting up with the sergeant major somewhere down the line and I said, 'Were there many casualties?' He said, 'No, nothing further.' I think, myself and my runner must have been well forward of the others. I said, 'Well, make the men safe! No reinforcements come up?' He said, 'No!' The next thing I knew I was in some dressing station. They said I was demanding to see the CO![24]

Major Alan Hay, 'A' Company

Hay was evacuated due to his wounds, but also suffering from battle exhaustion and problems with his sense of physical balance. After hospitalisation and convalescence, he would rejoin the Durhams in December 1944.

Alan Hay would never forgive Colonel Dennis Worrall, as was more than evident in our interview in 1993. From his perspective, men that he had trained, his friends among them, had been sacrificed because he had not received the proper support, whether it be artillery, tanks, mortars, Bren carriers, or whatever. But military matters are not guided by humanitarian concerns. The battle was intended to establish the 46th Division up on the Gridolfo Ridge. That was not negotiable as far as the High Command were concerned. And in the end that aim was largely achieved, as both 139 Brigade and 128 Brigade on its right had managed to carve out positions on the Gridolfo Ridge. High Command was optimistic that a few more solid blows would crack the Gothic Line wide open. In huge military operations there are always winners and losers, even on the 'winning' side. Military resources like tanks and artillery could not be spread out equally; they were concentrated to maximise their impact. That meant in some places that there would be a lack of the support and units would suffer. Sacrifices had to be made; their losses had been considered a price worth paying to take the ridge. Furthermore, although it is difficult to swallow, tactical mistakes were inevitable in the stress and confusion of battle. Perhaps Worrall had made mistakes, perhaps he could have done more. Hay certainly thought so.

That night, 'C' Company attacked 'The Triangle', managing to overrun it before a German counterattack flung them back out. They too suffered casualties. It had been another painful reverse. Next day, 1 September, saw a renewed effort to take the Triangle, this time by 'D' Company, with 'C' Company in support. Douglas Tiffin was sent forward on a recce patrol.

> We were ordered to go up and reconnoitre a white house and, if possible, occupy it. We picked our way through vineyards, and I was leading the platoon. About 10, 20, 30 yards in front of me, I saw a movement. I suppose instinctively I just rushed forward because I was so close. I had a Tommy gun which was a very effective weapon at this sort of thing – and I opened fire. To my surprise after some shouting and screaming, one or two people had been hit, getting in amongst this there was a platoon of Germans, about fifteen, sixteen, came out with their hands up. Why hadn't they fired on us? Probably they hadn't seen us, because we were coming through the vineyards which were fairly full of leaves; perhaps we were just out of their line of fire? I'm quite sure that if we hadn't fired and dashed forward, they would have been able to enfilade us. They got such a shock to find people charging around and spraying them with bullets, that they put their hands up and came out. It sounds like something out of Boys' Own Paper but they did, literally, say, 'Don't shoot, Tommy!' And out they came. This warrant officer came up to me saying, 'Don't shoot!' Because they were still obviously apprehensive that we weren't going to ask any questions and keep on firing. He pulled his wallet out and showed me his wife 'Frau' and children, 'Don't shoot! Don't shoot!' He had a lovely Luger, so I took it and stuffed it in my belt, and I thought, 'Well, there's a good souvenir!' There were five or six Germans haring back. We had our Bren gun and I suppose they were a couple of hundred yards off. We were firing at them – and we didn't hit them. I suppose in all the best books you would have done. It was quite a clear target.[25]
>
> 2nd Lieutenant Douglas Tiffin, 'D' Company

Tiffin felt that they had surprised the Germans and at first felt that there might be a chance to exploit the position. He asked for reinforcements, but none were forthcoming, instead, the Germans began to increase their pressure on the isolated platoon. In the end, Tiffin was told that his position was untenable.

> Somebody came up and said, 'You've got to pull back!' I said, 'OK!' I went up to the forward section to bring them back. Moving to get myself at the head of the platoon. I thought I was under cover, I was fairly careful, I thought, but they must have had a line of fire. The next thing I knew I was hit, I felt as if a sledgehammer had hit my left thigh, with excruciating force. I shot down the bank down amongst the vineyards. I didn't lose consciousness. What I do remember is finding my left leg across my body. The bone was completely shattered, so the muscles contracted, and the leg comes across. The first thing I did was wiggle my toes because I thought the leg was off. I had enough medical knowledge to know that if you can't wiggle your toes – the leg's a goner. But everything was working – incredible as the bone was completely and absolutely shattered. It must have hurt but I can't say I was writhing in agony. Two or three of the blokes came round. I told the sergeant to take the platoon back as we'd been told to. We pulled the leg straight. It wasn't bleeding all that much, it missed the femoral artery or else I would have been dead in two or three minutes. I suppose that's only a millimetre either way. In hindsight, I suppose I'm the luckiest man alive. We stuffed it with a couple of field dressings, put two entrenching tools on and bound it up. That was that. I was conscious, but then I did feel a sort of blackness coming over me, obviously it was loss of blood and shock, but I thought, 'You're going to die; you're dying!' You laugh now, but I thought, 'No, I mustn't, I mustn't!' The blackness came over and then it went away again. This was about eleven o'clock in the morning. I was too badly wounded to move. I had some water, two or three people left water bottles. The platoon went back; two blokes said, 'We'll stay with you!' One of them was this fellow Tuck, the other was Askill. There we were – stuck in this vineyard. I thought, 'Somebody will be along shortly!'

Time went on and we just lay there for three or four hours. The Germans were shelling and mortaring the road which was just at the bottom. I saw two of our tanks, they passed right in front of us. Tuck was trying to attract their attention, but it was hopeless. They soon came back again, because there was a lot of shelling on the road. A lot was falling in the vineyard, you could hear the fragments whistling through. Tuck said, 'I'm going to go back, get somebody up to get you out, Sir!' Off went Tuck – he didn't come back. Tuck subsequently told me that he couldn't find anybody who would go forward – it was considered too dangerous – he did his best I'm sure. I lay there until dusk fell.[26]

2nd Lieutenant Douglas Tiffin, 'D' Company

Askill and Tiffin were completely stranded and faced a terrifying experience. Sounds are magnified in the relative still of the night and Tiffin could hear the Germans all around them.

You could hear Jerry voices, they'd put patrols out nosing their way forward, they passed within a few yards of us. You could hear them whispering. We were tucked into a vine, we tried to cover ourselves with leaves. It was pitch dark by this time – midnight. What I really feared was that if they saw us, they'd shoot first and ask questions afterwards. Anyhow they never saw us! That was quite a terrifying experience. After midnight, the patrols stopped. At one or two o'clock in the morning, they started shelling again, very heavily, along the road, but they were falling in this vineyard. The vineyard came down to the road and where it met there was a ditch. The shelling really was bad, and it was a matter of luck whether you were hit or not because you could feel the shell fragments whining through the vineyard. I said to Askill. 'We'll have to get in that ditch or we're going to be hit!' It was 20 yards away and I dragged myself down there with his help. It was excruciatingly painful. People say, 'That is impossible!' It isn't impossible – if it's a matter of life or death. By this time, it was three or four o'clock in the morning, so I'd been out there getting on for sixteen hours without any medical attention. But I was still conscious. It was

> obviously getting near dawn, so Askill said, 'I'm going back! I'm going to bring somebody up if I have to bloody well drag them up!' So off he goes. That was perhaps the worst part of it; there I was on my own. Now if he didn't come back, what the hell was I going to do? Even if I was found by the Germans and I didn't get shot and they treated me decently – which I'm sure they would have done – one fear I had got fixed in my mind was that I didn't think they had medical treatment as good as ours and that they would probably amputate my leg. I lay there with all these thoughts for maybe an hour and a half, and I was beginning to get annoyed. Suddenly I heard voices – and there was Askill, with two stretcher bearers from the Leicesters. They said, 'Come on, get on! This bugger's practically dragged us down at rifle point!'[27]
>
> 2nd Lieutenant Douglas Tiffin, 'D' Company

Tiffin was carried back to the nearest regimental aid post. After suffering a serious wound followed by eighteen hours without medical treatment, he was in a terrible state. He was evacuated by hospital ship to the UK and would spend most of the rest of the war in Ryhope Hospital.

> If you've been in bed for five or six months the only thing is, 'When am I going to get up?' They kept saying, 'Well you can get up when your calliper comes!' This was a be all and end all of your life, 'When's the bloody calliper coming?' Eventually, about March, it arrives and tentatively I get up on my feet with this calliper on and a pair of crutches. For about a week I was just allowed to walk round the ward. Then, after a bit, one of the first things was going down to the pub in Ryhope, illicitly I think. Nevertheless, down to the pub we went. Eventually, they said, 'All right, you can go home!' Still with my calliper on.[28]
>
> 2nd Lieutenant Douglas Tiffin, 'D' Company

For many more years he would be in and out of hospital.

Back on the Mondaino battlefield, the 16th DLI were relieved when they realised the Germans had withdrawn. On 2 September, the 2/5th Leicesters pushed into Mondaino from the west, breaking the German stranglehold. Always pragmatic, they immediately pulled back. A rapid follow up meant that the next strongpoint at Saludecio was overrun without fighting. But once again, the Durhams came under heavy shellfire.

> The Germans pulled out and we occupied it. They shelled it something rotten. We went into the crypt of the church, most of the adult population were there – men and women – shouting as the Italians do. We were in there for some hours, and we were absolutely shelled something rotten. That was quite frightening, but nobody was killed. The noise effect was the worst of it.[29]
>
> Private Ronald Elliott, 'D' Company

The advance continued and the Durhams' Carrier Platoon managed to burst through to seize Serra Ridge, where a Mark IV tank was destroyed, twenty-nine POWs were taken, and an 88mm gun captured. 'C' and 'D' Companies followed up and the ridge was soon firmly in British hands. The left flank was exposed as 56th Division had still not managed to take the dominating heights of Monte Maggiore. When 'B' Company attempted to move further forward, it was soon repulsed and the company commander, Major Ray Mitchell, was wounded. He was replaced as a temporary measure by Captain Jimmy Coutts. The 2/5th Foresters and 5th Leicesters moved through the Durhams, and the advance resumed. The progress of 139 Brigade was matched by the rest of 46th Division, as 128 and 138 Brigades had taken Mondaino itself, and secured a bridgehead across the Conca river at San Clemente. On the night of 3–4 September, the 139 Brigade was relieved and the 16th DLI moved back to Saludecio.

The polite term for the men's state during the brief rest period that followed was 'knackered'. They had been almost dropping with exhaustion; now at last they could sleep. It was also a chance for a programme of entertainments to try and bolster morale, with visits from the divisional concert party and dance band, the mobile cinema, and of course the men made their own amusements in the local bars. In the background there was process of considerable reorganisation, with the arrival of more new replacement drafts, and as senior NCOs and officers were juggled around to replace casualties. Les Thornton, as company sergeant major of the Support Company, found he was part of this process.

> I picked up the field telephone and it said, 'Sergeant Major Thornton?' I said, 'Aye!' 'I'm afraid we've got news for you! Sergeant Major Mattin has been killed[30] and you've got to go immediately to take over as 'C' Company sergeant major – urgently!' I said, 'What about the company here?' 'Forget about that, we will sort that out, off you go!' A jeep was sent, and I got my kit together and off I went to report to 'C' Company. I was not very pleased actually. I knew I was going to be more liable to be killed than I was before! I mean, I was more liable to be killed by small arms fire or mortar fire. I wasn't very pleased, but of course there was a job to do – and it had to be done.[31]
>
> Company Sergeant Major Leslie Thornton, 'C' Company

Another example of a man recognising and accepting what his duty was. He didn't want to do it; but he did it.

12

THE BATTLE OF GEMMANO RIDGE

> Mortar shells were raining down upon us. I always remember there was a bloke who was dying to one side of this path. Nobody could do anything for them, or nobody did. He was just bleeding away. People were being wounded – and there was just this rain of mortar shells.[1]
>
> Private Ronald Elliott, 'D' Company

THE ALL TOO SHORT REST of the 16th DLI at Saludecio was brought to an abrupt end on 10 September 1944. The fighting had moved into the Gemmano sector, a steep rocky ridge line, running from the villages of Villa and Gemmano, up through the almost connected small village of Borgo. The ridge then ran up to the round topped Hill 414, on which stood a single farmhouse. There was a slight dip down to a cemetery, between Hill 414 and the highest point of Hill 449, which was marked by an old white cross on the summit. Gemmano and Villa had already been cleared by the 56th Division, while the rest of the ridge had just been captured by the 2/4th KOYLI and 6th Lincolns of 138 Brigade during the afternoon of 10 September. But the situation was still precarious in the extreme. That night, the 16th DLI was to relieve the 2/4th KOYLI, with 'C' and 'D' Companies occupying Villa with the battalion headquarters, while 'A' and 'B' Companies moved into Gemmano itself. Unfortunately, on the same night the Germans launched an effective surprise attack and had wrested back control of both Hill 449 and Hill 414, even penetrating as far as the northern buildings of Borgo.

It was evident that the Germans would not give up Gemmano Ridge without a severe fight.

As they prepared to move up the track to Gemmano, Les Thornton and Major Pat Casey found they had a difficult decision to make when one of their men lost his nerve and was unable to go on. There was a difficult balance to be struck. After all, none of them wanted to go; but they had to. Yet what good would be served by forcing a 'broken' man to be in action?

> This young lad came to me and said, 'Sergeant major, I can't go up the line!' I say, 'What do you mean, you can't go up the line?' He said, 'Well if I go up the line, I won't come back! I'll get killed!' I said, 'Don't be silly, you've as much chance as everybody else!' 'No, I won't come back!' 'Well come on, get in front of the major then!' I took him in front of the major – Pat Casey from Jarrow. I said, 'He won't go up the line!' The padre was visiting, he said to the boy, 'Look, son, who's going to do your job if you don't go up the line – your mates?' The major said, 'Well, you're going up the line with me! I'll take you up on the end of this!' And he held up his pistol. Anyhow that lad went up next day and he was killed by shellfire. Premonition or not – I don't know. With him was a good sergeant, Sergeant Dabner. He was killed as well.[2] You feel, 'Should I have sent him up; or should I have sent him sick?' But when you lose a few men, then every man is necessary to do a job of work.[3]
>
> Company Sergeant Major Leslie Thornton, 'C' Company

The men of 'B' Company set off, marching up the track that climbed up towards Gemmano. Just before they reached the village of Villa, Richard Hewlett's platoon took a short break.

> We stopped at this barn and brewed up and I was having a cup and a private of Headquarters Company, a company runner or something like that, was sitting beside me. A mortar bomb landed right in front of us – not 15 yards away. We both fell back, forced by the blast. He was blown to bits. His legs were broken, his arms were broken, everything was broken. All the contents of his cup of tea went all over me and I thought, 'Oh

my goodness, it's blood!' But it wasn't; it was tea. I thought
I must have been hit, I thought, 'Oh my God, it's the end of
my war!' I couldn't believe it – it missed me – he was as near
as touching me and he was blown to bits – and I didn't get a
scratch, I couldn't believe it, most extraordinary. There was
straw on the floor of this barn so there was a horrible mess of
tea, blood and straw.[4]

Lieutenant Richard Hewlett, 'B' Company

After passing through Villa, they continued the climb up to Gemmano at the top of the ridge. Almost as soon as they arrived, 'B' Company came under a torrent of shells.

> Our platoon got in this cellar. There was shells landing all
> the time, clouds of dust coming in and there was nothing
> you could do. You kept hearing cries above, 'Stretcher bearer!
> Stretcher bearer!' Calling for stretcher bearers when somebody
> else had been hit. A chap was laid there; he'd just been covered
> with a gas cape. His lips were protruding through it – just as
> though the gases out of his stomach had dissolved the cape.
> There must have been people buried in some of the ruins
> because it stank – a terrible stench. It was hot weather – the
> bodies soon putrefied. It was a sickly, sweet smell – if you think
> now – you can actually bring it back.[5]

Corporal William Virr, 'B' Company

On the bare, rocky hillside, cover was at a premium, so they were forced to take what shelter they could in the stone-built houses and farms. But Hewlett and his men encountered an unusual natural obstacle.

> This cow was stopping us getting into the barn. We tried
> to push it further in and it just wouldn't! When the shelling
> started, we thought, 'Well, we've got to get some cover!' I said,
> 'There's only one thing to do – to kill this cow!' And we shot
> it, put quite a few bullets into it! As it started to die, we pushed
> it further in so that we could all get into the barn. I felt so out
> of touch with everybody that I left my platoon there and went

> round to Gemmano – I went to see Jimmy Coutts to try and find out what was happening. The house on the left had been largely destroyed and Jimmy Coutts was sort of underneath a house; he had his company headquarters there. He said, 'Bring your platoon up to the village and occupy that house on the right! And send out a patrol to see what's going on ahead!' I went back to my platoon, they were being shelled like mad, and I ducked down, waiting for it to finish. I heard somebody near me hit by a shell – and I never found them – I could hear them dying a horrible noise. I don't know who it was. Then we moved forward, and we occupied a house right on the very edge of the village. We were in a sort of semi-basement occupying a defensive position in case of a counterattack.[6]
>
> Lieutenant Richard Hewlett, 'B' Company

They had already suffered several casualties and it was soon evident that some of the men were not physically or mentally strong enough to endure these horrors – and who can blame them.

> There was a lot lying dead in there. They'd got their heads blown off, there was packs and that covered in bloody blood. Bill Virr says, 'If you want any tea, they've got the tea and sugar!' We went through the village a bit; we got shelled. We got into this house, down in the cellar. I got dysentery. Things were just going straight through me. I had to crawl away, all the way back down. I ended up in an ambulance.[7]
>
> Private Eric Murray, 'B' Company

Murray's dysentery soon cleared up, but he developed shell-shock symptoms and then had a full-blown nervous breakdown. He was subsequently medically downgraded to B1 and had a posting as a POW camp guard. He would never return to active service. Amid such terror and confusion, there was also a moment of pure surrealism.

> I met Sergeant Jerrison – he was 'A' Company, I think. I was probably asking for information. I remember his standing to

attention as he spoke to me and there were chickens all over the place. One was on each shoulder – and one on top of his steel helmet. It didn't seem to worry him at all! Extraordinary sight! The chickens needed company! You couldn't push them away – they came back. I don't know whether they wanted food, or they just didn't want to be shelled by themselves! I thought this is something we are going to laugh about one day.[8]

Lieutenant Richard Hewlett, 'B' Company

Sadly, next day Joseph Jerrison was killed.[9] There was a sharp contrast between chuckling at friendly chickens and the stench of the corpses that littered Gemmano from the previous fighting. It was enough to turn anyone's stomach.

The stench was terrible. We passed British and German soldiers, great shell holes in them, bloated from being lying there three days, more or less. We got up into this building. The company commander said, 'Right-ho, we'll stop here! The rations will be coming up!' I said to two lads, 'Right, come on, we'll go and get the rations!' I had my Tommy gun and they had their rifles. We went down and there was two petrol cans full of water and the rations. Now I carried my Tommy gun and the two cans of water. Now a can of water was 4 gallons. Now, they got heavy and by the time I'd passed all these bodies – with a stench – I had to drag myself up backwards up the incline to get these tins of water up to where the major was. They issued the rations out – it was steak and kidney pudding – and I couldn't eat a bite. The stench from these bodies and the terrible sights. I could have wept. It was lovely stuff, steak and kidney pudding, but I couldn't eat it, I was just about sick.[10]

Company Sergeant Major Leslie Thornton, 'C' Company

This is the story of the 16th DLI, but it would be invidious not to reference and commend the heroic fighting of the 2/6th KOYLI who time and time again made heroic attempts to cross the bullet-swept wasteland between Gemmano and Hill 449. But it was all in vain. It did not seem humanly possible. At the end of that terrible day, Hill 449 was still in German hands, looking down on a company of the KOYLI below them in the cemetery. By this time, three battalion headquarters were located in Gemmano, as its strong stone building provided the only feasible safe harbour. Tom Lister remembered being ordered to drive Colonel Dennis Worrall's jeep up to the village. Worrall was clearly somewhat stressed.

> Colonel Worrall's own jeep was out of commission, and he told the captain quartermaster that he would have his – and grabbed me to drive it. He'd got the reputation of 'Mad Worrall'. He said, 'Drive up to Gemmano!' We got round the corner all right at the bottom, got halfway up the hill and there was a sudden shower of mortar bombs. It wasn't a very wide road, there was a deep ditch on the left-hand side, and I stopped the jeep, which was the natural thing to do, and dived in the ditch. He played holy hell with me, 'Get back in the jeep! Drive on. I'll tell you when to stop!' He got into the ditch with the idea of digging me out and we got back on the road – and the entire windscreen had disappeared and there was water squirting out of the radiator. But it went and he insisted on going on. I got behind the remnants of a house at the bottom end of the village and he pressed on. He threatened me with God knows what! Some time after, he said I'd probably done the right thing, but in the heat of the moment he'd been very annoyed.[11]
>
> Private Tom Lister, MT Section, Headquarters Company

Something else had to be tried, and on 12 September, 139 Brigade was ordered to act as a flank guard and push round to the right, with the 16th DLI feeling their way across the series of ridges and gullies which led down from the Gemmano Ridge heights right down to the Conca river. Meanwhile the 138 Brigade would renew the main assault on Hill 449. The next two days proved a chastening experience for Les Thornton.

> We made an attack on a group of buildings on this little hill. The platoons were spread out, to attack. We got there without a lot of trouble. But when we got in, the Germans gave us hell, knocking the building down bit by bit. The company

headquarters were the only ones in the building, the platoons were outside, in open ground. The OP gunner officer was wounded with shellfire. I heard him say, 'I'm choking! I'm choking!' Obviously, he was dying.[12] One of my corporals came in shot through the foot. He was in the corner moaning and the company commander was saying, 'For goodness sake, try and keep him quiet!' Then Pat Casey he got on the wireless to the CO and said, 'Somebody's got to do something about this! We are being absolutely cut to bits by shellfire!' He must have got through and there was counter-battery fire. We heard our own guns firing over the top of us and clearing the enemy out.[13]

Company Sergeant Major Leslie Thornton, 'C' Company

Being under shellfire like this was a terrible, earth-shattering experience that physically and mentally battered the men. Only when the German shellfire died down could they move forward.

> I had my company headquarters following me, the major and the platoons on each. As I went up, there was a German soldier sitting in a pool of water just off the path. Obviously, he was very badly wounded. I was going over to him, and the major said 'Don't, sergeant major, don't go, leave him!' I had to leave him.[14]

Company Sergeant Major Leslie Thornton, 'C' Company

Major Pat Casey obviously feared the man might have a concealed weapon or grenade. But moments afterwards it was irrelevant, as their positions were counterattacked by a strong force of Germans.

> Well, they were too much for us, so we had to get back quickly. We were caught unawares. The major said, 'Get back! Get the men back!' Because he knew that we would have got slaughtered. As we went back, we heard this noise. It was funny noise – and we knew what it was – it was the nebelwerfers winding up. They were electrically controlled six-barrelled mortars – and they were horrors. They caught us in the middle of this open ground. We were all flat on our faces in a ditch full

> of water. When you get a battery of six-barrelled mortars it's all hell let loose. They stopped and we got up again. I looked over and the German soldier had gone – he'd been blown to pieces by his own mortars. We got back into this building and started to reorganise ourselves. But it was a sticky time. When you take a place, you don't see many Germans, you don't see your enemy a lot. You only see them when they're running away. You can't say how many you've killed. Your shellfire killed a lot – it accounts for most casualties in a war like that.[15]
>
> Company Sergeant Major Leslie Thornton, 'C' Company

The counterattacking Germans then seemed to pull back and, after a short period to reorganise, the 'C' Company advance once more resumed. Crossing a small river, they came across another farm building.

> It was a building with an open front to it, or an open back. It was like a stable. We bedded down there – we didn't go to sleep – we just stayed there. And then he started again, shelling us! God, we were shelled rotten. A few hours later, the company commander got through to the CO. He said, 'Well, look, you're being relieved! Just get the men out of the road!' I got the men in this cellar – it was pretty deep. I started to detail my sentries, but I didn't put them upstairs. I put the sentry at the bottom of the cellar steps. They started shelling again – and it went on all night. We were safe. Next morning it stopped. We got up and there was no building there at all, there was just the cellar. You can imagine what would have happened if I'd put the sentry at the top or we'd stopped in the building – it was completely demolished.[16]
>
> Company Sergeant Major Leslie Thornton, 'C' Company

'D' Company was charged with making forward patrols round the side of the Gemmano Ridge. As an acting platoon sergeant, John Lewindon was ordered to carry out a recce and he was soon made aware of the grave nature of his responsibilities.

We set off and we hadn't been going long, when all of a sudden to the right there was a burst of machine gun – Schmeisser – George Pauly was on the right. Everyone went down of course, and then there was a single rifle shot. I knew what that was; that was one of ours. I made my way over and one of the blokes in that section said, George Pauly[17] had been shot! 'He's down there! There's a German down there as well, they're both dead!' I thought, 'This is a brilliant start!' George was lying on his back, and he had this burst all across him – he must have been dead before he hit the ground. I got hold of the lance corporal with the sections and said, 'Well, you'll have to take the section now! We have to keep going!' With that, off we went again.[18]

Sergeant John Lewindon, 'D' Company

They were moving towards a row of trees. Lewindon had called a stop about 50 yards in front of them ready for the next bound.

There was a lot of shouting across to the right. The ground was sloping down to the riverbed and the section on the right had found one or two Jerries over there, hit some of them and chased the rest of them out. I called them back, I said, 'Let them go!' Stop where you are – don't go too far down!' In the meantime, Corporal Goldstone had gone forward. I heard a lot of hullabaloo from his section. I heard a grenade go. I made my way over there and he'd got right to the fringe of the trees – it was him who'd thrown the grenade – he'd found a mortar – he'd destroyed that. The Jerries were on the run – going down the hill. I called Goldstone back, but he never heard and kept on going. The Germans, one or two of them stopped running, turned round and grabbed hold of him – he was outnumbered – and took him with them. There was a sound of a lorry starting, so they must have had a vehicle of some sort down there – down by the river somewhere.[19]

Sergeant John Lewindon, 'D' Company

They then retraced their steps. Goldstone was reported missing and was later listed as a prisoner of war.

Tony Cameron found himself on a similar mission trying to clear the Germans from the northern slopes of Gemmano Ridge. He was accompanied by his platoon commander, 2nd Lieutenant Frank Johnson, whom he had known previously when they were both gunners before Johnson had been commissioned. Cameron was still inexperienced as an infantryman.

> I don't know really what we were supposed to do, except that we had to go and clear this farmhouse down in a dip towards the Jerry. We were on one hill; Jerry was on the other hill; Jerry must also have been down in the valley. Frank said, 'It would help if you gave defensive fire on the stretch of farm track on the bottom of the Jerries' hill!' I had a section, with my own lance corporal, and a corporal in charge of the Bren. We moved out that night, went a roundabout way and came along this farm track between our positions in Gemmano and the Jerries' position on the hilltop where there was a big black cross. It was quiet, so I told my lads, 'Right, line up here, get the Bren down there!' Frank had said, 'Now, you'll hear us move into that farmhouse!' which was right in the dip. There was a lot of bangs and cracks went off, you could hear grenades exploding. I said, 'Fire on the farmhouse!' We started firing, and then the bloody Spandau machine gun fire came at us. We were on the track, and they must have had fixed lines somewhere on the hill. I rolled back over. I never saw where the other lads went. Everybody dispersed, luckily nobody was hit! I lay there for quite a while. I had a Tommy gun hugged in on me, and the Spandau bullets were hitting along the track. I could practically see them, the splashes of dirt. When they stopped, I lay there quite a while, no idea where the rest of the platoon was or anything. I didn't know whether to follow Frank, but I couldn't, because there was no one to follow him with! I didn't know which way he'd gone, so I went back the way I'd come![20]

Corporal Tony Cameron, 'A' Company

When Cameron got back, he was in for a real surprise.

> I got back on my own – and there was half my section still there – where the other half went, I don't know. They must have done the same as me, doubled back, and the other half disappeared. At the time the infantry were like that – lads who'd been right through Italy, they'd had a bellyful of that. At the first real thump, a lot of them used to disappear! After that experience I thought, 'Well, I can look after myself better as a private – it's no good me being a corporal, when I can't control these blokes! Never mind looking after them. I'm going to be a private, the same as them and look after me!' I asked to revert the rank – right back to private after Gemmano. It seemed to me sensible to find out how to be an infantryman from scratch. Never mind starting halfway up! I wanted someone else to have the responsibility. I didn't want to have charge of a bunch of blokes that I couldn't trust. I'd sooner be under a bloke myself – and know that he could trust me! To be a team-leader is no good if the team aren't behind you![21]
>
> Corporal Tony Cameron, 'A' Company

At this stage, Ronnie Sherlaw was beginning to encounter some quite natural reluctance among his subalterns and senior NCOs to lead patrols.

> From that position we kept sending out small fighting patrols to deal with bits of German opposition in the area some 200 to 300 yards ahead. All the time we were in that position we were shelled. There was never a major attack, but there were skirmishes as they were attempting to deal with our advanced positions. It was very unpleasant indeed. The biggest difficulty was we had to continue sending out these fighting patrols and of course it got to the stage where the chaps were very reluctant to go! You would say to a platoon commander, 'I think you'll have to take a couple of your sections this time!' He would say, 'Oh God! I've been out so many times!' I don't ever remember anybody saying, 'I won't go!' But they had to be persuaded – there was a job to do – and the job had to be done. By the time we came out we were too weak to do very much at all. I think as a company we lost something like eighteen

to twenty killed. We certainly lost a good deal more than that wounded. When we came out, only about twelve of us walked out![22]

Major Ronnie Sherlaw, 'D' Company

These two days struggling round the Gemmano Ridge proved to be one of Ronald Elliott's worst experiences of a terrible war. As a signaller it was his responsibility to maintain communications, whether by wireless or by a telephone cable connection back to the battalion headquarters. Elliott preferred the wireless – it was simpler and safer. Telephone cables were easily broken.

> It was a gully – a very steep gully indeed, on the far side of this hill. As a company we were spread along this gully, no more than about a couple of yards wide, very steep shoulders on it. It was beautifully designed for mortar fire – the Germans had it marked out as a mortar target. And it was hell! We took the radio set in, and we were on the radio. The first night, two or three lads from base came over the lip of the hill and said, 'We've brought you a cable and a telephone handset!' I said, 'You can get bloody stuffed with that! I don't want it!' They said, 'You've got to take it!' So, we were in touch on the telephone, and we shut down the set. Of course, during the night, the line went 'DIS'[23] as I knew it would do, because the shelling around there was absolutely horrible. There was only Jackie Wells and I there – I said to Jackie Wells, 'All right, I'll go back and look at the bloody thing!' I wandered back with this line in my hand and at the top of the hill there was a break in the line! This was in the pitch dark! I looked around for the other part of the line and it had been blown by a shell yards and yards away. I found it. I've got that in that hand, got the other one in the other – and the two lines were about a yard apart. I said, 'Well, shit it! I'll bugger off! I'm not going to do anything about this!' So, I threw the cable away and went back down into the gully and told, 'Giff' Footer, 'Your bloody cable's out of order! We'll have to go back on to radio.' They weren't at all charmed in headquarters. I said, 'Well, if you want to repair it, you can bloody repair it!' We were in a hellish position. Really.

It was absolutely impossible. We weren't serving any useful purpose and we're just being chopped to pieces here – I was quite panicky, I guess.[24]

Private Ronald Elliott, 'D' Company

Then suddenly it was all over. The 16th DLI had not been the main assault; they were the flanking operation and other units gradually encircled and encroached on Hill 449, so that in the end the Germans had no option but to pull out. As so often with the infantry, the 16th DLI did not see the 'end of the story'; they had played their part and were then moved out to a well-earned rest. They needed it.

13

MORE BLOODY RIDGES

> We got across this range of hills – and that's the end of it. Then you cross the next range, then the next range, you went from one line to another. They took some budging at that time, the Germans. You gradually got them out of their positions, and they withdrew, only for you to find that they'd got another line somewhere behind it. It was a very frustrating period.[1]
>
> Private Tom Lister, MT Section, Headquarters Company

THAT AUTUMN, SKIRMISH FOLLOWED SKIRMISH, sometimes flaring up into a fully-fledged battle, which swelled the trickle of casualties into a veritable torrent. As each river was followed by the next ridge, the men joked that the Germans had a fleet of bulldozers working flat out to create ever more obstacles in their path. But it was assuredly no joke for those in the front line. In the next phase, the 139 Brigade pushed towards San Marino on 18 September, taking over the advance from 138 Brigade. The 16th DLI concentrated at Tavernia, then crossed the Marano river to assist the 6th York and Lancasters in the capture of Verucchio. Few recalled this period in any detail, but Tony Cameron certainly remembered the advance on Point 235 near the town of Serravalle in San Marino on 21 September 1944.

> There was only about twenty of us left in the platoon. We were moving in file up this road, and we came under fire from the village at the top of the road. Everybody hit the deck straight away, we pulled back down the hill, and then there was

only about twelve of us left, because there were a few hit on the road. We pulled back, reorganised, and we were moving forward to take the three white farmhouses, to the right side of the village. In the distance, you could see the peaks of San Marino. We formed up in line, headed up the hill across open fields for these farmhouses. The platoon sergeant, Frank Bousefield, passed me and as he passed me, he said, 'Tell the platoon commander I've been hit, I'm going back!' When the firing really started heavy, we moved up within 50 yards of these white houses and there wasn't many left. The section corporal who was in charge of the Bren, he had a Tommy gun, he was standing up against a tree. I was lying down with a rifle. I could see Frank Johnson, the platoon commander, 10 yards in front of me. The corporal got a mark across the head, flashed red, down he went, but he started crawling away, so I knew he was all right. I looked up and Frank's still going forward, so I jumped up to follow him. They started mortaring then – and when I looked round – I couldn't see no one else. I shouted, 'Frank, there's only the two of us!' Well, he couldn't hear me. The mortaring had bloody started. He got down behind a burnt haystack. I thought, 'That's bloody silly, that's not going to stop nowt – a heap of burnt straw!' It was 'BANG! BANG! BANG!' bits of stuff flying all over and that's the last thing I remember. When I came to, I was lying there, no sign of Frank, no sign of nobody, but it was quiet. I'd been hit by mortar fragments. I was in a state of bloody shock – and I was sore – I had no idea where I was![2]

Private Tony Cameron, 'A' Company

He had a wound in his back but managed to make his way back down the hill, where he encountered the three Sherman tanks and elements of 'C' Company who would ultimately take the objective as the Germans retreated. Cameron was evacuated on a Bren carrier to the regimental aid post, where he had an operation to remove the shrapnel from his back. Hospitalisation followed in southern Italy and Cameron would only rejoin the 16th DLI in Greece in January 1945.

Over the next few days, the 16th DLI crossed the Marecchia river, then the Uso river, formerly known as the Rubicon – forever linked with Caesar in the popular memory – although few would remember exactly why! Then on 28 September came another battle that seemed to stick in the memory of many of the participants. The depleted battalion was reduced to just two companies when the 16th DLI was ordered to take Casa Ricci Ridge. Major Ronnie Sherlaw, commanding 'D' Company, which had been combined with 'A' Company, was ordered to assault a church, codenamed 'Dryden'. Ronnie Elliott remembered the mood was grim.

> Morale was pretty low. We were down to two companies; companies [were] being amalgamated. Everyone was pretty pissed off one way or another. The operations started with two platoons being led by Captain Ronnie Sherlaw, who was then in charge of the company. He attacked 'Dryden', which we managed to take without too much problem. The whole of company headquarters went into this area, and we thought that was as far as we would go.[3]
>
> Private Ronald Elliott, 'D' Company

But Sherlaw had been ordered to push on further and take a group of farmhouses identified as 'Johnson' up on Casa Ricci Ridge.

> We went over open ground in open order. Fortunately, at that stage we didn't have any casualties. We reached these outbuildings of a farm, about halfway to the objective. I'd got the artillery FOO to put down a lot of smoke on our left flank, where the fire was coming from. Hoping that when the smoke was down, we could advance. When we moved out of these outbuildings to go towards the objective, there was a tremendous 'stonk' during which a small piece of shrapnel went in the back of my leg. The difficulty was that we were on a hill, and I found that I couldn't walk up the hill.[4]
>
> Major Ronnie Sherlaw, 'D' Company

Behind him, back at 'Dryden', Ronnie Elliott had also been ordered to go forward, ready to provide communications. As he did so, he encountered a symptom of the declining morale that was sometimes occurred in any battalion that had been in action too long.

> On the way there, there was this hollow by some trees – and there were a lot of people there. What we called at the time 'bomb happiness' and shell-shock cases, genuine or feigned. People reacting to having to go into action by opting out – a fair number of them. We two signallers and the company sergeant major were going forward past these people, not too much we could do about them. We moved on up the hill up towards this 'Johnson' feature. Shells and bullets stormed down upon us – it was a rain of fire. We dropped to the ground. It seemed to go on for a while. So we just came back again, to this hollow an area that obviously couldn't be seen, because there wasn't any firing. We were then confronted by Ronnie Sherlaw in an absolute fury, he had a wound on his leg. Playing merry hell with us and the sergeant major for not going up and bracketing us with these other cowards – or worse than that! Which we took great exception to because we had seriously tried to go forward but had been prevented.[5]
>
> Private Ronald Elliott, 'D' Company

Sherlaw was left seething in that hollow, where he was eventually picked up and evacuated back to the regimental aid post by Tom Lister in his jeep. It proved a memorable journey for them both – though it did not improve Sherlaw's mood.

> He was wounded in the leg. He was on the roadside, waiting for somebody to pick him up. We had these frames to bring wounded down on the jeep where you couldn't get a truck or an ambulance. They bunged him on. He wasn't in such a terrible state I don't think, but he most forcibly reminded me the first chance he got after he got back to the battalion, that he'd suffered more from my driving than he did from being hit in the leg! He said he had, 'A headache for a fortnight after

bouncing my head!' It was a bad narrow road to start with, strewn with boulders, the jeep wasn't particularly well sprung, and you were making the best pace you could in case you got stonked! You tended to put your passengers last and yourself first! That was perhaps not the attitude you should have had![6]

Private Tom Lister, MT Section, Headquarters Company

Notwithstanding, Sherlaw was safely delivered back to the regimental aid post. Here his wound was bandaged, but it was relatively minor and he was able to remain with battalion on light duties for a couple of weeks. It was perhaps fortunate that the platoon commanded by the dynamic Russell Collins was still up on Casa Ricci Ridge. His increasing stature in the battalion was reflected in the responsibility that was thrust upon him.

When we got about halfway up the hill, Ronnie Sherlaw got hit – not for the first time! Orders were given that I was to take over command of the assault, although I may say I was not the senior subaltern – Tim Perriam commanding a neighbouring platoon was senior to me. The assault was launched by then and we had to get on with it! The idea was the tanks were to fire smoke cannisters, to put down a smoke screen to protect us as we charged the buildings. As we faced the two buildings, we were approaching the one to the right of the road. In fact, the whole of our force was coming in by the right flank. I led the men through this smoke area, but the tanks were still firing these smoke cannisters – they were things weighing about 5–6 pounds, dropping on you from perhaps a 100 feet in the air – it would have been very nasty! There was nothing for it but to press on – nobody was hit by them luckily. We burst through and we got into the right-hand farmhouse. Then there was the problem of clearing the farmhouse. The enemy who had been occupying it, quite unsurprisingly, had gone into the rear rooms, and I think they ran away. Some of the Italian family were still there in the building.[7]

Lieutenant Russell Collins, 'A' Company

He knew he had to consolidate the position if he was to have any chance of resisting a German counterattack. He was in desperate need of signals contact with battalion headquarters and hence with the supporting artillery units who could rain down a protective screen of shells. Once again Ronald Elliott had to force himself forward up the hill to 'Johnson'.

> Part of the difficulty was that there were vineyards with wires strung out with mines. It was bloody impossible to travel through those with the wireless set aerial. We dropped down two or three times because of the fire and eventually we all came to the conclusion 'Look ... if we're going to get bloody killed!' So we stood up and walked through it. We came through unscathed and arrived at 'Johnson' at about midday. The set was in absolute dire need, because they were being counterattacked by upwards of fifty Germans with tanks and self-propelled guns. We were to direct artillery fire into areas where the Germans were – infantry concentrations, the guns or tanks.[8]
>
> Private Ronald Elliott, 'D' Company

The Germans were determined to go down fighting and to Elliott it was a desperate business.

> Perriam's platoon was in one of the houses and 'Winkler' Collins was in the one that we were in – we were in a barn at the back. Fairly safe, really, apart from the shelling. The Germans attacked us throughout the whole of that night and the best part of the next day as well. We hung on. Communications came and went, but we always managed to get through, to call down artillery fire when it was needed. They fired phosphorus bombs at us, 88mm guns and mortars. There was hand-to-hand fighting at one stage. The Germans got into Perriam's house – there were Germans in one half of the house and English in the other half![9]
>
> Private Ronald Elliott, 'D' Company

When Collins was confident that he had got a firm base he darted across the rough track, accompanied by a few men, to help Lieutenant Perriam clear the last Germans out of the neighbouring farm building.

> Somehow, we got up a staircase. The Germans were all concentrated in a downstairs room and looking down the stairs, they were obviously in the room, which was just out of sight to me, I could see the doorway to it, but I couldn't see in. They were down there, and we were in the upstairs room. Obviously, it would have been very foolhardy to go down those stairs, so we lobbed down the odd grenade. Then we communicated by radio with the tanks. We made a little plan that we would get out of there and the tanks would blast the building. I gave orders for all our chaps who were in and around this second building, to withdraw to the other building, to clear the way. When we went across to the other building, we could see the aspect of the left-hand building which the tanks were going to fire at. They started firing and as soon as they started firing, a man came and appeared at the upstairs window. I felt it was one of our chaps who had been left behind in there. One of these nightmarish visions, which I've never been able to rationalise or get out my mind since – he was waving his arms desperately – but the next shell went through the window and that was the end of him. That picture is engraved on my mind.[10]
>
> Lieutenant Russell Collins, 'A' Company

The British tanks then edged their way forward up on to Casa Ricci. But just as the German infantry in a building were helpless in the face of a tank's main armament, the tanks were helpless if exposed to the deadly German artillery. Tanks were not shellproof.

> The tanks then started to move forward and tried to gain the crest, get a view over the crest – they like to fire from a hull down position. This tank came up, and when it got about level with us, it became just exposed. The German 88 anti-tank gun from only a couple of hundred yards ahead, it got a direct hit right on the front of the turret. We had a bird's eye view, because it was only about 15–20 feet from us just outside the

window. That shot went straight through the turret, it must have killed the commander, then the hatches went up at the back and the rest of the crew baled out quicker than you can say 'Jack Robinson' in case it brewed up. Then went back down the hill like scalded cats.[11]

Lieutenant Russell Collins, 'A' Company

Another tank seems to have been knocked out, and the remaining tank retired back down the hill. The situation was getting desperate and there was no sign of any meaningful reinforcements, or even better, relief by a fresh battalion. Their only real hope was that the supporting artillery could break up any German counterattack before they were overwhelmed.

> We were in a very tenuous position. We put around such defences as we could, but the right tactic would be to exploit beyond the objective, to anticipate a counterattack. Although we'd gained the objective, we were really very insecure there. They were massive buildings, and they weren't on the very top of the hill. Obviously, the Germans hadn't given it up, they'd just withdrawn to regroup. There was a sense of foreboding. I put out such machine gun posts as I could and observation posts. Our gunner OP was a chap called David Purnell, he had the whole thing under observation, he controlled the battery, and he did it extremely well. He came up on the blower to me. We had reasonable radio contact then because I had a company net 18 set then. He was asking what protection we had, because he was planning supporting fire. 'How close could our shells fall? Were we sufficiently protected?' I just had to use my judgement about that, but he actually made the calculations and directed the fire.[12]

Lieutenant Russell Collins, 'A' Company

The Germans could choose their moment; only when they were ready would they strike.

> When the Germans did counterattack – they arrived in numbers, mainly from the left-hand side – they got back into the

> building which we'd evacuated. Then they got in the building I was in! We were in a kitchen, and there was an ordinary standard doorway about 8 feet high and a kitchen dresser blocking across it. I became aware suddenly of a great excited conversation going on the other side. I could hear an Italian woman's voice and a German man's voice. I got hold of a chair and got up on this chair and I looked over the top of the dresser. There, as close to me as I am to you – about 8 feet – was this very large German officer, with his steel helmet, haranguing this poor woman as to where we were: 'Where were the British?' What to do? I had no option really; I wasn't going to draw attention to my presence. I drew my pistol and fired at him. You always have to aim a little bit low, I tried to fire at his head, but I got him in the throat actually. He fell like a sack of coal, the woman screamed, and they hid under the table. I called to one of my soldiers, 'Give me your Tommy gun!' I put that over the top and tried to make sure that I'd finished him off. He fell partly behind the door, so I then had to fire the Tommy gun through this rather thick door. A rather brave German orderly or soldier, only just visible around the doorway, dragged the officer away out of sight. That was how close the contact was there.[13]
>
> Lieutenant Russell Collins, 'A' Company

It all seemed hopeless, but then their only real hope of a successful defence opened up: the massed guns of the Royal Artillery. Not just a battery or a regiment, but the mailed fist of the whole of the divisional artillery struck home.

> David Purnell brought down this divisional concentration of fire all around us. Really it was very good infantry and artillery cooperation, because I knew exactly what our situation was, and was able to convey it to him. He did extremely well and he got a Military Cross for the way he brought down that concentration. The attack was repulsed, I had one or two machine guns, but the main thing that broke it up was the artillery fire. We were really hanging on quite honestly by the skin of our teeth and were really pretty insecure.[14]
>
> Lieutenant Russell Collins, 'A' Company

Then – at last – there came a very welcome message, one they had begun to give up hope of getting.

> My signaller was trying to receive a message on the radio from the intelligence officer and he couldn't make head or tail of it! He couldn't understand it! I took over the handset and the intelligence officer, 'Giff' Footer, was saying, 'Peter. Mike. For figures: 69, read 43!' Now it didn't mean anything to the signaller, but it did to me! All units, for convenience of identification of their vehicles, had a code number. The code number of our vehicles in the 16th DLI was 69; and the code number of the Divisional Recce Regiment was 43 and I knew that 'Peter. Mike.', is just of course p.m., in other words this evening. So, what he was saying to me was, 'This evening you're going to be relieved by the Recce Regiment.' So that was very good news indeed.[15]
>
> Lieutenant Russell Collins, 'A' Company

The 46th Reconnaissance Regiment was badly delayed and would only take over early next morning. Ronnie Elliott was delighted to see them, although he was in for a shock.

> The captain of the Recce troops came up and 'Winkler' Collins showed the position – and told him where to put his people. He came in to see us and said, 'Well, this is the signal terminal if you want to put your set in here!' The Recce officer said, 'I haven't got any signals yet!' I looked at Jackie Wells and he looked at me! 'Jesus Christ! We're gonna get landed here!' But 'Winkler' Collins said, 'Fair enough this set belongs to the DLI, so it was on the DLI network!' Therefore, he would have to take it with him – for which we were devoutly grateful. We pulled out of there as fast as we could go! I'd just about come to the end of my tether. I was nervous and on edge. Very hysterical at times. A bit distracted. I was conscious that I'd been pushed a wee bit too far. I'd had a couple of pretty bad experiences. This was about the culmination of it.[16]
>
> Private Ronald Elliott, 'D' Company

Collins was aware that the position he was handing over was by no means secure, but he knew his men could do no more. Nor in fact could he.

> I couldn't help feeling rather sorry for them because it was a rather precarious position. But you know we had gained it and we had hung on there. I showed them the position and the problems. I started pulling out some of my chaps, sending them back. I was the last one left, which is the right and proper thing. Then I set out and by then I was absolutely on my uppers – exhausted. I just staggered back down the hill on my own, wondering how I was going to get back to the rallying point, when along came a jeep. I recognised Harry Craggs, the battery commander of the battery that supported us. Dear Harry Craggs, he stopped and hauled me aboard, and so we got back to the rest area. I collapsed and slept the clock round, absolutely exhausted. Unfortunately, when I eventually came to, the first thing I was told was that the Recce Regiment had lost the feature. They'd been driven off soon after we'd handed over. They'd come to it, they hadn't got the feel of it, they hadn't a cat in hell's chance really, at night. It was very bad luck on them. Whether we would have been driven off if we'd stayed there, I don't know![17]
>
> Lieutenant Russell Collins, 'A' Company

As was so often the case, they had played a part in the bigger story, but never really saw how it ended. Small cogs in a big wheel, but they had played their part. After such a series of experiences they needed a rest, and on 29 September, the remnants of the 16th DLI were pulled back near the village of Verucchio. The rest periods tended to blur together for the men we interviewed. By their very nature, periods out of the line are not as important to the military historian. But to the men they were everything, this was their chance to finally relax, to recharge body and soul for the inevitable challenges that would lay ahead of them. And to find out what had happened to their friends.

> When you come out of the line, one of the first things you see a soldier do was make sure his mates in the platoon were safe. Then if he had friends in other platoons, he used to go and try to find out if they were alright! They kept a great bond amongst each other. I think it helped a lot.[18]
>
> Sergeant William Cowans, 'C' Company

It was such a relief to be free for a while from the fear of death and maiming, the responsibilities of command, of the physical burdens, of the necessity to kill or be killed. It was as if a great weight had been lifted from them.

> You were so relieved to be alive, that all you wanted to do was sit down and be happy, and sing, and plenty of local wine! You do absolutely nothing: just lie down. Sleep! I've come out and slept the clock round. Clean your clothes of course; clean your weapons. Just have a relaxing time. Tim Kelly would tell the same old jokes time and time again – always got a big laugh! Every man had a good feed. You had all the little kids round you, the little bairns from the village, wanting something to eat! 'Mangiare?' Kelly would get up and start his spiel, his patter! 'Silencio, bambinos!' He didn't know what he was talking about. That was his Italian! That's where I learnt to speak my first Italian, because we had the Union Jack army newspaper, and they had a little box with Italian phrases: 'How much is a bottle of wine?' 'How's your mother!' You learnt the basic words. It was easy to pick up.[19]
>
> Corporal Edward Grey, 'D' Company

There is no doubt that alcohol was a priority for the men. Something to dull the senses, allay their fears of what lay ahead, to blur away the pain of lost comrades. The local Italians were a common source of extra wine and spirits, although the quality was variable in the extreme.

> We were all right; we in the sergeants' mess got our ration of spirits – the men very seldom got any beer. The only time they got anything to drink really was if they got into a village and

> the inhabitants had a wine cellar. I've seen a chap in a place when we'd been at rest. The place was covered in mud. It had been lousy weather. We went into this little barn and there was a little Italian lad in a barrel – stamping! I said, 'What's that, what's he doing?' The Italian explained – he was pressing the grapes with his feet. We just turned the tap on, put a glass underneath it. It wasn't even fermented; it was just pure grape black grape juice, but they would drink it![20]
>
> Company Sergeant Major Leslie Thornton, 'C' Company

Women were also in demand – as was understandable for men in their position.

> They wanted a woman if they could – they were all human. They'd been in action and probably hadn't seen a woman for six months. Naturally – if they had the chance – they would. Half the company lined up for one woman![21]
>
> Company Sergeant Major Leslie Thornton, 'C' Company

The men had chance to write home, and to receive the letters from the home they craved. News from their families and friends, no matter how trivial, was essential to the maintenance of a man's morale; after all it was a reminder of what they were fighting for.

> Our battalion took notice of the people who hadn't any letters come regularly. They sent their names and addresses back to Britain to the YMCA for people to write to them. 'This soldier hasn't got any family. Can you give him a pen pal?' One chap, three times we came out of the line, and he never had a letter from home. Poor bugger! I really felt sorry for the man! I says to him, 'Are you not courting, not married?' He says, 'No! I found out me Mam had died before I came abroad!' I sent his name back. He came to me and says, 'I've got a letter from a girl! She's going to be a pen pal! Thanks – I've got somebody to write to now!' He was really pleased to get a letter from somebody.[22]
>
> Sergeant William Cowans, 'C' Company

Of course, human nature and sexual infidelity were not limited to men at the front; back home there were temptations and lapses for their wives and sweethearts. This led to a plethora of 'Dear John' letters from girlfriends or wives, informing the soldier that their relationship was over. The officers monitored the situation through their censorship duties, checking outgoing mail to ensure no military secrets were revealed.

> There were some heartrending stories of infidelity; quite a few pretty dreadful GI (American soldier) problems. What we saw was not the incoming mail, but the mail going back from the man to his wife. I used to give the parson a list of men that I could see were having, or were likely to have, severe trouble. He would make it his business to 'bump into them' and then develop a conversation, to see what could be done. In fact, he had contacts, and he did at times write to fellow vicars and curates and ask them to call round and see what the score was. But there were a lot of very sad cases. They used to get very depressed. When I saw what they were writing home, I used to make it my business to go down the lines of an evening and have a chat, 'How are things?' This and that and so forth. He knew I'd read his letters so he would tell me, and I would say, 'Well, are you sure it's as bad as that?' 'Yes,' he'd say, 'It's no good, it's all over!' And we'd talk about this. He'd say to me, 'Are you married?' I'd say, 'No!' 'Have you got a girlfriend?' 'Yes!' 'Is she alright?' I'd say, 'I don't know, I hope so!' Then I'd say, 'Have you had a word with the padre?' 'No!' 'I wonder if you'd do that – have a word with the padre – nothing to lose!'[23]
>
> Major Arthur Vizard, Headquarters Company

During rest periods, the officers would try their best to keep the men amused, with a variety of sports and games, designed to soak up the men's extra energy and take their minds of the next operation. They also had the regimental dance band.

> Out of the line, if we couldn't go anywhere, they used to always have the band, all the instruments in a wagon at headquarters. They used to send for it, bring it up and the

band lads got together. We'd say, 'Can we have a bit of music for the troops! Give them a bit of a lift. A bit of a singsong and whatnot!'[24]

Sergeant William Cowans, 'C' Company

One specialist came into his own in the rest periods. Truly, they also serve who dig and check latrines!

> We had a battalion sanitary man, a Lance Corporal Hall, who was responsible for the commanding officer's latrine and checking up on the latrines of the companies when we were out at rest. The CO came round inspecting one of these positions where we were at rest – and he sent for Lance Corporal Hall and said, 'Corporal, the men are not using the toilets! It's all in the hedgerows.' Lance Corporal Hall, being the man he was, said, 'Sir, I've inspected that. It does not belong to our men! It's Eyties!' After that we called him, 'The Connoisseur'![25]

Company Sergeant Major Leslie Thornton, 'C' Company

Of course, it was amusing, but sanitation was important, otherwise dysentery or other infections could spread like wildfire.

During the rest at Verucchio the battalion was substantially rebuilt, aided by the arrival of a draft of some 130 men from the 14th Sherwood Foresters who had been a lorried infantry unit in the 1st Armoured Division. This allowed a return to a three-company structure. A new group of replacement officers also arrived, the most significant of whom was Major Laurie Stringer, who was placed in command of 'B' Company. Stringer was the son of a farmer, who had worked in banking before joining the extended family business in Spitalfields market. He was called up as a private soldier in early 1940, but was soon identified as a potential officer and commissioned into the Essex Regiment in 1941. He specialised in battle drill training and became an instructor at the battle school at Barnard Castle. By 1943, he was a major and was posted to the Military Mission in Durban, South Africa, where he helped establish a battle school near Pretoria. By this time, he was razor keen to gain real battle experience to add to his years of theoretical training. When offered an active service posting he jumped at it.

> I said yes immediately! The desire to stop talking about war and having the opportunity to participate was so strong at that stage that I almost felt it was hypocritical to keep on talking without any experience. I saw this as an opportunity to get some battle experience. The battalion had just come out of the line in a fairly sort of tired and demoralised state. I wondered whether I would identify with the North Country soldier, and I can only say that I found I established a rapport with them very quickly. Simply by being interested in them, their welfare, and their personal lives. Trying to attend to their needs, complaints, requirements when it was necessary. Being fair in the administration of justice. One can never gain popularity as an officer by any other means, other than by personal examples. I think that is vital in every stage of military life, but none more so than when you're in action.[26]
>
> Major Laurie Stringer, 'B' Company

Although considered a somewhat conventional officer and a stickler for strict standards of appearance, most of his fellow officers and men seem to have had a high regard for Stringer. He may not have been tactically brilliant in the heat of battle, but he proved to be sound enough, and personally brave.

★

ONE OF THE MOST VIVIDLY RECALLED BATTLES fought by the 16th DLI took place on Balignano spur on the evening of 10 October 1944. All the worst battles seemed to start quietly, and at 14.45 on 9 October, the 16th DLI were ordered to move up from Verucchio to relieve the 2nd Hampshires of 128 Brigade on the recently captured Montilgallo spur. Surprise, surprise they were faced with yet another valley and ridge line. Next morning, Russell Collins was ordered to patrol forward to the village of La Crocetta lying beneath the Balignano spur.

> I'd taken a bit of a gamble in going across a rather open space in open formation. We had all our heavy weapons and when we were in the middle of this open space, the Germans opened up with artillery fire. It's an exceedingly terrifying thing to be lying there, just cringing on the ground, really hoping that the ground will open up – the shells are falling within feet all around. You just think, 'My God, the next one is going to land on me!' But somehow, miraculously, I don't think anybody was hit, there was a little lull in the firing and we got back under cover again. I had the greatest difficulty in persuading my chaps that we had to go on after that! My chaps were beginning to say 'Well, we're not going to go out there again!' I promised them we would go round a more secluded way. Which we did. We got up into La Crocetta. I didn't see any mine. We just carried on and got to our objective up in the village. We were shattered to hear later on that our company headquarters followed us up and poor old Ray Mitchell, the company commander, trod on one of these things and had his leg blown off. But the whole of my platoon had gone up the same track – so his number was on it and not mine.[27]
>
> Lieutenant Russell Collins, 'A' Company

Laurie Stringer and 'B' Company moved up into La Crocetta, but when another patrol was sent further forward up on to Balignano spur, they got a bloody nose, and it was then clear the Germans were there in strength. At this point Colonel Dennis Worrall arrived and assessed the situation.

> We had an 'O' Group and Dennis Worrall said to me, 'Laurie, I want your company to go into the attack at 19.00 hours. You will have artillery support, and you will be able to call for artillery support once the operation starts.' This was a company attack and I had supporting me a platoon from another company commanded by 'Winkler' Collins. He was one of the finest soldiers in the battalion, who'd already got a Military Cross. He was attached to me, because the feature I would have to attack was a very large one. It had to be a frontal attack, although I did ask Collins to go round on the right flank, whilst

my company went forward. You had a battalion 'O' Group, then you would have a company 'O' Group. I was going to attack with two platoons forward, and one platoon in reserve. 'H' hour was to start with a barrage at 19.00. The two platoons were to be divided by the sunken road. I was going to have a creeping barrage in front of me. I was between the two leading platoons, just a little bit back behind them, and Dick Hewlett and his platoon were behind me. I didn't have a FOO with me, but I was told he was at a vantage point and that if I wanted to call for fire, I could call for extra fire with a Very Pistol.[28]

Major Laurie Stringer, 'B' Company

Stringer ordered a newly arrived officer, Lieutenant Stanley Waymark, to take his platoon to the left, Sergeant Norman Reading would lead the right-hand platoon, while Lieutenant Dick Hewlett's platoon was held back in reserve. But Russell Collins was not happy to be thrown into action again so soon. By this time, he was beginning to show signs of 'wear and tear' from being constantly flung into the battle at the sharp end.

> We'd had a fairly taxing day, and then it was announced that 'B' Company was going to put in an attack on this Balignano spur, but they had to be reinforced by an additional platoon. And guess whose platoon was deputed to reinforce them? Mine! I felt that was really decidedly unfair and I thought Colonel Worrall had really presumed upon us a bit too much. I said so to the 'B' Company commander, Major Laurie Stringer. I protested and he upheld my protest. He went and complained to the colonel, but Colonel Worrall wouldn't hear of it and he said, 'No, his platoon has got to go!' When I told the lads that we were going to have to do this attack, there were groans all round, because we'd been the leading platoon all day – and there are nine or ten platoons in a battalion! Then one of the older soldiers in my platoon, a man called Corporal Vick, a very nice, quiet gentlemanly man, a section commander, took me on one side, and said, 'You know, Sir, I don't think I can go on, I've had enough. I don't think I can make it; we've had so much.' I said 'Well, I know the feeling, Corporal Vick, I feel just the

same, but I've also already represented to the CO that we ought to be relieved of this and they've said, "No we've got to do it, we can't let the side down now, we must go ahead!"' He said, 'Well, all right!' And so off we went.[29]

Lieutenant Russell Collins, 'A' Company

These men were tired, they had no wish to go forward yet again, but Collins and the phlegmatic Corporal Harry Vick could have stood for their whole generation. They couldn't let the side down; so off they went into the maelstrom again.

Laurie Stringer was with his headquarters section, behind the two leading platoons, as they all set off up Balignano Ridge. By now it was getting towards dusk.

> At 19.00 we fixed bayonets and started advancing. 'Winkler' Collins went off round to the right. We started going up the hill behind the barrage. It was pretty colossal; it was a pretty heavy barrage. It was moving, and we got to within about 20 to 25 yards of it. On the way up the hill, we took quite a lot of German prisoners. They came out of their slit trenches with their hands up. I remember feeling, 'Oh well, that's not too bad!' We took a substantial number of prisoners initially. They were an embarrassment, because you've only got one objective, and that is to get to the top of the hill and deal with the opposition there. But they had to be dealt with, so I told two or three men from Hewlett's platoon to round up the prisoners and take them back, get them out of the way. We had to carry on the action.[30]

Major Laurie Stringer, 'B' Company

Hewlett was close by Stringer, in fact too close for comfort given an unfortunate incident with his Thompson gun.

> I was towards the rear, in the middle, with Laurie Stringer. I had a Tommy gun and – guess what – it didn't work – in fact trying to make it work I very nearly shot Laurie Stringer early on. Tommy guns are very sensitive to mud, they're all right as long as the weather's good! We had had an enormous amount of rain. I chucked it away and got my pistol out.[31]

Lieutenant Richard Hewlett, 12 Platoon, 'B' Company

So far so good; but once they had pushed some 400 yards up the hill the German resistance began to increase. Like so many officers before him, Stringer found that he was too busy leading his men to feel much personal fear.

> We were under small arms fire and nebelwerfers. Terrifying, high trajectory mortars which the Germans had recently brought out. They made a whizzing, terrifying noise and their explosive fire was quite substantial. They were on the reverse slope, and they were coming right over. I say this with very, very great humility; when you are leading men in action, you cease to be concerned about yourself and you are worried solely about your men. To say that I wasn't frightened would be an exaggeration, no human being would like to be in that set of circumstances, but I didn't let it worry me, because I was concerned about managing the men that I had under command and trying to keep the casualty level as low as possible. The job had to be done and I was going to do it to the best of my ability. It looked to me that we were having success on the right-hand platoon, that was Sergeant Reading's platoon on the other side of the sunken road. Yet we were beginning to find the opposition stronger, and I called for more artillery fire with my Very pistol, firing the range coloured Very lights. Quite a heavy 'crunch' came down onto the top of the objective. It was splendid.[32]
>
> Major Laurie Stringer, 'B' Company

Meanwhile, Russell Collins had embarked upon his flanking attack. He was still upset, but doing his best, even though his experiences of battle thus far had made him sceptical of Colonel Worrall's plan of attack.

> A ghastly error was that a frontal attack was made on this spur. The company was set out in line to approach this on a broad front. It was a hopeless plan; it must have been the CO's plan. My platoon was put on the right flank. On the top of the crest was a church and all these other buildings along the street to the left. We set off on the due signal and made our way forward

and up around to the right, heading towards the church. There was a tremendous lot of shooting on the central part of the attack, but there was no direct opposition where we were, which was obviously the better line of approach. We should have gone for an objective like that at one end and then sweep through the village from one end to the other.[33]

Lieutenant Russell Collins, 'A' Company

Covered by the main attack, they proceeded undisturbed until they were almost up to the village of Balignano on the ridge spur. Collins then prepared his men for the final assault.

When we got within about 50 yards of the church I deployed some of the heavy weapons, the anti-tank projector (PIAT) – because that's quite good to give covering fire amongst buildings and machine gun positions. I sent one section, led by Corporal Vick, because he just happened to be in the right place, to lead the assault on the church and, if possible, to get in it. Everything went well, exactly according to plan, we were ready to move forward. The poor chap, Corporal Vick,[34] he got up there – whether it was the stress, and he just forgot his drill at that moment – instead of taking some precautions, a quick look round the door, throw a grenade in, to establish whether there was somebody in there before you go in – he just walked in the church door. I could see him. They were waiting for him inside and he was shot – that was the end of him.[35]

Lieutenant Russell Collins, 'A' Company

The main German defensive fire was still concentrated on 'B' Company as they struggled up the hill.

I couldn't see what Collins was doing, there was a lot of heavy undergrowth, and he was well away at the church end of the spur. Mine was more open, there were haystacks. I got up to them and I saw some Germans go into the haystacks and I fired into them. We made progress and I was feeling reasonably happy. Then from the left-hand platoon one of Waymark's men came to me and said, 'Mr Waymark has been hit, Sir!' 'Carry on, carry on, you can't do anything about it!' Seeing success on the right, I thought, 'Now one of the principles of war is that you reinforce success where you can and not failure. Well this is the time when I ought to launch my reserve platoon to support Sergeant Reading who had made initial progress on the right-hand side of the road.' So I got the message to Dick Hewlett and he went into action on the right-hand side.[36]

Major Laurie Stringer, 'B' Company

This was not quite how Richard Hewlett remembered the course of events, but it is near enough not to disturb the trajectory of our narrative.

There was a machine gun firing towards us from over on the right. Laurie Stringer said, 'For God's sake take your men and go and silence that machine gun!' He must have gone on – still on the track as far as I knew. We had to climb up out of the sunken road on to the hill. We were all running, hopefully in the right direction, perhaps slightly more to the right than we should have been. There didn't seem to be any way one could approach it absolutely direct – the only cover of any sort was on the right! I was hopefully making for these small trees and bushes and things – to get some sort of cover to get up the hill. I had difficulty in keeping my men together because there were vineyards on it with wires stretching out. People's small packs got caught in the wires and I was concentrating on trying to help them to disentangle them and get them in a state where they could be firing their weapons. This slowed the progress down but there was good deal of haste. As any infantry officer will tell you, the most difficult thing in the world is to get your men to fire back once they get fired on. One is inclined to sort of freeze up so that you can't do anything, but the only thing to do is to fire! It doesn't matter where you fire.[37]

Lieutenant Richard Hewlett, 'B' Company

Here was another officer, busy trying to give leadership and an example to his men, almost oblivious of personal risk. But the threat was always there; always ready to strike him down. And it did.

> It was whilst doing that that I got hit – it was like being hit by a double-decker bus. The weight of a bullet is unbelievable when it hits you, you can't shake it off. It hit solid bone, like a sledgehammer right through the knee joint. That was real agony, the leg bones were broken, and it was hanging off at the wrong angle, any move was agony – as you can probably imagine. I said, 'Don't leave me here – dump me down in the sunken ditch!' And they did. Appleby must have been one of them. But when we got to the ditch somebody had taken some prisoners. Appleby and two German prisoners were carrying me on this old shutter – that's what they put me on. It was then that mortar bombs started – and Appleby was hit – as were the two Germans prisoners carrying me. They dropped me immediately. Darkness was approaching. It got pitch dark – I was completely alone! I could hear Germans walking around looking for their own wounded and I thought, 'Oh my God, they're going to find me! I'm going to end up a prisoner of war unless I die from lack of blood first! What a way to end the war!' That was the awful depressing feeling I had. I was losing quite a lot of blood, lying to the right-hand side of this road.[38]
>
> Lieutenant Richard Hewlett, 'B' Company

With Hewlett down and out, other men had to take over the fight. Ken Lovell was one of those charged with taking out the machine gun that was causing so much trouble.

> We hit very heavy opposition and my platoon took a number of casualties including Lieutenant Hewlett. Another officer told me to take the remainder of the platoon to the other side of the sunken road and to try and work round from there. I led the chaps to go across the sunken road and I jumped down straight into a trench with three Germans in it. They got their hands up before I got mine up, so I took three prisoners. It was a machine gun post covering the advance up the sunken road, only 50 to 60 yards up the road, from the house where we were, but

it was concealed by a slight curve, and it was well dug in and couldn't be seen from the house. If we'd gone up the sunken road, because of the confined space, we'd have had very much heavier casualties.[39]

Corporal Ken Lovell, 'B' Company

The attack was almost successful; almost but not quite. Just as they seemed to have almost gained the summit of the ridge, the Germans struck back hard.

> By this time, we had got up fairly close to the crest of this feature, within 50 yards of the crest, when the enemy counterattacked from the reverse slope and from the left-hand side of the feature. They had a machine gun firing in enfilade, I was beginning to have a lot of casualties and the situation was beginning to look serious. The whole advance had been stopped and we were beginning to fall back. I could see we were having heavy casualties, so I gave the order to withdraw. To describe that situation now in cold blood is very difficult. It was pretty chaotic. I had actually got up to the top of the feature and [then] I came down the sunken road.[40]

Major Laurie Stringer, 'B' Company

On his way back, Laurie Stringer earned the undying gratitude of the abandoned Richard Hewlett.

> Some way down, I almost kicked someone, and I saw that it was Dick Hewlett. I stopped and I could see that part of his leg had been shot away. He was still conscious, and he said, 'Leave me, Sir, leave me, leave me, leave me!' I didn't leave him. I lifted him, I was strong then, I lifted him and put him over my shoulder and I shall never forget, the blood went right the way through my clothing, my vest and on to my body as well. The Germans weren't coming down towards us, but they were firing from the tops of the slope – a distance of about 50 to 60 yards. I carried him, he was screaming with pain, I carried him for about 50 yards and then he became too heavy. Fortunately, I happened to see my sergeant major and there was an old Italian

outhouse there, with a door. I put Dick Hewlett down on the ground and we lifted him on to this barn door, and we carried him back to the start line.⁴¹

Major Laurie Stringer, 'B' Company

It is not surprising that Richard Hewlett's version of events at this stage is fairly confused.

I don't know how long it was before Major Stringer and Company Sergeant Major Clarke came up. I might well have been unconscious. I can't remember if I said, 'Leave me!' Shock, I suppose. I must have been mad, if I said that! They had difficulty in carrying me because I was in such agony with any movement of my leg. They decided to tie my legs together with my own boot-laces, which was a very good idea, because it kept the whole thing more or less solid. The only thing I remember then is getting to a regimental aid post, where I was lying on a stretcher. With the best intentions in the world Padre Meek poured scalding hot tea all over me – as a blessing and a comfort! It was too hot; I couldn't swallow, and it went all down my front!⁴²

Lieutenant Richard Hewlett, 'B' Company

He was in a bad way, with a fractured femur and kneecap, which required several operations and blood transfusions, all complicated by the onset of dysentery that further ravaged his weakened body. His weight dropped from 12 stone to 7 stone and evacuation back to the UK was inevitable. He would be in hospital for the rest of the war.

Not far away from the helpless Hewlett, Ken Lovell found Roger Appleby, who had been badly wounded in the initial attempt to rescue Hewlett.

I found Private Appleby, who was Lieutenant Hewlett's batman. He was in a terrible state, he had a great big hole at the base of his neck, and he told me that he and a couple of others had got Lieutenant Hewlett on a door, using the door as a stretcher. Whilst they were carrying him down, a mortar bomb had dropped near them, and he'd been badly wounded. He didn't know what had happened to the others. He just wandered. I broke my field dressing out, stuffed his wound and did the best I could to staunch the blood, but it was almost impossible, it was such a gaping wound. There appeared to be nobody else on the left side of the sunken road. I had about four other men with me, so we decided to go back to the bottom of the hill and find out what was going on. We carried Appleby back, and as we got back to the house that we'd occupied, Sergeant Winterhausen, our pioneer sergeant came along. I said, 'Can you get Appleby back to the regimental aid post?' This was about a mile in the rear. He did, but Appleby[43] died virtually on the doorstep of the RAP.[44]

Corporal Ken Lovell, 'B' Company

Up to the right, Russell Collins was still up in the village, when it became obvious that the main attack had failed.

> There we were at the church; we hadn't actually taken it. I had to think of what to do. Suddenly, I became aware that everything was very quiet. I listened and looked to my left, and I couldn't see anything. I'd had no message over the 'blower', but it became apparent that the company had withdrawn, aborted the attack and all the rest gone home. I'd got no message and there I was with my solitary platoon on the edge of the village. We returned to the start line when we realised we were alone in the battle.[45]

Lieutenant Russell Collins, 'A' Company

It had been a sobering experience for Laurie Stringer, the theoretical tactical expert required to carry out an unsubtle frontal assault by Colonel Dennis Worrall.

> My company had been cut about quite a lot, twenty or thirty wounded and eight or nine killed. Sergeant Reading[46] died, Stanley Waymark[47] was killed, and Dick Hewlett was wounded. Collins actually got up into the church area. They eventually had to retire as well because of this German counterattack. I

think Russell thinks that if we'd handled it better, we might have got the feature the first time. He thinks we might have done the whole operation as a right flanking attack, rather than attacking from the front, then we might have had a greater degree of success – and he might well be right. I was very depressed, but I didn't let it influence my outward attitude too much, because I was still in control of these men. I had to get them together again; get them ready for the next battle.[48]

Major Laurie Stringer, 'B' Company

The painful saga came to an ignominious end when next day it was found that the Germans had retired from Balignano spur. Shortly after this, Russell Collins was posted to the Carrier Platoon, Support Company. Although they were fighting dismounted, without their Bren carriers, they still boasted an impressive augmented Bren gun firepower.

★

AFTER BALIGNANO, the 138 Brigade took over the lead role in the never-ending advance across the myriad ridges of Italy, pushing forward and up on to Monte Romano. Then, when 139 Brigade took over the lead role, the 16th DLI were held back as the brigade reserve, before moving forward to relieve the 2/5th Leicesters at Celincordia, which they reached early on the morning of 19 October. The battalion was then tasked by Brigadier Allen Block with the capture of Cesena, a fairly big town lying astride the Savio river, which was crossed by several bridges. As a first stage in the operation, Colonel Worrall ordered 'C' Company to capture the Abbey of Maria del Monte, a formidable looking building up on a hill overlooking the town. William Cowans was relieved that it proved to be easier than it looked.

> My company was told to take the monastery. There was very little fighting. I took my platoon into the monastery. I was amazed. The nuns came out this big door and opened it. They said, 'Tedeschi! [Germans!] Tedeschi!' We knew straight away there must have been some Germans left behind. There must

have been hundreds of kids and women. They were glad to see the British, 'English! English!' We had to try and quieten them down the best way we could. Trying to keep them back! The first German we saw came out of one of the rooms with his hands up. That was a good start! We went round the corner and there were these two Germans just sitting as though they were waiting for a bus! They weren't going to leave; they knew where they were best off![49]

Sergeant William Cowans, 'C' Company

Then it was on to Cesena as 'B' and 'C' Companies moved down the ridge to attack the town itself, assisted by the Sherman tanks of 'B' Squadron, 10th Hussars. Ronnie Elliott had been posted to the Signals Section with Headquarters Company, but for this operation he was required to liaise with the Shermans.

Cooperation between tanks and infantry wasn't particularly good, so they decided they should have a company signaller in a tank on the company network, to provide an immediate communication with the troops that were attacking. Because Jackie Wells and I were spare, we went into the tank on this attack on Cesena. We'd always thought that the tanks had this marvellous life because every evening they pulled back to some sort of reserved position and laager up, have food and get their heads down. We thought that was great, the poor infantry man tends to get stuck up where they were. I was in this tank and the communication side of it didn't work particularly well because communications were pretty bloody, but it didn't really matter because the battle went quite well. The tanks and the infantry cooperated by some form of hand signals. The part that really intrigued me was that I was more afraid inside the tank than I would have been outside the tank. You're more conscious of shot and shell inside a tank, the shrapnel pinged on the side – it made a noise. It was claustrophobic. It was noisy. You felt as though you were the focal point of any likely attack – and that you were vulnerable inside. Outside, you felt that you had a fair bit of room in which to be 'evasive'; but you felt specifically in the line of fire inside this 'tin can'. Although the infantry hadn't a great deal to commend it, I think on balance I preferred the infantry to a tank man's life!⁵⁰

Private Ronald Elliott, Headquarters Company

The attack developed with 'B' Company on the left, 'C' Company on the right. Laurie Stringer was with his headquarters section.

> In a lot of Italian towns, the houses are built right on to the road and there are no gardens on the side – the houses were cheek by jowl on to the road itself. We moved forwards under a certain amount of desultory machine gun fire from a distance. We were walking along, and the tanks were in the centre really. We were just slightly ahead of the tanks on either side. I was walking along by the side of the tank. I got to within 60 to 70 yards of the 'T' junction in Cesena itself, and suddenly, from the other side of the 'T' junction a Spandau opened up and fired on me and my chaps.⁵¹

Major Laurie Stringer, 'B' Company

Somewhere not too far away was William Cowan and his platoon. He too remembered a shocking moment when the Germans opened fire at close range.

> We had to join Major Stringer and his company. I went out with Lieutenant Brown and took four blokes up this narrow street. We heard a 'Click!' I shoved Brown out of the way and I got down! This Schmeisser fired. I could see the bullets going between my legs, the ricochets, hitting the ground! It's a good job I went down! The click of a German machine gun was handy! When I got to look at Lieutenant Brown, a bullet had caught his ankle. We passed the word back to the lads who were in the shops further up, that there was a machine gun at the far end.⁵²

Sergeant William Cowans, 'C' Company

With bullets splattering all around, Laurie Stringer had to come up with a plan of attack. He decided to lead the way.

> There were no gardens, so we were really sitting ducks. The tank commander saw what was happening – but I had got to within 25 to 30 yards of the 'T' junction. There was no cover on either side. I said, 'Follow me, sergeant major!' My idea was to run round into the main street, then get into the house through the front door – it was the only cover I could possibly get. Sergeant Major Clark,[53] instead of following me, he crouched up against the wall and stayed there – the Spandau picked him up and killed him without any trouble at all. Meanwhile the tank commander of the leading tank had seen what had happened and his cupola swung round, and he fired an HE shell at this house where this Spandau was firing from – and the whole of the house came down into the road. It was a fantastic thing. That finished that particular machine gun – it could have been two – because the fire was intensive. But there was a lot of machine gun fire coming from other directions at this stage.[54]
>
> Major Laurie Stringer, 'B' Company

Will machine gun bullets smashing into the walls all around him, Stringer had to get out of sight and under cover.

> I ran round, got into the main road, ran across the garden into the front of this house on the left-hand corner. If you go to the house today, you will see machine gun bullet holes all the way round the entrance to the house – how they didn't hit me I shall never know. I flung myself at the door and fortunately it gave way! When I got inside the house, I was met by ten screaming, hysterical women! Without being dramatic about it, imagine the situation! I was expecting a German counterattack at any moment and I had these women to deal with! They were absolutely hysterical. Just a little way down the passage there was a cellar of some kind, so I put my arms round all these women, and I pushed them down this cellar – there were stairs obviously! This all happened in the space of a few minutes. Some of my men got into the house and I stationed them round the windows, because I expected the Germans to counterattack. I couldn't move forward because there was so much machine gun fire outside.[55]
>
> Major Laurie Stringer, 'B' Company

Much of the fire was apparently coming from the high ground at Abbadesse to the south-west of the town, which controlled the approaches to the bridges spanning the Savio. Meanwhile, Les Thornton and 'C' Company had been slowly street fighting their way through Cesena.

> We were starting to clear up houses on the way where the Germans might be. Obviously, you're not going to rush straight in! You've got to take it easy – make sure there's no booby traps – they could be anywhere. The best thing to do was to throw a grenade in! If there was a booby trap it would go off with the shock of the grenade. Mostly they would come out, we didn't have a lot of trouble winkling them out. One was an old Wehrmacht soldier. When I say old, older than we were! He was an ordinary German soldier who obviously looked as though he didn't want to fight in a war. He got on his hands and knees and thought I was going to shoot him – and prayed. Another one was a younger chap who was very cocky. The usual, bombastic German, who started to give us a lot of patter that we didn't understand. On his back was one of our British soldier's gas capes. I took them up to hand them over to the major for onward transmission to prisoner of war camp. The major got hold of this gas cape and gave him a clout right across the face – and took it off him. He knew he'd got it off a dead British soldier.[56]
>
> Company Sergeant Major Leslie Thornton, 'C' Company

Although they made some progress into Cesena, for a while the situation was somewhat fraught and Stringer was hoping that he might get some relief from the Shermans. But the tank commanders had their own problems.

> The tanks happened to see a German Tiger tank covering that road – they were very vulnerable to the Tiger with their 88mm shells – so they couldn't come into the main road. The bridge over the Savio I was supposed to get to was still some way down the main road to the left. I reported to the CO. I had signallers with my company. I told him what the situation was, and I had instructions to stay for the while and that we were

going to be relieved. Then later to pull back slightly from the main road area. It was getting down towards dusk. Tanks can't stay in a built-up area during the darkness, because they're so subject to attack, so they had to withdraw to a laager. We had had a fairly strenuous day one way and another! I think it was at about ten o'clock I was called to the set and the CO said, 'You will maintain contact!' Which was devastating really because it meant that we weren't going to be relieved.[57]

Major Laurie Stringer, 'B' Company

In the end, he needn't have worried, as the Germans blew up the various bridges over the Savio as they withdrew overnight. In the aftermath of the final throes of fighting, Arthur Vizard witnessed an example of the fanatical nature of some of the Germans soldiers.

> There were some virulent troops. The medical officer moved up a forward regimental aid post and a mortally wounded corporal from the German 91st Light Regiment was brought into the RAP. He'd been blown up in one of the houses in Cesena. It was quite clear he wasn't going to last the distance to the clearing station. I lit a cigarette and bent down to put it between his lips – and he spat at me! This man was within minutes of death, and he wouldn't even take a cigarette from me. There were some like that. Most of them were perfectly normal people like ours; they just happened to be Germans instead of British.[58]

Major Arthur Vizard, Headquarters Company

Not all German soldiers would fight to the death; some were only too pleased to surrender, as Laurie Stringer would discover next day.

> I saw a barber's shop. We'd been fighting in the town twelve hours before that, and I happened to notice that this barber's shop was operating. I pushed the door open; I'd got my pistol at the ready and my chaps had got their Tommy guns. There in this barber shop was seven chairs, with seven people occupying

the chairs, with barber's robes round them. I walked round to the front, and I looked at the feet of these seven people – and I saw they were all wearing German army boots! Then it was really very funny. I said, 'Up!' Some of them had got lather over their faces, some were half-shaved, some had half haircuts. I got them all up, took off their white sheets and I marshalled them out and sent them back as prisoners of war. Their war was over! It made Eighth Army News because the paper said, 'Durham major captures seven prisoners in a barber's shop!' My men were quite delighted.[59]

Major Laurie Stringer, 'B' Company

He was also touched at the reception they got from the Italian civilians, who treated the 16th DLI as liberators.

This was the first big town the division had captured. The welcome given to the battalion by the joyous population was one of tremendous enthusiasm. Women and children clapped and shouted and even flung their arms around the necks of the troops. Partisans paraded the streets proudly displaying their armbands. The older folks were rather more subdued but showed their gratitude by placing bunches of flowers on the bodies of those who had given their lives in effecting the relief of the town. In the main square lay shattered busts of Mussolini which had been thrown from the windows of the Fascist headquarters. This was a great day for the Durhams and for the people they had liberated.[60]

Major Laurie Stringer, 'B' Company

In all they managed to take seventy-three prisoners.

There was good news coming for the men of the 16th DLI: the 46th Division was being relieved by the 4th Division and was going back for a well-earned period of rest and recuperation. On 21 October, the battalion left Cesena and moved back to the small town of Montefiore, quite near the scene of the Gemmano fighting. Bill Virr recalled at how shocked he was when he saw the state they had been reduced to.

> I was there when they came out of the line. That was the time when I realised what we actually looked like after we'd been in action. It was the only time I'd not been in with them myself! Their faces looked ashen and drawn. You don't realise when you're in yourself – it shocked me did that![61]
>
> Sergeant William Virr, 'B' Company

This would prove to be a proper rest, with a mixture of concert parties, film shows, dances, showers, but above all, no necessity to fight their way up to kill Germans high on the next ridge. But their morale was fraying at the edges: how much longer could this go on?

14

COULD *YOU* HAVE COPED?

> I shall live for today and to hell with tomorrow! That was given to me by a soldier at Brancepeth – Sergeant Dalton. I can't see anybody living for tomorrow when they didn't know what was going to happen tomorrow! Especially where we were![1]
>
> Sergeant William Cowans, 'C' Company

MEN NEED GOOD LEADERSHIP IN BATTLE at every level of the command chain. The Durhams generally considered themselves fortunate in their officers. It wasn't just a matter of them being popular, but they wanted them to have tactical acumen, and the guts to stand up for them when their lives were unnecessarily put at risk.

> What makes a good officer? Not to panic! That was the main thing, not to show that he was worried. That's the worst thing that could happen. Pat Casey was a chap like that. He looked after his men. You can't explain it in a lot of words, but you can tell when you've got a good efficient officer who knows what he's doing – a man that can turn around and tell the CO that he cannot take this position until he gets what he wants. A good officer can tell a higher rank that it cannot be done unless he has smoke laid down, or a tank in support or mortar support. That is not going bald-headed into a position.[2]
>
> Company Sergeant Major Leslie Thornton, 'C' Company

Preston's successor, Lieutenant Colonel Dennis Worrall, was

not as universally admired, but he still had the respect of most of his men. But some of the other officers were little more than boys, with insufficient military skills to guide them in moments of extreme tension.

> New lieutenants came in fresh from England as reinforcements, quite young, without any experience, they went right to the front of the battle in charge of platoons. Until they had learned their trade, they were dependent upon their NCOs – the people that were carrying them were the platoon sergeants. Some of the officers were very good, learned a trade and did very well, others were not up to it. If you were good as a platoon commander, before very long they would take you and make you a company commander. But quite often they were killed or captured – the turnover was quite horrific. You were very much dependent on the quality of your NCOs. They often lasted longer being more experienced and provided continuity to a greater extent than the officers.[3]
>
> Private Ronald Elliott, 'D' Company

The NCOs knew the importance of their role in and out of action. The two were intrinsically linked as the men were far more likely to follow a popular and competent NCO who looked after them out of the line.

> You were responsible for the wellbeing of the lads. We always said, that when you were in action with blokes, you would have been in a right pickle if you'd come too much of the heavy hand with them. If you'd been on a patrol and things got sticky, they would have left you, but if you were all right with the lads, they were all right with you. I seem to keep my nerve, thank God, but I think that when you're an NCO, you kept your nerve because you didn't like to show it. Nobody can say that they're never frightened – I wouldn't believe anybody that told me that they were never frightened! You did things automatically, but at the same time you were always a little bit afraid inside.[4]
>
> Corporal Tom Turnbull, 'B' Company

Every time any soldiers went into action, they knew that some men would die, they just hoped it wouldn't be them, or their pals. In Italy there seemed to be a never-ending sequence of attacks. This took a real toll as men were gradually ground down.

> The word went round the battalion that the officers had been called to an 'O' Group. Then you could feel people tensing up. The word would come back, 'We're moving up tomorrow morning, back into the line!' Then you could see the people were no longer steady – what I noticed in the eyes – they couldn't look you in the eye. A sense of silence came over the company. Hi-jinks and horseplay seemed to cease. The whole thing seemed to quieten down. People were wrapped up in their own thoughts about what they felt; how they were coping. As people were going through these abnormal experiences, their resistance was being diminished as time went on.[5]
>
> Private Leslie Brown, 'B' Company

The last few hours before they went into action were a real test of their courage.

> Everybody was nervous until they got under fire. The time before was the worst. They'd say, 'Look here, you're going in at eleven o'clock tonight!' Well, those four hours were the worst four hours! Everything went through your mind. The loss of a limb was the main thing. We all had a dread of that. Everybody said they'd rather go straight out. That was the worst part of it. The waiting. Once you were under fire it just left you, it was just self-preservation. I would rather they just came to us at five minutes to eleven o'clock, saying, 'Right, you're going in, lads!'[6]
>
> Private James Corr, 'B' Company

Men reacted in a hundred different ways to the news of an imminent attack. Ronald Elliott thought a lot about his own personal reactions, trying to work out what kept him going when every prospect seemed bleak.

> Not bravery, not even fear of a court martial. More the fear of a loss of self-respect; that you think that you're a man – that you ought to be able to do this sort of thing. And then you'd be less than a man to yourself if you didn't. You didn't think of 'King or Country' or anything like that. It was also respect for your mates that were with you. You were supporting one another. You did it for them. You did it perhaps sometimes for an officer for whom you had a high regard. He was doing it – he was there with you. You were part of it; you were supporting him. One reason not many officers were shell-shocked was that it was useful to have some responsibility, if you had responsibility for others, this gave you an extra determination, not to let them down, or yourself down.[7]
>
> Private Ronald Elliott, 'D' Company

They had a collective responsibility to go forward together – all of them. But what happened when individuals cracked or simply refused could be a brutal business, as James Corr revealed.

> I went to Major Casey with a despatch, and he was in this little room in a farmhouse. 'Right!' I gave him his despatch and he said, 'I'll only be a second, stand there!' Then he says to this lad, 'You're going into action! I'm telling you. Never mind you're feeling bad, you're going in!' And he started whipping him across the face; started hitting him! The lad straightened up, 'All right, Sir! All right! I'll go in, I'll go in!' Casey said to me, 'What's your name?' 'Corr, Sir!' He wrote it down, 'What Company?' '"B" Company!' 'Right, you'll be wanted as a witness!' I thought he was going to charge the lad. I couldn't say nowt. 'Right, Sir!' About a fortnight, three weeks later, Casey sent for me, 'Yes, Sir!' He says, 'You remember the incident? Well, I put myself on a charge, but the private has not pressed charges. He says he was in the wrong, I was right to do it, and he thanks me very much because he's a good soldier again!'[8]
>
> Private James Corr, 'B' Company

Major Casey clearly realised his conduct was close to the edge, but on this occasion at least, it seemed to have worked.

The Durhams knew they would be facing an intimidating opposition.

> We all respected the Germans as marvellous fighting men. There were the elite ones – and some of them were bastards like the SS! But the ordinary German soldier was someone like ourselves; in that he was having to do the job. A war situation is rather like a triangle. With some poor individual at the very point of that triangle, right at the forefront of the battle. And behind them is all the backup: all these base people, and all the generals, who are all pushing this poor bugger forward in fear and trembling – he's the one that's going into action. And the same is true of the other side. At the points, although they have to fight one another, they have a lot more in common. They have a lot of respect for one another. They are both people put into a position of having to fight each other because of pressure from behind. In a sense, we detested rather more the hierarchy of the army establishment that were pushing us forward than we did our immediate enemy.[9]
>
> Private Ronald Elliott, 'D' Company

Elliott himself was a signaller and as such was a specialist responsible for keeping open the lines of communication during any battle, while others around them did most of the fighting.

> We would keep them in touch, providing the communications which were absolutely essential. There were three signallers, usually, in a company. You had to carry the 18 set, which was quite heavy, 30 to 40 pounds. You had to have the aerial out, which stuck up about 5 feet, and walking along through vineyards with an aerial really was quite impossible at times! We had to carry two spare batteries, which were big thick things – like bricks – and some spare equipment like headsets. Together with all of our usual equipment, although there was a concession that whoever was carrying the 18 set usually didn't have his personal weapon. We would have one Tommy gun man and a rifle amongst the three of us. In theory, we used to take it in turns carrying the set, then someone behind plugged

into him with a headset on, and then the other fella would be protecting them. Quite often the person carrying the set had the headset on as well. In the signals, we believed ourselves to be 'non-combatants'; we saw ourselves as providing a service to the company. There was a tacit agreement that the signals didn't do very much in actual fighting, unless things were quite desperate.[10]

Private Ronald Elliott, 'D' Company

Wireless sets were not reliable in 1944, but it was all they had in the early stages of an action. The signallers had to 'tune in' to a network, just as people used to tune in to a radio station in the days before pre-sets.

At the beginning of an operation usually you were given a wavelength on which you would all operate. That was known as a network. Someone from battalion headquarters would at any given time send out a call signal, which usually meant pressing the button on the side of the microphone, and you tune your radio in to that. Then you called up, 'Able Company reporting, over!' They will report hearing you loud and clear. Then you would go through the whole of the network. Whenever you called up after that, you were 'Able Company' or 'Baker Company' or 'Charlie Company' or whatever. You were given instructions of the call signs and code words for particular places that you were going to attack. Against which you might want to draw down artillery fire, when it was quite critical. Reception was mostly pretty bloody – that didn't work terribly well. You were working in difficult conditions, in mountainous areas. Our range was very small anyway. Even in a very flat situation, I think about 5 miles would be about our limit. If you settled down to a semi-permanent site, you would put in a cable and telephone sets. We were always very unhappy about laying cable because the cables got churned up by tanks and shot apart by mortars, shells and so forth. It really was quite a hectic job going along the line and repairing it.[11]

Private Ronald Elliott, 'D' Company

The pioneers were in another category of specialist personnel. They had many different roles, but one dangerous task was the requirement to clear mines. The Germans had many different types of anti-personnel mines, which they would scatter liberally behind them as they retreated.

> They had a thing we called 'The Debollocker': a small pipe about 9 inches long. They put it in the ground, unscrewed the barrel and put a bullet in, screwed the barrel back on. It was on a small platform; they put it in the ground at an angle. When you stood on it the bullet fired, up your leg – and that was why it was called 'The Debollocker!' And the 'schu' mine. It was a little wooden mine and when you stood on it, it blew your foot off – sometimes both feet! When anybody had their foot blown off, they knew there were mines there; they sent for the pioneers! And the stretcher bearers of course! You took the appropriate action. You used the bayonet, just scratch the ground, took the surface away – gently! Very, very gently! We had a mine detector – but it meant you couldn't carry a weapon – it was heavy, and you had the batteries too. Anti-tank mines were comparatively easy. The Germans were very particular about how they laid their mines – in alternate rows – every fourth one was booby trapped! You could walk on anti-tank mines easy! I've seen motorbikes go over them! We had hundreds of Teller mines. We used to pull them up, from a safe place, just take the detonators out and that was it! They were easy to handle.[12]
>
> Sergeant Edward Grey, Pioneer Platoon, Headquarters Company

Anti-personnel mines caused real mental anguish as the pioneers could not clear them all. Sometimes they were in clearly defined minefields with barbed wire and warning signs. But more often they were not. Doug Tiffin found himself in a terrible situation.

> We found ourselves in a minefield. Goodness knows how we got there! All round us except for the way we'd come in. We hadn't suffered any casualties. Now we had to get out, so we had to go back the way we came in – that's not to say that

we'd laid a white line or anything. If they were the heavier
tank mines, they may not have exploded, but these places
were full of 'schu' mines. It was simply a case of retracing our
steps a couple of hundred yards through this minefield. We
walked back in single file and 'Muggins' went first! That was
my job, everybody expected me to, apart from anything else!
And that was one of the most terrifying experiences that I can
remember. We'd walked into the thing, but once you knew
you were in a minefield that was a different matter. As they
say, 'We proceeded cautiously back!' Fortunately, without any
casualties.[13]

2nd Lieutenant Douglas Tiffin, 'D' Company

Some of the men were trained in the PIAT anti-tank weapon.
It was effective, but it had many disadvantages that rendered it
unpopular.

> The PIAT was horrible! It took you all your time to load it for
> a start off. It had a compression spring – it must have been 6
> inches across. I don't know how thick it was, must have been a
> half inch! You had to have a strong back to cock it! You had to
> put your feet on the shoulder pad, get hold of the guard, twist
> it, and you pull it – like being on a rowing machine – until it
> clicked. When you fired it, it knocked you back about a yard!
> It was supposed to re-cock itself if you held it properly. If you
> didn't hold it tight, it didn't re-cock itself, and then of course it
> was too late. You couldn't stand up to load it if there was a tank
> coming on you! Nobody cared much for them – plus there were
> the bombs to carry about. The bomb itself was OK if you hit
> the tank square on. Later on, it was improved and had a 'graze'
> fuse which meant you could hit the tank a glancing blow and it
> would still explode, whereas before it could skim off. We did a
> few practice firings at a knocked-out tank and saw the results –
> only a small hole, but of course it went into the turret and all
> those bits of steel were flying about the turret.[14]

Lance Corporal William Virr, 'B' Company

Lionel Dodd was an officer with the Mortar Platoon which was equipped with 3-inch mortars. He had worked in farming before call up and after service with the Royal West Surrey Regiment had been posted to the 16th DLI back in March 1943.

> I never thought that the Mortar Platoon was used to the best advantage. We could have been used a lot more. That was because we didn't get the orders; the CO had his priorities and the mortars weren't one of them. We could have supported the infantry. The effective range was about 1,700 yards. We had 'Charge One' up to a 1,000 yards; and 'Charge Two', up to 1,700. We used to range on a target, you got your compass bearing, and you lined it up. You fired a ranging shot and you observed where the shot went. If it was short, you used to say, 'Up, 100!' If it had overshot the target, 'Down, 100!' And, 'Left one degree!' or, 'Right one degree!' That's how you did it.[15]
>
> Lieutenant Lionel Dodd, Mortar Platoon, Support Company

There were also some 2-inch mortars which came in handy at times.

> That was OK, although we used it mainly for laying smoke. We did have high explosives. If you were putting a small attack in you could put a bit of a smoke screen down with it. Although you were restricted with the number of bombs you carried. You used to carry a pack of cardboard tubes with a handle on the top. Perhaps six bombs. When you'd fired those, that was it until you got some more bombs from somewhere![16]
>
> Lance Corporal William Virr, 'B' Company

There were a few specialist snipers, trained marksman who were charged with dealing with their German opposite numbers.

> The company sniper would be with company headquarters. If at any time a section or platoon was held up by somebody holed up, then they would inform the company commander. I would say to the sniper, 'Right, I'm going to take you round to see what the position is!' I would try and locate this 'obstacle'. If you could – fair enough – then I'd say, 'Right ho!' Because he would have his telescope on his rifle, and he would see it better.

If he could dispose of this 'obstruction', as we liked to call it, then he would carry on and do it. After that, I would take him back to company headquarters again. The one I had was called Rattigan, a north country lad.[17]

Company Sergeant Major Leslie Thornton, 'C' Company

Very little could help them if there was a devastating burst of machine gun fire from a concealed position – a terrible surprise.

I saw a fellow hit by burst of bullets. He caught a full burst in his body; there were bits of tissue flying all over the bloody place. It wasn't like seeing somebody lying dead. I didn't know where to go or what to do, and somebody shouted, 'Come here!' And I went and laid down behind a wall – lying down taking cover. The riflemen from another section silenced this bloke [firing at us]. Anyway, I got through it all right. After the first time things do become – I couldn't say easier – but you become more attuned to it.[18]

Corporal Edward Grey, 'D' Company

But even in a life or death situation, when actually under machine gun fire a soldier's sense of humour could still sometimes prevail.

We were advancing as a company along the edge of this wall and the Germans had a fixed machine gun firing along the top of the wall. I had this set with the big aerial. We all bobbed down behind the wall as best we could. Then the bloke in front of me farted! Now, I really didn't know what to do: whether to stay down and be gassed because the stench was absolutely horrible, or stand up and be shot to death![19]

Private Ronald Elliott, 'D' Company

Although the fire was rarely as concentrated as that which their fathers and uncles had braved in the Great War some twenty years before, it was still a lethally dangerous business – for both sides.

> A patrol had found a strongpoint at a junction of fields – a couple of hedges and a track in between, ending in a sort of copse, with a hill rising away above it. At the corner of this track there was a bunker which had been used by the Germans, covered over with railway sleepers and things like that. This had been found to be unoccupied and we had to go through and occupy it! As we passed through there were some German dead around. I was a bit surprised that these 'Glorious Dead' just looked like bundles of old rags. I thought how dreadful that was. We got to this corner of the field and the main group went into this copse. Bill Wade went down into the bunker with the company commander, and Fitz and I were outside. We started digging in. As it got dark – suddenly, you looked up – there were German helmets coming along the other side of the track. All hell let loose![20]
>
> Private Leslie Brown, 'B' Company

The exchange of fire let the Germans know exactly where they were. What followed was almost inevitable as the German mortars and nebelwerfers opened up. The distinctive wailing sound would long haunt the memories of veterans.

> For the rest of that night, it was mortars and machine guns. Screams of, 'Stretcher bearers!' from this copse. Fitz and I were furiously digging in at the back of one of the hedges. That went on all night. That was my first meeting with the nebelwerfers – they had a horrible noise when they were mounting up. You knew when you heard that noise, in a matter of seconds there'd be mortars. In the morning, when it got light, there was this line of trenches that we were digging, and it seemed just about a yard behind the slit trenches there was a row of mortar holes. I don't think training can prepare you – as a rule. Being new to it maybe helped! Because I think as time goes on you build up these experiences. Courage is possibly expendable, and you get tired and more fearful as time goes on. I can't remember being terribly frightened – but I was frightened – and I was certainly digging like mad to get as far down as possible. It's no use saying you weren't frightened at all! I think what's more

frightening is that you cannot do anything about it – you're just stuck there and you're being shot at.[21]

Private Leslie Brown, 'B' Company

When the Germans had pinpointed a defensive position, the prospects were bleak.

> Jerry brought his mortars down on us! I've never been under shellfire like it before – or after. He tossed everything at us that afternoon. We had a string of blokes went shell-shocked – just lost their nerve – they were crying, then laughing, crying one minute, laughing the other. Just babyish. I felt terrible, but I got through it. We just had to crouch down in the slit trench, because there was nothing else you could do. It was just pouring down. One time, there was two of us in the slit trench and one shell fell that close to the bank side that it nearly covered us up! We just sat in the bottom of the slit trench and waited till it quietened down. It was just going through your mind, 'When am I going to get out of this? Is the next one going to come down here?' Our CO, or the company commander, had the presence of mind, as soon as the dark came in, he moved us about 300 yards further into the wood. And believe me the next morning the Germans brayed hell out of the positions where we'd been before. So, we were lucky we'd left there![22]

Corporal Tom Turnbull, 'B' Company

Artillery fire could reach out all across the battlefield, with shells hurtling back even as far as the company and battalion headquarters.

> We were in the cellars; they knew we were there because they were shelling it. Nobody likes it! 'Well, we'd better get out of the road – or we'll get hurt!' If you heard the whistle of a shell, you knew it wasn't for you! Because it had gone past! If a shell bounced near you, you didn't hear it – you never hear the shell that kills you! The sound hasn't reached you.[23]

Company Sergeant Major Leslie Thornton, Support Company

It seems strange but life had to go on, even when under fire. Men had to eat, drink and sleep – against all the odds. Eric Murray had a close escape due to the British soldier's eternal obsession with his tea break.

> We went into this village on the hillside. Anyhow we got bloody shelled. There were hens running around! I got into where the houses were. It was like our ten o'clock break, so we were making a cup of tea! We came out and had the cup of tea. We were [still] getting shelled and when we went back into that house – a shell had gone straight through the window and blown all the floor out. I thought, 'Bloody hell! We've been lucky there!'[24]
>
> Private Eric Murray, 'B' Company

And shellfire was no respecter of even the most private bodily functions, as Les Thornton almost found to his cost.

> We were in this position where we were being heavily shelled with mortars and artillery. Naturally, we wanted to go to the toilet sometime and there was no toilet around! The shelling died down and I decided to go outside near a tree to do what I wanted to do. Well, I got my trousers down and started – and so did the Germans! There I was, lying flat on my stomach with my behind facing the sky and I daren't move. I had to remain there until the shelling ceased. Then I finished what I was doing and went back to my company headquarters. It's a laughable thing now, but it was serious then![25]
>
> Company Sergeant Major Leslie Thornton, 'C' Company

Although at times they felt helpless when under heavy fire, the Durhams did have some loyal support and the ability to strike back at their tormentors by means of the 25-pounder guns of 449 Battery, 70th Field Regiment, Royal Artillery.

> We became so integrated with them it was almost as if we were in the same unit. We knew them all extremely well, personally, and I think that's why it worked so well. They were brilliant. There was a regiment supporting each brigade and a battery

supporting each battalion. In the division there were three field regiments and probably a medium regiment as well. They would all register, so they could lay on a particular target at a moment's notice. If they were divisional targets, they had the letter 'U', the phonetic name for 'U' then was 'Uncle', so they were 'Uncle' targets. If you had a concentration down on 'Uncle' target, my goodness, you knew nothing moved in that area.[26]

Lieutenant Russell Collins, 'A' Company

The gunners and the infantry worked together as best they could, with the gunners aware that if they failed to hit the targets, then their own infantry would die. But the front-line troops had to help them in locating their targets. Collins long remembered an initially unsuccessful shoot, which ended in a triumph of good fortune.

> The forward observation officer couldn't be everywhere and they might not be able to see a particular target. If we had identified a target and thought that artillery support was suitable, we would communicate it by radio – we gave our own position and the compass bearing to the target – and the estimated range. They know where their guns are, and they had all the maps and the ability to compute and convert from one set of references to another – the range and bearing from their guns. They would then put down a round of fire and it may be eight or ten seconds before the shell arrived and then you heard a crump in the distance – you looked around and you couldn't see it, or it might have been quite close. In that very, very difficult and close country, the gunners felt that we weren't always terribly sure where we were, because the maps weren't perfect, they weren't like ordnance survey maps. It was a matter of speculation to a degree. So they had to play safe; they had to make quite sure that they didn't drop the shell on you because you'd miscalculated where you were! A particular incidence of this was when I could see quite distinctly through my binoculars an enemy machine gun post under a tree about 400 yards away. I asked for artillery support. Well, the gunners

> wouldn't have it that I knew where I was – but I thought I did! The first shell they dropped was absolutely nowhere in sight. I said, 'Well, you'd better try again!' They tried again and got one closer. Now the drill is, once you see a shell, then, taking the axis of the observer – one's self – to the target then, in relation to that, you say, 'Go right, 200 yards, go up 100 yards!' And of course it was a total fluke, rather like a hole in one at golf, but the next shell fell slap on the machine gunner under the tree. Of course, the gunners were delighted and so was I – but it was a pure fluke![27]
>
> Lieutenant Russell Collins, 'A' Company

In the course of the fighting, prisoners were often taken. The circumstances varied from cases of outright heroism, to the rather more farcical, as Bill Virr discovered.

> We didn't see many Germans. The following morning it was daylight and we all gathered at the church at the far end of the village. The village main street was a pile of rubble really. I was taken short and all I could do was go back up the street – there was nobody there – and squat down in this rubble. I was squatting down, this door opened, and two Germans came out and put their hands up! I've never felt so silly in my entire life, pulling my trousers up and trying to sound authoritative! One of them had a pistol and gave it to me. I was trying to fasten my trousers up at the same time![28]
>
> Corporal William Virr, 'B' Company

Far less amusing were the cases where Germans had caused significant casualties to the Durhams before trying to surrender. In the heat of battle, with feeling red raw at the loss of friends and comrades, there were regrettably occasions where not many prisoners would be taken. Edward Grey put it succinctly.

> If you'd lost your best friend, it's no good some bugger putting his hands up, you have to kill them.[29]
>
> Corporal Edward Grey, 'D' Company

If an attack succeeded, with the German opposition for the moment stifled or crushed, then consolidation was all important, especially given the known German propensity to counterattack. This is where all the training invested in young officers like Russell Collins paid dividends.

> The most important thing is the security of your own defended locality. You're responsible for deciding where the most likely threat is and setting up your weapons – light machine guns and so on. Then deciding what regime of sentry guard you wanted. You just get a sense about it – I mean I was never attacked and overrun in all that time. It's really just a question of having a sense of how to set up these interlocking arcs that are mutually supporting and then having a good, responsible regime of keeping people on the alert all the time. I would give orders as to what the strength of the sentry guard was to be – whether or not there would be two men awake at a time, or half a section, or whether the whole section would stand-to. We always manned the machine gun. Whoever was on sentry would move into the position where the machine gun was, and the others would be resting. We always had a stand-to drill at dusk and dawn, everybody stood to their posts with their weapons. Those were theoretically the most likely times for an attack. You had to make sure that you gave people enough rest, otherwise they would fall asleep at their post, and of course that's hopeless. Mark you, chaps who fell asleep got a pretty severe rocket, but they weren't shot any more. I mean you couldn't do that because people are only flesh and blood after all. But some people were more slack than others and they had to be made aware of their responsibilities. I was very strict about checking on them. You just can't leave it to chance.[30]
>
> Lieutenant Russell Collins, 'A' Company

When a battle was finally over, there was time to think, to try and process what had happened, to try and regain some sort of mental balance. Such mind-blowing visceral experiences were not easy to forget. Especially when they knew that they would soon be undergoing the same trials again, and again, and again.

Sometimes there was just a trickle of casualties, but men could see the chance of death or serious injury getting statistically closer.

> People got whittled away – your platoon got whittled away without any particular action. A couple of casualties whilst being shelled or mortared; two or three blokes standing on a 'schu' mine moving through a field. A lad on my left screaming out – he'd stood on a 'schu' mine. People were always frightened of getting their balls blown off. This was this fellow's main shriek, 'How's me balls? Oh God!' He was all right as it happened, he was badly cut in the lower thigh. They were nasty things. A fellow used to drop off here and there, no serious casualties, but fellows with shrapnel wounds. Even in two or three days you lost four or five men.[31]
>
> 2nd Lieutenant Douglas Tiffin, 'D' Company

Those that remained could not help but fear for their future. Over time it got worse; very few men got 'used to it'. A gut-clenching raw primeval fear took all their self-control to conceal. And of course, they had good reason to be frightened.

> One was just afraid; one was afraid all the time. Fear in that context is not just a mental thing; it's a physical thing. You really have almost like indigestion or someone gnawing at your insides all the time that you're in action, because of fear – or even the thought of going to action. This is what you have to live with. That really is what is the quintessence of bravery. Not doing something remarkable at any one time, but continually having to go in. Because you're continually being pushed into action. People are killed; your friends are killed. And it's a state of attrition. Eventually, it will be you that will be killed. The sheer inevitably of it all, this is the thing that gets you, and then ultimately, comes a point where you can't go on anymore.[32]
>
> Private Ronald Elliott, 'D' Company

Men became miserable, or more accurately clinically depressed. Doubtful as to whether they could go on. With danger all around them, men resorted to religion or superstitions, making 'bargains' to try and forestall their fate.

> I was on the point myself, when you felt yourself giving in, losing it. I suppose everybody else felt the same at various times. Anybody that didn't must have been made of stone. You had to get a grip of yourself. Partly it was the fear of showing yourself up. In my case I thought of what my father would think about me. He went through the First World War, and I thought, 'What a disgrace it would be!' It helped pull you together. I had a New Testament that my aunt sent me, and I used to open that at any page and read whatever it said and try to apply it to the position I was in! When we were going into the line, I used to tie my bootlaces into about twelve knots. I thought, 'Well, if I come out all right, I won't mind untying all those knots! And if I don't, it doesn't matter.' Silly things like that. To try and boost your own morale![33]
>
> Corporal William Virr, 'B' Company

The officers and NCOs would be constantly monitoring the state of their platoon, working out how individuals were coping.

> As I got to know them better, there would be ten, eleven or twelve people that you could rely on in any circumstances. There would be another ten, eleven or twelve who if everybody else was doing their duty could be relied on to follow suit. Then there was five or six that were not particularly reliable.[34]
>
> 2nd Lieutenant Douglas Tiffin, 'A' Company

But morale was not a static business; even the bravest would crumble over time, or after a particularly bad experience. People would note the change in a man's overall demeanour, as they approached the brink.

> You could tell if a bloke was 'going'. He kept asking, 'How long are we going to stick in this part? Are we going to go in the line shortly? Are we going to be pulled back?' You knew then he was getting on the verge. Somebody would say, 'What's happened to Private So-and-So? He hasn't come back!' 'No, he's been sent

to an institution. He's gone crackers! Gone bomb happy!' It was forgotten then.[35]

Sergeant William Cowans, 'C' Company

The medical officer had to deal with many of the cases reported to him. He tried his best.

> A large number complained of 'nerves'. Some reported sick just before a battle, or attended with trivial complaints. There were many cases of 'physical exhaustion', some were genuinely 'bomb happy', others one couldn't be sure whether they were genuine or not. In such cases the medical officer was the last chance of an honourable escape from their 'difficulties'. However, we were able to sort these men out and I think we were pretty fair to them all. Bomb happy cases exhibited gross tremor of the hands, arms and legs, and often of the whole body. They gave little if any response to proffered help. These cases were seen by psychiatrists, and most were downgraded and given posts in base units.[36]

Captain Huw Jones, Royal Army Medical Corps

In many cases, no one doubted the courage of individuals that fell by the wayside; they had been known to be good, or even exceptional soldiers.

> I think Ray Sykes went by the same route that Frank Duffy did – 'bomb happy' was the common phrase. I think he was probably a bad case of battle fatigue. But they got to him in good time, same as they did with Duffy. They don't shake or anything like that, but you could see the change in them. They don't react. They get slow to react. If some plan is being put to them whereas most people would only want to hear it once, maybe twice, they would want to hear it more. It's the slowness. If you know them well enough, you can see it. Duffy looked as if he was permanently tired; he didn't have the same sort of bounce as he had. Before he was bouncing about all over the place, but now he was just the opposite – it had that effect on him. You get to the stage that everything's too much trouble

and you just haven't got much interest in anything. He just didn't seem himself at all.[37]

Sergeant John Lewindon, 'D' Company

When men snapped it was a terrible business. Shaming, humiliating, terrifying for them; it could be a brutal business for those required to get them to pull themselves together; and chastening for witnesses, many of whom were often compassionate as they were teetering on the same abyss of humiliation.

> We were in a farmhouse and this lieutenant was out on a patrol. I was on guard outside this farmhouse, and I heard this shouting and screaming. I went to investigate. They gave the password – and it was our lads coming back. They were dragging the lieutenant back. There was one of our lads lying wounded further out. We got them into the farmhouse and Stringer said, 'I want some volunteers to go back and pick the lad up!' About four volunteered. Major Stringer said, 'Come on, pull yourself round, lieutenant, pull yourself round!' Slapping him across the face. We gave him a couple of hot cups of tea. They shifted him the next day. We had every sympathy.[38]
>
> Private James Corr, 'B' Company

Few of the men mentioned it, but there were also occasional cases of self-inflicted wounds, where men would rather shoot themselves, or incur a deliberate injury to avoid going 'over the top'.

> Our sergeant shot himself through the foot. I didn't see him do it, but I saw him come in after it had been done. One of the lads says to me, 'He did that himself – I saw him!' It wasn't common, but there were cases of it. It was bad enough letting the Germans do it to you without doing it to yourself![39]
>
> Private James Corr, 'B' Company

Tommy Chadwick was the son of a coal miner from Accrington in 1924. A bit of a troublemaker as a youth, he had ended up working down the pit before he was called up, and after training posted to the 16th DLI in the late autumn of 1944. He was keen to make his way in the army and gain promotion, but he was occasionally a little shocked by the reactions of those who had come to the end of their tether.

> This private he was a very jovial character, came from Manchester. I took a shine to him. When we were out on rest, I was talking to him and I said, 'What were you in Civvie Street?' He said, 'A burglar!' And he was! And he had 'burglar' in his paybook!! We were going up the line and you used to get nights pouring with rain. Move forward to this hill! Soaking wet. Just started to dig in! 'On your dogs! Move again!' He said, 'If we move again that's the last straw!' Well, we did get the order to move again. So he picked up the 2-inch mortar which has a spade base plate on it, put his hand on a rock and gave it a 'WHACK!' Smashed his hand! Then the word came round, 'Dig in! We're in the position we're going to be!' We wouldn't have moved again anyway He came back to the battalion, but his hand was one hell of a mess as you can imagine![40]
>
> Private Tommy Chadwick, 'C' Company

There were some cases of desertion, which was still a serious offence even though the threat of the death penalty had been removed.

> Now we did have quite a few deserters – say two or three at a time. This was probably after shelling. You could be shelled and dispersed. You would check and find each platoon would report so many missing. They had nowhere to go except out of the firing line. When you came out of the line, they would turn up again. That meant when we were at rest, I spent my time with the platoon sergeants on court martials having these deserters tried. Giving evidence about what had happened. There was only one reason – they were frightened – a man had had enough. You believe me, if you're under shellfire, you've got lads that can't stand it. They're not entirely to blame, but if they've gone then they've deserted. The charge is deserting His Majesty's Forces – not going absent. They listened to the chap's

excuses, listened to the evidence, and then gave the punishment out. If the desertion was proved it would be three years.[41]

Company Sergeant Major Leslie Thornton, 'C' Company

When wounded, the men needed to feel that they would get the best possible medical care. This was of crucial importance to morale. The medical officer sums up his duties.

> During battle conditions, to organise the collection of the wounded, to treat the wounded to the best of one's ability, and with the help of the field ambulance to arrange the speedy evacuation of the casualties to forward surgical units. During the battle, the medical officer sets up a regimental aid post (or RAP), the site being determined after consultation with the commanding officer. Where possible, twenty regimental stretcher bearers are available for the collection of casualties, four being attached to each rifle company and four remain at the RAP. It is their work to collect and carry the wounded to the aid post. If they fail in their dangerous task the whole scheme of evacuation of casualties and their treatment falls to the ground. Their courage and high standard of devotion to duty are deserving of high praise.[42]

Captain Huw Jones, Royal Army Medical Corps

If they were wounded, then the men had a respite from the tension and pressure that dominated their lives: a chance to recuperate from physical wounds, but also a chance to recharge their mental batteries.

> The first time I was wounded, I was getting a bit sick of doing little patrols at night with half a dozen men. It was quite unnerving. Initially, they didn't worry me too much, but as time went on, the more I did, the more I was apprehensive as I went out. It's like all of these things, once you set out, you get on with it, but the apprehension before you set out is always just that little bit unnerving. At the time I got that second wound I was a little bit on edge. But it was nothing that a fortnight off didn't put right and I was in quite good form after that. It

never got easier! I don't know anybody who didn't find that the repetition of action didn't affect them one way or another. The funny thing was, it very often evidenced itself out of the line, rather than in the line. People got involved in excesses of one kind or another, they started being silly over drink, doing daft things. If you were never wounded, you never got a rest! It's a strange thing to say, but often the wound gave you two or three weeks out of the line and improved you. Stress just got on top of them.[43]

Major Ronnie Sherlaw, 'D' Company

Once they had recovered then many were keen to get back to their comrades in the 16th DLI. Perhaps in their heart of hearts, they would rather have been sent home to 'Blighty' for a long respite from war, but if they had to resume the fight, then they wanted to fight alongside their mates.

I think the majority of people I came across who had wounds were a good deal more concerned about getting back to their own battalion than anything else. You made relationships in an infantry battalion which were quite unique. Somehow or other, to have to start again, to make the same sort of relationship, was something you didn't want to face up to.[44]

Major Ronnie Sherlaw, 'D' Company

As to their own mortality, there were far too many reminders on the battlefield of what could lie ahead for them. Some men were even involved in the grim business of gathering up the corpses and preparing them for interment.

I'd never been on a burial party before; it scared the death out of me to tell you the truth! I think there was about ten of us on the burial party. The sergeant was there and the padre. We had to collect them, pull them out of this ridge, put them on a stretcher, fetch them up, search them, get all their stuff out – if they had any stuff on them like pay books and identity discs – the padre collected them. I'd seen dead lying before, like, but when you come to pick them up, blokes that have been lying out in the sun and the rain for two or three days – the smell was terrible. They were rancid, man, their blood was dried on their faces. As we were fetching them up this bloke kept rolling off! I don't know if he was a Panzer Grenadier, but he must have been about 6 foot 3 and about 14 stone. This bloke from Houghton le Spring said, 'He's trying to get away! Get hold of him!' We brought them up and laid them in a flat field. We had to put them on blankets, roll them in blankets, take all their gear off them.[45]

Private George Bland, Carrier Platoon, Support Company

Once the bodies were ready to be buried, they were taken to the nearest burial point, though this was not always easy as George Bland recalled. They were given a 3-ton lorry and a jeep to transport the remains.

We lifted all the blokes and put them on their truck – and the smell! There was a bloke in the 3-tonner with all the bodies, sitting on top of them! I wouldn't get on the truck, I got on the jeep, there was about ten of us hanging on to the back. We went to the 56th Division cemetery. They wouldn't have nowt to do with us, 'No, no, they're not our blokes try somewhere else!' We tried another cemetery, the 78th Division – and they were the same. We got a burial place at the finish, we had to start digging, but it was teatime then! They more or less kicked them into the ground. The graves were that shallow – only about 2 foot down. We knew they had to be picked up later – the Graves Commission used to come and lift them. I can remember the medical sergeant saying to me, 'There's no reason to be frightened of them, lad, they're dead men – they're just sleeping like! You shouldn't be frightened of the dead!' It was just the idea of lifting them and the smell was on your hands for weeks after. I couldn't eat nowt for about three weeks. It was horrible.[46]

Private George Bland, Carrier Platoon, Support Company

Arthur Vizard saw many of the burials.

> The Reverend Meek [was our padre], the Roman Catholic was Father Fury! We had Meek and Fury! Burials were his speciality of course. He moved about with the regimental aid post. He was on hand when people died; he went out and helped bury the dead. Collect up the identity discs. If you had a battle, Gemmano for example, there were thirty or forty bodies lying there – and nobody could get to them for three weeks. Well, the two parsons went out with the burial parties, gas masked! Getting the identity discs – the flesh would have swollen and closed over the disc. You had to get them out, cut them out. If you got it out and the green disc would give your number, name and religion punched on it. If you were the Protestant parson and you came across a Catholic – and the Catholic parson was several hundred yards away – you're not going to call him. They used to bury each others. The troops didn't mind. You're all going to the same place![47]
>
> Major Arthur Vizard, Headquarters Company

Meanwhile, it was the officers' task to write the letters of condolence to the relatives of all their men that had died. This was a task that they took exceedingly seriously, although the letters were formulaic and avoided revealing the often painful and agonising truth of the circumstances of their demise.

> I wrote letters to the relatives of every one of my men who was killed – not one did I miss. That was a feature of the Durhams. One expressed the greatest sorrow and emphasised the fact that the husband, the son, had died very bravely, and that he would be buried eventually in a suitable place. If there had been a failure in any direction as far as the individual was concerned, I would not mention it. I wouldn't pile on the agony. I would try and make the situation as easy for the dependents, the loved ones, as I possibly could.[48]
>
> Major Laurie Stringer, 'B' Company

It should never be forgotten that it was not only the men at the front that suffered, but also those back home that waited for them. Feeding off scraps of news from the newspapers, radio and cinema newsreels, hoping against hope that all would be well. That there would be a happy ending. Too many would get the notification from the War Office and the letter from an officer that would end for ever their hope of a return by their son, brother, lover or husband.

15

LAST RITES AT COSINA

> I was faced with close fighting which didn't always allow for the application of 'battle drill' tactics. The principles of fire and movement applied, but I can't say I ever applied the 'battle drill' techniques in actual fighting.[1]
>
> Major Laurie Stringer, 'B' Company

TIME RUSHED BY AND SOON – TOO SOON – it was time for the 16th DLI to leave the rest idyll at Montefiore and return to the front line. They found a new divisional commander, as John Hawkesworth had been promoted and given command of X Corps. In his place was a New Zealand officer, Major General Stephen Weir. While 139 Brigade was out at rest, there had also been considerable progress, with the 4th Division and 10th Indian Division battering their way across the Ronca river and taking the town of Forli, while the rest of 46th Division had got across the Montone river. On 6 November, the 16th DLI moved up to the concentration area at La Fratta. On arrival the men found it was another case of 'hurry up and wait' as a session of training followed, with work on tank–infantry cooperation, a flamethrower demonstration and the practicalities of winching a 2-pounder anti-tank gun across a river. It was only on the night of 14 November that the 16th DLI moved forward to relieve the 128 Brigade in the San Varano sector. Now at last they were on the great northern plain of Italy. No more ridges, but plenty of rivers and canals still dogged their progress. The weather was also a considerable handicap, as it teemed with rain and the drenched men were soon marching ankle deep in glutinous mud. Yet at first all went well: on 15 November, 'A' and 'C' Company put in a successful attack across the Lazaro river, assisted by tanks. The battalion moved forward to take up defensive positions along the Balzanino river, ejecting the last German rearguards holding houses south of the river. Here the logistical problems multiplied, as it was impossible to get the jeeps or lorries forward from 'B' Echelon on the cratered and mined roads with deep cloying mud all around. Necessity is the mother of invention and mules, augmented by oxen 'borrowed' from an Italian farmer, were pressed into service to carry forward rations and ammunition, with only moderate success. Apparently, 'Even these poor creatures found the going very hard and were inclined to be unnerved by the incessant shelling'.[2] A small further attack was made by 'A' Company to distract attention from the Royal Engineers, who were constructing a Bailey bridge across the canal on the front held by the 2/5th Leicesters to the left of the Durhams. The attack failed, but the Bailey bridge was reported complete by 06.00 on 16 November. The advance then resumed with 'A' and 'C' Companies pushing forwards, but it again fell apart and only minimal gains were made. That night, 'B' Company took over from 'A' Company. Shortly afterwards, Bill Virr was called to the company headquarters.

> Major Stringer showed me these houses on these aerial photographs and said, 'I want you to go out there and make some noise – a nuisance patrol you could call it. If you can, take a prisoner!' It was about three o'clock in the morning. It was pitch dark. I don't think there was a moon or anything. I took about four men, that's all. I and one of the other lads had Tommy guns. We went out past a pile of rubble after we'd gone about 200 yards. We could see where it was because we could see flames burning, flickering in this house. We carried on and finished up going through a soggy, wet field. We got more or less up to the farmhouse. One of the lads was deaf, he shouldn't have been there, but he used to play hell with you if you didn't pick him to go on patrol! I said to him, 'Right, cover me, I'm

> going to go forward to try and see if I can hear or see anything!' I was just going to set off and this lad says, 'What did you say?' I had to stop – I went back and told him again! But just as I was going to set off again, a door opened and this German came out with his coat down to his ankles, his rifle, smoking, just finishing his ciggie off. He was waiting for his mate, who came out, and then they were coming towards us. So we opened fire on them, threw a grenade – we were supposed to make a noise and we did do! Then we set off back. The Germans opened up with this machine gun and this mortar although they didn't know where we were. We got back to our old positions, and I reported to Major Stringer. He didn't believe me that I'd been right out there! As I got back to our house there was these two Germans – they had followed us wanting to surrender! They couldn't catch us we must have been going that fast! I took them to Major Stringer![3]
>
> Sergeant William Virr, 'B' Company

On 16 November, the Leicesters put in a concerted attack accompanied by tanks pushing from the Bailey bridge towards a bridge over the Cosina river. At first all went well, in fact they even crossed the Cosina, but then the inevitable German counterattack hurled them back. In support, Major Laurie Stringer had been ordered to attack a group of farmhouses near the Cosina which was codenamed 'Sleep'. The attack was to start at 13.30 and it was a fearsome prospect.

> My plan was to send one platoon to an intermediate objective to make that 'firm', then to take the two other platoons, slightly left-flanking round on the left-hand side, supported by fire from the intermediate position – and I had a troop of tanks under command. The intermediate objective was a group of very ramshackle buildings which were hardly standing, they were almost razed to the ground. Very little cover at all, but it was slightly raised from the rest of the surrounding countryside. There was something like 800 yards of almost open country that I had to travel over to get to my objective. Artillery and mortar support were to come down just after 'H' hour. Just

prior to crossing the start line, the Desert Air Force were to come over and dive-bomb the enemy lines.[4]

Major Laurie Stringer, 'B' Company

What happened then was incredibly irritating to the long-suffering infantry.

> Unfortunately, the Desert Air Force mistook our line for the enemy line, and they came over a minute before 'H' hour and dive-bombed and machine gunned my forward position. Which was most unpleasant! Dennis Worrall, who happened to be forward, saw what was happening and he stood in the middle of the road waving his stick at these aircraft to try and let them know they were machine gunning the wrong line. There he stood in the middle of that Italian road – he hadn't got a steel helmet on – and he was unperturbed and really didn't bat an eyelid. Fortunately, they didn't create many casualties as far as my company was concerned and we were able to move forward. None the less it was a distraction and an unpleasant incident at a time when everyone was keyed up to go forward.[5]

Major Laurie Stringer, 'B' Company

The dive bombers were flying low at eye blurring speeds, often with relatively poor visibility, and they were faced with a fluid situation on the ground. In these circumstances, mistakes were inevitable and hence frequent – but they were no less annoying for all that. Notwithstanding this interruption, the attack went in as planned at 13.30, with Stringer watching anxiously from his headquarters. Bill Virr was far more anxious – he was one of those going 'over the top'. He soon had plenty to worry about.

> We set off. We got almost as far as this pile of rubble; it had been an outbuilding of some sort that had been hit. There was a long drainage ditch running right the way from our house, past this rubble. Then they opened fire on us, so we dropped. There was a tank at the side of us. The ground was that soft he got bogged down – he couldn't move. We got down and had a smoke, you couldn't do anything else. There were snipers firing

from these houses. We had two brothers in our company, both in the same section. It was while we were amongst this rubble that the younger one lifted his head up and the sniper hit him straight through the head. His brother was there at the side of him.[6]

Sergeant William Virr, 'B' Company

Stringer soon realised that things had gone awry. He became concerned that the second lieutenant charged with leading the attack was not pressing forward.

I watched with my binoculars to see what sort of progress he was making. After he'd gone about 300 to 400 yards, he stopped, and there was no further move forward. I couldn't understand why this was! I said, 'Sergeant major, I'm going forward to see why Mr X's platoon is not moving forward!' I went forward to where his platoon was lying along a bank and I said to him, 'Why aren't you moving forward?' He said, 'I can't, Sir!' I said, 'Why not?' He said, 'We're heavily pinned down by fire!' I said, 'You've got a troop of tanks on your right giving you fire support – you are to move forward!' He said, 'I can't move forward! I can't do it!' I took him by the arm, I didn't get excited, I said, 'You must move forward!' With that he left me and ran in the opposite direction! I had given him a direct order; that was disobeying the order of a senior officer in battle; it was unforgivable. It was a very, very tricky situation. I was worried because the men had seen this incident and I wondered what their reaction would be. I decided to go myself. Hale and Kent were Bren gunners on the ground beside me and I said, 'Well, I am going on to the objective!' Hale turned to Kent, 'If he can go, we'll go!' We moved forward – slowly – and got on to the objective. I couldn't raise my head, because as soon as you moved, the machine guns started opening up again. That is where I saw a small family of rabbits around their mother just nearby – and I said to myself, 'If I get out of this situation, I will never complain again!'[7]

Major Laurie Stringer, 'B' Company

They reached the farmhouses, but it was hopeless. There was no chance of holding on if – or rather when – the Germans counterattacked.

> Suddenly on my right I saw quite a heavy contingent of Germans moving forward and there was no doubt about the fact that they were going to counterattack me on that position. It became untenable. There was a ditch running just away from this intermediate objective, and I took the men into the ditch. We were able to crawl along the ditch and into a deep pond some way away. One of the tanks had been knocked out, but the other two were quite superb. They didn't pull back; they fired everything they'd got and covered our retreat back to this pond. We eventually got back at about 17.00 to the start line.[8]
>
> Major Laurie Stringer, 'B' Company

Bill Virr remembered that sodden ditch in considerable detail. His experiences in it were a strange mixture of terror and surrealistic humour.

> The only way back was along this ditch which was half full of water. The Germans were firing, clipping the top of the ditch. When I got in, the driver from the tank was in front of me. You were stretched out full length. You couldn't get up because they were firing across the top. They used to wear like a boiler suit, and it was gradually filling with water. I said, 'Go on!' He said, 'I can't move, I'm like a Michelin man!' I pulled his trousers out of his gaiters and said, 'Right, unzip it and crawl out!' I held his trouser bottoms, and he crawled out of his tank suit. He just had his underpants on underneath – and a revolver! That was how we finished up at the other end of the ditch. We were relieved then and we were in these houses drying our clothes off. One of the lads went out to parade or something – and he just had his overcoat, long johns and boots. The company sergeant major said, 'I'll put you on a charge – you're improperly dressed – you haven't got your hat on!' He was kidding him really![9]
>
> Sergeant William Virr, 'B' Company

More serious were the consequences for the inexperienced young officer who had lost his nerve. He had shown signs of mental strain before, by 'overreacting' to the sounds of distant machine gun fire. He would subsequently be court martialled, but in truth it was clear that he should not have been on front line duty with the infantry in the first place.

At 19.00 on 16 November, the 16th DLI were relieved by the 2/4th KOYLI and sent back for three days as the brigade reserve based at Villagrappa. The 46th Division was faced with the necessity of breaching the outer defences of the German Gerhild Line – in particular, the defences based on the Cosina river. In this task the 139 Brigade was well to the fore. First, on 20 November, the 5th Leicesters launched a successful operation to capture the village of Castiglionne on high ground on the Allied side of the Cosina, assisted by a crushing artillery bombardment coupled with the bombing of the Desert Air Force. On 21 November, the 16th DLI pushed forward to the Cosina.

Here Russell Collins and his Bren Carrier Platoon were posted in a farmhouse close to the riverbank, where they could see a group of farm buildings occupied by the Germans, just 200 yards across the Cosina. If they were to make an attack in the near future, then Collins was keen to establish the details of the opposing defensive positions.

> We tried to sally forth to make an exploratory probing patrol across the river, and they opened fire and drove us back. What we observed was that the enemy were dug in on the far side of the river. In other words, they weren't just in the buildings. Then I went upstairs in the farmhouse to look through a window to try and locate their machine gun posts. I was standing there with my binoculars searching the ground – and suddenly there was a great clattering and a long burst of machine gun fire, which spouted all around this window – broke through the lath and plaster walls on either side, through the window – and none of them hit me. They might have done! You get to the point where you think, 'My gosh! I'm leading a charmed life!'[10]

> Lieutenant Russell Collins, Carrier Platoon, Support Company

When night fell, he led another patrol to try and sneak across the river.

> We got down into the riverbed. Then it was clear that there was a German machine gun dug in only about 20 yards the other side. We were in the riverbed, so we were all right. We had some grenades, and I gave orders that we would try and knock this thing out with grenades. There were two or three of us trying to lob these grenades into the machine gun post. Every so often they would fire back, so we had to nip up very quickly, throw our grenades and get down again. We did that alternately and there was a soldier standing next to me, I can see him very clearly, he was closer to me than you are now – about 3 or 4 feet away. Turn and turn about we stood up and threw a grenade. When we had done that four or five times, there was a searing burst of fire when it was his turn – it went right through his head. That was really shattering; he was obviously dead before he hit the ground. That again was the luck of the draw, you see. I had a fifty-fifty chance there.[11]
>
> Lieutenant Russell Collins, Carrier Platoon, Support Company

That night had a disastrous ending for Bill Virr. His luck finally ran out when he was ordered to accompany Lieutenant Gray on a recce patrol.

> We went down the road, then we had to cross a deep dyke, up to your chest in water. We followed the path at the other side of the dyke. It went along a gully, with a steep embankment up to the right, then the ground dropped away into a valley. The Germans had cleared everything, so they got a field of fire. Cut all the trees and bushes down and chucked them into this bit of a ditch. We were walking on – and I was leading man – I didn't want to, but I had to because I was leading the patrol. We were going along this gully, and it sort of bore round to the right. As I went round there was a dugout dug into this embankment. At the entrance was a German sat on a chair – bored to death! We both saw each other at the same time; we were both for a second flabbergasted! He jumped up, ran inside and hid. I

> thought, 'I'm not coming running in after you, you've probably gone in and picked your rifle up waiting for me!' I shouted at him to come out. He wouldn't, I could hear him inside, he was frightened to bloody death, whimpering, probably expecting me to throw a grenade in. I shouted at him to come out, said I wouldn't shoot, 'Nicht schiessen!' But at the top of the banking, they also had a bloke in a slit trench – he popped over with his Schmeisser and hit me. I immediately fired back at him. His head was just stuck over the top. Then I jumped, leapt into all this brushwood, in case he fired again. He never fired again. I don't know whether I hit him, or not. I knew I'd been hit, and I said to the lads, 'Give us a pull up out of this ditch, I've been hit!' The officer then said, 'You'd better get back!' A couple of the lads walked me back. I said, 'Have a look, just see if my balls are all right!' I'd been hit at the back of my leg and it had come out – grazed my scrotum – into the right leg and then it must have hit the bone. They got me at the side of road, ripped my pants and said, 'You're all right!' Then two lads came running down with a stretcher, I climbed on it and they carried me back to the farmhouse where we set off from.[12]
>
> Sergeant William Virr, 'B' Company

He was evacuated to a casualty clearing station where the bullet was removed from his leg. After hospitalisation and a short period of convalescence he would rejoin the 16th DLI in April 1945.

The big attack all along the line by X Corps was launched at 20.00 on 22 November. Major Laurie Stringer was attacking with his 'B' Company on the right, while 'A' Company went in to his left. In every way the prospects were grim.

> It was an appalling night; it was raining cats and dogs. Just near to my start line, which was just south of the Cosina river, there were two enormous haystacks. The Germans set light to these haystacks, and they blazed away, lighting up the area for hundreds of yards in all directions. The plan was for a barrage to come down just before I crossed the start line, and then move forward, a creeping barrage on to my objective,

> a group of buildings called Corla, the other side of the river. The ground led down to the river slowly, and then the river was about 20 yards wide – that's all – it was a very small river, but it was quite deep, strangely enough. Then the ground rose slightly on the other side, 400 to 500 yards the other side of the river to Corla.[13]
>
> Major Laurie Stringer, 'B' Company

At this stage in the campaign many of the men were at the end of their tether. But officers could not afford to be overly sympathetic in moments of crisis – as Stringer demonstrated.

> The barrage started and a few of the shells dropped short. This didn't help matters and one of my men started screaming at the top of his voice, absolutely hysterical. It only wants someone to do that and it has a very adverse effect upon the rest of the company who are already tensed up. I went up to him, caught hold of him by the front of his battledress and said, 'Stop that noise!' It didn't make a scrap of difference at all to him; he just kept on screaming. Imagine it: rain, two haystacks alight, ground soggy, going into the attack and there was this man creating an unpleasant situation. I knew there was only one thing I could do – I hit him with my fist on the chin hard enough to stop him! I never regretted doing that, if I was faced with the same situation again, I would do exactly the same. It was the only way that I was able to stop him. As far as he was concerned that was the end of his fighting. He went back as a battle exhaustion case – and I didn't ever see him again.[14]
>
> Major Laurie Stringer, 'B' Company

Time passed slowly but at last the time came to go over the top.

> At 'H' hour we moved forward. I was in the middle of the company, with two platoons up and one back. David Buchanan, a Scottish subaltern, was commanding one of the two platoons. He was an excellent officer. We moved down to the river. There was machine gun fire, Spandaus – they were firing the whole time. We got across the river. It was not easy because

the Germans had positions that were covering the river and the company on the left weren't able to cross at all, because the Germans had Spandaus covering almost every 30 or 40 yards of the river. I was right up, and I said, 'David, take your platoon on to Corla, see what you can find out and let me know!' David went forward and there then commenced some quite heavy fighting.[15]

Major Laurie Stringer, 'B' Company

With 'A' Company apparently failing to get across the Cosina, 'B' Company were vulnerable to counterattack. Corporal Ken Lovell had been sent back to 'B' Company headquarters and thus was there when Corporal Pettifer arrived with a situation report from David Buchanan. According to Lovell, Stringer sent him off to pass orders to Buchanan to fall back as they were very exposed in their forward position towards Corla.

We set off, went over the river and I fell in a bomb hole going over! I'm not a very good swimmer and I came up spitting water. What I didn't realise at the time was that my Tommy gun had gone into the clay mud. Having got out of the river, we went forward and got to the edge of this ring of light, almost like daylight, from haystacks on fire. When the Germans withdrew from farmhouses, they used to set fire to the haystacks to give their mortars and artillery an aiming point if they needed to counterattack. The stacks really were blazing at this farmhouse we'd taken. There was about 150 yards of really open ground in front of the farmhouse. We jumped into a bomb hole, and I said, 'Right, hang about Pettifer, let's see what's happening. We don't know whether the platoon's still there.' Pettifer said to me, 'I can hear Sergeant Thompson over there!' A little chap called Joe Thompson, I don't think he would have been much more than 5 foot 2 inches; he had a very deep voice, a Yorkshire accent. I listened and sure enough it sounded like Thompson. So, I said to Pettifer, 'Keep me covered, I'll go over and ask Joe where Lieutenant Buchanan and the rest of the platoon is.' He stayed in the bomb hole and kept me covered. I crept forward, 100 yards, maybe 150 yards, and there was this short chap, and I couldn't make it out; it was in the dark, outside the ring of fire, but it sounded a deep voice. I thought, 'Oh, Joe Thompson!' Then I got up, walked up and tapped him on the shoulder, and I said, 'Hey Joe, where's Mr Buchanan?' The German soldier turned round and said, 'Ist ein Tommi! Hande hoch!' Well, I pulled the trigger of my Tommy gun and it virtually exploded – the breech block and the covering blew back just past my arms. It's lucky I wasn't holding it in my stomach otherwise it would have taken my insides out. The gases couldn't escape because it had been stuffed up with clay. So, I was taken prisoner.[16]

Corporal Ken Lovell, 'B' Company

His adventures were not yet over, however.

I was sent off with a German in front of me and a German behind me. They were taking me to their battalion headquarters. As we went along this road, our artillery put down a 'stonk', which was supposed to have preceded our attack on the next objective. It really was a frightening 'stonk'. It stopped for a moment, and we got into the farmyard – and this 'stonk' opened again. Right round the farmhouse. I took a flying dive and I dived headfirst into a bloody cesspit! The shelling stopped and I got out – I stank to high heaven. I scraped what I could off me! They bunged me in a room with some straw, a sentry outside and locked the door.[17]

Corporal Ken Lovell, 'B' Company

Lovell would spend the rest of the war in a German POW camp. But even in the first few hours of that long trial, he had a strange insight into the links between infantrymen on opposite sides in a vicious war.

The corporal who was in command of the company that captured me, I don't think he could have been much more than seventeen and a half, or eighteen. They were all kids. I wasn't very old myself; I was only nineteen and a half! I was very young looking, but beside me, these looked like school kids!

> They really were very young indeed! Fervent Nazis obviously. I was asked how many men were holding the position, various other questions, and I feigned to understand no German whatsoever. They didn't persist. Apart from pinching my fags, my watch – the sort of things we did when we took German prisoners – they were quite reasonable to me. It's amazing: you are enemies, you'll kill each other; and yet between infantrymen fighting each other there is nevertheless a bond. It's the bond of all being in the shit together![18]
>
> Corporal Ken Lovell, 'B' Company

Behind him, Laurie Stringer was becoming frustrated, while waiting for news from Buchanan's platoon. He decided to go himself to see what was happening. When he got near Corla, his experiences were not dissimilar to Ken Lovell's – he was just marginally luckier.

> I said, 'I'm going forward to see what's happening!' I got up to Corla and I went round into a farmyard. I saw a section of men in a slit trench, or bomb hole. I got to within 20 yards and I shouted out to them, 'Which section are you!' Imagine my surprise, when seven German helmets popped their heads above this hole! I just managed to gain the cover of some buildings on my left-hand side! The Germans counterattacked pretty strongly, and they drove us back to the other side of the river. We had to retreat. There was some heavy and very confused fighting. Grenades and small arms fire – small arms fire mainly. It was in the middle of the night – I think it was a very disorganised retreat really. Sometimes you just don't know what is going on. When the men realised what the situation was, and the enemy started advancing, I gave the order for the platoons to retreat across the river. I got into the river again and the water was up to my chest. We got back across the river and the fighting died down. Things began to stabilise.[19]
>
> Major Laurie Stringer, 'B' Company

As he took stock of the situation, he became aware that Buchanan was missing. Stringer may have been a little 'stiff' in his manner, but he certainly did not lack courage.

> My men told me that David Buchanan had been hit and I decided I would try and find him. Circumstances were with me, because I took two men and a stretcher and there, just my side of the river, he must have got back somehow or other, I saw David lying in a furrow. He couldn't move. I went up to him – and I heard then the best words that I heard during the whole of my military career: 'Sir, I knew you would come!' You might say it's sentimental, you might say there wasn't much importance to that statement, but to me there was! He'd been shot through the leg, and we were able to get him onto this stretcher and back to safety. Dear David, he was a splendid officer and that was the end of his fighting days.[20]
>
> Major Laurie Stringer, 'B' Company

The attack had been a failure, but the 5th Sherwood Foresters to their right had far more luck and had established a firm bridgehead across the Cosina. This enabled an Ark bridge to be thrown across next to the bridge demolished previously by the Germans. Aided by this, on 23 November, 'C' Company, supported by tanks, exploited through the bridgehead in the direction of Corla, and the village was finally captured. The whole of the 16th DLI then advanced on Casa Bruciati.

By this time Russell Collins began to realise that he had drawn too deeply on his 'bank' of personal courage. He had made his reputation as a daring young officer – 'Winkler' Collins – seemingly afraid of nothing and always leading his men from the front by example. But it was all getting a bit much: so many close escapes.

> From my own experience one has got a reserve, or pool, of courage and endurance. At the beginning of the campaign in September 1943, I didn't worry about it at all, but by the end of November 1944, rather than saying 'Come on chaps, follow me!' I was rather saying, 'Now look, I'm going to put my headquarters here, and you go there, and you go there!'

> Which many people had done from the beginning – but that was not my way! It comes to some sooner than others. The thing that really weighed on my mind – it's sheer rationality really – the number of officers and soldiers who'd been killed, wounded, or missing from the start of the Italian campaign until the end. As a platoon commander I was in the front echelon the whole time. I mean I used to regard a company headquarters as a place of comparative safety because it was a 100 yards behind. You reached a point, 'Come in now; your time is up!' You think, 'Well look, this can't go on!' Everybody else that I could think of had been killed. There was nobody who had survived as a platoon commander as long as I had – and it weighs on your mind in the end, that your turn must be just around the corner.[21]
>
> Lieutenant Russell Collins, Carrier Platoon, Support Company

During the last phase of fighting, he was ordered to attack a small group of farm buildings. With his nerves wound tight by his two recent escapes with the smashed window and in the riverbed of the Cosina he just couldn't go on.

> I had to make the plan to do it. I remember agonising with myself, but I decided on that occasion I really couldn't! I couldn't be the first man forward there! I'd done it so many times and I'd really got to the end of my tether then. Had it been a rifle platoon I certainly would have led it, or been very near, but I did have four sections, each commanded by a sergeant. If there ever was a man who never showed any fear, it was Sergeant Chilvers, who led that attack then. We very quickly followed up, with my platoon headquarters and the other sections, surrounded the place and got right in. There was not much firing and the first thing you have to do is to secure the place, exploit through the objective, make sure they have not just gone back 20 yards and are waiting to jump in on you again. Then you immediately make an all-round defence, by saying 'Right you, Sergeant, cover that sector, from there to there; Sergeant, you cover that sector over there! Go and find some fire positions and I'll come round in a minute to see you!'

> Off they went and then I started on my rounds. It was dusk, and I came around one corner, and a voice said, 'Halt, who goes there?' 'BANG!' All in one movement. It was a carrier driver, who was shaking like a leaf and had his rifle at the hip. He was called 'Yorkie' Streeton and that was the last shot that was ever fired at me in anger in Italy! Once again it missed, and that's why I'm here and able to tell the tale.[22]
>
> Lieutenant Russell Collins, Carrier Platoon, Support Company

Shortly afterwards, blessed relief as the 128 Brigade took their place in the forefront of the advance on the Lamone river. On 27 November, the 16th DLI moved back to Forli. Here there was a small indication that their luck might be changing.

> Word came through that the New Zealanders had captured a vinery, where they made the wine. They were the biggest [wine] butts I'd ever seen! Talk about a butt of Malmsey! They were as tall as this room, and they must have held thousands of gallons. I took a carrier up there and as many empty 4-gallon jerry cans as I could find. There were numerous drunk New Zealanders. 'Where do you want it, sport?' this New Zealander said. He got this 2-inch pipe and he said, 'Hold your can!' I held the can out and of course half of it went over me! My army issue macintosh was never quite the same! I got about 24 gallons of vermouth! We were drinking it for quite some time![23]
>
> Lieutenant Lionel Dodd, Mortar Platoon, Support Company

Doubtless in part fuelled by the vermouth, wild rumours began to spread as to what lay ahead. But this time something new really was upon them. Something they could never have guessed.

16

GRECIAN ODYSSEY

In my childhood, I'd always been reading the classics and the thought of going to Athens was quite remarkable. Something that I thought I should never be able to take advantage of. That night, 'C' Company was placed on the Acropolis itself. Nothing much happened and next morning I said to the signaller, Tony Sacco, 'How was it, Tony!' He said, 'Nothing else but bloody stones up here and it's freezing cold! And I thought, 'Well, that's the practical view of what the Acropolis was like!'[1]

Private Ronald Elliott, 'A' Company

IN A NOT SO FAR AWAY COUNTRY, something was stirring. The Greek People's Liberation Army (Ellinikós Laïkós Apeleftherotikós Stratós or ELAS) was the para-military body of the Communist controlled National Liberation Front (Ethnikón Apeleftherotikón Métopon or EAM) and it had been at the very heart of resistance since the German invasion in April 1941. Resistance operations against the Germans began in June 1942, but were greatly boosted when officers of the British Special Operations Executive parachuted in. They were to assist in attacks on rail routes, while at the same time promoting cooperation between ELAS and the right-wing National Republican Greek League (Ethnikós Dimokratikós Ellinikós Sýndesmos or EDES). EDES was far more palatable to the British, but ELAS was the more popular and powerful grouping – and beggars cannot be choosers. These British officers actively trained the insurgents and arranged for supplies of weapons. Throughout

1942–43, ELAS grew in popularity and their guerrilla bands had considerable success launching raids from their hiding places in the mountainous regions. As it became evident that the Allies would ultimately win the war, ELAS began an internecine warfare with EDES, which simmered in the background throughout 1944. By this time, ELAS numbered over 50,000 partisans, and in conjunction with EAM, had the potential to create a Greek government capable of rivalling not only the puppet government set up by the Germans in Athens, but also the 'official' government in exile residing in Cairo.

> The ELAS organisation was structured well – command headquarters, brigades and so forth – it had been trained and equipped by the British to harry the Germans in Greece. It was only after the Germans had pulled out and the 'vacuum' existed that these people tried to seize control of the country. They had strong communist tendencies. It was a sad situation in many ways, the ELAS used to use their bullhorns at night and shout out, 'Tommy, Tommy, we are your friends, we were trained by your people!' And it was true. But it was to make life difficult for the German occupiers.[2]
>
> Major Arthur Vizard, Headquarters Company

By this time, more confident of ultimate victory, and hence no longer 'beggars', the British government gave free reign to its preference for the monarchist elements within EDES, with the ultimate aim of returning the Greek government in exile, led by Prime Minister Georgios Papandreou, to Athens. This was duly achieved when Papandreou arrived in Athens in October 1944 to form a government of 'National Unity', accompanied by some Greek Army units and British forces under Lieutenant General Sir Ronald Scobie. Many of the ELAS forces still saw the British as liberators from the hated Germans, but this natural gratitude co-existed with a natural suspicion as to the motivations of the British Empire. A major trigger for the fighting that followed was Papandreou's orders for all partisan forces not under his command to completely disarm. This, ELAS considered, would render them defenceless in a hostile world. A compromise ELAS proposal involving mutual disarmament by all partisan forces was rejected, and an ultimatum issued that ELAS should disarm by 10 December. The writing was on the wall and the EAM ministers serving in Papandreou's National Unity government resigned. This was followed by the calls for a general strike and the organisation of a huge protest demonstration in Athens on 3 December. At least 200,000 people attended, marching through the city and heading for Syntagma Square. Their way was impeded by British soldiers and tanks, but there is controversy over who fired the first shots. Many believe it was the work of the Greek police, many of whom had been collaborators with the Germans and thus had no love for ELAS. It is estimated that some twenty-eight demonstrators were killed and hundreds injured. The ELAS movement was then portrayed – fairly or unfairly depending on political perspective – as having launched a coup d'état. This the British could not allow; they had no intention of allowing a Communist regime to be established in Greece. In essence, we can now see the conflict that followed as the first 'proxy war' of the Cold War.

British reinforcements had already been called for, of which 139 Brigade was one of the first. The 16th DLI and 2/5th Leicesters were both sent to Athens, while the 5th Foresters were despatched to Salonika. The main body of the Durhams flew out on Dakotas from Bari to Kalamaki airport, Athens, on 3 December 1944. This would be the first time that most of them had ever flown. As they arrived, George Bland seems to have caught sight of one of the protests that day.

> It was a Sunday morning and there were thousands of them coming along the coast road. They were chanting; a demonstration, like. We had a bloke called Lieutenant General Scobie that was in charge, and they were coming along shouting. I was saying to myself, 'What are they saying?' They were saying, 'Scobie is a bastard! Scobie is a bastard!' Chanting like that! I think that the royalists that wanted the King back were in a minority! Or if they weren't they didn't dare say anything![3]

Private George Bland, Carrier Platoon, Support Company

The 16th DLI was initially based at various police stations around the Athens area. There was some confusion as they tried to get their bearings in travelling around a large and unfamiliar city. This wasn't helped by some elementary navigational errors!

> I got an instruction from headquarters to go and occupy the hill on which the Philopappos Monument stood. I was told that we were unlikely to have any particular opposition. I detailed a platoon to go down the road about half a mile, turn right, climb the hill, find the Philopappos Monument, sit down, and let me know when they got there. I eventually got a runner back who said that they had occupied the Philopappos. So I said, 'Right-ho, I'll go and join them!' We got out a jeep and couple of chaps and we went down the road. I turned right and the runner said, 'This isn't where we went!' There was nobody at the Philopappos, we were the first there! I discovered that the platoon commander obviously didn't know his right from his left. He had turned left and occupied the Acropolis![4]
>
> Major Ronnie Sherlaw, 'D' Company

The situation was still tense after the outburst of violence during the 3 December demonstration. Sporadic fighting occurred between the ELAS guerrillas and the Greek police, but at first the British were mere bystanders. Gradually they were dragged in: first a few snapshots at them, then a somewhat clumsy retaliation; more shooting until the situation spiralled out of control. One example was witnessed by Tony Sacco.

> You would try and ask them politely, 'Give me your gun!' If they said, 'No!' Just carry on! Don't attempt to drag it from them. We were in this big mill. Then the order came round, 'Get dressed in your best khaki! Get everything polished up!' Then we got on trucks and went to Athens. They put about three of us on each corner – looking as smart and as tough as we could! But there was nothing happening – the streets were deserted. In the end they said, 'Back on the trucks!' We were going up the main street in Athens, then turn right on our way back to the billets. There was a crowd of people there. We pulled up. Next thing I

knew, Major Casey, he'd got out and he demanded this gun from this chap, 'Give me that gun!' This chap started to scream, and as soon as he starts screaming, the whole crowd came round. We'd just got round the corner and there was this window up above, the first storey, that window went up and there's this man sitting with a great big old-type Vickers machine gun, with a man at either side of him! He was screaming at us, and we were in the back of this truck, only about 20 yards away! He had the gun on us! We were shouting, 'Give him his pistol back!' But Major Casey didn't want to lose face! Oh dear! I thought, 'Well, I'm not going to sit and take it!' There was only four or five of us on the back of the truck. I got out of the back of that 3-tonner in slow motion – no hasty moves. There was a yard with the gate recessed and I [got under cover] – doing everything in slow motion! In the end I used some bad language to Casey! He gave him his pistol back – and the crowd started to cheer![5]

Signaller Tony Sacco, 'A' Company

Recognising that the overall situation was deteriorating, the British reorganised, pulling the 16th DLI back from Athens to join Block Force, named after Brigadier Allen Block, in the Piraeus area, alongside the 2/5th Leicesters, a squadron of tanks and some RAF armoured cars. As the trucks drove down through the narrow streets, they passed along one where the ELAS and the Greek Police were engaged in fighting. All they could do at this stage was accelerate to full speed and hope they would get through! The ELAS reaction was a mixture of cheery waves and isolated shots.

Many of the Durhams were still dubious about their role in Greece. They were aware that the ELAS had taken a major part in fighting the mutual enemy the Germans, with all the painful sacrifices and losses that that entailed. Now it seemed that they were the enemy; it did not seem quite right. This was not helped by gangs of ELAS supporters shouting slogans which appealed to many of the men: 'Liberty and Justice!' 'We want freedom!' and 'Down with the fascist Scobie'. Ronald Elliott was one of those that were concerned.

> All of the army by that time was pretty well socialist. Everyone was of the view that the Conservatives were to blame for all sorts of ills that we had in the war, the general level of the economy. Even though I think people admired Churchill for his ability to lead the country, his politics were completely suspect. He was Conservative and was blackened with the rest of the Conservatives! We felt that what the government was trying to do in Greece was to restore the monarchy, which we also surmised was really not what the people wanted, but it was just going to be imposed upon them. In the beginning, there was a fair amount of favourable feeling towards this insurgency.[6]
>
> Private Ronald Elliott, 'A' Company

They may not have had the ingrained discipline of regular soldiers, but these men were still soldiers who did what they were ordered to do – in the end their personal inclinations were put aside.

The Leicesters were based in Piraeus itself, while the Durhams were entrusted with taking up defensive positions strung out along the seafront around Phaleron, and tasked with keeping open the coastal road stretching back into Athens. The first proper skirmish occurred when Lieutenant T. C. Periam of 'C' Company encountered a group of ELAS attempting to set up a roadblock. Both sides opened fire and the obstruction was removed, with some casualties reported to have been inflicted on ELAS. The situation then calmed down again for a couple of days, although there was a considerable amount of ELAS sniping. One victim of this was the popular officer Lieutenant Frank Johnson, who was shot on 8 December and died next day.[7]

> There were a few of us who were quite musical, and we used to sing in the mess in the evening just for fun. We used to sing in little quartets; hymn tunes were about all we knew! Frank Johnson was one of four of us, Ronnie Sherlaw, was another, 'Giff' Footer and myself. Poor old Frank went out to try and sort out somebody, and one of the ELAS snipers got him. A very dear friend indeed.[8]
>
> Lieutenant Russell Collins, Carrier Platoon, Support Company

On 9 December, a local truce was established with some help from Alan Hay and an intermediary.

> I was lucky in recruiting a girl who had excellent English. She put me in touch with the chap who was the leader of the ELAS in that area. He said that if we would agree not to shoot at them, he would agree not to shoot at us for a period of a week, when we could perhaps come to some terms. I said I wasn't in position to do that sort of thing, but that I would have a word with the colonel. The colonel agreed that we should have a local armistice. Every morning, for about three days, I would start at this bottom end of Phaleron, I would take out my pistol and put it on the ground. [The ELAS leader] would put his gun down and we'd walk up and shake hands. We had about three days of peace. Then on the third night, the ELAS broke the peace and attacked one of my platoons – and in fact killed somebody. So that ended the peace. We were very fed up about it! The colonel felt that I'd been a bit optimistic about what we could do with these chaps – and I think I probably was.[9]
>
> Major Ronnie Sherlaw, 'D' Company

The breakdown of the truce was preceded by intelligence that ELAS were planning an imminent attack. On 13 December, full-blown hostilities recommenced. First, during the day a couple of Bren carriers were shot up causing three casualties. But the real attack was planned for that very night. Movements in the surrounding streets gave a good indication that an attack was due and most of the battalion was on high alert, 'standing to' ready for immediate action. Sadly, one of the platoons in 'B' Company seems to have been an exception to this rule.

> One night the sergeant major came to us. He says, 'Right you are, we're going out to the Lieutenant Whitwell's billet, I've heard word there's going to be an attack and I want to warn him!' By this time it was about half past ten at night, so it was dark. We went in front of our barrier, very careful, to go to his house. They were to the left of us, about 50 yards in front of the barrier, in a little side street. The first house on the right

was a big house and they were all in there. We go in and all we could hear was the piano playing and drunken singing! I'll never forget the song this lad was singing, 'If I had a Paper Doll to call My Own'! The sergeant major bustled his way in and there was the lieutenant as drunk as a kitty cat, honestly, he was – he was paralytic. They had got some vino and they were all drunk! No guards on the door. The sergeant major tried to get some sense into them, but he couldn't and at the finish the lieutenant ordered him away. He came back and he said, 'Well, I've done my best!' We manned the barriers all night and, sure enough, there was an attack, and the house he was in was blown up. The lieutenant got taken prisoner with a full platoon in the house, all drunk![10]

Private James Corr, 'B' Company

This is not how this incident was reported in either the 16th DLI war diary, or the subsequent battalion history. Here there is a heroic tale of a desperate fight against a ferocious mob, who are held at bay until the defenders had run out of ammunition, at which point ELAS managed to place an explosive charge against the front door, blowing it open and then rushing the building. In this account Whitwell and twenty men were taken prisoner, although Whitwell himself would escape after a few days in an ELAS hospital. All of the company positions were attacked that night, with ELAS taking several more prisoners, although no more positions were overrun. George Lyons was one of those taken prisoner.

> The house that we occupied was on a corner and the whole platoon was happy. There was a knock on the door and as I was on night duty, I asked the corporal in charge what to do. He said that he would talk to them. I opened the door, which was fatal as they were well-armed, and they took us all prisoners. With the captors being local, they knew how to get us out of the town and into the country where we set off for days on end. The only food we had was a type of rye bread and water and we stayed when possible at a small village. There the residents jeered at us – and we had laid our lives down

for them to protect them from the Germans – but people forget. The weather was starting to get colder the further north that we went, and we ended up at a farm with a foot of snow down and we had no warm clothes! The sleeping quarters were a cowshed and we had to clean it out and put straw down, but they were stone floors, and we couldn't get warm. The food was the usual rye bread and water. When we celebrate Christmas, my mind goes back to that Christmas in the cowshed. We hadn't had a wash since we were captured. Our only wash, or should I say swill, was in the duck pond outside and we had to break the ice to get at the water! After what seemed to be weeks, we had lost all sense of time. Two American officers appeared, and they had obtained our release, but they said the transport was about a mile down the road and could we make it? We assured him that we would make it, come what may! Once we were all aboard, the transport moved off – we were free at last![11]

Private George Lyons, 'B' Company

They would all be given a month's compassionate leave after their rough experiences as POWs.

Back on 13 December 1944, the most serious attack was made on the battalion headquarters. Colonel Dennis Worrall was briefly away, so Major J. C. Denny was in charge, while Major Alan Hay was temporarily standing in as second in command.

Our headquarters was in a small villa on the sea front. Just next door, there was a block of flats, where the cooks and clerks were. The ELAS decided they would drive us out; they got right down to the house immediately behind us; hundreds of them with all sorts of weapons had congregated in this open area, behind a stone wall. Major Denny asked me to go and take command of this block. I had to go into this house next door to organise the defence. It was a three-storey apartment with concrete stairs and a flat roof which overlooked the headquarters. I said, 'What ammunition have we got?' Well, being battalion headquarters, they didn't have [much] ammunition, and I said, 'Well, look round for anything you can get!' I collected what grenades I could. We then came under very heavy attack. These people were shouting, it was just a rabble. I put what men I could find in open positions. We were firing from windows, but we were getting casualties, so we got up on to the flat roof, because there was a little more protection. There was a parapet you could keep behind; so unless they'd had mortars, they couldn't catch us. They attacked the headquarters building, but they didn't get to it because our flat roof overlooked it. A family with two kids was still on the top floor; they were interpreting, trying to tell us that ELAS were telling us to surrender because they would blow the block up. We could hear them hammering and knocking, there were so many, and we really couldn't disperse them, because the angles for rifle fire from the top were really too acute – they were down underneath. We didn't know how many at that time but there was an awful lot – hundreds. They were all raging and shouting – a real mob. They were going to drive us into the sea! I waited and waited and then threw another grenade. These people were screaming and shouting that they were going to blow us up. We were by that time all on the roof. There were concrete stairs coming up, so I thought, 'I'll keep this one grenade as a last resort when they charge the stairs!' There was this hammering going on down below, then the explosion went off! The whole of the outside of the flats collapsed, just like a cardboard box. The outer floors collapsed – we were a bit further back. I was stunned by some masonry; I can't have had my tin hat on because I had a gash across my head. Then they charged – but they were just making a noise – I don't think they were effective in anything. White flags appeared shortly from the mob, and they wanted to collect their wounded. By this time, it was getting towards morning. They came with barrows and bits of sheet with red crosses painted on them, to get their dead and wounded. I would think that casualties there could have been about a hundred. Then we started to count the cost. We didn't have any casualties, except the sergeant cook and some others were buried in the rubble, and we had to get them out. They were all right, they had cuts and bruises. I think I was the worst with the gash across the top of my head![12]

Major Alan Hay, Headquarters Company

Daylight brought a day of relative calm, but it had certainly been a night to remember. It was also evident that ELAS must have suffered severe casualties, with subsequent reports of thirty-six dead and sixty wounded. Shortly afterward Dennis Worrall returned, and Alan Hay was posted to command 'A' Company.

By this time the Durhams had become cynical as to the nature of the insurgency tactics practiced by the ELAS guerrillas who had been used to fighting an enemy – the Germans – who did not acknowledge any rules of warfare in dealing with civilians. They had thus learnt to seek any advantage they could in conflict situations. This led them to adopt many methods which to British eyes were cowardly. Even men like Ronald Elliott, who had initially been sympathetic to ELAS, found the realities of the situation were fast changing his perceptions.

> The ELAS tended to use women. They would have women coming along the street, just as though they were housewives having a demonstration – followed by armed men behind using the women as a shield. Or even having children around, so you couldn't fire at them. It got very dirty in that sense. As will always happen in these situations, the soldier's attitude changed from being politically favourable to being militarily against them. Because they weren't playing particularly fair. Before very long, it was just that they were 'them' and we were 'us' – it was just a combat situation. We tended to feel that they were communist, they probably weren't out to do any more for the population, they weren't particularly supported by the ordinary man on the street. Churchill was trying to reimpose the King; the communists were trying to impose communist rule, so that one was almost as bad as the other. And we were somewhere in between![13]

Private Ronald Elliott, 'A' Company

It was very difficult to pinpoint exactly who their enemies were as few of the ELAS guerrillas wore uniform.

> There was always this problem of knowing who they were. If someone shot at you, you shot back at him. Although people were quite glad to be away from the main battle front, and certainly it wasn't as hard as fighting the Germans. There were aspects of it that people felt uneasy about. Your average infantryman, one of the first questions that you ask when you're going to a new battle position is, 'Which way is the front?' So that you know, if the worst comes to the worst, which way you can go to get out to the bloody place. Now, in this sort of urban battlefront, it's all around you and one feels somewhat unhappy about that, because there's no clear-cut way out. Fighting amongst houses was not really the sort of warfare that we've been used to.[14]
>
> Private Ronald Elliott, 'A' Company

It was a difficult period for the Durhams. However, reinforcements in the shape of elements from the 4th Indian Division were beginning to arrive to tip the balance in favour of the British. On 15 December, Lieutenant General Sir John Hawkesworth, their old divisional commander, arrived to take over command of the British forces.

On 18 December, the 16th DLI began clearing the streets and houses in front of them, slowly edging their way forwards day by day towards the main railway line to Athens. This was a difficult business in the narrow streets.

> A lot of the houses had no windows, so that made life a lot easier. The success rate of the house clearing was about 10 per cent because they weren't in uniform. They could ground their arms and walk out of the back door down the street, most likely with a pistol in their pocket! So, it was treacherous more than vicious; that's the words I would use.[15]
>
> Private Tommy Chadwick, 7 Platoon, 'C' Company

Chadwick watched with amusement when the august figure of Company Sergeant Major Les Thornton, launched a one-man offensive.

> One night I saw Les was a little 'tipsy', for want of another word. He decided to go and settle the war himself, so he ups and waltzes down this street firing at everything he saw. Some of these [ELAS] chaps were on rooftops, firing from behind chimney pots. How he wasn't shot that night I will never know! He was fated. He ultimately came back, and Casey was waiting for him. He said, 'I want you!' Les said, 'I have been carrying out my duties. Sir! A one-man fighting patrol, I have nothing to report, Sir!'[16]
>
> Corporal Tommy Chadwick, 7 Platoon, 'C' Company

Thornton had been lucky.

As a new area of houses was cleared, it was wired off each night and patrolled to prevent ELAS infiltration. The battalion was also engaged in some 'hearts and minds' operations as they cleared the streets of the insurgents. Food and medical supplies were sent up to be distributed among the Greek civilians. As Colonel Worrall later wrote in his report, 'Lessons learnt from recent fighting': 'The soup kitchen may be a better weapon than the rifle. A great interest should be taken in the distribution of food.'[17] Tom Lister was on these regular food runs.

> I drove a lorry, or I went as an armed second driver, to the base and drew rations to be distributed wherever it had to go. You never went out in a vehicle alone, you always had to take somebody with you. It was always done under the supervision of our quartermaster Captain Newman, who was responsible for trying to feed women and children. Trying to ease the situation, because they had nothing at all, no sort of income and no means of supply. So, it fell upon the army to distribute whatever food was available to them. They were very, very grateful.[18]
>
> Private Tom Lister, MT Section, Headquarters Company

Many of the men remembered that once ELAS had been ejected, the local population were friendly and indeed welcoming.

Christmas Day, 25 December 1944, was rendered special by a visit by the Prime Minister Sir Winston Churchill, Foreign

Secretary Anthony Eden, and Field Marshal Harold Alexander, who broke their journey to the Yalta Conference, staying aboard *HMS Ajax* in Piraeus harbour. Churchill came ashore and toured the 'secured' area, where he was reportedly given a great reception by the Greeks. Alexander visited the battalion on Boxing Day, taking the time to brief the officers and men at headquarters and emphasising the importance of their role in Greece. More prosaically, Arthur Vizard managed to create some sort of festive feeling.

> Christmas was spent where you were! As president of the mess committee, I managed to open up a 'honky-tonk', I think it was the only one working at the time. We had music – the battalion's seven-piece septet of drums, piano, guitar, saxophone, clarinet and so on – plus our little mascot who was a seven-year-old Greek boy in national costume. They operated in this honky-tonk. There was tea and 'wads' [buns] and a limited amount of Greek wine! Not retsina, but a nice red wine which came in these great carboys.[19]
>
> Major Arthur Vizard, Headquarters Company

The British pushed ELAS well back beyond the railway line and further down the Athens–Piraeus main road. On New Year's Day, there was a large pro-British demonstration in the Moschaton sector, of Athens. There was much cheering and waving of Greek and Allied flags, culminating in twenty selected prominent citizens drawing up a statement subsequently presented by the mayor.

> The whole population of Moschaton having been concentrated today, the 1st January, 1945, instinctively condemn the exorable crimes of internal convulsion effected by a few Greeks, organs of strange propaganda, and declares its gratitude to the great ally Great Britain and its heroic army for its deliberation; also declare its unlimited devotion and adoration to their ally, Great Britain.[20]
>
> Major Laurie Stringer, 'B' Company

By this time the bulk of 4th Division had arrived, which

accelerated the process of taking control of Athens. On 3 January, the Durhams began operations in an industrial area on the outskirts of Athens. There were still occasional casualties.

> The CO told me to move forward. There was a heap of metal, rubble and tin – all sorts of stuff there. Some of my men got over the top of this rubble, and then the enemy opened up with Bren guns! Weapons that had been left by the British Army for the use of ELAS against the Germans! They were now using them against us! Two of the men were hit. I went forward, to try and get to these men. Whilst I was bending down over them, I too was hit, in my leg. We managed to get these men out, behind a 2-inch mortar smoke screen. We went back in my jeep, with these two wounded men and myself.[21]
> Major Laurie Stringer, 'B' Company

He had been shot in upper right thigh, which could have been serious. but luckily his wound was relatively minor. After a brief hospitalisation, within a couple of weeks he was able to rejoin the battalion.

That same day, 3 January, an attack was launched on a former Red Cross supply depot in an old factory held by ELAS. It was a substantial building, about a quarter of a mile square, with a wall around it. The operation did not begin well for Les Thornton.

> Intelligence had reported that about sixty of these ruffians were holed up in a factory area on the outskirts of Athens. We were ordered to go and sort them out. We had to attack before light, but, unfortunately, the lads had been doing a bit of drinking the night before – and when I got up expecting to see the sergeants and men ready to move, there was nobody there – they'd slept in. The major was going off his head and he said, 'We'll never get there now before light!' We got them ready in double quick time and off we set with our interpreter, a student type of a lad, he was frightened to death. We were dodging along paths and hedgerows – and it started to get light. Now in front of the factory was a great big open space, there was no cover at all. That's the reason we were supposed to have got there before light. We carried on and got to the factory wall.

> The major went in and fortunately they'd done the same as we had – they'd slept in! I was following the major and suddenly I was fired on by a machine gun with my two lads and we had to dodge behind a column in the wall. We stayed there; we couldn't get out. The firing came from a very high tower in the factory. I said, 'This is no good!' I took a running dive through the hole in the wall where we'd got through, dashed up the side of the road behind the wall, got a tank commander and said, 'Just see him off will you!' He put a round in his gun and blasted that chap up there. That was the end, we got them all out. Some had been shot, a sorry lot of dirty people, bearded, one with his jaw shattered with a bullet. We loaded them up into trucks ready for interrogation.[22]

Company Sergeant Major Leslie Thornton, 'C' Company

When Tony Sacco got into the former factory, he found it was in a mess.

> We went through all of the different rooms in the place. What they couldn't eat themselves, they'd jabbed with knives and destroyed all the stuff in the place. Clothing was burnt! The place stank! We got the whole lot out as prisoners – about 135 of them. We lined them up and we had an interpreter with us, this young Greek interpreter from Athens, only a lad of about twenty. They were glaring at him as if to say, 'When this is over, you're for it!' Next thing I knew he'd disappeared; he'd done a bunk! He was terrified.[23]

Signaller Tony Sacco, 'A' Company

Les Thornton and his men were ordered further up the road to take another factory premises. Again, there was opposition that could have been dangerous.

> We were fired on; the bullets were coming straight down the road. We had to get to this factory across the road. So, we had to jump across two at a time. As soon as there was a lull in the firing where we thought the chap was changing his magazine, then I would send two men across. Now this was a cognac factory,

with two great big doors. I was organising something and one of the young officers got hold of my PIAT man and said, 'Fire your PIAT and burst those doors open!' He was inexperienced about PIATs, you were supposed to be under cover to fire a PIAT because it has a terrible blast, a blow back. He fired this PIAT at the doors, hit the doors and finished up in hospital because he got the backlash. I had to tell the young officer a couple of home truths about the use of a PIAT – that it was dangerous if not handled properly. We got the cognac factory. The soldiers filled their water-bottles up with this cognac. It was pure, bloody poison really – one signaller went blue in the face and finished up in hospital. We had to get all their water bottles emptied. But some of them managed to smuggle them away![24]

Company Sergeant Major Leslie Thornton, 'C' Company

Tommy Chadwick remembered that the several of Thornton's men had indeed managed to ignore any instructions to abstain.

We took a factory that had barrels of booze. We ran in and we were squirting the barrels with Sten gun fire. Of course, the stuff was pouring out all over the place, so we were filling water bottles with it. Within half an hour we had about six men unconscious – so that put the mockers on it – but we kept our water bottles. Word got back to Major Casey and he banned it – all the drink we had in our water bottles was to be put in jerry cans and kept till the end of the war![25]

Corporal Tommy Chadwick, 'C' Company

Later they found the raw spirit had burned its way through the jerry cans!

The ELAS resistance collapsed in Athens, but it would prove to be the end for Pat Casey. He had finally come to the end of his tether, worn out by the stress of command.

They said, 'Major Casey's leaving and all available "C" Company, he wants to say his farewell message!' He's had a few that morning, he said, 'Well, the time has come, I'm going to see goodbye to you lot! No doubt a lot of you will fall by the wayside in the Brenner Pass! I want to thank you all for the support you have given me!' The normal jargon you get – and off Casey went. That was the last I ever saw of him. He was over the hill – his nerves. Like every other company commander, he took a hell of a lot of responsibility. He had had enough. They sent him home.[26]

Corporal Tommy Chadwick, 'C' Company

With Athens secured, the Durhams were optimistically hoping for a rest period, but the existence of several other pockets of ELAS resistance meant that their services were still required. On 7 January, they were despatched at short notice to deal with an ELAS group based around Patras on the Peloponnese Peninsula. The road route was impassable as the guerrillas had blown up the bridge over the Corinth Canal and they still controlled much of the route. Hence the 16th DLI and the 2/5th Leicesters once more took to the seas. Many of the men were pondering the question of whether they would have to land under fire at Patras, but Brigadier Allen Block had a cunning plan!

> The big question was what we were going to do? Because ELAS were in occupation. We'd arrived there in numbers, but we weren't deployed militarily – there weren't assault craft – just a cargo boat. We were all in there like so much luggage! When we arrived there, our brigadier brought off a tremendous psychological coup. Brigadier Block, who was a terrific man, went ashore, called for the local commander and issued an ultimatum that if they weren't out of the town of Patras by first light the next morning, they would have all hell knocked out of them by this 'great army of troops' that were in these ships. He bluffed these chaps into getting out of Patras completely, so we just disembarked in a complete non-tactical way. We would have been helpless if they'd jolly well opened fire on us.[27]

Lieutenant Russell Collins, Carrier Platoon, Support Company

On 10 January, the 16th DLI moved into their assigned billets. Although ELAS had departed, they left behind what could have been a very nasty surprise.

> We went into a flour mill, massive: great big bins with unground wheat, or corn. There was a big boiler house with some vertical boilers. They were made by a Scottish firm! Somebody decided that it would be a good idea to light these boilers up. They started to clean the firebox out to start the fire, and it occurred to me that it wasn't a very good idea from my limited knowledge! Was there enough water in them? Furthermore, had they been booby-trapped? Which was a possibility! It suddenly dawned on the officer – and he turned quite pale and decided it wasn't such a good idea at all! One of the boilers had some sticks of dynamite taped together fastened to the dome of the firebox! It's just as well they didn't light it up.[28]
>
> Private Tom Lister, MT Section, Headquarters Company

There was a minor engagement on 13 January, when the 16th DLI passed through the 2/5th Leicesters' positions and advanced to take Araxos airfield in the north-west corner of the peninsula. There was minimal resistance and next day a general truce was announced with ELAS across the whole of Greece, as ELAS withdrew back into agreed areas. With peace established, the 16th DLI returned to Patras, were they stayed for a month. Patrols and detachments were sent out to various locations in the peninsula and the mountainous regions, but the truce held and there was no trouble.

This marked a complete change of emphasis, from a situation where everybody seemed to be at risk from a 'faceless' enemy all the time, to a far more relaxed existence. No longer in fear of their lives, the soldiers looked to enjoy themselves. Drinking was a common pursuit, although they had to get used to very different choices than they had back in England.

> We were on guard duty on the coast, and somebody had seen a light and we went to investigate. It was a wooden hut made of railway sleepers. Nobody there. We tried to open the door and it was fastened. We kicked the door; they opened it, and we went in! It was very gloomy; they had hurricane lamps. First impression was of all these characters seated on either

side of a long trestle bench with wooden forms. Great big bottles of retsina, and bowls of raw cauliflower and salt! All around the walls were fishing nets and tackle. It was obviously a fishermen's haven. They made us welcome and invited us to have a drink. I thought, 'Oh, I hadn't liked retsina!' But you dip this raw cauliflower in the salt, then take a swig of retsina – and it revolutionised it – made it very good! Had we been able to do so we would doubtless remained there for ever![29]

Private Tom Lister, MT Section, Headquarters Company

Sam Cawdron was the son of a coal miner from Rotherham who had been serving with Heavy Anti-Aircraft Regiments in the Middle East and Mediterranean areas before being retrained as infantry. He was posted as a fitter to join his brother who was already serving as a stretcher bearer in the Durhams. He never forgot his amusing reception on joining the regiment at Patras.

An officer met us and gave us a lecture of what to do – and what not to do in Patras – all about the women. All the 'loose' women had been put inside barbed wire and there was only one entrance and that was through the actual gate – and that was out of bounds for troops to control VD. While he was telling us, there was two women on the roof of their house performing all sorts of things for our benefit – amazing![30]

Corporal Sam Cawdron, MT Section, Headquarters Company

Drink and women were both of considerable interest to the average young soldier.

The cafes were open and everything – and the brothel was there. There was a way to the brothel which was over the roofs of the outhouses to this factory into the brothel. The girls used to be at the main windows of the brothel which faced the factory windows – they were more or less face-to-face across an intervening distance of about 50 yards. The girls would be there with nothing on, just enticing the soldiery with ribald remarks. You couldn't go in the front because there were people guarding it. I never did, but one or two of the lads reckoned that there was a route over the outhouse rooftops so that you could get into the brothel by the back door of the brothel. This route, lay beneath the window of the officers' mess and this fella came back one night absolutely steaming and wet. When he'd been going past the officers' mess, one of the officers had pissed all over him from the window![31]

Private Ronald Elliott, 'A' Company

Arthur Vizard noticed one essential truism about some of his best soldiers in the thick of the fighting.

> My chaps used to come back, and they were the worse for wear and the provosts used to throw them into a truck and bring them back to the guard room. Next day they used to come up in front of me and I nearly always found that the fellows who were the biggest offenders were the best soldiers.[32]

Major Arthur Vizard, Headquarters Company

One dramatic incident occurred when a serious fire broke out in one of the billets.

> We were billeted upstairs in part of the station buildings. There was a lot of local children, mostly little nippers, three or four years old, little girls, always asking you for chocolate! One afternoon the kids were messing about, we never bothered, they never tried to steal anything. There were great big bales of jute that burst into flames. Somebody saw the smoke pouring out and the kids were shouting and screaming! Three of us rushed up the wooden staircase, grabbed them and got them out. Then we had bucket chains to put the fire out.[33]

Private Tom Lister, MT Section, Headquarters Company

No doubt this helped improve their standing in the local Greek community, and in the end, despite initial fears, the Patras experience had been a rest period for the Durhams.

Meanwhile the arrival of the rest of 46th Division was due, and advance parties were received from the 138 Brigade, who were to take over the Patras area. On 11 February, the 16th DLI began the journey to Athens, this time by road, as the bridge over the Corinth canal had been repaired. The views over the Gulf of Corinth were spectacular, but the roads were in dreadful condition and Tom Lister did not enjoy the drive.

> I was at the tail end of the convoy. The roads were atrocious in parts, all white chalk dust and the further behind you were, the worse it was. You could hardly see out of the windscreens, you had to keep stopping and wiping this damned stuff off. It affected your breathing. The MT officer was conducting the convoy riding a motorbike – going to the head of the column, going back to the rear. We got about four fifths of the way and he decided to call it a day! He took my place in the truck and bunged me the motorbike. But unthinkingly, I'm sure he didn't do it on purpose, he didn't give me his goggles. I never thought about it. I was riding this bike and within a couple of kilometres I was virtually blind. I rubbed it, made it worse and I just couldn't go any further – I couldn't see – and I stopped.[34]
>
> Private Tom Lister, MT Section, Headquarters Company

Peering about through watering eyes, he could just about see a railway signal box and what looked like a farmhouse.

> I thought, 'Well, I'll go in here, see if I can get some water and wash my eyes out.' I rode the bike into this entrance into a yard – and was surrounded by armed Greeks! They made me get off the bike and rather roughly pushed me into the house. They started to ask me a load of questions, which I couldn't understand! I couldn't see very well, and I asked for some water to wash my eyes from somebody who spoke English. He told them to give me it and I sluiced my eyes out. They were very, very sore. I'd never met the man, but I got the immediate impression that it was General Grivas [a senior commander in ELAS]. He was dressed like that. He said, 'I'm afraid you have to be kept here. We're going away, you'll have to be kept here until we've gone. We'll leave your bike, you stay in this room, it will be under guard, give us your word that you won't

> try to escape, and we'll let you off in about an hour or so.'
> Which they did! By then the battalion was long settled back in
> Phaleron. When I arrived there was a hue and cry, 'Where had
> I been? What had I been doing?' I could barely see properly,
> and it was dark when I got there. I went to the medical aid
> post, they syringed my eyes out and put some drops in. Then
> it suddenly occurred to me that I ought to report this. I asked
> where the intelligence officer was and went and reported
> this – and I got another roasting because I hadn't reported it
> immediately my suspicions that Grivas was there. Subsequently
> it turned out it was him; he had been there! Of course, the
> contention was that if I had reported it straight away, they
> might have been able to do something about it. I never agreed
> with that because I didn't know where he was going – he could
> have been anywhere.[35]
>
> Private Tom Lister, MT Section, Headquarters Company

In the end he was none the worse for what could have been a fatal experience.

The battalion was now based in Old Phaleron, where they soon settled in. Arthur Vizard was proud, if a little bemused, by the sheer malleability of his men to new circumstances.

> Looking back on all this, the one thing that sticks out in my
> mind is the adaptability of the British soldier. You can pick him
> up and put him down into a totally unfamiliar alien atmosphere
> where he doesn't understand what people are talking about,
> he's highly suspicious of all the people around about – and
> they're hostile, or they're friendly, or they're in between. But
> within the space of at the most forty-eight hours, he will have
> completely adapted himself to the new surroundings like a
> chameleon. Before you know where you are, chickens appear,
> eggs, tomatoes, melons and so forth. Washing is being done
> by Greek women, the men are talking to them – how they do
> it I don't know, but there is this tremendous ability to adapt. It
> happened over and over again, whatever the circumstances –
> hostile, difficult, cold, wet – yes, never mind – you'd still get this
> adaptability to the environment. It was one of the great assets.

> I suppose it always has been one of the great assets: the British soldier is basically friendly and gets on with people.[36]

Major Arthur Vizard, Headquarters Company

Be that as it may, but there was still an underlying impact on the men of the terrible experiences they had faced over the last two years: certain inbuilt reactions that it would take years not weeks to eradicate.

> You're glad you're out of trouble. It gradually wore you down – you just got fed up with day after day you would be facing the unexpected. You just lived from day to day. We used to say, 'Live for today and let tomorrow take care of itself!' I think to a certain extent your nerves did crack up at times. You got edgy at times – the least little bit of sound you were on edge. One time in Greece we were going along a road and there was a 'BANG!' And you're never seen so many blokes go to ground as sharp as what we did! It was only the exhaust of a lorry! Anything like that and you automatically got down out of the road just in case anything happened. When you got up you felt silly.[37]

Corporal Tom Turnbull, 'D' Company

Although they had some duties, including training the Greek National Guard, there was much time for relaxation. The officers organised dances and a fully-fledged inter-company sports day based in one of the Athens athletics stadiums. Two days later, the deciding cross-country race with ten men from each company started off from the battalion headquarters and headed off into the local countryside' but there was a surprise in store for the entrants.

> We went down a straight road and then came back cross-country about 8 miles. Up and down gullies, ploughed fields, everything. What we didn't know was the Signal Section had put wires up right the way round the circuit. They were sat on poles, each had got a blinking microphone, all the way round, with speakers in the finishing circle! They were broadcasting

all what was going off to all the others who were waiting for us finishing! I'd done short races, but I'd never done a long one. I thought, 'Well I'll stick it out!' Anyway, I finished up twenty-sixth! So that wasn't bad! There were between sixty and eighty running. I had a fantastic day![38]

Corporal Sam Cawdron, MT Section, Headquarters Company

'B' Company won the shield trophy as champion company, to the evident delight of Major Laurie Stringer who waxed lyrical in his Battalion history. Regimental Sergeant Major Thomasson, a superb sportsman, won the award as 'champion athlete'. By this time the weather was improving, the sun was coming out and the men were relaxing.

> That's where everybody headed for every night. You'd do a little sightseeing and then finish up in one of the cafes. I drank retsina! Very strong! We used to say, 'A shilling a fire-bucket full!' It was that cheap! And the drachma – I think there was about 9 million to a pound! There was the odd bar brawl, but not a lot, nothing serious! I found that the morning after what I call a heavy session, I had such a proverbial hangover that I invariably always said, 'That's it – I'm leaving that alone!' But by midday, you were young and fit, you'd recovered quite well, so with a little encouragement from your pals, they were all going – so off you went again![39]

Corporal Tommy Chadwick, 'C' Company

Les Thornton had taken a liking to the Mavrodaphne dessert wines that originated in the Patras region.

> We were going to town down to the cafes. I'd got a taste for this wine called Mavrodaphne. It was a black wine and it was a tourist attraction, packed for tourists and export. It was a semi-sweet and I loved it! I used to drink a lot of it, and that's how I got a nickname, 'Sergeant Major Mavrodaphne', it was even in the 16th Battalion Journal![40]

Company Sergeant Major Leslie Thornton, 'C' Company

The more relaxed military situation allowed the commencement of the home leave under the 'Leave in Addition to Python' system. (LIAP). For Tony Cameron, it was not a moment too soon.

> A lot of blokes had been out overseas, three, four, five years. The war hadn't finished but it had quietened down in the Mediterranean theatre. PYTHON was mainly for regular soldiers; they had done their time overseas and they were sent home to England. On LIAP you got a month's home leave and then you went back to your unit. That worked on how many months you'd been overseas. My time came up to come home; it was in April. It took me a month to travel from the battalion to home! We got on a 'trooper', and we were sailing up the Atlantic when the war finished. I was bloody pleased about it, like, but more so as we were on our way home! We landed at Gourock on the Clyde. We went into a camp there and they kitted us out with train passes and leave certificates – and paid us! We had the evening in Gourock, and there was a fish and chip shop about 100 yards outside the camp. Of course, everybody was off as soon as we'd been paid. Outside that fish and chip shop there was a queue at least 300 yards long! All blokes off the ship! We'd never had fish and chips for years! It was a sight worth seeing that! Aye, we enjoyed them! Then next morning we got on a train and were sent down home to Tyneside. But we had all our kit with us – the bloody lot! Rifle, greatcoat, field service marching order, kitbag, the whole lot! And I'm only 5 foot 4! It was a Sunday morning when I got home. I'd got into Newcastle, got off the train, with all that bloody gear! I had to get a bus and when I got off the bus it was just about ten minutes to twelve, and they were all standing outside the local, all the local blokes! Waiting for the pub to open! I hopped off that bus, got my gear on, big pack, kitbag on my shoulder, rifle on the other one. I could see all the heads looking! It was 500 to 600 yards from that bus stop down the hill into my street where I lived. I'd written to say I was on the way home, but that was a month ago, and I hadn't written since. I

> got to my street end, walked round the corner, my mother was standing at the backyard door, with the broom – she'd been sweeping the step. She came dashing along that bloody street, 'Oh, my lad! My lad!' There are tears in my bloody eyes now![41]
>
> Lance Corporal Tony Cameron, 'A' Company

Back in Athens, the 16th DLI began to recommence proper military training with special company camps organised, with weapons training, field firing and tactical exercises. All this prompted the question as to what new battles might lie ahead of them. They would not have been human if they did not hope to avoid going into action again.

> All the talk and speculation was, 'Where were we going next?' We were hoping against hope that we were going to be selected to go to north-west Europe, to join the much more glamorous party that was going on there. We abhorred the thought of going back to Italy again, where we'd fought two previous campaigns and had left a lot of our dead. We envied the chaps that had all the glamour – in any case it would mean going home first! It seemed to be a very much more straightforward show there altogether. But in the event, we were told we were going back to Italy. Everybody was depressed about it; it didn't do much to improve morale.[42]
>
> Lieutenant Russell Collins, Carrier Platoon, Support Company

But they were in the army and there was no choice, no freedom of action.

17

WHAT A RELIEF, 8 MAY 1945

> I don't know whether the nightingales were glad because the war was over, or whether it was just we happened to be there when it was there time for singing, or mating, whatever it was, but not just one, dozens of nightingales were singing away at night. Marvellous singing.[1]
>
> Corporal Sam Cawdron, MT Section, Headquarters Company

THE 16TH DLI WERE ALL AT SEA having boarded their ship, the *Ville d'Oran* at Phaleron on 13 April, landing at the port of Taranto on 15 April. In Italy it was all over bar the shouting. On 9 April, the Eighth Army under the command of General Sir Richard McCreery had launched a successful major assault, which had smashed its way through the German lines on the Senio and Santerno rivers, before pressing hard towards the Po river with the intent of capturing Verona. Although it was going well, there was a concern that the Germans would still provide fierce resistance on a last line of defence based on the Adige river. It was for this that the Durhams and the rest of their comrades in 46th Division had been recalled to Italy.

> A lot of them weren't keen, which is understandable. To coin their phrase, 'It was a bit late to get a wooden topcoat!' They'd gone so long! We just missed going in the line by two or three days. They must have said, 'There's no future in pouring more troops in! Just leave the ones who were there!' So, we bivouacked just a few miles back.[2]
>
> Corporal Tommy Chadwick, 'C' Company

After a period of route marches and normal routine training, the main party returned to Taranto and were re-embarked on a coastal ship for the run to Ancona. It proved a terrible experience for Tommy Chadwick.

> Horrific. It took about forty-eight hours. It was really, really rough. We couldn't stand up; we were lying on the floor. The buckets where the troops had been sick in were flying across the floor. Honest to God it was like a fairground ship! It was the roughest trip I've ever had in my life. Fortunately, I wasn't sick, but most were. Some just laid there and never even moved. It was that bad![3]
>
> Corporal Tommy Chadwick, 'C' Company

The 16th DLI reassembled at the concentration area at the village of La Fratta near Bertinoro. One sobering shadow was the realisation that this was the very village where they had concentrated before the Cosina crossings; but on the other hand, good news continued to flow in from the front, with reports that the Eighth Army had battered their way across the Po. Nevertheless, many of the men were still convinced that one last terrible trial lay ahead of them.

> They still hadn't officially declared that that was the end of the war. We always felt that we were being held back, that Hitler was going to make a last desperate stand in the Alps. They knew all the passes. We thought, 'Now we are being saved for this!' We'd not been given any other jobs; we were just told to be in readiness. We thought, 'This is our job – to invade the Alps!'[4]
>
> Major Alan Hay, 'A' Company

Once again normal training resumed, but everyone was on tenterhooks awaiting the 'call to arms'. Then on 8 May 1945, at last the great day dawned – Victory in Europe – VE Day.

> We were called all together to sit on the grass and we heard Churchill's speech, 'The European War is ended!' You can't express it. The rum ration came out, half of us didn't know

where we were! That night I issued out all the mortar green, white and red flares, all the red Very lights – and we had a Guy Fawkes night. Got the 2-inch mortars out, popping the parachute flares in, red flares, white flares, green flares. Very light pistols were being fired. Nobody cared. Even shots were fired! But nobody worried.[5]

Company Sergeant Major Leslie Thornton, 'C' Company

It sounded like a battlefield. Ronald Elliott was in a more thoughtful frame of mind as he tried to appreciate just what it all meant to himself and his comrades. He had found the declaration of war back on 3 September 1939 a damp squib, now he was once again somewhat underwhelmed by the moment.

> We could hear people letting off rifles and machine guns in agony and ecstasy at the end of the war. When it came it was an anti-climax actually – something you'd been looking forward to all your wartime career and when it came it really didn't give you all of the kick that you thought it ought to have done. It was just as though it fizzled out rather towards the end. They did say that it was as dangerous in Forli that night as it was on any battlefront. So, there it was. It was the end of the war, and everybody was able to breathe a sigh of relief. For the first time you could feel the pressure was off you; you didn't have this feeling in your stomach that you could be going into dangerous situations.[6]

Private Ronald Elliott, Signal Section, Headquarters Company

But for most of the Durhams minds one thing dominated their thoughts – the need for drink to celebrate! There was an air of sheer euphoria in the air.

> It was, 'Get your hands on any vino!' We had a party, first of all firing off all the Very Lights, the flashes and signals. I suppose some live ammunition went off, but not officially, but all the lights went up in the air and we had quite a party. It was just a huge laugh, drinking and absolutely relaxing. Those static units in that area that had nice camps with flagpoles and whitewashed stones – who were not even supporting troops –

we then sent out parties to pinch their flags. Anything that was stupid we were very good at – and I was in the thick of it!⁷

Major Alan Hay, 'A' Company

Soon the locally available sources of beer, wine and spirits had run out and alternative sources were sought out.

> We all clubbed our money together. The 15cwt driver said, 'I'll go down to Forli and get a carboy of wine!' It was about eight or nine kilometres, so he came back very, very, slowly on the bumpy roads, with two in the back holding the carboy down. It was a great big glass carboy – massive! He just came in this farm gate, and he went down in a ditch. 'CRASH!' And there was the wine pouring out of the side. He was out of that cab, and he was away! We never saw him for two days. That was our celebration! We lost our wine.⁸

Private James Corr, 'B' Company

This was not the only accident that night. A party was laid on by the officers and during the festivities, Ronnie Sherlaw came to grief.

> Myself and two of my officers went down in my jeep. It was on the other side of a very small stream where the bridge had been blown and a diversion had been made. During the course of the evening, they ran out of drink, which was a very serious matter, and somebody said to me, 'Is there anything you can do?' I said, 'Oh, yes, I've got some, we'll go and get some!' One of my officers, Freddy Dries said, 'I'll take you!' I said, 'OK!' He got into the jeep driving seat, I was next to him, and he shot away. Of course, he'd be half tight! He shot away from the headquarters – he didn't notice the bridge had been blown – and went straight across with that jeep. It is no exaggeration that as the jeep was in the air, I stepped out of it on to the other side, the jeep went over – and Dries was underneath it. The jeep wasn't in very good shape and Dries was in less of a good shape. He had a broken leg. So, it wasn't a good VE Day for us at all!⁹

Major Ronnie Sherlaw, 'D' Company

Jackie Milburn had gained some renown for his ability to recite the popular monologues of the day, so he attended the officers' party.

> I could do a few dirty monologues: one was 'The Nudist Camp', I gave them that – and they liked that one. They were giving me a whisky or two now and again. I gave them 'The Shooting of Dan McGrew'! When it comes to the end, 'Two guns blazed in the dark!' Well, I got that out – and then flopped down! When I came round, I got straight up and carried on, 'Two guns blazed in the dark' – as if I'd not been 'away'. They enjoyed that.[10]
>
> Private Jackie Milburn, 'C' Company

Next day the festivities continued with a Grand Fete with each company putting on two sideshow stalls, music from the dance band and decorated jeep and fancy-dress contests. Even the normally straitlaced Russell Collins found himself somehow inveigled into participating in a manner he might not have anticipated.

> Harry Mynheer got hold of one of the locals and borrowed an oxcart, a covered wagon sort of thing. They put on the side 'Off to Blaydon Races!' He said, 'Well, you two dress up!' Russell Collins and I – because we were only young! We borrowed frocks and stuffed some socks in – mine kept sagging! He was quite the part! Harry Mynheer got some old hat, and we were all going to the Blaydon Races! Everybody was drinking everything they possible could! Later, I don't know what time it was, but I can remember Russell firing a Bren gun up in the air – I said, 'Now come off it – it'll only come down on us!'[11]
>
> Lieutenant Lionel Dodd, Mortar Platoon, Support Company

In the evening there was a massive bonfire, and an effigy of Adolf Hitler was ceremonially burnt, followed by a communal singalong of the favoured songs of the day. And, of course, more parties! Russell Collins was a hero, who had come close to breaking in the final stages of the Gothic line campaign, so for him this was all a glorious release.

> There was general mayhem for forty-eight hours or so. I was absolutely relieved, particularly as then we didn't have to go into action a third time in Italy. There was a great sense of euphoria; it was really marvellous.[12]
>
> Lieutenant Russell Collins, Carrier Platoon, Support Company

The war was over. They would after all be going home. But when?

*

AUSTRIA BECKONED FOR THE men of the 16th DLI and on 11 May they began the long journey through northern Italy. Travelling in trucks they crossed the Po and Adige rivers and stopped overnight near Padua. Then on again. They passed through Treviso and Udine, to arrive at Caporetto. Here they found a deeply disturbing situation, as everywhere there seemed to be gangs of Yugoslav partisans seeking to establish control over this area of Italy for the regime headed by the leader of the Communist Party of Yugoslavia (KPJ), Josip Tito, who had also led the Yugoslav guerrilla movement following the German invasion of Yugoslavia in 1941. With the end of the war, he had taken power over Yugoslavia, but sought to extend his control over the border zone with Italy, an area that had long been the focus of dispute. The partisans were an intimidating bunch.

> We were there to deny the Yugoslav partisans the opportunity to move any further. We had head-on confrontations with Tito's people. They looked like soldiers, well – like partisans anyway! Tough, very antagonistic, bristling with weapons, they had bandoliers of bullets, half a dozen of them strung around their necks. We were there, sometimes with our rifles, sometimes not. We had no intention of fighting any more – as far as we were concerned the war had finished. Nobody was going to fire a gun in anger again if they could help it! We were eyeball to eyeball, and the position got quite nasty for a while. There was mistrust – snarling at one another! It wasn't that we

wouldn't have been capable of fighting them, but we were in no mood to fight them. It was the end of the war as far as we were concerned – we weren't ever going to fight again![14]

Lance Corporal Ronald Elliott, 'A' Company

Luckily the Yugoslav partisans were content to infiltrate into the disputed areas, and to counter the movements of the opposing Italian partisans.

> The Yugoslavs were claiming all the smaller villages and they had painted signs, 'Tito'. They were very much in command of the smaller villages and towns. The only firing was against the Italian partisans, whose noses were being pushed out. There were clashes between them, but it wasn't our concern![15]
>
> Major Alan Hay, 'A' Company

That night, just as they were settling down to sleep, orders came that they were to push on next day at 02.00, to get across the Alps and into Austria as quickly as possible. It proved a tough journey, with a long chain of lorries heading up into the mountains over the Caparetto Pass and crossing the Austrian frontier at about 05.30 on 14 May.

> We went over this winding pass, which the Germans had done their best to have destroyed. There were makeshift repairs, and it was quite frightening! I don't think we had any real casualties; there were some broken down vehicles [that] had been shunted off the road. At dawn we were over the top of the pass, the sun was rising, and we saw this green and pleasant land of Austria.[16]
>
> Major Alan Hay, 'A' Company

They arrived at Villach, which was a decent sized town. Austria was classified as 'enemy territory' and there was a non-fraternisation policy with civilians, which was at first strictly enforced. As they drove through, the evidence of the German defeat was all around them, for the roads were packed with dispirited German soldiers plodding along on their road to nowhere. They would gradually be gathered up and put in prisoner of war camps.

After brief stops, the Durhams convoy motored on northwards, via Klagenfurt, to Unzmarkt, to the temporary demarcation line agreed with Russians along the Mur river. They had heard much of the exploits of the Red Army, but most found them underwhelming in the flesh.

> In the main street there was a bridge at the top that was absolutely full of Russians. Not in any arrogant postures, but as though they were having the afternoon off! Leaning against the bridge, but there were a lot of them! They had been told they hadn't to come across the river. We were given company areas and I went into a very nice little guesthouse. The lady couldn't have been more polite to welcome us. I put the officers in there. Meanwhile we'd found billets for the men. We settled down for the night. It was the first time I'd slept between sheets with my clothes off![17]
>
> Major Alan Hay, 'A' Company

However, he wasn't given the chance to enjoy such luxury for long. On 16 May, he was given an urgent task that required him to backtrack across Austria.

> At about two o'clock in the morning, I was awakened, told to go to battalion headquarters and ordered to take my 'A' Company with 'D' Company and given a route to Bleiberg. I said, 'But that's way back from where we've just come!' They said, 'Yes, there's some trouble there!'[18]
>
> Major Alan Hay, 'A' Company

The crisis in the Bleiberg region originated from the presence of large numbers of both Croatian and Yugoslavian forces, which was creating a great deal of tension and the potential for large-scale violence; the two sides nursed mutual hatreds that originated in their respective roles for and against the Nazi invasion of Yugoslavia. Hay was told to report to the headquarters of the 38 (Irish) Brigade in Bleiberg Schloss, where he was given a background briefing and told he had to somehow diffuse the situation. Above all, he was to prevent a clash between the huge number of Croatians who had gathered in a nearby valley, and the Yugoslav partisans in the surrounding woods. In among the Croatians were some prominent leaders whom the Yugoslavs were desperate to capture. Hay went to judge the position for himself.

> I was on this high ground looking down this valley at this vast mass of people with vans, horses, cows even. Civilians, troops, there could have been well over about 200,000. Erecting bivouacs and settling in. I said to Ronnie Sherlaw, take up positions, don't do anything, but just spread yourselves around so that these people can see you, to show that they were surrendering to the British, that they were then on 'British' territory. I didn't know where the actual border was, but they had come to surrender to the British to get away from Tito's troops who were out to annihilate them. I didn't see many of Tito's Yugoslavs to start with, but once we came, they seemed to come out of the woods and almost surrounded us – a scraggy looking lot with all sorts of weapons and bandoliers. They were firing over the heads of these crowds for no reason at all. They weren't shooting to kill; they were doing it to intimidate. Whilst nobody spoke English, they wanted to know if we'd brought them food and cigarettes. The 'Jugs' – Tito's lot were known as Jugs – started to take up positions between us and the Croatians – and there were a lot of them; they outnumbered us.[19]
>
> Major Alan Hay, 'A' Company

Hay hurried back to report to Brigadier Pat Scott at the schloss. The only other British forces in the area seemed to be a battery of four guns and a few armoured cars from the 46th Recce Regiment. The rest of 38 Brigade was already occupied in establishing a POW camp for the surrendered Cossack Kolonoff Brigade. There was also a complication – for all unknown to Hay, Brigadier Scott was under instructions from Lieutenant General Sir Charles Keightley, (Commanding V Corps) to secure the surrender of the Croatians to British forces – but then to return the Croatians by deception to Yugoslavian territory. Underlying everything was a fear of annoying the Soviets or their Yugoslavian allies, and thereby starting a Third World War! If Alan Hay expected some advice or assistance from Scott, he was soon disabused of the notion.

> In the brigadier's own words , 'It was a complete donkey's breakfast!' What was he expected to do? 'We've just got to play this as we see it: we can't wish for this, that, or the other, let's hope that this works!' We moved down into the valley. All this time the Yugoslavians were pestering us, threatening and just being thoroughly objectionable. We spread ourselves along the woods to just see what happened next. No sooner had we done that, then the civilian refugees started to come across and wanted to talk to us. Waving bits of paper. Everybody seemed to be a doctor or professor, with papers. There were women with kids, nice and respectable, pleading with us. I said to them, 'It's going to be all right!' Darkness came and then Tito's lot were coming down and raping the women. The screams during the night, the shots, it was quite unnerving. There was no rest for us.[20]
>
> Major Alan Hay, 'A' Company

They moved along the valley assisted by the armoured cars from 46th Recce Regiment. Next day came the formal surrender of the Croatians. What followed was a disgrace to everyone concerned. But what could they do? It is easy to criticise, but difficult to think of a course of action that avoided abandoning the Croats to a terrible fate.

> After a while we saw some white flags going up from the Croats, yes, they were going to surrender. Word was passing through the crowds, and you could see the bivouacs coming down. They were marshalling themselves, there were soldiers on the outside of the road piling up their arms. It was very slow. It took a lot of time for the word to get round; they had no method of communication other than by word of mouth. I took our men back from the edge of the woods, a position I didn't like at all, back to the hill we first stood on. Tito's lot

were down in the village about half a mile away – we could
hear them roistering and singing. We didn't go anywhere near
them. By this time a flagpole had been put up behind us and a
few more of our lorries were stationed behind it. The Union
Jack was flying – all for show! These Croatians were getting
themselves organised. The order was that soldiers would line
up five abreast on the side nearest the woods, the civilians
would line up and they would march down this Bleiberg road.
After a while the column started to move down the road
with their horses, carts and animals. Just before they got to
where the road branched off to Bleiberg, Tito's soldiers got
amongst them and started to pinch everything they had from
the column – the Croatian soldiers weren't armed. They told
them to leave everything. Those who didn't were attacked and
beaten. There were no actual shootings out of hand, but shots
were being fired to intimidate them to leave everything. The
Yugoslavs were in full command – we had nothing to do with
it. I didn't understand the language, but it was being put to
them that, 'You do not take anything with you!' They looked
really dejected and to make matters worse it started to rain – it
was really pouring. The road went straight on Klagenfurt, but
they branched off round Bleiberg village, swung round and
went back across the Yugoslav border. We were standing there,
and somebody said, 'I thought they would be going straight
up there?' 'Oh, no this is the route they're taking them!' Well.
I frankly didn't know the geography of the place. By this time,
word had passed down the column that they weren't going
straight up to Klagenfurt. There was absolute panic. Then
people started to break away from the column, to run into
the woods, run back towards the border. That's when there
was a certain amount of shooting to get them back. There
were some casualties and some escaped. We had fought a
war – fighting Germans – we'd fought eyeball to eyeball – that
was warfare. But this was civilians – it was horrendous. There
we were – soldiers – and here we were standing spectators.
There was nothing we could do for them. We were totally
outnumbered, and my instructions were not to do anything

provocative, unless we were personally attacked. Those were my instructions. It was traumatic; I'm still sickened to this day.[21]

Major Alan Hay, 'A' Company

By this time the whole battalion had arrived and was based at Bruckle. Here they assisted in rounding up the Cossack Kononoff Brigade. This was another unsavoury business for it resulted in the forcible disarmament and repatriation of the Cossack troops to the Russian sector. Laurie Stringer was involved from the start.

> We were responsible for rounding up and disarming the Cossack Kononoff Brigade. They had a unique history as it consisted mainly of Russians who the Germans had persuaded to fight for them against their fellow countrymen. As soon as peace was declared it is to be understood that Stalin showed great interest in this particular brigade – and wanted to ensure that they would be returned to him – lock, stock and barrel. They started to come into a cage that I had constructed, in which they were to be rounded up until the next move took place. We handled something like 3,000 Cossacks a day, together with their horses and their camp followers. As the Cossacks arrived, the majority of them presented a rather picturesque picture! They weren't aggressive, they were mounted and many of them were wearing flowing cloaks. They looked quite dignified. I stood at the gate of the POW cage and the officer in charge of the whole party stopped his horse and I demanded that he handed over his sword. He wasn't at all pleased about that! But I was perfectly within my rights. I still have that sword as a memento.[22]

Major Laurie Stringer, 'B' Company

The mood in the POW camp was jovial, but they had no idea what the Allies had planned for them.

> They were well behaved: they had a band and sang very well indeed. They lit fires at night and danced round their fires. No problem to us at all. We had searchlights which played on the

cage. There was no attempt at any escape at all. Lorries came, provided by the division, and these were loaded up with these Cossacks – and they were taken away. Many of them still under the impression that that was the commencement of their journey to Canada. That's what some of them had been told. I'd heard rumours – and I was very unhappy about the whole situation. I know it is the subject still of a lot of dissension and disagreement. Neither my men nor I were quite certain what was going to happen to these people, but at the back of our minds was a feeling of great concern as to what might happen. The lorries were driven to the banks of the River Dra, which was the line of demarcation, passed over the river, then emptied their cargo on the other side and the lorries came back. We heard some of these poor fellows committed suicide on the way over the bridge. When you're in the army, you have orders and those orders come to you from Higher Command. You obey those orders; there is no question of you questioning those orders. I was in that situation. It was the unhappiest episode in the whole of my military career.[23]

Major Laurie Stringer, 'B' Company

What followed after the 'handover' to the Russians was the stuff of nightmares for the Durhams involved. To the Soviets the Cossacks were nothing more than traitors, and they showed them no mercy. Tom Lister was one of the lorry drivers.

It was really quite heartrending in some ways. A lot of them were good soldiers; a lot were forced to serve under the Germans. They had the choice of serving under the Germans or dying. A number committed suicide rather than be handed back to the Russians; they knew they were going to certain death, or harsh imprisonment. It appeared obvious to me that the majority of them weren't going to last long, because as soon as they got them out of the back of the waggon, they used to be kicking them, pushing them, battering them with the butts of rifles. Driving them in. They would be shouting and pleading with you not to hand them over, but you had to do what you had to do. It was Allied policy to hand them over and handed over they were.²⁴

Private Tom Lister, MT Section, Headquarters Company

James Corr was another witness to the shameful handover.

I went away on the bike with them, partly from curiosity. When we get to this big high bridge, where we were due to hand them over to the Russians, they realised they were going back to Russia, from 100 yards away, I saw them diving over the top – killing themselves. I turned and came away then. It was a betrayal as far as I was concerned.²⁵

Private James Corr, 'B' Company

Many of the Durhams were deeply compassionate to the terrible plight of these men, but after all 'they were only following orders'. Such a defence never resonates well, especially not in the aftermath of the concentration camps. But what else could they do?

*

AMID THE MISERY OF THESE BETRAYALS there was the strange juxtaposition of the story of the hundreds of horses gathered up by the 16th DLI from the Cossacks and the various German units, many of whom still relied on horsepower for logistical support. The horses were rounded up and kept in pens, where they were an irresistible temptation to soldiers brought up on 'western' cowboy films at their local cinemas.

I wasn't by any means a trained horseman, but everybody that could find a horse that seemed reasonable, used to clap a blanket on, fasten it on with some webbing for a saddle, a couple of bits of rope for reigns – and ride round like cowboys. It's a beautiful part of the country and virtually everybody was riding around on horses!²⁶

Private Tom Lister, MT Section, Headquarters Company

Although many promptly fell off and gave up, others became proficient, and the horses were even used on patrols.

> You can't go through woods and forests on trucks, so Captain Tom Reynolds said, 'Why not use the horses!' We all started getting used to horses. You had to find out yourself! We had a couple of officers who knew something about horses, they used to tell you the fundamentals: how to put your reins on, how to saddle a horse up, how to ride a horse. Then sections went out on patrols, to see if there was anything in these woods – clear these woods out. We were travelling a good few kilometres by horseback, which was very uncomfortable until you got used to them – I'll tell you![27]
>
> Sergeant William Cowans, 'C' Company

They also had horse races, where the officers could show their prowess and the men could have a flutter on the result.

> Horse mania! We had a flat race meeting; we had officers who had ridden horses before. By that time, I was never off a horse's back! There was betting and I was a firm favourite to win. I'd never been in a race before. I never knew that horses could throw up so much dirt! I was getting almost knocked out by the clods coming up from the horse! I was more concerned about saving my face from these clods! In the end, my horse took its own way and just narrowly lost – so I wasn't very popular. They said, 'You had the thing in your hand!' I said, 'Yes, but I was getting muck thrown at me!'[28]
>
> Major Alan Hay, 'A' Company

It couldn't last, and after a while all the horses had to be handed in. Once again the 16th DLI was an infantry regiment!

At this stage the non-fraternisation orders were still having an impact and it was difficult to establish good relations to the local Austrians when they weren't allowed to speak to them. And of course, the Austrians had been the enemy. However, in the absence of any active resistance, on 15 July the non-fraternisation orders were lifted, which reduced any incipient tension and allowed a more natural relationship to develop with the Austrian civilians.

On 23 July, the 16th DLI began the move to the Wildon area in the Styrian region of Austria, which they took over from the Soviets as part of the arrangements negotiated at a higher level under Operation Fanfare. The departure of the Russians meant that the British were received by some Austrians as liberators, with reports of flowers strewn in the streets. The battalion companies were distributed around Wildon, and neighbouring villages, although the process of finding billets did cause a little initial friction.

> We got off on the wrong foot, as you go into somebody else's country and into their towns. Because you had to billet the troops! This meant the 'old story' of doubling up – go into a house – through the door you'd go! Then without even asking, you'd walk up the stairs, look at the number of bedrooms, and say, 'Right, there are twelve rooms in this house, you have six we have six!' It doesn't get you off on the 'right foot' when the grandma has to be moved out, carried downstairs and put into another room! It all causes a certain amount of resentment! But this didn't last very long! Because the British soldier with his unbeatable talents for getting to know people, whether he's instructed to or not, meant it wasn't long before a much more friendly atmosphere prevailed![29]
>
> Major Arthur Vizard, Headquarters Company

Gradually the atmosphere warmed up as both sides found that the other was not as bad as they might have feared. In contrast to the former Russians occupiers, the British soldiers appeared relatively benign and willing to help the Austrians where they could. Tom Lister and his section found themselves billeted in the Rosenhof Brewery, which had formerly brewed schnapps but was now unoperational. For some reason, Lister and his chums were more than keen to help, when asked to help restore this vital part of the local infrastructure.

> The Russians had smashed everything up, so they were trying
> to get it going again. The manager came to the fitters of the MT
> Section, appealing if we could help him getting this still going.
> They wanted a couple of tubes. We raked around and got a
> wrecked vehicle, got the brake piping out of it and steam cleaned
> it all up. We bent it the way they wanted it into circles, got them
> some rubber tubing to link up here and there. We got it going!
> They made some very rough schnapps with brewed fruit – there
> was ample apples and pears in the orchards. It was drinkable
> within three or four days! They were absolutely over the moon
> with the result. We had a good relationship with the locals based
> on the old principle of you scratch my back and I'll scratch yours!
> It worked very well. From then on, they began to dig up bottles
> of schnapps from here and there – they had a lot buried to hide it
> from the Russians. It eased the situation. We had our own little
> recreation place which we called the 'Drop Inn' – we had a big
> sign up[30]
>
> Private Tom Lister, MT Section, Headquarters Company

A lot less savoury was the attitude of some soldiers to the local Austrian women.

> The 'frat' ban was lifted. The soldiers could now go out with a
> German woman. But the Burgomaster warned the women, 'If
> you get pregnant with a British soldier, you can't marry him!
> He's not forced to marry you!' It did happen, of course. One of
> my sergeants got one of them pregnant – and of course he left
> her![31]
>
> Company Sergeant Major Leslie Thornton, 'C' Company

The result of such 'romantic' entanglements was more ruined lives. But, sadly, many of the men saw women as fair game. On the other hand, some of the Austrian men had several reasons to dislike the interlopers and they, too, could behave badly.

> There were quite a few of the Austrian young men who we
> considered a bit dodgy. You couldn't trust them as far as you
> could throw them! There was a mountain stream came down

> and there was this beautiful pool. We used to go swimming and then someone dumped some German mines, grenades, things like that on the bottom – in the hope that they might do some harm. It had to be cleared.[32]
>
> Private Tom Lister, MT Section, Headquarters Company

Indeed, the 16th DLI still had work to do as they were required to send out patrols to search out and detain former Nazi figures that had been identified from intelligence briefings.

> The next job we had was to round up the SS, which was an interesting job. I was given a list of names and addresses – and an interpreter, a 15cwt truck and seven men. I visited all these farms to dig out these SS. We went around these farms picking up these people, mothers crying through the interpreter, 'What will happen to them?' I said, 'Well if he hasn't done anything, he'll come back. If he's done any atrocities, he won't come back – and that's the end of it!' Now the SS were all tattooed under their arm. I went to the farm and this chap came to the door and I said in German. 'Ist du Carl Collinger?' He said in perfect English, 'No, I'm not Carl Collinger. I'm a discharged German soldier! I fought against you in Italy – you were the 46th Division with the oak tree [badge]!' I said, 'Now, go and get [Collinger]!' He came out with this young lad! I said, 'Right, take your shirt off!' And the lad had burnt the tattoo off! 'Get him in the truck! And you – any more from you and you'll go in a truck as well! Don't you talk to me about how you fought against me!'[33]
>
> Company Sergeant Major Leslie Thornton, 'C' Company

On 30 July, there came the announcement of the breaking up of the Eighth Army. From this time the army of occupation in Austria was unimaginatively known as British Troops Austria [BTA]. Then came the news of the dropping of the atom bomb on Japan on 6 August.

> I was listening to a cricket match on the radio. Then this thing came on about the 'atom bomb'. I went in to see my mate, I says, 'Hey, they've dropped this bomb in Japan, and it's cleared

the decks – cleared the town out, like!' He says, 'Ahhhh! It'll be a play!' Nobody had heard of an atom bomb.³⁴

Private George Bland, Carrier Platoon, Support Company

On 15 August 1945, came 'Victory over Japan Day' (VJ Day). At last, the war was really over and there were no residual fears of being sent to fight in the Far East. But for the Durhams nothing much changed as they continued their patrols and kept fit with keenly contested sports days. More and more men were being sent home on leave under LIAP, while the first demobilisations were also removing men, to such a degree that the battalion was reorganised on a three-company basis.

Then on 9 October, the 16th DLI were honoured to be the first unit from the 46th Division to be chosen to act as garrison troops in Vienna. They were billeted in the Boerhaavegasse.

> We were billeted in a big Red Cross hospital; it wasn't far from the Imperial Palace. It had been used as a hospital, and also partly as a Gestapo headquarters. It was about three stories high, a wing to the left rear, a wing to the right rear, and a big area in the centre. It had probably been a garden or lawn, with a great big mound of earth overgrown with grass and weeds. When we went there, the whole place was filthy – it stank! We had a lot of cleaning out to do. We finally got what had been an upstairs ward cleaned out and the lot of us were billeted in there. There was this pervading smell – and there were hundreds of bodies buried under this mound. Nobody knew anything about them – they'd just got there, according to the Austrians. Obviously, they had been people eliminated – missing persons.³⁵

Private Tom Lister, MT Section, Headquarters Company

The city was divided into four zones, controlled by the British, French, American and Russian forces. Each month a new supreme commander of the city was appointed from one of the four powers, while that nationality's forces also provided the guards for the separate 'International Area' of the city. On 15 November, General Sir Richard McCreery became Supreme

Commander, taking over from the Americans, so from that point it fell to the Durhams to provide the required guards. This was perceived as a great honour and every effort was taken to make sure they looked the part.

> We were kitted out. An issue of a different type of battledress, more like the 'Yank' type of stuff. Where ours was rough khaki, this was finer, like a serge. They fitted us all up with this fancy battledress. We pressed it and put our Africa Star ribbons up, cleaned up, polished and shined rifles, cap badges and everything. My guards were twenty-four hours on, twenty-four hours off at the main building where the Four Powers occupied. There were offices for the Yanks, the British, the Russians and the French. We had a twelve-man guard there, myself and Sergeant Bert Scully. We had two sentries at the front of the main building. They were ceremonial, and we had to do a drill similar to what the guards do at 'Buck House'. I used to march the two sentries out to change them at the two sentry boxes. All the civvies used to stop and have a look. There were two entrances at the back where the sentries just had to stand at the door with a pistol on a belt.[36]
>
> Lance Corporal Tony Cameron, 'A' Company

Vienna was a mysterious place, wreathed in a sort of romantic gothic noir darkness. The British still had one inestimable advantage here in their relations with the Austrians – they were not Russians.

> The Austrians were very pleased to see the British, the Americans and the French! We got on very well with them. It was seedy because there was the black market about, and if you've seen *The Third Man*, that is exactly what it was like. It was an odd mixture of joi de vivre mixed with this seediness. They were short of money and the occupying troops did have the wherewithal. So there was a lot of bartering going on and black-marketing activities. They were starting up the opera and the music of Vienna. All of the spectacle was returning. I first saw *Die Fledermaus* there, and one or two Austrian musical

concerts. It went along with all sorts of criminal activities, nefarious activities. We never spent any money in Vienna. We had our rations of cigarettes, chocolates and soap – and we used to give them to an intermediary: one of the blokes who was a 'Mr Fixit' – he was one of the lads – a headquarters orderly. He could get you anything; we never paid for anything. We were happy to have somebody else to do it for us; we didn't want to get involved with it. We all felt it was immoral – that's why we didn't want our own hands to be sort of blackened with it![37]

Lance Corporal Ronald Elliott, Headquarters Company

The Durhams were slightly apprehensive of the Russians, a combination of awareness of all they had done to win the war, coupled with a growing awareness of the political schism that would become the Cold War, and a revulsion at the stories they heard of brutality to civilian populations in their path.

> We never went in the Russian sector. We never went in any of the other sectors, we stayed in the British sector – that was our orders. The Russians were supposed to stay in their sector, but they didn't. You'd get the odd ones coming across the Danube – and they all carried bloody small arms, normally machine guns. Often enough you'd hear a bloody burst go off – the Russians getting drunk – and they'd rattle off a few rounds. But they never had any trouble with us – we stayed out of trouble with them, it was only common sense![38]

Lance Corporal Tony Cameron, 'A' Company

Like the British, the Russians were trying their best to create a good impression.

> The Russians produced 'the cream': very smartly dressed, beautiful new uniforms! Immaculate officers and NCOs! A very stern discipline. I recall getting on a tram to go into the centre of Vienna. A woman started to scream and accused this Russian of trying to rape her. The tram stopped and two Russian military police boarded the tram, grabbed him, and took him

out. There was an officer questioning him. He took his revolver out and shot him there and then in the street. Shot him dead! That was the way they were.[39]

Private Tom Lister, MT Section, Headquarters Company

On 15 November, control of the International Area was passed to the French. Shortly afterwards, the 16th DLI were relieved by the 2nd Hampshires and returned to their billets in Wildon.

The focus had now moved on to providing lumber for a country that was desperate for fuel as winter loomed. A battalion lumber camp was established, and thousands of trees were chopped down to cheery shouts of 'Timber!' Another sign of winter was the introduction of ski patrols, with skiing courses to train the men in this new skill.

> They sent us right up in the hills. Snow on the top. We were stationed in one of those chalets. There was nowt there but bunk beds and washing facilities. We slept there and we ate in the guesthouse at the bottom of the hill. We had a young Austrian, about nineteen years old, teaching us to ski. We got fitted out with all this gear with these fancy boots with a thing at the back where the spring of your ski fitted. Teaching us how to go up hill – that was bloody hard work! Coming downhill you had to fall over for to bloody stop at first! This youngster was bloody amazing on a pair of skis, he'd grown up with them. We never got to be experts, but it was bloody good fun! Take your skis off and into the guesthouse. And we'd eat anything they put in front of us! With the fresh air, we would have eaten the table, I think![40]

Lance Corporal Tony Cameron, 'A' Company

They practised on the nursery slopes, but Tom Lister got a touch overconfident, to his cost.

> We were told not to go on the main ski run, especially if it had been raining. One Saturday afternoon, we had a few Schnapps and half a dozen of us decided to go. We got our skis and went on this run. I went down this main run and I couldn't make a

righthand turn at the bottom. I shot over the embankment and about 30 feet down into the top of some pine trees – and I broke all the fingers in my right hand, my right forearm, dislocated my right shoulder! I was covered in scratches and God knows what![41]

Private Tom Lister, MT Section, Headquarters Company

When the trainees got back to the regiment, they never carried out a single ski patrol.

As part of the 'hearts and minds' campaign, the 16th DLI put on a Christmas show for the Austrian civilians. It was all well intentioned, but some of the performances seem to have caused tears of regret in the audience.

We put on a fine Christmas show for the villagers. A performance, a sort of pantomime! We had a number of performers. We had our little septet augmented, a small orchestra, we had two violinists, and we also had some rather good musicians in the working group – and we invited them to come in – it being Christmas. The hall would hold about 150. The villagers came in and they sat down, and we put on this performance. The last item was one of the German prisoners of war, who was a good violinist, would play to them solo, 'Vienna City of my Dreams'. And all these Austrians were weeping. The Anschluss, the arrival of the German troops, the German occupation of Austria – all that had happened ever since. Here they were now in the grip of another foreign group of people – albeit humanitarian – but nonetheless occupied and likely to remain occupied for a long time. I think hearing 'Vienna City of my Dreams' upset them all.[42]

Major Arthur Vizard, Headquarters Company

As with every regimental history, every wartime story, peace brought nothing but an anti-climax, with everyone marking time, their thoughts concentrating on demobilisation and a return to real life. Peace also meant a gradual return to 'parade ground' soldiering,

> We were getting back to peacetime army standards. You could not impose the original pre-war standards of discipline, because people that have been through the war just wouldn't stand it. But you were returning to something fairly close to that – as close as one could do with a civilian army. You were back to parades, the old mounting of guards with all of the 'bull'! Everything had to be cleaned and polished.[43]
>
> Lance Corporal Ronald Elliott, Headquarters Company

Week by week, the 16th DLI dissolved before their eyes. The younger ones were sent off to serve with the 1st DLI in Greece, but many did not feel the same 'family' connection with these 'strange' Durhams. But most were being demobilised as 'their number came up'.

> There was always the fear of losing friends that had been forged over many years in difficult situations, I had a number of friends in the signals. Gradually, the older more senior members were leaving to be demobbed. You were saying goodbye to people – one by one you would be losing friends.[44]
>
> Lance Corporal Ronald Elliott, Headquarters Company

It is sad to think of the battalion breaking up and friendships lost, but remember they were going home to resume their 'real' lives. This was the freedom they all sought.

> The shrinking process continued throughout January – releasing them all the time. We were losing officers, many of the younger ones were in higher release groups, they were going away to different units. People shaking hands, exchanging home addresses, waving each other goodbye. 'Have you got your UXPDR?' Your unexpired portion of the day's rations, which usually consisted of a cheese and bully beef sandwich! And 15cwt trucks moving off. It was very sad actually. A very sad time; the breakup and disbandment of the unit. The colonel went, he was due for discharge as a Dorset farmer. I was senior major, we began to 'close in' grouped round Wildon – there was plenty of accommodation for the shrinking numbers. In

the end I was the only officer left – they'd all gone. Then my turn came! Sent the last radio message to brigade. I gathered up all the loose paper, in the orderly room, stuffed it into bags, turned out the lights and locked the door. It was the 16th February at 10.30 in the morning. [45]

Major Arthur Vizard, Headquarters Company

Among the officers to depart was Laurie Stringer, who had become a true 'Durham', when he formally changed his commission to the DLI from the Essex Regiment. He was determined to preserve the spirit and history of the battalion and since September 1945 had been producing a regimental magazine called the *Geordie* filled with a mixture of articles on their mutual wartime history, contemporary news, gossip and humour. But he was determined to do more and set about writing a full-fledged history.

> For some time, I had been aware of the fact that if someone didn't take the trouble to record the history of the battalion, it might in the process of time be lost. I felt it was right that someone even as unqualified as I was, should do something about it! No one else had said they were going to do it, so I got down to writing the history. The War Diary was the main source of information. The other thing was Colonel Johnny Preston, who commanded the battalion in the early days. He maintained a very close connection, although he was a KOYLI officer, because he loved the battalion. When he got to know I was trying to write the history, he said 'Laurence, come and stay with me.' I stayed with him – and we talked for hours – he gave me a lot of material – answered a lot of my questions.
> I got other information from people in the battalion. Johnny Preston offered to pay for the majority of the expenses. I made a smaller contribution, but the credit in the main should got to Preston, who arranged 1,500 copies should be printed. It was a difficult job to do, because when it was eventually published it was done by printers in Graz, who didn't understand a word of English! You can imagine the problems that that presented! I think the fact the history was printed went a long way towards

keeping the battalion together after it was disbanded. The book was dedicated to the officers and men of the Durham Light Infantry who gave their lives in the fighting.[46]

Major Laurie Stringer, 'B' Company

The result was *The History of the Sixteenth Battalion The Durham Light Infantry* published in 1946. The battalion had gone for ever, but the men had something to cherish, something to remind them of their time in uniform. They had played their part, and that part had been commemorated by Laurie Stringer.

18

END OF DAYS

> When you commit a murder in the King's name it never leaves you. Never, ever, leaves you. It was murder. You shouldn't do it; you shouldn't have been there. I suppose a lot of them would feel the same. It never leaves you. You live a life of regret when you've done that sort of thing. You never forget the faces. I'm seventy-two; those lads should have been seventy-two now. But that's the way it was.[1]
>
> Edward Grey

DEMOBILISATION WAS MUCH DESIRED by one and all, but how was it to be achieved? There were some 5 million men and women in the armed services, and they had to be released back into society in a fair and equitable manner. A system was devised by Ernest Bevin, the Minister of Labour, whereby they would be released in groups based on their age and the number of months they had served in uniform. When a man's 'Group Number' came up, he would say farewell to his comrades and make the long journey back to England. Here, at one of the demobilisation depots, he would be fitted out with a 'demob suit' – a subject of much post-war hilarity among ex-servicemen.

> The next thing was to be fitted out with a suit. I was greeted by a warrant officer who said, 'Alan Hay, what on earth are you doing?' It was a man who had a furrier's shop in South Shields! I said, 'Great! Now I want your best suit!' He said, 'Certainly!' I said, 'We've all talked about it and Burton's suits are the best!'

> He said, 'That may be! But come with me and I'll deal with you personally!' I got a nasty shock! There was somebody amongst the suits and he said, 'Major Hay wants a portly forty-four!' I'd never been a portly forty-four!²
>
> Alan Hay

Many of the men harboured dark thoughts and suspicions as to the honesty and integrity of the storemen charged with running the depots.

> I had a bit of trouble there, like! You were going round picking your things, and I saw someone come out with a smashing gabardine coat. I says, 'Oh, I want one of them!' 'You cannot have one!' I said, 'I'm entitled to one as much as he is! We're all entitled to the same; now I want one!' He wouldn't give me one, so I caused a row about it! A major came over and said, 'What's the trouble?' I said, 'I want one of them coats, he won't give me one!!' He said, 'Why won't you give him one? Give him one!' I got my own way there! Then they wanted half a crown for wrapping it up! I wouldn't pay them. I said, 'I'm away for the major again!' They couldn't wrap it up fast enough! They were trying to make a living out of the lads!³
>
> James Corr

Adorned with their 'demob suits' they were finally free of the army, looking forward to a brave new world. Many of them would soon be disabused. The financial pressures and debts of wartime meant that the UK was in economic distress, lacking the money to provide the massive investment in housing and the national infrastructure that was needed to make a real difference to the prospects of returning soldiers.

> Everybody's looking forward with a feeling of anticipation that there would be lots of changes, that life would be totally different. There was a feeling of hope. One had come through the war unscathed, that you were still alive, thank God! With the Labour government, things would change politically. It would be a better life for everyone and a fairer life – more

> equitable and, eventually, there would be a better economic climate. But things were still quite tough for some years and there were still shortages.[4]
>
> Ronald Elliott

Men returned to their families to face a variety of problems, many exacerbated by the difficulty in re-establishing relationships with family members who were strangers. James Corr found his brothers were unrecognisable.

> Quite honestly, my brothers had grown up! When I went away, I was twenty-one, one was seventeen, one was fifteen, one was thirteen. They'd grown old! I didn't recognise them. Three years had made all that difference![5]
>
> James Corr

Many had parents who had died in the long years they had been away. Some found their wives had 'moved on' in their long absence. A few found unexpected additions to their family that could not have been their progeny. But most resumed their lives, a return to normality if you like.

On his return to civilian life, one man, Arthur Vizard, could not settle until he had paid tribute to the men who had fought and died under his command. A self-imposed mission, but one that he devoted a huge amount of energy to accomplishing.

> It was a sort of haemorrhaging. I lost seventy-three men killed in those three and a half years. My first job was to go round and call on the wives and mothers of those seventy-three – as many as I could track down. I managed to call on fifty-eight – the remaining fifteen I could never locate. I explained the circumstances to them, going over the ground and explaining how it all happened. I never told them of any agonising end; I always said it was 'clean'. They'd got over the initial shocks, but there was a lot of sadness.[6]
>
> Arthur Vizard

His actions show he was a very special officer – and a true

gentleman. His recognition of the suffering of the families of casualties strikes a real chord.

One civilian that might symbolise the ordeal of wives and families in the war years is Maria Shutt, who was married to Sidney Shutt. She was born Maria Boldersera of Italian émigré parents who owned an ice cream business in Wheatley Hill and Thornley. After leaving her convent school, Maria worked in the family ice cream shop, where she met Sidney Shutt, who was working in a nearby greengrocer's shop. They got married on 7 July 1937. By then Sydney was working in the local Cooperative store and their son – David – was born in February 1939. The reality of war struck home when Sidney was called up in August 1940.

> There was talk of a war, things were bad. Lots of them thought it would never happen! It came as a shock to lots of people – it did to me! You tried to keep happy – it's not going to happen – but it did! When he went away, he didn't want me to go with him – I wanted to go all the way to Darlington. He didn't want that. It was sad. David and I – we just waved to him till he was out of sight. It was frightening. You didn't know what was going to happen.[7]
>
> Maria Shutt

At first all was well, but then came dreadful official news that Sydney Shutt had been reported missing during the Battle of Sedjenane in March 1943.

> I was down at the shop. My mother got the letters that morning, which she couldn't read. She must have seen by the letter that it was sad news! 'Presumed killed!' She didn't show me the letter until the afternoon! When she showed me, I was shocked. I felt terrible; my dad cried. You didn't like to look at them two words 'Presumed killed!' You wanted to think he wasn't killed; there was hope! Then we went down to tell his Mam; she didn't live far away. It was a very sad day. It was a funny feeling, every day, I kept thinking about him, 'Well, I should hear something; if he's not dead, I should hear something!'[8]
>
> Maria Shutt

It was three long anguished weeks before she had a letter through from the Vatican informing her that Sid Shutt was alive and a prisoner of war. That was some consolation, but she still had plenty to worry about for the rest of the war. Could he survive in a German prisoner of war camp? Then at last it was all over.

> We got this telegram that he would be home in May. Everyone, if their husbands or sons were coming up, they put the flags out! So, we got a flag and put it out of the upstairs window! David didn't know who his dad was! He wasn't as excited as I was! I always pictured the scene when Sid was coming home, you know. What would it be like? This poor old man that had lost his son, he lived opposite. On the Sunday morning he looked up the bank, then he looked up at my window, he did it twice – and I knew it was Sid coming home! But I felt sorry for the old man. To me he was old – then – he might not have been very old! When Sid came in it was early Sunday morning – and I was getting ready to go to mass. Sid just came in and he was worn out – he just sat down in the chair, he looked round, and he says, 'The kings and queens live in palaces!' I made his breakfast![9]
>
> Maria Shutt

After his demobilisation, Sid Shutt returned to his work at the Cooperative stores. It was a return to normality.

*

THE RETURNING SOLDIERS HAD CHANGED, many out of all recognition. Some teenage livewires had calmed down; others had been brutalised by war and were no longer recognisable to their 'nearest and dearest'. The reactions to a return to peacetime life were varied, with some gaining a confidence and a will to better themselves. One such was Ronald Elliott, who returned to his work as an accountancy clerk, but found he had gained a little more ambition than most ex-soldiers. He did not want to 'settle', he felt he could do more. And he did.

> I took the easy way out and just went straight back and they did find me a job. I wasn't too unhappy with it – it was fairly senior. They came along with schemes whereby you could transfer to teacher training and get grants because they were terribly short of teachers. I was very, very tempted to be a teacher. But I had become interested in economics and although I ought to have taken in an accounting qualification, I did an economics degree in my spare time at home. So, there I was in an accounting career with only an economics degree. Then I saw an advert advertising a job with Rowntrees, the chocolate people, for someone with an economics degree. I applied and I got that job in the personnel department researching into labour statistics, so I moved to York.[10]
>
> Ronald Elliott

In the years that followed he had a successful career and rose to be head of his department, before leaving to be the chief accountant for a factory in Fordham. I used to see him every year at the lectures I gave at the DLI Museum. A truly wonderful man.

Charles Bray was one who emerged older and wiser from the army, but determined to put the whole thing behind him as best he could.

> I went in the army when I was twenty, and I came out when I was twenty-six. I'd grown up a lot in those six years. I'd seen a lot of things which I wouldn't have believed in 1939. It gave me a much wider and broader image of life and the world. When I came back to Buckingham, a small town like this, I looked at things rather differently. I realised there were other places in the world outside Buckingham. It widened my understanding of things tremendously. But I don't think it unsettled me. Rather that it settled me. When I moved back in 'Civvy Street' I thought, 'Well this is it; this is what I'm going to do – I just want to settle down. I don't want to do anything more exciting! Or go racing around. I just settled down and had a quiet life!'[11]
>
> Charles Bray

Tom Lister was another who opted out of the 'rat race'. He took work driving a butcher's van before becoming a salesman.

> The war changed my outlook. I'd always thought of furthering my education. I knew it was unlikely I'd ever get to university, but I thought about taking some courses, getting some reasonable qualifications. But after the war, I'd lost the ambition to do that – I was quite happy to make a reasonable living and muddle along.[12]
>
> Tom Lister

When Jimmy James was demobilised, he at first had little choice but to go back to living with his parents in Rhymney. He had done well in the army, rising to become a company sergeant major. He had held a responsible position; he had commanded men in action and been respected within the battalion. Now it seemed he was as nothing.

> I was a single man. I just couldn't settle down. Where was I going? My parents were getting on – they didn't want me there! I didn't want to be a burden to them! I sometimes wonder if I was a little bit deranged after all these experiences in the army. I had to 'get over myself'! I missed all the comradeship. You sold yourself to the army; but the army looked after you! I missed all that! You didn't have that protection, the army umbrella. I was like a fish out of water for a long time.[13]
>
> Jimmy James

He stuck it out, although he was tempted at times to rejoin the army as a regular soldier. He decided to move to seek employment and rebuild his life in Birmingham, where he worked in a semi-clerical job in an electrical factory.

> The bloke who was the manager was a corporal in the army – and he hated my guts because I was a warrant officer! He had been badly treated by his warrant officer, he hated the army, and he hated warrant officers – and there was I saddled to work with him! He stopped my promotion. I eventually learned not to tell [people] what I was, I kept it dark! I wouldn't tell

> anybody because I knew that company sergeant majors and regimental sergeant majors were not popular![14]
>
> Jimmy James

Some men struggled when their wartime careers might have led one to believe they would thrive. One such was Alan Hay, who soon realised that he was still suffering from the effects of his various wartime wounds, but found it difficult to get anyone to take him seriously.

> I still wasn't fit. Even on 'demob' leave I was blacking out from the head wounds. I had blacked out twice digging in the garden. I saw my doctor and he said, 'Well you've just come back from the war, with these wounds!' And I had my disabled right hand – I found writing was difficult. I thought it would be easy enough. I applied for a disability pension, and they found nothing wrong with my head. They looked at my hand and assessed it at £160. I said, 'But this isn't my trouble! I'm blacking out!' I went back for more examinations; they couldn't find anything. They said, 'Take your £160 or leave it!'[15]
>
> Alan Hay

As if this wasn't enough, it was evident on his return to work that he should have secured his accountancy qualifications before he joined up.

> I tried to do accountancy work – I got back into my civilian job. There was a mature secretary she said, 'Nice to see you, Mr Hay! You did well and you'll soon lose that tan here as well as your rank!' That was the only comforting remark. I hadn't passed my final examination. Through my army courses, I got a secondary degree, but it wasn't the one I wanted. I was really having trouble. In the end I had a nervous breakdown in 1952. I just couldn't cope.[16]
>
> Alan Hay

Yet despite all this, when I asked Alan Hay whether he regretted what he had done by joining up so early and fighting so long and hard for his country, he said, 'Not at all!'[17]

Gerry Barnett also had problems in gaining his professional qualifications on his demobilisation. Although he was able to resume his studies at the School of Architecture, Liverpool University, his overall poor health because of his serious leg wounds meant that he had to drop out from the course. When he finally took his architectural qualifying examinations, he found his wartime experiences had given him an enviable inner calm.

> When I was in the trenches, I used to lie there, frightened to death, thinking, 'How dreadful this is! What's the worst experience in civilian life?' And I thought, 'Well the worst experience is examinations! That's the thing I hate most! When I next sit down in an examination room, I'm going to remember this and enjoy the exam!' And by gum I did! Sitting an examination, on a lovely summer day, the sun streaming in through the window, and I was sitting at a desk with a question paper in front of me. I thought, 'Well, how comfortable this is – what a delight – it's all quiet!' It cured me of a lot of grief.[18]
>
> Gerry Barnett

Such a determination to make the best of things is quite inspiring.

One man who had to face returning to civilian life bearing the deep scars of battle was Richard Hewlett. His leg was left in a terrible state, and he had to wear an iron calliper for a long time. His previous dreams of becoming a regular soldier after the war were clearly hopeless. He was also upset by the lack of understanding shown by his pre-war employer. His subsequent civilian career in customer services and management would be greatly hampered by his injuries, to such an extent that he felt his disability pension of some 60 per cent was no real compensation.

Douglas Tiffin was another officer who had to cope with the after-effects of severe wounds.

> There were still a few patches, where the stitches had been, that hadn't completely healed over. I stayed on leave having this

> physiotherapy through July and August. I threw the crutches away and had two sticks – still with a calliper. I threw one stick away – I had one stick and a calliper. By September, the calliper was taken off, but I still had a stick. So, it took me a year to get anything like back to normal. It was never completely better. I'd been a good athlete, a good rugby player. I asked the doctor, 'Will I play rugby again?' He said, 'Laddie, just wait and see – and just be thankful that you'll be able to walk!' It was soon obvious to me I would never play rugby again! But the longer I've gone on, the more I've said to myself, 'By God, you were a lucky bloke!' I am – that would have been the end of me if it had hit the artery! Seventeen hours without medical attention. A couple of blokes who were willing to stand by me! That's luck![19]
>
> Douglas Tiffin

His philosophical acceptance is quite marvellous.

Many men found that their army experiences had unsettled them, made them reluctant to return to a civilian job that they now detested. In Tony Cameron's case, this was the prospect of resuming work as a coal miner.

> You could go back to your own job, that was for sure, because that was guaranteed. All you had to do when you finished your leave was go and report and they had to find a place to set you on – which in my case was the pit. I had no intention of going there; not if I could avoid it![20]
>
> Tony Cameron

But you couldn't always choose your destiny in post-war Britain, and Cameron would have to suffer a couple of years as a coal miner before he rejoined the army in 1947. He served in Palestine, Greece and Germany before marriage convinced him he had to settle down, and he returned to work down the pit in 1952.

Les Thornton was another who decided to rejoin the army. The trigger for him was that his father died in an accident just as the 16th DLI moved to Vienna. As a result, Thornton was sent back to England for twenty-eight days compassionate leave. From there he reported to Brancepeth Castle depot, where he was 'talent-spotted' as an experienced NCO.

> Colonel McBain was the colonel there; he was my company commander before the war. I was due to finish in the army. I'd signed on for seven years, when I first signed, but I'd done eight by the time the war was over! Colonel McBain said, 'Are you going to sign on, Sergeant Major?' I said, 'Well, I don't know! If I can stop here for a couple years, I suppose I will!' A thing came out that said, 'Anybody signing on for the full time plus three, that's for twenty-two years plus three, will get £25 and a civilian suit'. Well, that was a lot of money then! I thought about that – spoke to my wife, 'What about it?' So, I signed on for twenty-five years![21]
>
> Leslie Thornton

He had a successful career, eventually transferring to the Somerset Light Infantry with whom he would serve in Korea in 1951. Following the same path was his friend Tommy Chadwick, who thrived in the army, serving in both Malaya and Korea, and rising to be regimental sergeant major with 1st DLI before his eventual retirement in 1966.

One young man to make the grade as a soldier should be no surprise: Russell Collins. He served with 2nd Duke of Cornwall's Light Infantry in Greece from 1946–7, where he made a successful application for a regular commission. After a long career, he finally retired as a lieutenant colonel in 1973. His whole life would be bound up in the army and service to his country, but one thing is certain as the interviews at the IWM demonstrate – the men he commanded and inspired in the 16th DLI never forgot 'Winkler' Collins.

Yet others, equally distinguished soldiers, went in an entirely different direction, seeking to forget the army and all they had experienced at war. One such was James Drake, the man who had been awarded the DCM for exceptional gallantry at the Battle of Sedjenane in 1943.

> Once I moved out of the army – that was it! I didn't want to know any more. I never joined the British Legion or any of them – I washed my hands of it completely. I didn't even join the Salvation Army![22]
>
> James Drake

He moved to join with his brother in setting up a successful painting and decorating business in Blackpool, where he became a prominent figure in society and a Conservative counsellor for many years. His soldiering days were over.

★

ONE IMPORTANT ASPECT OF THEIR POST-WAR lives for most of the veterans interviewed was the formation and enduring success of the 16th Durham Light Infantry Association. Regimental associations had been formed all over the country after the Great War and the Second World War was no different. They were the best way for old comrades to maintain contact with each other in a world without the internet or even many telephones in the years immediately following the war.

> I hadn't been home long, and I went down to Dorset to see the colonel with Alan Hay and Ronnie Sherlaw. We got together and I had the Nominal Rolls – and we created the first edition of the 16th DLI address book which was sent to every man. It contained a note from Colonel Worrall, saying how proud he had been of us. Because we'd never really had a proper farewell parade.[23]
>
> Arthur Vizard

Sam Cawdron remembered the first meeting of the 16th DLI Regimental Association. At the time he was working on the railways based in Bradford. It seemed he was doomed to miss out!

> The association officials made the first one in Leeds, because that was the centre of England; there were so many people in the Durham Light Infantry from all over England. Leeds was

easy for transport – all the trains went to Leeds from all over the country. It was in town hall, a lovely summer's day in August 1947. I wasn't going because I couldn't afford the rail fare. At work, we were doing a repair on one of the mining engines on the Saturday – we'd been working all morning on this engine. I was talking to this man, he was a lot older than me, he'd been in the First World War, I says, 'I never ought to be here today, struggling about with this blinking job! My brother's gone to Leeds and it's our 16th Battalion, Durham Light Infantry reunion dinner – the first one!' 'What, army reunion?' I says, 'Yes!' He says, 'Well, look, I'll tell you now, Sam, put them tools down. I'll look after the rest of the work, we've done what's necessary, you get off!! You've got plenty of time to get there, there's plenty of trains got to Leeds from Rotherham – get off! You'll thoroughly enjoy it, something you'll be sorry you missed if you don't go! All those pals you're going to miss them! If you miss the first one, you'll not go to the next one! You'll forget all about it'! He'd been to quite a few of his own regiment reunions. He says, 'You'll never be sorry for going – you go!' I went! [24]

Sam Cawdron

The reunions soon switched from Leeds to Durham, but Sam Cawdron went from then on – indeed he had attended the fiftieth reunion at time of interview. The regimental associations allowed them to mix together, reliving old experiences, but also remembering those they had lost.

Ken Lovell worked post-war as a teacher, but he never forgot the comradeship of the 16th DLI.

Although the war was pretty terrible and I had some pretty rough experiences, I don't think it's something I would have missed. It taught me an awful lot about other people; it taught me an awful lot about myself. I think it made me a much more compassionate person than I was. A much more understanding and tolerant person. Certainly, the comradeship that existed isn't found anywhere else. The comradeship of battle is something that lives with you for the rest of your life. [25]

Ken Lovell

DON'T REMEMBER THEM AS OLD OR FRAIL; REMEMBER THEM AS THEY WERE! Determined men, sometimes frightened, but fighting as best they could for their country and a cause they believed in. Plenty of people exude cynicism these days, but I still believe that, amid all the other cross-currents of twentieth-century politics, the Second World War *was* a war against fascism. To me these men are true heroes, more so for being ordinary men. For they were ordinary men who did extraordinary things, things that I cannot imagine having the physical or mental strength to endure. I was going to put the dates when these men finally died, but it seemed morbid, somehow, overly sad to think that these wonderful men are no more. When I look at the idealised bronze statue representing all the soldiers of the DLI standing proud in Durham market square, it is men like Ronald Elliott and Russell Collins that come to mind. And now they have nearly all gone. What an amazing generation they were. We must remember them. But how few of us seemed to really care while they were still alive.

> Nowadays you can't talk to other people about it – in the main they don't want to know, and you don't want to become a bore. It's only with people that have been through it that you can talk to and understand what it's all been about.[26]
>
> Leslie Brown

Laurie Stringer was a relative latecomer to the 16th DLI, but he had played his part in some hard-fought battles. As we have seen, he was also the first 'historian' of the battalion and chronicled their career. He was a true patriot, and even when I interviewed him in his old age, he was still proud of what he and the men had achieved.

> I will always regard it as a privilege to have played a very small part in helping to resist – to fight against – one of the greatest evils that the world had ever known. That really sums it up. I would not have missed my army experience and I'm grateful

for having had it! If the same situation came again, this is foolish of course because of my age, I would do precisely the same thing as I did before!²⁷

Laurie Stringer

ACKNOWLEDGEMENTS

Any book like this is an exercise in teamwork. First, I must thank the veterans who put so much of themselves into the oral histories they recorded – after all, this is their book. Then my skilled fellow interviewers who helped draw out and record their memories: Harry Moses, his son Michael Moses, and Tom Tunney. Several of the photographs in this volume are also featured on Tom Tunney's website at 16dli.net. Tom would like to thank all the ex-16th soldiers and their relatives who provided these over the nearly twenty years of the site's existence. Paul Errington was incredibly generous with his time and supplied much materiel from his DLI collections. My colleagues at the Imperial War Museum were all incredibly supportive throughout my time there, but I must single out Margaret Brooks, Tony Richards and Bryn Hammond who had the dubious pleasure of being my line managers. Then all the team at Profile: my editor, Georgia Poplett; the production manager, Penny Daniel; the wonderful copy editor Penny Gardiner and Martin Kulikowski who drew the maps. Then I would thank my brilliant agent Ian Drury, who keeps me on the relatively straight and narrow. My good friends, Gary Bain, John Paylor, Warren Smith and Phil Wood all read various versions of the text and their critical input was invaluable. Thank you all.

Picture Credits

The author and publisher wish to thank the Imperial War Museum for permission to use the follow photographs: page 1, bottom; page 2, top left, top right, bottom; page 4, top and bottom; page 5, top: all ©IWM. All other images were kindly provided by Tom Tunney.

While every effort has been made to contact copyright-holders of illustrations, the author and publishers would be grateful for information about any illustrations where they have been unable to trace them, and would be glad to make amendments in further editions.

NOTES

1. Close Encounters

1. IWM SOUND: James Drake, AC 020791, Reel 12.
2. IWM SOUND: James Drake, AC 020791, Reel 12.
3. IWM SOUND: James Drake, AC 020791, Reel 12 and 13.
4. IWM SOUND: James Drake, AC 020791, Reel 12 and 13.
5. IWM SOUND: James Drake, AC 020791, Reel 13.

2. Learning their Trade

1. IWM SOUND: Tom Turnbull, AC 12680, Reel 1.
2. IWM SOUND: Jimmy James, AC 20793, Reel 7.
3. IWM SOUND: Gordon Gent, AC 18255, Reel 2.
4. IWM SOUND: Gordon Gent, AC 18255, Reel 2.
5. IWM SOUND: James Drake, AC 020791, Reel 3.
6. IWM SOUND: Sidney Shutt, AC 18511, Reel 2 and 3.
7. IWM SOUND: Thomas Atkinson, AC 17618, Reel 3.
8. IWM SOUND: James Drake, AC 020791, Reel 4.
9. IWM SOUND: Thomas Atkinson, AC 17618, Reel 3 and 4.
10. IWM SOUND: Thomas Atkinson, AC 17618, Reel 3.
11. IWM SOUND: Gordon Gent, AC 18255, Reel 2.
12. IWM SOUND: Thomas Atkinson, AC 17618, Reel 3.
13. IWM SOUND: Thomas Atkinson, AC 17618, Reel 3.
14. IWM SOUND: Jimmy James, AC 20793, Reel 8.
15. IWM SOUND: James Drake, AC 020791, Reel 5.
16. IWM SOUND: James Drake, AC 020791, Reel 5.
17. IWM SOUND: Thomas Atkinson, AC 17618, Reel 3.
18. IWM SOUND: Thomas Atkinson, AC 17618, Reel 4 and 5.
19. IWM SOUND: James Drake, AC 020791, Reel 5 and 6.
20. IWM SOUND: Jimmy James, AC 20793, Reel 14.
21. IWM SOUND: Jimmy James, AC 20793, Reel 14.
22. IWM SOUND: Henry Harris, AC 18256, Reel 1 and 2.
23. IWM SOUND: John Lewindon, AC 20349, Reel 13.
24. IWM SOUND: Tom Turnbull, AC 12680, Reel 1.
25. IWM SOUND: Tom Turnbull, AC 12680, Reel 1.
26. IWM SOUND: Tom Turnbull, AC 12680, Reel 1 and 2.
27. IWM SOUND: Oswald McDonald, AC 30342, Reel 4.
28. IWM SOUND: Tom Lister, AC 12825, Reel 5.
29. IWM SOUND: Tom Lister, AC 12825, Reel 5.
30. IWM SOUND: George Forster, AC 122824, Reel 3.
31. IWM SOUND: George Forster, AC 122824, Reel 3.

32. IWM SOUND: George Forster, AC 122824, Reel 3.
33. Private Tom Anderson was killed aged twenty on 13 October 1943. He is buried at Minturno War Cemetery in Italy.
34. IWM SOUND: Jimmy James, AC 20793, Reel 18.
35. IWM SOUND: Thomas Atkinson, AC 17618, Reel 6.
36. IWM SOUND: Tom Lister, AC 12825, Reel 5–6.
37. IWM SOUND: Oswald McDonald, AC 30342, Reel 4.
38. IWM SOUND: Tom Tunney, AC 19129, Reel 6.
39. IWM SOUND: Charles Palmer, AC 16709, Reel 6.
40. IWM SOUND: Tom Lister, AC 12825, Reel 5–6.
41. NATIONAL ARCHIVE, KEW: R. F. Ware, 16th DLI War Diary October 1942: Appendix 2, Battalion Efficiency Competition, p. 3.
42. NATIONAL ARCHIVE, KEW: R. F. Ware, 16th DLI War Diary October 1942: Appendix 2, Battalion Efficiency Competition, p. 3.
43. NATIONAL ARCHIVE, KEW: R. F. Ware, 16th DLI War Diary October 1942: Appendix 2, Battalion Efficiency Competition, p. 3.
44. IWM SOUND: Russell King, AC 18512, Reel 8.
45. IWM SOUND: Charles Bray, AC 20349, Reel 4.
46. IWM SOUND: George Forster, AC 122824, Reel 3.
47. Alfred Akester died aged twenty-eight on 21 October 1942. He is buried in the Driffield Cemetery.
48. Harold Wright died aged twenty on 21 October 1942. He is buried in a family grave at Water Orton churchyard.
49. IWM SOUND: Russell King, AC 18512, Reel 9.
50. IWM SOUND: Tom Turnbull, AC 12680, Reel 2–3.
51. IWM SOUND: Jimmy James, AC 20793, Reel 22.
52. IWM SOUND: Oswald McDonald, AC 30342, Reel 4.
53. IWM SOUND: James Drake, AC 020791, Reel 7.
54. IWM SOUND: Jimmy James, AC 20793, Reel 22.
55. IWM SOUND: Russell King, AC 18512, Reel 9.
56. IWM SOUND: Jimmy James, AC 20793, Reel 22.
57. IWM SOUND: George Forster, AC 122824, Reel 3.
58. NATIONAL ARCHIVE, KEW: 16th DLI War Diary, 18 December 1942.
59. IWM SOUND: George Forster, AC 122824, Reel 4.

3. The Great Adventure

1. IWM SOUND: George Forster, AC 122824, Reel 4.
2. IWM SOUND: George Forster, AC 122824, Reel 4.
3. George Gates, *Geordie Magazine*, Christmas Issue 12/1945.
4. NATIONAL ARCHIVE, KEW: 16th DLI War Diary, 25 December 1942.
5. IWM SOUND: Gordon Gent, AC 18255, Reel 7 and 8.
6. IWM SOUND: Tom Lister, AC 12825, Reel 6.
7. IWM SOUND: James Drake, AC 020791, Reel 10 and 11.
8. IWM SOUND: James Drake, AC 020791, Reel 10 and 11.
9. IWM SOUND: James Drake, AC 020791, Reel 10.
10. IWM SOUND: George Forster, AC 122824, Reel 4.
11. IWM SOUND: James Drake, AC 020791, Reel 11.
12. IWM SOUND: George Forster, AC 122824, Reel 4.
13. IWM SOUND: George Forster, AC 122824, Reel 4.
14. IWM SOUND: Jimmy James, AC 20793, Reel 24.
15. Crook is a village in the Wear valley in County Durham.
16. IWM SOUND: Russell King, AC 18512, Reel 9.

Notes

17. IWM SOUND: George Forster, AC 122824, Reel 4.
18. IWM SOUND: Tom Turnbull, AC 12680, Reel 3.
19. IWM SOUND: George Forster, AC 122824, Reel 4.
20. IWM SOUND: George Forster, AC 122824, Reel 4.
21. IWM SOUND: Jimmy James, AC 20793, Reel 25.
22. IWM SOUND: Gordon Gent, AC 18255, Reel 9.
23. IWM SOUND: George Forster, AC 122824, Reel 4.
24. IWM SOUND: Tom Lister, AC 12825, Reel 8.
25. IWM SOUND: Jimmy James, AC 20793, Reel 26.
26. IWM SOUND: Thomas Atkinson, AC 17618, Reel 7.
27. IWM SOUND: George Forster, AC 122824, Reel 5.
28. IWM SOUND: Russell King, AC 18512, Reel 10.
29. IWM SOUND: James Drake, AC 020791, Reel 11.
30. IWM SOUND: Oswald McDonald, AC 30342, Reel 9.
31. IWM SOUND: John Douglass, AC 25211, Reel 12
32. Private John Fox died aged twenty-two on 22 February 1943. He is buried at Tabarka Ras Rajel War Cemetery.
33. IWM SOUND: Thomas Atkinson, AC 17618, Reel 7.
34. IWM SOUND: George Forster, AC 122824, Reel 5.
35. IWM SOUND: Gordon Gent, AC 18255, Reel 9.
36. IWM SOUND: Jimmy James, AC 20793, Reel 26.

4. Battle of Sedjenane

1. IWM SOUND: Thomas Atkinson, AC 17618, Reel 8.
2. IWM SOUND: Tom Turnbull, AC 12680, Reel 3.
3. IWM SOUND: Jimmy James, AC 20793, Reel 27.
4. IWM SOUND: Tom Turnbull, AC 12680, Reel 3.
5. IWM SOUND: Thomas Atkinson, AC 17618, Reel 8.
6. Company Sergeant Major George Broadhead died aged thirty-two years old on 28 February 1943. He is commemorated on the Medjez-el-Bab Memorial in Tunisia.
7. IWM SOUND: Russell King, AC 18512, Reel 10 and 11.
8. IWM SOUND: Thomas Atkinson, AC 17618, Reel 8.
9. IWM SOUND: Tom Turnbull, AC 12680, Reel 3 and 4.
10. IWM SOUND: Thomas Atkinson, AC 17618, Reel 8.
11. IWM SOUND: Tom Tunney, AC 19129, Reel 8.
12. IWM SOUND: Tom Tunney, AC 19129, Reel 8.
13. IWM SOUND: Sidney Shutt, AC 18511, Reel 6.
14. IWM SOUND: Sidney Shutt, AC 18511, Reel 6.
15. IWM SOUND: Tom Tunney, AC 19129, Reel 8.
16. IWM SOUND: George Forster, AC 122824, Reel 5.
17. IWM SOUND: George Forster, AC 122824, Reel 5.
18. IWM SOUND: Tom Tunney, AC 19129, Reel 8.
19. IWM SOUND: John Douglass, AC 25211, Reel 14
20. Tom Tunney Collection: http://16dli.awardspace.co.uk/ Harry Craggs, Account.
21. IWM SOUND: Sidney Shutt, AC 18511, Reel 6.
22. IWM SOUND: Oswald McDonald, AC 30342, Reel 9 and 15.
23. Captain Jeffrey Bavington-Jones died on 9 March 1943. He is buried at Massicault War Cemetery, Tunisia.
24. IWM SOUND: James Drake, AC 020791, Reel 14 and 20.
25. IWM SOUND: James Drake, AC 020791, Reel 14 and 20.
26. IWM SOUND: James Drake, AC 020791, Reel 14 and 20.
27. IWM SOUND: James Drake, AC 020791, Reel 14 and 20.

28. IWM SOUND: James Drake, AC 020791, Reel 14 and 20.
29. IWM SOUND: James Drake, AC 020791, Reel 15.
30. IWM SOUND: James Drake, AC 020791, Reel 15.
31. P. Welch, quoted by Anon, *North Irish Horse Battle Report: North Africa and Italy* (Belfast: W & G Baird Ltd, 1946), pp. 10–11.

5. Advance to Tunis

1. IWM SOUND: James Corrs, AC 13080, Reel 5.
2. IWM SOUND: Tom Lister, AC 12825, Reel 7.
3. IWM SOUND: Arthur Vizard, AC 16601, Reel 6.
4. IWM SOUND: Charles Palmer, AC 16709, Reel 8.
5. IWM SOUND: Arthur Vizard, AC 16601, Reel 5.
6. IWM SOUND: Arthur Vizard, AC 16601, Reel 6.
7. IWM SOUND: Arthur Vizard, AC 16601, Reel 6.
8. IWM SOUND: Arthur Vizard, AC 16601, Reel 6.
9. IWM SOUND: Arthur Vizard, AC 16601, Reel 6.
10. IWM SOUND: Tony Sacco, AC 18744, Reel 4.
11. IWM SOUND: Tony Sacco, AC 18744, Reel 4.
12. Sergeant Major Wilson Wales died aged twenty-six on 22 April 1943. He is buried at Massicault War Cemetery, Tunisia.
13. IWM SOUND: Jimmy James, AC 20793, Reel 29.
14. IWM SOUND: Tony Sacco, AC 18744, Reel 4.
15. Major Arthur Martin died aged thirty-four on 22 April 1943. He is buried at Massicault War Cemetery, Tunisia.
16. Private Frank Chambers died aged twenty-five on 22 April 1943. He is commemorated on the Medjez-el-Bab War Memorial, Tunisia.
17. IWM SOUND: Tony Sacco, AC 18744, Reel 4.
18. IWM SOUND: Arthur Vizard, AC 16601, Reel 6 and 7.
19. Private John Crosby died aged twenty on 22 April 1943. He is buried at Massicault War Cemetery, Tunisia.
20. Edited from account and correspondence by George Lyons from the private collection of Paul Errington.
21. IWM SOUND: James Corr, AC 13080, Reel 3.
22. IWM SOUND: Charles Palmer, AC 16709, Reel 9.
23. IWM SOUND: James Corr, AC 13080, Reel 3.
24. Author's Collection: H. Jones, Personal Account.
25. IWM SOUND: Jimmy James, AC 20793, Reel 30.
26. IWM SOUND: Arthur Vizard, AC 16601, Reel 7.
27. IWM SOUND: Arthur Vizard, AC 16601, Reel 7.
28. IWM SOUND: Gordon Gent, AC 18255, Reel 10.
29. IWM SOUND: Russell Collins, AC 13878, Reel 5.
30. IWM SOUND: Ronald Sherlaw, AC 12436, Reel 4.
31. IWM SOUND: Gerry Barnett, AC 12238, Reel 3.
32. IWM SOUND: William Virr, AC 17621, Reel 7.
33. IWM SOUND: Kenneth Lovell, AC 13251, Reel 6–7.
34. IWM SOUND: William Virr, AC 17621, Reel 7.
35. IWM SOUND: William Virr, AC 17621, Reel 7.
36. IWM SOUND: William Virr, AC 17621, Reel 7.
37. IWM SOUND: Gerry Barnett, AC 12238, Reel 4.
38. IWM SOUND: Kenneth Lovell, AC 13251, Reel 7.
39. IWM SOUND: Robert Ellison, AC 18743, Reel 9.
40. IWM SOUND: Robert Ellison, AC 18743, Reel 9.

41. IWM SOUND: Gordon Gent, AC 18255, Reel 10 and 11.
42. IWM SOUND: Kenneth Lovell, AC 13251, Reel 8.
43. IWM SOUND: Arthur Vizard, AC 16601, Reel 9.
44. IWM SOUND: Arthur Vizard, AC 16601, Reel 9.
45. IWM SOUND: John Lewindon, AC 20349, Reel 20.
46. IWM SOUND: Russell Collins, AC 13878, Reel 5.
47. Author's Collection: H. Jones, Personal Account.
48. IWM SOUND: William Virr, AC 17621, Reel 7.
49. IWM SOUND: Russell Collins, AC 13878, Reel 5.
50. IWM SOUND: Gerry Barnett, AC 12238, Reel 4.
51. IWM SOUND: Gerry Barnett, AC 12238, Reel 4 and 5.

6. Landing at Salerno

1. IWM SOUND: William Virr, AC 17621, Reel 8.
2. IWM SOUND: Arthur Vizard, AC 16601, Reel 9.
3. IWM SOUND: Kenneth Lovell, AC 13251, Reel 9.
4. IWM SOUND: Jimmy James, AC 20793, Reel 33.
5. IWM SOUND: Arthur Vizard, AC 16601, Reel 9.
6. IWM SOUND: Kenneth Lovell, AC 13251, Reel 9–10.
7. IWM SOUND: Arthur Vizard, AC 16601, Reel 9.
8. IWM SOUND: Tony Sacco, AC 18744, Reel 6.
9. IWM SOUND: Jimmy James, AC 20793, Reel 33.
10. IWM SOUND: Arthur Vizard, AC 16601, Reel 9 and 10.
11. IWM SOUND: Ronald Sherlaw, AC 12436, Reel 5.
12. IWM SOUND: Arthur Vizard, AC 16601, Reel 10.
13. IWM SOUND: William Virr, AC 17621, Reel 7 and 8.
14. IWM SOUND: Robert Ellison, AC 18743, Reel 9.
15. IWM SOUND: Robert Ellison, AC 18743, Reel 9.
16. IWM SOUND: Arthur Vizard, AC 16601, Reel 10.
17. IWM SOUND: Arthur Vizard, AC 16601, Reel 10.
18. IWM SOUND: Kenneth Lovell, AC 13251, Reel 10.
19. IWM SOUND: Gerry Barnett, AC 12238, Reel 4.
20. IWM SOUND: Gerry Barnett, AC 12238, Reel 5.
21. IWM SOUND: Gerry Barnett, AC 12238, Reel 4.
22. IWM SOUND: Ronald Sherlaw, AC 12436, Reel 5.
23. IWM SOUND: Gerry Barnett, AC 12238, Reel 4.
24. IWM SOUND: Tom Lister, AC 12825, Reel 9.
25. IWM SOUND: Gerry Barnett, AC 12238, Reel 4.
26. IWM SOUND: Kenneth Lovell, AC 13251, Reel 10.
27. The 'A' Company Platoons were numbered Nos 7, 8 and 9. However, this was not standard and Vizard has clearly remembered it otherwise.
28. Captain Thomas Logan died aged twenty-three on 14 September 1943. Buried in Salerno War Cemetery, Italy.
29. IWM SOUND: Arthur Vizard, AC 16601, Reel 10.
30. IWM SOUND: Arthur Vizard, AC 16601, Reel 10.
31. IWM SOUND: Arthur Vizard, AC 16601, Reel 10.
32. IWM SOUND: Arthur Vizard, AC 16601, Reel 11.
33. IWM SOUND: Gordon Gent, AC 18255, Reel 12.
34. IWM SOUND: Arthur Vizard, AC 16601, Reel 11.
35. IWM SOUND: John Lewindon, AC 20349, Reel 22.
36. IWM SOUND: Robert Ellison, AC 18743, Reel 9 and 10.
37. IWM SOUND: John Lewindon, AC 20349, Reel 22.

38. IWM SOUND: Kenneth Lovell, AC 13251, Reel 11.
39. IWM SOUND: John Lewindon, AC 20349, Reel 23.
40. IWM SOUND: Gerry Barnett, AC 12238, Reel 6.
41. IWM SOUND: Gerry Barnett, AC 12238, Reel 6.
42. IWM SOUND: Gerry Barnett, AC 12238, Reel 6.
43. IWM SOUND: Gerry Barnett, AC 12238, Reel 6.
44. IWM SOUND: Gerry Barnett, AC 12238, Reel 6.
45. IWM SOUND: Ronald Sherlaw, AC 12436, Reel 5.
46. IWM SOUND: Gerry Barnett, AC 12238, Reel 6.
47. IWM SOUND: Ronald Sherlaw, AC 12436, Reel 5.
48. IWM SOUND: Russell Collins, AC 13878, Reel 5.
49. IWM SOUND: Russell Collins, AC 13878, Reel 5 and 6.
50. IWM SOUND: Russell Collins, AC 13878, Reel 5 and 6.
51. IWM SOUND: Russell Collins, AC 13878, Reel 5 and 6.
52. IWM SOUND: Russell Collins, AC 13878, Reel 5.
53. IWM SOUND: Russell Collins, AC 13878, Reel 5 and 6.
54. IWM SOUND: Russell Collins, AC 13878, Reel 6.
55. IWM SOUND: Russell Collins, AC 13878, Reel 6.
56. IWM SOUND: Robert Ellison, AC 18743, Reel 10.
57. IWM SOUND: Alexander Gray, AC 22081, Reel 9.
58. IWM SOUND: Jimmy James, AC 20793, Reel 34.
59. IWM SOUND: William Cowans, AC 17622, Reel 8.
60. IWM SOUND: Tom Lister, AC 12825, Reel 10.
61. IWM SOUND: Ronald Elliott, AC 10167, Reel 5.
62. IWM SOUND: Ronald Elliott, AC 10167, Reel 5.
63. IWM SOUND: Ronald Elliott, AC 10167, Reel 5.
64. IWM SOUND: Ronald Elliott, AC 10167, Reel 5.
65. IWM SOUND: Ronald Elliott, AC 10167, Reel 5.
66. IWM SOUND: Ronald Elliott, AC 10167, Reel 5.
67. IWM SOUND: James Corr, AC 13080, Reel 5.
68. IWM SOUND: Ronald Elliott, AC 10167, Reel 5.
69. IWM SOUND: Tom Lister, AC 12825, Reel 10.

7. Naples and River Crossings

1. IWM SOUND: Ronald Sherlaw, AC 12436, Reel 7.
2. IWM SOUND: William Virr, AC 17621, Reel 9.
3. IWM SOUND: Robert Ellison, AC 18743, Reel 10.
4. IWM SOUND: Ronald Sherlaw, AC 12436, Reel 6.
5. IWM SOUND: Tom Turnbull, AC 12680, Reel 5.
6. IWM SOUND: Ronald Sherlaw, AC 12436, Reel 6.
7. IWM SOUND: Kenneth Lovell, AC 13251, Reel 12.
8. IWM SOUND: Tom Turnbull, AC 12680, Reel 5.
9. IWM SOUND: Ronald Sherlaw, AC 12436, Reel 6.
10. J. Hawkesworth quoted by L. Stringer, *The History of the Sixteenth Battalion The Durham Light Infantry*, (Graz, Austria, The DLI, 1946), pp.28–9.
11. IWM SOUND: Ronald Elliott, AC 10167, Reel 6.
12. IWM SOUND: Ronald Elliott, AC 10167, Reel 6.
13. IWM SOUND: George Bland, AC 17619, Reel 7.
14. IWM SOUND: Gordon Gent, AC 18255, Reel 11.
15. IWM SOUND: Kenneth Lovell, AC 13251, Reel 13.
16. IWM SOUND: Ronald Elliott, AC 10167, Reel 7.
17. IWM SOUND: Robert Ellison, AC 18743, Reel 12.

18. IWM SOUND: Kenneth Lovell, AC 13251, Reel 13.
19. Lieutenant Wilson Whitehead died on 10 October 1943. He is buried in Naples War Cemetery.
20. Lance Sergeant George Ferrell died aged thirty-three on 12 October 1943. He is buried at Naples War Cemetery.
21. IWM SOUND: Robert Ellison, AC 18743, Reel 12.
22. IWM SOUND: John Lewindon, AC 20349, Reel 26.
23. IWM SOUND: Ronald Elliott, AC 10167, Reel 7.
24. PUBLIC RECORD OFFICE: War Diary, 9 October 1943. The War Diary maintains the other patrol was actually commanded by Lieutenant W. A. Mitchell.
25. IWM SOUND: Russell Collins, AC 13878, Reel 6.
26. IWM SOUND: Russell Collins, AC 13878, Reel 6.
27. IWM SOUND: William Virr, AC 17621, Reel 9.
28. IWM SOUND: Russell Collins, AC 13878, Reel 6.
29. Private Tom Anderson was killed aged twenty on 13 October 1943. He is buried at Minturno War Cemetery in Italy.
30. IWM SOUND: Russell Collins, AC 13878, Reel 6 and 7.
31. IWM SOUND: Tony Sacco, AC 18744, Reel 7.
32. IWM SOUND: Edward Grey, AC 16719, Reel 5.
33. IWM SOUND: Tom Turnbull, AC 12680, Reel 5.
34. Private Joseph Tuck was killed aged twenty-four on 12 October 1943. He is buried at Minturno War Cemetery in Italy
35. IWM SOUND: Tom Turnbull, AC 12680, Reel 5.
36. Private William Crummack died aged twenty on 13 October 1943. He is buried at Minturno War Cemetery, Italy. Ranks are not always substantive.
37. IWM SOUND: Kenneth Lovell, AC 13251, Reel 14.
38. IWM SOUND: Russell Collins, AC 13878, Reel 7.
39. IWM SOUND: Russell Collins, AC 13878, Reel 7.
40. IWM SOUND: Russell Collins, AC 13878, Reel 7.
41. IWM SOUND: Russell Collins, AC 13878, Reel 7.
42. IWM SOUND: Kenneth Lovell, AC 13251, Reel 15.
43. IWM SOUND: Ronald Sherlaw, AC 12436, Reel 5.
44. IWM SOUND: Ronald Sherlaw, AC 12436, Reel 7.
45. IWM SOUND: Robert Ellison, AC 18743, Reel 13.
46. IWM SOUND: Tom Turnbull, AC 12680, Reel 5.
47. IWM SOUND: Ronald Sherlaw, AC 12436, Reel 7.
48. IWM SOUND: Russell Collins, AC 13878, Reel 11.
49. J. Hawkesworth quoted by L. Stringer, *The History of the Sixteenth Battalion The Durham Light Infantry*, (Graz, Austria, The DLI, 1946), p33.
50. PUBLIC RECORD OFFICE: War Diary, 3–6 December 1943.

8. Monte Camino

1. IWM SOUND: Charles Palmer, AC 16709, Reel 11.
2. IWM SOUND: William Virr, AC 17621, Reel 9.
3. IWM SOUND: William Virr, AC 17621, Reel 9 and 10.
4. Lieutenant Fred Strothart died aged twenty-five on 3 December 1943. He is buried at Minturno War Cemetery, Italy.
5. Major George Ballance died aged twenty-seven on 4 December 1943. He is buried at Minturno War Cemetery, Italy.
6. Lance Corporal Albert (Bill) Holder died aged thirty on 3 December 1943. He is buried at Minturno War Cemetery, Italy.
7. IWM SOUND: William Virr, AC 17621, Reel 9 and 10.

8. IWM SOUND: Leslie Thornton, AC 10421, Reel 17.
9. IWM SOUND: Leslie Thornton, AC 10421, Reel 17.
10. IWM SOUND: Russell Collins, AC 13878, Reel 8.
11. IWM SOUND: Ronald Sherlaw, AC 12436, Reel 7.
12. IWM SOUND: Russell Collins, AC 13878, Reel 8.
13. Private Ronald James Baglin died aged thirty-five on 15 December 1943. He is buried at Minturno War Cemetery, Italy.
14. IWM SOUND: Russell Collins, AC 13878, Reel 8.
15. IWM SOUND: Russell Collins, AC 13878, Reel 8.
16. IWM SOUND: Russell Collins, AC 13878, Reel 8.
17. IWM SOUND: Russell Collins, AC 13878, Reel 9.
18. IWM SOUND: Tony Sacco, AC 18744, Reel 8.
19. Private Clifford Millett died aged twenty-five on 6 December 1943. He is buried at Minturno War Cemetery, Italy.
20. Private Bernard Davenport died aged twenty-five on 6 December 1943. He is buried at Minturno War Cemetery, Italy.
21. IWM SOUND: Tony Sacco, AC 18744, Reel 8.
22. Sergeant Douglas Kennedy died aged twenty-six on 6 December 1943. He is buried at Minturno War Cemetery, Italy.
23. IWM SOUND: Leslie Thornton, AC 10421, Reel 17.
24. IWM SOUND: Leslie Thornton, AC 10421, Reel 17.
25. IWM SOUND: Leslie Thornton, AC 10421, Reel 17 and 18.
26. IWM SOUND: Leslie Thornton, AC 10421, Reel 17 and 18.
27. IWM SOUND: Alan Hay, AC 13079, Reel 8.
28. IWM SOUND: Alan Hay, AC 13079, Reel 8.
29. IWM SOUND: Gerry Barnett, AC 12238, Reel 7.
30. Lieutenant Albert Critchley died aged twenty-three on 23 December 1943. Buried at Cassino War Cemetery, Italy.
31. IWM SOUND: Alan Hay, AC 13079, Reel 8.
32. IWM SOUND: Alan Hay, AC 13079, Reel 8–9.
33. IWM SOUND: Alan Hay, AC 13079, Reel 9.
34. IWM SOUND: Alan Hay, AC 13079, Reel 9.

9. Across the Garigliano

1. IWM SOUND: William Virr, AC 17621, Reel 10 and 11.
2. IWM SOUND: Gerry Barnett, AC 12238, Reel 7.
3. IWM SOUND: Gerry Barnett, AC 12238, Reel 8.
4. IWM SOUND: Gerry Barnett, AC 12238, Reel 8.
5. Private Arnold Mawson died aged twenty-one on 30 January 1943. He is commemorated on the Cassino Memorial, Italy.
6. IWM SOUND: Russell Collins, AC 13878, Reel 9.
7. IWM SOUND: Tom Turnbull, AC 12680, Reel 5.
8. Sergeant Joseph Makepeace died aged thirty-three on 30 January 1943. He is commemorated on the Cassino Memorial, Italy.
9. IWM SOUND: William Virr, AC 17621, Reel 10.
10. IWM SOUND: Ronald Elliott, AC 10167, Reel 8.
11. IWM SOUND: Leslie Thornton, AC 10421, Reel 19.
12. IWM SOUND: Leslie Thornton, AC 10421, Reel 19.

10. A Middle East Sojourn

1. IWM SOUND: Leslie Thornton, AC 10421, Reel 19.
2. IWM SOUND: Leslie Thornton, AC 10421, Reel 19.

3. IWM SOUND: Leslie Thornton, AC 10421, Reel 19.
4. IWM SOUND: Leslie Thornton, AC 10421, Reel 19.
5. IWM SOUND: James Corr, AC 13080, Reel 5.
6. IWM SOUND: William Virr, AC 17621, Reel 11.
7. IWM SOUND: Arthur Vizard, AC 16601, Reel 12.
8. IWM SOUND: Richard Hewlett, AC 18688, Reel 4.
9. IWM SOUND: Alan Hay, AC 13079, Reel 10.
10. IWM SOUND: Alan Hay, AC 13079, Reel 10.
11. IWM SOUND: Alan Hay, AC 13079, Reel 10.
12. IWM SOUND: Tom Lister, AC 12825, Reel 11.
13. IWM SOUND: Alan Hay, AC 13079, Reel 10.
14. IWM SOUND: Tom Lister, AC 12825, Reel 11.
15. IWM SOUND: Douglas Tiffin, AC 12257, Reel 5.
16. IWM SOUND: Alan Hay, AC 13079, Reel 10.
17. IWM SOUND: Leslie Thornton, AC 10421, Reel 19.
18. IWM SOUND: Richard Hewlett, AC 18688, Reel 4.
19. IWM SOUND: Alan Hay, AC 13079, Reel 10.
20. IWM SOUND: Alan Hay, AC 13079, Reel 11.

11. Gothic Line Horrors

1. IWM SOUND: Tony Cameron, AC 12918, Reel 9.
2. IWM SOUND: Ronald Elliott, AC 10167, Reel 8.
3. IWM SOUND: Arthur Vizard, AC 16601, Reel 14.
4. IWM SOUND: Tony Cameron, AC 12918, Reel 9.
5. IWM SOUND: Tony Cameron, AC 12918, Reel 9.
6. IWM SOUND: Tony Cameron, AC 12918, Reel 9.
7. IWM SOUND: Arthur Vizard, AC 16601, Reel 13.
8. IWM SOUND: Douglas Tiffin, AC 12257, Reel 5-6.
9. IWM SOUND: Douglas Tiffin, AC 12257, Reel 5-6.
10. IWM SOUND: Richard Hewlett, AC 18688, Reel 5.
11. IWM SOUND: Douglas Tiffin, AC 12257, Reel 6.
12. Lance Corporal Harry Senior died aged thirty on 29 August 1944. Buried at Montecchio War Cemetery, Italy.
13. IWM SOUND: Charles Palmer, AC 16709, Reel 11.
14. IWM SOUND: William Virr, AC 17621, Reel 12.
15. IWM SOUND: Richard Hewlett, AC 18688, Reel 5.
16. IWM SOUND: Alan Hay, AC 13079, Reel 11.
17. IWM SOUND: Alan Hay, AC 13079, Reel 11.
18. IWM SOUND: Alan Hay, AC 13079, Reel 11.
19. 2nd Lieutenant Stanley Marshall died aged twenty-five on 31 August 1944. He is buried at Montecchio War Cemetery, Italy.
20. IWM SOUND: Alan Hay, AC 13079, Reel 11.
21. 2nd Lieutenant William Hood died aged thirty-one in August 1944. He is buried at Montecchio War Cemetery, Italy.
22. IWM SOUND: Alan Hay, AC 13079, Reel 11-12.
23. IWM SOUND: Alan Hay, AC 13079, Reel 12.
24. IWM SOUND: Alan Hay, AC 13079, Reel 12.
25. IWM SOUND: Douglas Tiffin, AC 12257, Reel 6.
26. IWM SOUND: Douglas Tiffin, AC 12257, Reel 6 and 7.
27. IWM SOUND: Douglas Tiffin, AC 12257, Reel 7.
28. IWM SOUND: Douglas Tiffin, AC 12257, Reel 7.
29. IWM SOUND: Ronald Elliott, AC 10167, Reel 8.

30. Company Sergeant Major Arthur Mattin died aged twenty-nine on 4 September 1943. He is buried at Montecchio War Cemetery, Italy.
31. IWM SOUND: Leslie Thornton, AC 10421, Reel 20.

12. The Battle of Gemmano Ridge

1. IWM SOUND: Ronald Elliot, AC 10167, Reel 9.
2. Sergeant William Dabner died aged twenty-eight on 12 September 1944. He is buried at Coriano Ridge War Cemetery, Italy.
3. IWM SOUND: Leslie Thornton, AC 10421, Reel 17 and 22.
4. IWM SOUND: Richard Hewlett, AC 18688, Reel 5.
5. IWM SOUND: William Virr, AC 17621, Reel 13.
6. IWM SOUND: Richard Hewlett, AC 18688, Reel 5.
7. IWM SOUND: Eric Murray, AC 17630, Reel 5.
8. IWM SOUND: Richard Hewlett, AC 18688, Reel 5.
9. Sergeant Joseph Jerrison died aged twenty-seven on 12 September 1944. He is buried at Coriano Ridge War Cemetery, Italy.
10. IWM SOUND: Leslie Thornton, AC 10421, Reel 22.
11. IWM SOUND: Tom Lister, AC 12825, Reel 13.
12. Lieutenant Ernest Smith, 70th Field Regiment, Royal Artillery died aged twenty-eight on 12 September 1944. He is buried at Coriano Ridge War Cemetery, Italy.
13. IWM SOUND: Leslie Thornton, AC 10421, Reel 21.
14. IWM SOUND: Leslie Thornton, AC 10421, Reel 21.
15. IWM SOUND: Leslie Thornton, AC 10421, Reel 21.
16. IWM SOUND: Leslie Thornton, AC 10421, Reel 22.
17. Corporal George Pauly died aged twenty-one on 12 September 1944. He is buried at Coriano Ridge War Cemetery, Italy.
18. IWM SOUND: John Lewindon, AC 20349, Reel 29.
19. IWM SOUND: John Lewindon, AC 20349, Reel 29.
20. IWM SOUND: Tony Cameron, AC 12918, Reel 10.
21. IWM SOUND: Tony Cameron, AC 12918, Reel 10.
22. IWM SOUND: Ronald Sherlaw, AC 12436, Reel 9.
23. Disabled – out of action.
24. IWM SOUND: Ronald Elliott, AC 10167, Reel 8 and 9.

13. More Bloody Ridges

1. IWM SOUND: Tom Lister, AC 12825, Reel 12.
2. IWM SOUND: Tony Cameron, AC 12918, Reel 10.
3. IWM SOUND: Ronald Elliott, AC 10167, Reel 9.
4. IWM SOUND: Ronald Sherlaw, AC 12436, Reel 9.
5. IWM SOUND: Ronald Elliott, AC 10167, Reel 9.
6. IWM SOUND: Tom Lister, AC 12825, Reel 10.
7. IWM SOUND: Russell Collins, AC 13878, Reel 11.
8. IWM SOUND: Ronald Elliott, AC 10167, Reel 9.
9. IWM SOUND: Ronald Elliott, AC 10167, Reel 9.
10. IWM SOUND: Russell Collins, AC 13878, Reel 11.
11. IWM SOUND: Russell Collins, AC 13878, Reel 11.
12. IWM SOUND: Russell Collins, AC 13878, Reel 11.
13. IWM SOUND: Russell Collins, AC 13878, Reel 11.
14. IWM SOUND: Russell Collins, AC 13878, Reel 11.
15. IWM SOUND: Russell Collins, AC 13878, Reel 11.
16. IWM SOUND: Ronald Elliott, AC 10167, Reel 9.
17. IWM SOUND: Russell Collins, AC 13878, Reel 11.

18. IWM SOUND: William Cowans, AC 17622, Reel 11.
19. IWM SOUND: Edward Grey, AC 16719, Reel 4.
20. IWM SOUND: Leslie Thornton, AC 10421, Reel 22.
21. IWM SOUND: Leslie Thornton, AC 10421, Reel 22.
22. IWM SOUND: William Cowans, AC 17622, Reel 11.
23. IWM SOUND: Arthur Vizard, AC 16601, Reel 12.
24. IWM SOUND: William Cowans, AC 17622, Reel 10.
25. IWM SOUND: Leslie Thornton, AC 10421, Reel 23.
26. IWM SOUND: Laurence Stringer, AC 16707, Reel 6.
27. IWM SOUND: Russell Collins, AC 13878, Reel 12.
28. IWM SOUND: Laurence Stringer, AC 16707, Reel 6.
29. IWM SOUND: Russell Collins, AC 13878, Reel 12.
30. IWM SOUND: Laurence Stringer, AC 16707, Reel 6 and 7.
31. IWM SOUND: Richard Hewlett, AC 18688, Reel 6.
32. IWM SOUND: Laurence Stringer, AC 16707, Reel 7.
33. IWM SOUND: Russell Collins, AC 13878, Reel 12.
34. Corporal Harry Vick died aged thirty on 10 October 1944. Buried Assisi War Cemetery, Italy.
35. IWM SOUND: Russell Collins, AC 13878, Reel 12.
36. IWM SOUND: Laurence Stringer, AC 16707, Reel 7.
37. IWM SOUND: Richard Hewlett, AC 18688, Reel 6.
38. IWM SOUND: Richard Hewlett, AC 18688, Reel 6.
39. IWM SOUND: Kenneth Lovell, AC 13251, Reel 20.
40. IWM SOUND: Laurence Stringer, AC 16707, Reel 7.
41. IWM SOUND: Laurence Stringer, AC 16707, Reel 7.
42. IWM SOUND: Richard Hewlett, AC 18688, Reel 6.
43. Private Roger Appleby died aged thirty-one on 10 September 1944. Buried Assisi War Cemetery, Italy.
44. IWM SOUND: Kenneth Lovell, AC 13251, Reel 20.
45. IWM SOUND: Russell Collins, AC 13878, Reel 12.
46. Sergeant Norman Reading died aged twenty-nine on 10 September 1944. He is buried at Assisi War Cemetery, Italy.
47. Lieutenant Stanley Waymark died on 10 September 1944. He is buried at Assisi War Cemetery, Italy.
48. IWM SOUND: Laurence Stringer, AC 16707, Reel 7.
49. IWM SOUND: William Cowans, AC 17622, Reel 11.
50. IWM SOUND: Ronald Elliott, AC 10167, Reel 9.
51. IWM SOUND: Laurence Stringer, AC 16707, Reel 7 and 8.
52. IWM SOUND: William Cowans, AC 17622, Reel 11.
53. Sergeant Major Arthur Clark died aged twenty-seven on 19 October 1944. He is buried at Coriano Ridge War Cemetery, Italy.
54. IWM SOUND: Laurence Stringer, AC 16707, Reel 7 and 8.
55. IWM SOUND: Laurence Stringer, AC 16707, Reel 7 and 8.
56. IWM SOUND: Leslie Thornton, AC 10421, Reel 22 and 23.
57. IWM SOUND: Laurence Stringer, AC 16707, Reel 7 and 8.
58. IWM SOUND: Arthur Vizard, AC 16601, Reel 15.
59. IWM SOUND: Laurence Stringer, AC 16707, Reel 8.
60. Laurence Stringer book
61. IWM SOUND: William Virr, AC 17621, Reel 14.

14. Could *You* Have Coped?

1. IWM SOUND: William Cowans, AC 17622, Reel 11.

2. IWM SOUND: Leslie Thornton, AC 10421, Reel 23.
3. IWM SOUND: Ronald Elliott, AC 10167, Reel 7.
4. IWM SOUND: Tom Turnbull, AC 12680, Reel 6.
5. IWM SOUND: Leslie Brown, AC 22603, Reel 9.
6. IWM SOUND: James Corr, AC 13080, Reel 3.
7. IWM SOUND: Ronald Elliott, AC 10167, Reel 7.
8. IWM SOUND: James Corr, AC 13080, Reel 5.
9. IWM SOUND: Ronald Elliott, AC 10167, Reel 9.
10. IWM SOUND: Ronald Elliott, AC 10167, Reel 6.
11. IWM SOUND: Ronald Elliott, AC 10167, Reel 6.
12. IWM SOUND: Edward Grey, AC 16719, Reel 4 and 5.
13. IWM SOUND: Douglas Tiffin, AC 12257, Reel 6.
14. IWM SOUND: William Virr, AC 17621, Reel 6 and 7.
15. IWM SOUND: Lionel Dodd, AC 18254, Reel 6 and 8.
16. IWM SOUND: William Virr, AC 17621, Reel 7.
17. IWM SOUND: Leslie Thornton, AC 10421, Reel 21.
18. IWM SOUND: Edward Grey, AC 16719, Reel 4.
19. IWM SOUND: Ronald Elliott, AC 10167, Reel 6.
20. SOUND ARCHIVE: Leslie Brown, AC 22603, Reel 5.
21. SOUND ARCHIVE: Leslie Brown, AC 22603, Reel 5.
22. IWM SOUND: Tom Turnbull, AC 12680, Reel 5.
23. IWM SOUND: Leslie Thornton, AC 10421, Reel 17.
24. IWM SOUND: Eric Murray, AC 17630, Reel 5.
25. IWM SOUND: Leslie Thornton, AC 10421, Reel 23.
26. IWM SOUND: Russell Collins, AC 13878, Reel 9.
27. IWM SOUND: Russell Collins, AC 13878, Reel 9.
28. IWM SOUND: William Virr, AC 17621, Reel 13.
29. IWM SOUND: Edward Grey, AC 16719, Reel 4.
30. IWM SOUND: Russell Collins, AC 13878, Reel 8.
31. IWM SOUND: Douglas Tiffin, AC 12257, Reel 5.
32. IWM SOUND: Ronald Elliott, AC 10167, Reel 7.
33. IWM SOUND: William Virr, AC 17621, Reel 11.
34. IWM SOUND: Douglas Tiffin, AC 12257, Reel 5.
35. IWM SOUND: William Cowans, AC 17622, Reel 10.
36. Author's Collection: H. Jones, Edited from Personal account and accompanying article 'The Work of a Battalion Medical Officer'.
37. IWM SOUND: John Lewindon, AC 20349, Reel 26 and 28.
38. IWM SOUND: James Corr, AC 13080, Reel 5.
39. IWM SOUND: James Corr, AC 13080, Reel 5.
40. IWM SOUND: Tommy Chadwick, AC 16593, Reel 5.
41. IWM SOUND: Leslie Thornton, AC 10421, Reel 21.
42. Author's Collection: H. Jones, Personal account and article 'The Work of a Battalion Medical Officer'.
43. IWM SOUND: Ronald Sherlaw, AC 12436, Reel 9.
44. IWM SOUND: Ronald Sherlaw, AC 12436, Reel .
45. IWM SOUND: George Bland, AC 17619, Reel 8.
46. IWM SOUND: George Bland, AC 17619, Reel 8.
47. IWM SOUND: Arthur Vizard, AC 16601, Reel 12.
48. IWM SOUND: Laurence Stringer, AC 16707, Reel 7.

15. Last Rites at Cosina

1. IWM SOUND: Laurence Stringer, AC 16707, Reel 11.

2. L. Stringer, *The History of the Sixteenth Battalion The Durham Light Infantry*, (Graz, Austria, The DLI, 1946), p48.
3. IWM SOUND: William Virr, AC 17621, Reel 14.
4. IWM SOUND: Laurence Stringer, AC 16707, Reel 9.
5. IWM SOUND: Laurence Stringer, AC 16707, Reel 9.
6. IWM SOUND: William Virr, AC 17621, Reel 14.
7. IWM SOUND: Laurence Stringer, AC 16707, Reel 9.
8. IWM SOUND: Laurence Stringer, AC 16707, Reel 9.
9. IWM SOUND: William Virr, AC 17621, Reel 14.
10. IWM SOUND: Russell Collins, AC 13878, Reel 12.
11. IWM SOUND: Russell Collins, AC 13878, Reel 12.
12. IWM SOUND: William Virr, AC 17621, Reel 14.
13. IWM SOUND: Laurence Stringer, AC 16707, Reel 9.
14. IWM SOUND: Laurence Stringer, AC 16707, Reel 9.
15. IWM SOUND: Laurence Stringer, AC 16707, Reel 9.
16. IWM SOUND: Kenneth Lovell, AC 13251, Reel 21.
17. IWM SOUND: Kenneth Lovell, AC 13251, Reel 21.
18. IWM SOUND: Kenneth Lovell, AC 13251, Reel 21–22.
19. IWM SOUND: Laurence Stringer, AC 16707, Reel 9 and 10.
20. IWM SOUND: Laurence Stringer, AC 16707, Reel 10.
21. IWM SOUND: Russell Collins, AC 13878, Reel 10 and 11.
22. IWM SOUND: Russell Collins, AC 13878, Reel 12.
23. IWM SOUND: Lionel Dodd, AC 18254, Reel 9.

16. Grecian Odyssey

1. IWM SOUND: Ronald Elliot, AC 10167, Reel 10.
2. IWM SOUND: Arthur Vizard, AC 16601, Reel 16.
3. IWM SOUND: George Bland, AC 17619, Reel 12.
4. IWM SOUND: Ronald Sherlaw, AC 12436, Reel 10.
5. IWM SOUND: Tony Sacco, AC 18744, Reel 9.
6. IWM SOUND: Ronald Elliot, AC 10167, Reel 10.
7. Lieutenant Frank Johnson died on 9 December 1944. Buried at Phaleron War Cemetery, Greece.
8. IWM SOUND: Russell Collins, AC 13878, Reel 13.
9. IWM SOUND: Ronald Sherlaw, AC 12436, Reel 10.
10. IWM SOUND: James Corr, AC 13080, Reel 6.
11. Account by George Lyons from the private collection of Paul Errington.
12. IWM SOUND: Alan Hay, AC 13079, Reel 13 and 14. Edited from 2 accounts.
13. IWM SOUND: Ronald Elliott, AC 10167, Reel 10.
14. IWM SOUND: Ronald Elliott, AC 10167, Reel 10.
15. IWM SOUND: Tommy Chadwick, AC 16593, Reel 9.
16. IWM SOUND: Tommy Chadwick, AC 16593, Reel 9.
17. NATIONAL ARCHIVES: 16th DLI War Diary. January Appendix, 'Lessons Learnt from Recent Fighting', p.1.
18. IWM SOUND: Tom Lister, AC 12825, Reel 14.
19. IWM SOUND: Arthur Vizard, AC 16601, Reel 16.
20. NATIONAL ARCHIVES: 16th DLI War Diary, Appendix A, 1 January 1945.
21. IWM SOUND: Laurence Stringer, AC 16707, Reel 10 and 11.
22. IWM SOUND: Leslie Thornton, AC 10421, Reel 24.
23. IWM SOUND: Tony Sacco, AC 18744, Reel 9.
24. IWM SOUND: Leslie Thornton, AC 10421, Reel 24.
25. IWM SOUND: Tommy Chadwick, AC 16593, Reel 9.

26. IWM SOUND: Tommy Chadwick, AC 16593, Reel 9.
27. IWM SOUND: Russell Collins, AC 13878, Reel 13.
28. IWM SOUND: Tom Lister, AC 12825, Reel 14.
29. IWM SOUND: Tom Lister, AC 12825, Reel 14–15.
30. IWM SOUND: Sam Cawdron, AC 17106, Reel 9.
31. IWM SOUND: Ronald Elliott, AC 10167, Reel 11.
32. IWM SOUND: Arthur Vizard, AC 16601, Reel 8.
33. IWM SOUND: Tom Lister, AC 12825, Reel 14.
34. IWM SOUND: Tom Lister, AC 12825, Reel 14.
35. IWM SOUND: Tom Lister, AC 12825, Reel 14.
36. IWM SOUND: Arthur Vizard, AC 16601, Reel 17.
37. IWM SOUND: Tom Turnbull, AC 12680, Reel 6.
38. IWM SOUND: Sam Cawdron, AC 17106, Reel 10.
39. IWM SOUND: Tommy Chadwick, AC 16593, Reel 10.
40. IWM SOUND: Leslie Thornton, AC 10421, Reel 24.
41. IWM SOUND: Tony Cameron, AC 12918, Reel 11.
42. IWM SOUND: Russell Collins, AC 13878, Reel 13.

17. What a Relief, 8 May 1945

1. IWM SOUND: Sam Cawdron, AC 17106, Reel 10.
2. IWM SOUND: Tommy Chadwick, AC 16593, Reel 10.
3. IWM SOUND: Tommy Chadwick, AC 16593, Reel 10.
4. IWM SOUND: Alan Hay, AC 13079, Reel ???.
5. IWM SOUND: Leslie Thornton, AC 10421, Reel 24.
6. IWM SOUND: Ronald Elliott, AC 10167, Reel ???.
7. IWM SOUND: Alan Hay, AC 13079, Reel 14.
8. IWM SOUND: James Corr, AC 13080, Reel 6.
9. IWM SOUND: Ronald Sherlaw, AC 12436, Reel 10.
10. IWM SOUND: Jackie Milburn, AC 12681, Reel 8.
11. IWM SOUND: Lionel Dodd, AC 18254, Reel 9.
12. IWM SOUND: Russell Collins, AC 13878, Reel 13.
13. IWM SOUND: Arthur Vizard, AC 16601, Reel 17.
14. IWM SOUND: Ronald Elliott, AC 10167, Reel 11.
15. IWM SOUND: Alan Hay, AC 13079, Reel 14.
16. IWM SOUND: Alan Hay, AC 13079, Reel 14.
17. IWM SOUND: Alan Hay, AC 13079, Reel 14.
18. IWM SOUND: Alan Hay, AC 13079, Reel 14.
19. IWM SOUND: Alan Hay, AC 13079, Reel 15.
20. IWM SOUND: Alan Hay, AC 13079, Reel 15.
21. IWM SOUND: Alan Hay, AC 13079, Reel 15–16.
22. IWM SOUND: Laurence Stringer, AC 16707, Reel 12.
23. IWM SOUND: Laurence Stringer, AC 16707, Reel 12.
24. IWM SOUND: Tom Lister, AC 12825, Reel 16.
25. IWM SOUND: James Corr, AC 13080, Reel 6.
26. IWM SOUND: Tom Lister, AC 12825, Reel 16.
27. IWM SOUND: William Cowans, AC 17622, Reel 13.
28. IWM SOUND: Alan Hay, AC 13079, Reel 16.
29. IWM SOUND: Arthur Vizard, AC 16601, Reel 17.
30. IWM SOUND: Tom Lister, AC 12825, Reel 16.
31. IWM SOUND: Leslie Thornton, AC 10421, Reel 25.
32. IWM SOUND: Tom Lister, AC 12825, Reel 16.
33. IWM SOUND: Leslie Thornton, AC 10421, Reel 25.

34. IWM SOUND: George Bland, AC 17619, Reel 14.
35. IWM SOUND: Tom Lister, AC 12825, Reel 16.
36. IWM SOUND: Tony Cameron, AC 12918, Reel 12.
37. IWM SOUND: Ronald Elliott, AC 10167, Reel 12.
38. IWM SOUND: Tony Cameron, AC 12918, Reel 12.
39. IWM SOUND: Tom Lister, AC 12825, Reel 16.
40. IWM SOUND: Tony Cameron, AC 12918, Reel 11.
41. IWM SOUND: Tom Lister, AC 12825, Reel 17.
42. IWM SOUND: Arthur Vizard, AC 16601, Reel 18.
43. IWM SOUND: Ronald Elliott, AC 10167, Reel 11.
44. IWM SOUND: Ronald Elliott, AC 10167, Reel 13.
45. IWM SOUND: Arthur Vizard, AC 16601, Reel 18.
46. IWM SOUND: Laurence Stringer, AC 16707, Reel 13 and 14.

18. End of Days

1. IWM SOUND: Edward Grey, AC 16719, Reel 4.
2. IWM SOUND: Alan Hay, AC 13079, Reel 18.
3. IWM SOUND: James Corr, AC 13080, Reel 7.
4. IWM SOUND: Ronald Elliott, AC 10167, Reel 13.
5. IWM SOUND: James Corr, AC 13080, Reel 7.
6. IWM SOUND: Arthur Vizard, AC 16601, Reel 18.
7. IWM SOUND: Maria Shutt, AC 26861, Reel 2 and 3.
8. IWM SOUND: Maria Shutt, AC 26861, Reel 3.
9. IWM SOUND: Maria Shutt, AC 26861, Reel 2.
10. IWM SOUND: Ronald Elliott, AC 10167, Reel 14.
11. IWM SOUND: Charles Bray, AC 20349, Edited from Reel 16.
12. IWM SOUND: Tom Lister, AC 12825, Reel 17.
13. IWM SOUND: Jimmy James, AC 20793, Reel 44.
14. IWM SOUND: Jimmy James, AC 20793, Reel 44.
15. IWM SOUND: Alan Hay, AC 13079, Reel 18.
16. IWM SOUND: Alan Hay, AC 13079, Reel 18.
17. IWM SOUND: Alan Hay, AC 13079, Reel 18.
18. IWM SOUND: Gerry Barnett, AC 12238, Reel 9.
19. IWM Sound: Douglas Tiffin, AC 12257, Reel 7.
20. IWM SOUND: Tony Cameron, AC 12918, Reel 12.
21. IWM SOUND: Leslie Thornton, AC 10421, Reel 25.
22. IWM SOUND: James Drake, AC 020791, Reel 20.
23. IWM SOUND: Arthur Vizard, AC 16601, Reel 18.
24. IWM SOUND: Sam Cawdron, AC 17106, Reel 12.
25. IWM SOUND: Kenneth Lovell, AC 13251, Reel 28.
26. SOUND ARCHIVE: Leslie Brown, AC 22603, Reel 13.
27. IWM SOUND: Laurence Stringer, AC 16707, Reel 14.

INDEX

A

Abbey of Maria del Monte, Cesena 272–3
Africa Star 192, 368
Aitcheson, Sergeant 73, 74
Akester, Sergeant Alfred 32
alcohol 24, 43, 60, 79, 97, 98, 103–4, 167, 176, 203, 210, 257–8, 302, 321, 335, 336, 338, 340–1, 346, 351–2, 353, 364–5
Alexander, General Sir Harold 193, 213, 335
Algiers 41–3, 44, 45, 65, 93, 94
   brothels in 43, 98–9
   16th DLI arrival in 41–3
Allied Forces units
   Allied Forces Mediterranean 193
   Central Force 44
   Eastern Force 44
   15th Army Group 193
   First Army 44–5, 58, 59, 84
   Supreme Headquarters, Algiers 45
   Western Task Force 44
Anderson, General Kenneth 45
Anderson, Private Tom 25, 161
anti-aircraft (AA) guns 17, 31–2, 100, 160, 214, 341
anti-malaria tablets 102–3
anti-tank guns 16, 20–1, 115, 147, 148, 160, 252, 266, 287, 306, 338
Anzio landings (1944) 152–3, 193–4
Appleby, Private Roger 268, 270–1
Araxos airfield, Greece 340
Ark bridge 319
artillery xii, 12, 21
   experience of being under fire from 285, 291–2
   gunners and infantry working together 76, 254, 293–4
   Italian campaign 118, 126–7, 131, 146, 147, 149, 151, 152, 175, 178–9, 180–1, 186–7, 191, 192, 194, 200, 215–16, 217, 222, 226, 248, 251, 252, 253, 254, 262, 265, 308–9, 312, 316, 317
   North Africa campaign 47, 48, 60, 63–4, 66, 67, 76, 82, 85–6, 87
   25-pounder guns 48, 149, 150, 179, 184, 292–3
assault craft 15, 339
Athens, Greece 323–39, 343–8
Atkinson, Lance Corporal Thomas
   Johnny Fox death and 54
   rats, on 50–1
   Sedjenane battle and 58, 61–2, 63–4, 65
   stretcher bearer 13
   training 10–11, 12, 13
   venereal diseases, on 25
   uniforms and kit, on 8, 9
atom bomb 366–7
Ausladung (Bulge), Operation (1943) 59
Austria, 16th DLI in 354–74
Avalanche, Operation (1943) 106
Avellino, Italy 115, 131

B

Bailey bridge 154, 307, 308
Bakelite Mk 69 grenade 15
Ballance, Major George 103, 177
Baldy Hill (Dj El Ajved), Tunisia 45, 46, 59
Balignano spur, Italy 261–72
Balzanino river, Italy 307
Bannerman, Major David 59–60, 63
Bare Arse Ridge, Italy 175, 178
Barnard Castle, battle school at 95, 260
Barnett, Lieutenant Gerry
   apprehension/dread, on 104
   Cedra advance and 194–7
   Hospital Hill battle and 127–8, 129, 130
   joins 16th DLI 96
   Monte Camino, on conditions on 189
   party before leaving for Italy, on 103–4
   post-war life 383
   Salerno landings and 116–17, 118, 119
   tea, on importance of 98
'base wallahs' 205, 210

Index

Bastardo, Italy 213
Bavington-Jones, Captain Jeffrey 72
Baytown, Operation (1943) 105–6
Bedlam, Operation (1943) 106
Béja, Tunisia 59
Ben Ihren, Tunisia 61
Bernard, Lieutenant Colonel Joseph Morrogh 5
Bernhardt Line 174
Bevin, Ernest 375
Bizerta, Tunisia 90, 99–100, 107, 137
Bland, Private George 153, 302–3, 324, 366–7
Bleiberg region, Austria 356–7, 359
Blida, Algeria 65, 93–9
Block, Brigadier Allen 218, 222, 272, 326, 339
Block Force 326
Boer War (1899–1902) x
Boerhaavegasse, Vienna 367
Bordj des Monopoles, Tunisia 60, 62
Bou Arada, Tunisia 85
Bou Arouda valley, Tunisia 59
Brancepeth Castle depot, DLI 6, 18–19, 94, 95, 137–8, 280, 385
Bray, Sergeant Charles 31, 380
Bren carrier 13–14, 15, 43, 47, 52, 89, 107, 115–16, 226, 272, 312, 328
Bren gun 2, 15, 19, 21, 23, 27, 29, 31–2, 42, 45, 51, 53, 61, 67–8, 69, 73–5, 94–5, 121, 124, 125, 126, 155, 156, 160, 163, 191, 199, 227, 242, 247, 310, 336, 353
Bristol Beaufighter 31–2
British Army units
  ARMIES
  Eighth Army 41, 44, 84, 106, 131, 140, 193, 213, 216, 217, 278, 349, 350, 366
  ARMY GROUPS
  Army Group Royal Artillery (AGRA) 131
  21st Army Group 193
  BATTALIONS
  9th Australian Battalion 80
  Dunkirk battalions ix, 5, 18, 32
  6th Battalion, Durham Light Infantry (6th DLI) 23
  8th Battalion, Durham Light Infantry (8th DLI) 23
  9th Battalion, Durham Light Infantry (9th DLI) 23, 139, 141
  14th Battalion, Durham Light Infantry (14th DLI) 5, 94, 95, 96, 137
  16th Battalion, Durham Light Infantry (16th DLI) ix

alcohol and *see* alcohol
Algiers, arrival in 41–5
Austria, deployment to 354–74
battles *see individual battle name*
Camberley billets 32–6, 213
Churchill visits 92–3
commanding officer (CO), first 5
demobilisation 372–4, 375–86
desertions in 34, 95, 124, 300–1
efficiency competition 28–31
Egypt, deployment to 203–5, 210–11
embarkation leave 32–3
end of war and 350–4
Folkestone hotel billets 21, 22
George VI inspects 34–5, 213
Greece, deployment to 322–48
History of 16th Battalion: The Durham Light Infantry 163, 373–4, 388
Italian campaign 105–201, 211, 212–321, 349–54
kit inspections 5
morale 92, 108, 191, 200, 213, 218, 224, 231, 248, 249, 258, 279, 297, 301, 348
NCOs 6, 10, 11, 16, 17, 18, 29, 30, 31, 40, 46, 51, 93, 95, 101, 107, 108, 166, 181, 200, 207, 214, 215, 216, 232, 243, 281, 297, 369, 385
North Africa campaign 44–104
North Africa, deployment to 32–44
128 (Hampshire) Brigade, attached to 85
origins of xi, 5–6
Palestine, deployment to 205–10, 384
prostitutes/brothels and 43, 98–9, 167, 205, 341–2
regimental dance band 259–60
regimental shoulder flashes 14
regional accents 17
return home 375–89
Rye and Winchelsea coastal defence role 22–32
Salerno landings 105–44
self-inflicted wounds in 25, 33–4, 54, 299
78th Division, 'loaned' to 84
16th Durham Light Infantry Association 386–7
Syria posting 209–10
tactical exercises 22, 23, 26, 94, 96–7, 190, 209, 213, 348
10 Brigade of 4th Division, transferred to command of 84
'The Wretched Durhams' 172–3

3 Brigade, 1st Division, farmed out to 85
training 1, 4, 6–7, 9–23, 27, 30–1, 58, 80, 82, 93–6, 101, 102, 110, 132, 137, 143, 159, 172, 197, 203, 208–10, 213–15, 226, 260–1, 287, 290, 295, 299–300, 306, 341, 348, 350, 370, 371
12 Brigade of 4th Division, brief attachment to 84
uniforms and kit, issue of 8–9
War Diary 39, 172, 329, 373
16th Battalion, Durham Light Infantry (16th DLI) units
  'A' Company 39–40, 46, 48–9, 55, 60, 61, 84, 85, 87–8, 91–3, 100, 101–2, 107, 108–9, 110, 111–12, 114–15, 120–3, 124, 132, 133–4, 135, 150, 153–4, 158–62, 165–7, 171–2, 179, 180–3, 184, 194, 197, 198, 200, 205–7, 208, 209–11, 212, 214–16, 217, 218, 219, 221–2, 223–4, 225–6, 236–7, 242–3, 246–7, 248, 250, 252–3, 254, 255, 256, 261–2, 263–4, 265–6, 271, 292–4, 295, 297, 307, 314, 316, 322, 325–7, 332–3, 337, 341–2, 347–8, 350, 351–2, 354–5, 356, 357, 358, 359–60, 363, 368, 369, 370
  'B' Company 20, 26, 33–4, 46–7, 60–1, 53, 54, 58, 59, 60, 61–2, 63–4, 65, 66, 67, 71–2, 78, 87, 89–90, 94, 96, 97, 98, 103, 105, 113, 115–16, 146, 147, 148, 149, 160, 163–4, 171, 176–7, 193, 194, 198–9, 200, 204, 205, 210, 218, 220–1, 231, 233, 234–7, 260, 261, 262–3, 264, 265, 266–72, 274, 275, 276–9, 281, 282, 283, 287, 288, 289–91, 292, 294, 297, 299, 304, 306, 307–11, 313–19, 328–30, 335, 336, 346, 352, 360–1, 362, 373–4
  'C' Company 22–4, 26–7, 31–2, 36–7, 38, 41, 42–3, 46, 47–8, 49, 51, 54, 55, 60, 63, 65, 66, 67–70, 72, 95–6, 98, 103–4, 108, 111, 112, 114, 115, 116–18, 119, 127–8, 129–30, 131, 136–8, 145, 147–8, 149, 150, 160, 168–70, 171, 180, 184, 185–6, 189, 194–5, 196–7, 222, 224, 227, 232, 234, 237, 238–40, 247, 256–60, 272–4, 276, 280, 288–9, 292, 297–8, 300–1, 307, 319, 322, 327, 333–4, 336–9, 346, 349, 350–1, 353, 363, 365, 366
  Carrier Platoon 1–4, 13, 34, 40–1, 42, 52–3, 73–5, 76, 114, 153, 231, 272, 302–3, 312, 313, 319–21, 324, 327, 339, 348, 353–4, 366–7

  'D' Company 25, 29–31, 32, 33–6, 43, 45, 46, 48, 50, 52, 55–7, 60, 62–3, 67, 68, 72, 85–7, 90–1, 94–5, 97, 98–101, 102, 107–8, 109–10, 113–15, 119–20, 124, 125, 126–7, 135–6, 144, 146–7, 149, 150–2, 154, 155–8, 162, 164, 167, 170, 184, 188, 189–92, 194, 200, 213, 218, 227, 228–30, 231, 233, 240–1, 243–5, 248, 249, 251, 255, 257, 281, 282–3, 284–5, 286–7, 289, 294, 296, 298–9, 301–2, 325, 328, 345, 352, 356
  'E' Company 5, 19, 20, 22–3, 80–3
  Headquarters Company 13, 14, 16–17, 18, 21–2, 25, 29–30, 38–9, 46–7, 63, 66, 72, 110, 136, 142–3, 172, 204–5, 214, 216, 234, 259, 273–4, 277, 304, 323, 332–3, 335, 342, 364, 368–9, 371–3
  Intelligence Section 27, 81, 85, 89, 95, 174, 219
  MT Section 21–2, 26, 28, 40, 49–50, 78–9, 118–19, 138, 144, 207, 208, 238, 246, 249–50, 334, 340–1, 342, 343–6, 349, 361–2, 365–6, 367, 369–71
  Pioneer Platoon 286
  Signal Section 345, 351
  Support Company 93–4, 102, 103, 114, 124, 153, 178–9, 184–5, 186–7, 200–1, 202, 203, 210, 232, 272, 288, 291, 302–3, 312, 313, 319–21, 324, 327, 339, 348, 353–4, 366–7
17th Battalion, Durham Light Infantry (17th DLI) 5, 187, 188
18th (Beach Brick Battalion) Durham Light Infantry (18th DLI) 137
BRIGADES
1 Parachute Brigade 79
38th (Irish) Brigade 84, 356
113 Brigade 16
128 Brigade 45, 85, 106, 107, 110–11, 151, 217, 226, 261, 306, 321
138 Brigade 45, 145, 153, 197, 231, 233, 238, 246, 272, 342–3
139 Brigade 14, 16, 17–18, 45, 57, 66, 77, 79, 84–5, 89, 99, 111, 135, 153, 154, 159, 170, 175, 178, 217, 226, 231, 238, 246, 272, 306, 312, 324
151 Brigade 23
167 Brigade 106, 178
169 Brigade 17–18, 106, 178
201 Guards Brigade 175
206 (Independent) Brigade 5, 14
CORPS
I Canadian Corps 213, 217

Index

II Polish Corps 213, 217
V Corps 45, 213, 216, 357
IX Corps 57
X Corps 45, 106, 159, 167, 201, 213, 306, 314
Royal Army Medical Corps 90, 103, 298, 301
Royal Army Service Corps 72, 205
Royal Army Pay Corps 95
DIVISIONS
1st (Airborne) Division 106
1st Armoured Division 89, 260
4th Division 84, 278, 306, 335–6
4th Indian Division 216, 217, 333
6th Armoured Division 89
7th Armoured Division 145, 151, 159, 173, 215
10th Indian Division 306
42nd Armoured Division 23
46th Division 14, 18, 36, 45–6, 84, 85, 101, 106, 139, 145, 151, 153, 159, 170, 172, 173, 175, 201, 216, 217, 226, 231, 278, 306, 312, 342, 349, 366, 367
50th Division 138–44
51st Division 138–44
56th Division 17–18, 106, 159, 169–70, 175, 178, 231, 233, 303
78th Division 84
REGIMENTS
Beds and Herts Regiment 5–7, 11, 18, 31
Cheshire Regiment 94
Coldstream Guards 79
Dorsetshire Regiment 80
Duke of Cornwall's Light Infantry 93, 385
Durham Light Infantry ix–xii
1/6th East Surrey Regiment 84
East Yorkshire Regiment 5
Essex Regiment 260, 373
70th Field Regiment, Royal Artillery 48, 60, 70–1, 131, 147, 184, 195, 209, 292
Green Howards 197
2/4th King's Own Yorkshire Light Infantry (KOYLI) 79, 82, 88, 94, 124, 145, 147, 197, 233, 237–8, 312, 373
1/4th Hampshire Regiment 107, 110–11, 113, 114, 217, 222, 224, 261
2nd Hampshire Regiment 107, 110–11, 113, 114, 201, 217, 222, 224, 261, 370
5th Hampshire Regiment 107, 110–11, 113, 114, 188, 217, 222, 224, 261
2/5th Leicestershire Regiment 14, 47, 154, 170, 176, 217, 221, 222, 230–1, 272, 307, 308, 312, 324, 326, 327, 339, 340

68th Light Infantry x
6th Lincolnshire Regiment 67, 72, 75, 84, 145, 197
5th Medium Regiment, Royal Artillery 60
8th Middlesex Regiment 80, 95
70th (Young Soldiers) Middlesex Regiment 80, 95
Oxfordshire and Buckinghamshire Light Infantry 205
North Irish Horse 75–7
46th Reconnaissance Regiment 255
23rd Regiment of Foot x
68th Regiment of Foot x
5th Royal East Kent Regiment (The Buffs) 46
Royal Fusiliers 96
40th Royal Tank Regiment 107
51st (Leeds Rifles) Royal Tank Regiment 217
4th Royal West Kents 47
Royal West Surrey Regiment 288
5th Sherwood Foresters 47, 72, 82, 83, 115, 154, 170, 176, 178, 194, 197, 217, 220, 260, 319
9th Sherwood Foresters 14
14th Sherwood Foresters 260
6th York and Lancashire Regiment 114–15, 144, 145–7, 150–1, 194, 197, 199
Royal Artillery xii, 48, 60, 71, 131, 209, 254, 292
Royal Engineers 45, 55, 154, 187, 307
Broadhead, George 24, 60, 62
Brooks, Margaret xi
Brown, Jimmy 61–2
Brown, Private Leslie 282, 290–1, 388
Buchanan, Lieutenant David 315–17, 318–19
burials 81, 302–4

C
Cairo, Egypt 202–5, 323
Calabritto, Italy 175–8, 186, 187
Camberley 32–6, 213
Cameron, Lance Corporal Tony
 Gemmano Ridge battle and 242–3
 home leave 347–8
 joins 16th DLI 212, 214–16
 Point 235, advance on 246–7
 post-war life 384
 ski patrols and 370
 Vienna, on 368, 369
Campo, Italy 187
Caporetto, Italy 354–5

Casa Bruciati, Italy 319
Casa Ricci Ridge, Italy 248, 250, 252–3
Casaluce, Italy 167
Casey, Major Pat 137–8, 206, 234, 239, 280, 283, 326, 334, 338–9
Castel Volturno, Italy 153, 159
Castiglionne, Italy 312
Cawdron, Corporal Sam 341, 343, 345–6, 349, 386–7
Cedra, Italy 194–6
Celincordia, Italy 272
Cesena, Italy 272–9
Chadwick, Corporal Tommy 299–300, 333–4, 336, 338–9, 346, 349, 350, 385
Chambers, Private Frank 87
Chilvers, Sergeant 320
Churchill tanks 75
Churchill, Winston 44, 92–3, 174–5, 327, 332, 334–5, 350–1
Clark, Sergeant Major Arthur 275
Clark, Lieutenant General Mark 106, 159, 175, 194, 212
Clatworthy, Jack 170
Cocuruzzo, Italy 175, 178
Cold War (1946–91) 324, 369
Collins, Lieutenant Russell 'Winkler'
  anti-malaria tablets, on taking 102–3
  Balignano spur fighting and 261–6, 271–2
  Cosina river crossing and 312–13, 319–22
  'Dryden' assault and 248, 249–50
  Frank Johnson death, remembers 327
  gunners and infantry working together, on 293–4
  Hospital Hill battle and 131–5, 158, 166
  Italy landings and 102
  Italy, on return to 348
  'Johnson' assault and 251–6
  joins 16th DLI 93–4
  MC, awarded 183
  mental exhaustion 319–22
  Monte Camino fighting and 179, 180–3
  Monte Siola recce patrol 198
  Patras landing and 339
  post-war life 385
  sentry guard, on 295
  Teano river crossing and 171–2
  25-pounder guns, on 292–3
  VE Day (8 May 1945) 353–4
  Volturno crossing and 158–62, 164, 165–7
Communist Party of Yugoslavia (KPJ) 354
'compo' rations 48, 49–50, 141
Corpo di Cava, Italy 146–9, 168, 211
Corps Francs d'Afrique 59

Corr, Private James
  Athens, on taking of prisoners in 328–9
  Cossack Kononoff Brigade, on forcible disarmament and repatriation of 362
  demob suit, on 376
  Djebel Bou Kournine fighting and 89–90
  Preston, on leadership of 142–3, 204
  reaction of men to news of an imminent attack, on 282, 283
  return home 377
  shellshock, on 78, 299
  Sidi Barka fighting and 88–9
  VE Day (8 May 1945) and 352
Cosina river, Italy 308–21, 350
Cossack Kolonoff Brigade 357, 360–2
Coutts, Captain Jimmy 205, 231, 236
Cowans, Sergeant William 137–8, 257, 258, 259–60, 272–3, 274, 280, 297–8, 363
Craggs, Captain Harry 70–1, 256
Critchley, Lieutenant 189–90
Croatian partisans 356–9
Crummack, Lance Corporal Bill 164

D

Dalton, Sergeant 280
Davenport, Private Bernard 183–4
Davidson, Captain 66
D-Day invasion (1944) 174–5, 193, 194, 216–17
'Dear John' letters 259
'Debollocker, The' 286
demob suit 375–6
Denny, Major J. C. 330–1
Desert Air Force 223–4, 309, 312
desertion 34, 95, 124, 300–1
desert sores 97
Dieppe Raid (19 August 1942) 44
Distinguished Service Order (DSO) 150
Djebel Aboid, Tunisia 59, 72, 77, 79, 81, 84
Djebel Bou Kournine, 'Twin Tits', Tunisia 89–90
Djebel Bou Lahia, Tunisia 84
Djebel Galb Sour, Tunisia 63, 67, 71
Djebel Grembil, Tunisia 84
Djebel Rachtouil, Tunisia 61, 63
Djebel Sincira, Tunisia 61, 62, 63
Djebel Guerba, Tunisia 67, 69
Dodd, Lieutenant Lionel 287–8, 321, 353
Doorman, Sergeant 2
Dorian, Lieutenant 67, 72
Douglass, Sergeant John 54, 69–70
Dragonea, Italy 145–6
Dragoon, Operation (1944) 216

Drake, Lance Sergeant James
  Bren carrier patrols 52–3
  Carrier Platoon, posted to 13
  desertion case and 34
  George VI inspection and 35–6
  joins DLI 7–8
  Military Medal 75
  North Africa, deployment to 40–2
  return home 385–6
  Sedjenane battle and 1–4, 48, 73–6
  Sedjenane relief operation and 48
  training 7, 12
  uniforms and kit issue and 8
'Dryden', Italy 248–9
Duffy, Major Frank 63, 87, 125, 127, 149, 187–8, 218, 298
Dunkirk, evacuation of (1940) ix, 2, 5
dysentery 91, 97, 99, 151, 171, 236, 260, 270

E
Eden, Anthony 92, 335
Eisenhower, Lieutenant General Dwight 44, 45, 193
El Aroussa, Tunisia 59
Elliott, Lance Corporal Ronald 388
  Acropolis, on posting to 322
  Athens, on ELAS in 326–7, 332–3
  Cesena, on cooperation between tanks and infantry at 273–4
  demobilisation, on 372, 376–7
  'Dryden' assault and 248, 249
  fear, on 296
  50th and 51st Divisions deployment of previously wounded soldiers, on 139–44
  Gemmano Ridge battle and 233, 244–5
  George VI inspection, on 213
  Germans, respect for 284
  'Johnson' fighting and 251, 255
  joins 16th DLI 139
  latrines, on 151
  Naples, on local reception in 152
  news of an imminent attack, on reaction to 282–3
  officers and NCOs, on quality of 281
  Patras, on brothel in 341–2
  post-war life 379–80
  Primosole Bridge battle and 139
  Saludecio, on coming under heavy shellfire at 231
  signaller responsibilities 284–5
  Siola attack and 200
  soldier's sense of humour, on 289
  VE Day (8 May 1945) and 351
  Vienna, on black market in 368–9
  Volturno crossing and 154, 155, 157–8
  Yugoslav partisans, on 354–5
Ellison, Corporal Robert
  Algiers to Bizerta sailing, on 99–100
  German soldier surrenders to while cleaning rifle 146–7
  Hospital Hill battle and 124–5, 136
  joins 16th DLI 94
  latrines, on 151
  Naples, on triumphal procession through 151–2
  Salerno landings and 113–14
  Teano river crossing and 170–1
  Volturno crossing and 155, 156–7
El Quassasin camp, Egypt 203–5, 210–11
Er Rama camp, Palestine 208–9
Eucalyptus camp, Maison Carree, Algiers 42–4

F
Fanfare, Operation (1943) 364
First World War (1914–18) x–xi, 33, 44, 50, 80, 86, 95, 131, 202, 289, 297, 386, 387
Fisher, Lance Corporal Jock 28
Folkestone 17–19, 21, 22, 95, 138, 187
Footer, Lieutenant 'Giff' 190–2, 244, 255, 327
Forli, Italy 306, 321, 351, 352
Forster, Private George
  George VI inspection of 16th DLI and 36–7
  guard duty 22–3
  No Man's Land patrols 51
  North Africa, deployment to 38, 41, 42–3
  Sedjenane battle and 46, 47–8, 49, 55, 68
  Winchelsea, on 23–4
  Winchelsea, on shooting down of RAF aircraft over 31–2
'The Fort', Italy 115
forward observation officer (FOO) 70, 76–7, 147, 293–4
Fox, Johnny 54
Francolise, Italy 168, 172
Free French 59, 77
Freeman-Attwood, Major-General Harold 45
Frewer, Mike 131
'friendly fire' 150, 224

G
Gaines, Company Quartermaster Sergeant George 24

Garland, Captain Len 147, 149, 150
gas attacks 15, 21, 42, 83, 185, 188, 235, 276, 289, 304
Gates, Company Sergeant Major George 39
Gemmano Ridge, battle of (1944) 233–45, 278, 304
Gent, Private Gordon
    Churchill, on visit of 92–3
    German air raids at Bizerta, on 100
    Italy landings and 123
    joins 16th DLI 6–7
    North Africa, deployment to 39–40
    Sedjenane battle and 48–9, 55
    sickness 153–4
    training 9–10
George VI, King 34–5, 75, 213
Gerhild Line, Italy 312
German Army units
    XIV Panzer Corps 106
    15th Panzer Grenadier Division 106, 175
    16th Panzer Division 106, 124
    129th Panzer Grenadier Regiment 178
    LXXVII Panzer Corps 216–17
    Army Group Africa 58
    Hermann Goering Panzer Division 85, 106
    Luftwaffe Fallschirmjäger Barenthin Regiment 59
    Panzer Army Africa 44, 58
    SS 284, 366
    Tenth Army 212
Gipson, Lance Corporal 74
Goldstone, Corporal 241
Golightly, Regimental Quartermaster Sergeant 55–6
Gothic Line, Italy 212–32, 353
Gray, Private Alexander 136
Greece 247, 322–48, 349, 372, 384, 385
Greek People's Liberation Army (Ellinikós Laïkós Apeleftherotikós Stratós) (ELAS) 322–40, 343
Green Beach, Antiferro sector, Italy 101–2, 107, 110, 111
Green Hill (Dj Azzag), Italy 45, 46, 59, 84
Grey, Corporal Edward 162, 257, 286, 289, 294, 375
Gustav Line, Italy 152, 174, 193–4, 212

H
Hall, Lance Corporal 260
Harris, 2nd Lieutenant Henry 17
Hawkesworth, Lieutenant General Sir John 106, 151, 172, 216, 222, 306, 333

Hay, Major Alan
    Austria, arrival in 355
    Austria, Croatian and Yugoslavian forces in and 356–60
    Austria, on horse races in 363
    end of war and 350, 351–2
    evacuated due to wounds 226
    Greece, on ELAS in 328, 330–2
    Italy, on return to 211
    Johnny Preston, on departure of 211
    J. Mezar camp in Syria, on tactical exercises at 209–10
    joins 16th DLI 187–92
    Palestine, on Kefar Yona camp in 205–7, 208
    post-war life 375–6, 382–3, 386
    'Triangle' attack and 221–6
Hertfordshire Regiment Depot, Kempston Barracks, Bedford 5–6
Hetherington, Company Sergeant Major 61
Hewlett, Lieutenant Richard 205, 210, 218–19, 221, 234–7, 263, 264, 267, 268, 269–71, 383
Hill 414, Italy 233–4
Hill 449, Italy 233–4, 237–9, 245
Hitler, Adolf 45, 350, 353
Holder, Bill 176, 177
Hood, Lieutenant William 223, 224
Hospital Hill, Italy 115–35, 139, 158, 166
Husky, Operation (1943) 105–6

I
infantry
    artillery co-operation with 76, 254, 293–4
    infantrymen on opposite sides of war, links between 317–18
    'ordinary' infantry battalions xii
    tank co-operation with 20–1, 76, 171–2, 209–10, 273–4, 306
Isola del Piano, Italy 216
Italy 105–201, 212–321
    See also individual place name

J
James, Company Sergeant Major Wyndham (Jimmy)
    Algiers bordellos, on 43
    company quartermaster sergeant 14
    embarkation leave 33
    evacuated 136–7
    George VI inspection and 35–6
    Italy landings and 108–9, 111

joins 16th DLI 5–6
lice, on 50
post-war life 381–2
Sedjenane air raids, on 55–7
Sedjenane battle and 60
Sidi Barka battle and 86
training 11–12, 17, 24–5
Tunis Victory Parade and 90–1
Jerrison, Sergeant Joseph 236–7
J. Mezar camp, Syria 209–10
Jobey, Major George 66, 70, 127, 170
Jobey's Bump 66–7, 68
Johnson, Lieutenant Frank 242–3, 247, 327
'Johnson' feature, Casa Ricci Ridge, Italy 248, 249, 251
Jones, Captain Huw 90, 102–3, 130, 298, 301
Junkers Ju 88 31

K

Kasserine Pass, battle of (1943) 58
Keddy, Jock 171
Kefar Yona, Palestine 205–8, 210
Keightley, Lieutenant General Sir Charles 357
Kellet, Sergeant Joe 125
Kesselring, Field Marshal Albert 106, 131, 152–3, 212
King, Sergeant Russell
  George VI inspection, on 35
  journey to the front 45
  No Man's Land patrols 52
  North Africa, deployment to 32
  Sedjenane battle and (1943) 62–3
  sergeant, on responsibilities as 30–1
Koursia, Tunisia 85

L

La Crocella hill, Italy 145–6, 147, 149, 150–1
La Crocetta, Italy 261–2
La Fratta, Italy 306, 350
La Mennola Mental Sanatorium, Salerno 115
La Murata, Italy 176, 178, 186, 197
Lamone river, Italy 321
Landing Craft Infantry (LCI) 107
Landing Ship Tanks (LST) 107
La Pechereie docks, Bizerta harbour, Tunisia 107
Lax, Lieutenant 2, 3, 73
Lazaro river, Italy 307

Leave in Addition to Python system (LIAP) 347, 367
Lee Enfield rifles 8, 29
Leese, Lieutenant General Sir Oliver 193
letters, soldiers sending 258–9
letters of condolence 304
Lewindon, Sergeant John 18, 102
  Gemmano Ridge battle and 240–1
  Hospital Hill battle and 124, 125, 126–7
  landing craft training 102
  shellshock, on 298–9
  Volturno crossing and 156–7, 158
lice 50, 55–6, 200
Lister, Private Tom
  Athens, on rations distribution in 334
  Austrian billets 364–6, 367
  'compo' rations 49–50
  Cossack Kononoff Brigade, on forcible disarmament and repatriation of 361–2
  'Dryden' assault and 249–50
  50th and 51st Divisions, on deployment of previously wounded soldiers 144
  Folkestone, on air raids on 21–2
  Gemmano Ridge battle and 238, 246
  Italy landings and 118–19
  Kefar Yona patrols 207, 208
  North Africa deployment 40
  north/south divide in English society and 22
  Patras billets 340–1, 342
  post-war life 381
  Red Army discipline, on 369–70
  Regent Cinema bombing and 28
  Rye air raids and 26
  ski patrols 370–1
  Tabarka Woods, withdrawal to 78–9
Logan, Captain Thomas 88, 111, 121, 122, 123
Lovell, Corporal Ken
  Atlas Mountains exercises and 97
  Balignano spur fighting and 268–9, 270–1
  brothels, on 98–9
  Casaluce, period of rest at 167
  comradeship of 16th DLI, on 387
  Corla fighting and 316–18
  Hospital Hill battle and 126
  Italy landings and 108, 109–10, 115, 119–20
  joins 16th DLI 94–5
  La Crocella fighting and 149, 150
  Volturno crossing and 154, 156, 164

Luftwaffe 16, 26, 59
Lyons, Private George 88, 329–30

M

Macdonald, John 83
McDonald, Private Oswald 20, 26, 33–4, 53, 71–2
Makepeace, Sergeant Joseph 199
Marano river, Italy 246
Marecchia river, Italy 248
Mareth Line, Tunisia 58, 84
Marshall, Lieutenant Stanley 223
Martin, Major Arthur 87
Mattin, Company Sergeant Major Arthur 232
McCreery, General Sir Richard 106, 179, 349, 367–8
medical care 301
Medjez el Bab, Tunisia 84, 89
Mejez El Bab, Tunisia 59
mepacrine 102–3
Messerschmitt 26, 53
Metcalfe, Captain N. 15
Milburn, Private Jackie 353
Military Cross (MC) 23, 150, 183, 188, 211, 254, 262
Military Medal (MM) 75, 82, 158
Military Mission, Durban, South Africa 260–1
Miller, Colonel Aubrey 114, 121, 122
Miller, Lieutenant W. A. 124
Millett, Private Clifford 183–4
Mills bomb 20
mines 53, 87, 89, 112, 113, 114, 219, 220–1, 251, 285–7, 296, 366
'The Mine', Tunisia 81
Mitchell, Major Ray 159, 161, 180, 181, 184, 224, 231, 262
Monastery Hill, Italy 175, 178
Mondaino, Italy 221, 223, 230–1
Monte Camino, Italy 173, 174–92, 193
Monte Cassino, Italy 152, 187, 193, 202–3, 212, 213
Monte Gridolfo Ridge, Italy 221
Monte La Difensa, Italy 175, 178
Monte Romano, Italy 272
Monte Siola, Italy 198
Monte Turlito sector, Italy 197
Montefiore, Italy 278–9, 306
Montgomery, General Bernard 26, 44, 58, 84, 106, 131, 193
Monti di Amici, Italy 146
Montilgallo spur, Italy 261

Morant, Major John 161–2
mortars xiii, 1, 2, 3, 15, 20, 38, 280, 285, 287–8, 290, 291, 292, 296, 300, 308, 316, 321, 331, 336, 351, 353
  Italian campaign, use of in 112, 117, 120, 121, 122, 125, 126, 132, 133, 136, 139, 149, 150, 165, 170, 176, 177, 184, 194, 199, 200, 225, 226, 229, 232, 233, 234, 238, 239–40, 241, 244, 247, 251, 265, 268, 270–1
  North Africa campaign, use of in 46, 47, 51, 52, 54, 62, 63, 64, 67, 68, 73, 76, 82, 86, 87, 88
Moses, Harry v, xi
Mosque spur, Tunisia 63, 67, 71, 72
Murray, Lieutenant Colonel A. S. P. 14, 17, 23
Murray, Private Eric 236, 292
Mussolini, Benito 105, 278
Mynheer, Harry 114, 353

N

Naples, Italy 106, 145–52, 154, 202, 213
National Liberation Front (Ethnikón Apeleftherotikón Métopon) (EAM) 322, 323, 324
National Republican Greek League (Ethnikós Dimokratikós Ellinikós Sýndesmos) (EDES) 322, 323
Nebelwerfers 117, 162–3, 239, 265, 290
Newman, Captain Bert 48, 50, 334
non-fraternisation 355, 363–4
Northolt Drill Hall 80
Norton Hall 5, 6, 11

O

Ochsenkopf (Ox Head), Operation (1943) 59
Olive, Operation (1944) 213, 217
Oued Zarga, Tunisia 90
Overlord, Operation (1944) 105, 139, 152, 193, 194

P

Paestum, Italy 106, 111
Palestine 205–10, 384
Palmer, Lance Corporal Charles
  Gothic Line fighting and 219–20
  Monte Camino fighting and 174
  Rye air raids and 27–8
  Sidi Barka fighting and 89
  Tamara fighting and 81
Palmer, Herbert 27
Papandreou, Georgios 323–4
Patras, Greece 339–43, 346

Pauly, George 241
Pearson, Company Sergeant Major Arthur 27
Peccia river, Italy 194, 197
Peninsula War (1807–14) x
Periam, Lieutenant T. C. 327
Perriam, Tim 250, 251–2
Petriano, Italy 217–18
Pettifer, Corporal 316
P14 rifle 8
PG53 prison camp, Italy 69, 72
PG66 prison camp, Italy 69
PIAT anti-tank projector 160, 266, 287, 338
Pillbox spur, Italy 175, 176, 178
'The Pimple', Italy 115, 116, 127, 128, 129, 131
Point 150, Italy 199
Point 231, Tunisia 67
Point 235, Italy 246–7
Point 400, Italy 197
Point 420, Italy 284
Point 430, Italy 284
Point 530, Italy 175
Point 683, Italy 180
Point 727, Italy 175, 178
Ponder, Captain 14
Pontecagnano, Italy 111
Poole, Jack 31–2
Preston, Lieutenant Colonel Johnny
   Calabritto basin frontal assault plan 178
   Distinguished Service Order (DSO) 150
   50th and 51st Divisions deployment of previously wounded soldiers and 142, 143
   Hospital Hill battles and 116, 131, 135
   Italy landings and 106, 114
   joins 16th DLI 79–80, 85
   La Crocella advance and 146
   leaves 16th DLI 211, 215, 280
   morale, knack of maintaining 92
   Sidi Barka battles and 87
   stands up for his men 204
   Teano crossing and 168, 172
   'The Wretched Durhams', on label 172
   Volturno crossing and 159, 165
   War Diary and 373
Primosole Bridge, battle (1943) 139
prisoners of war (POWs)
   Austria 355, 357, 360
   camps 69, 72
   Greece 329, 330, 337
   Italian campaign and 126–7, 130, 147, 151, 179, 182–3, 191, 195, 222, 231, 236, 241, 264, 268, 276, 278, 317, 318
   shooting 294
   Tunisian campaign and 51, 64, 65, 69–70, 72, 84, 88, 89, 90, 91, 378–9
Pritchard, Captain 132, 133, 134, 160
prostitutes/brothels 43, 98–9, 167, 205, 341–2
P60 rifle 8
Purnell, David 253, 254

Q
Quassasin Officers' Club 210

R
Raincoat, Operation (1943) 175
rats 50–1
Reading, Sergeant Norman 263, 265, 267, 271
Red Army 216, 356, 360, 361–2, 364–5, 367–70
Reggio, Italy 106
regimental aid post (RAP) 122, 135, 180, 181, 199, 230, 247, 249, 250, 270, 271, 277, 301, 304
Risborough Barracks, Shorncliffe Camp, Folkestone 17–18
Rocca Station, Italy 194
Rome, Italy 168, 174, 193
   Allied capture of (1944) 212
Rommel, General Erwin 44, 58
Ronca river, Italy 306
Rosenhof Brewery 364–5
Royal Air Force (RAF) xii, 32, 110, 131, 139, 309, 326
Royal Navy 118
rum ration 60, 67, 350–1
Rye and Winchelsea, East Sussex 22–6

S
Sacco, Signaller Tony
   Athens posting 322, 325–6, 337
   Italy landings and 110
   joins 16th DLI 85–6
   Monte Camino fighting and 183, 184
   Sidi Barka fighting and 85–7
   Volturno crossing and 162
Salerno landings (1944) 105–44, 145, 166, 189, 201
San Marino, Italy 246, 247
Santarcangelo, Italy 150–1
San Varano, Italy 306
Schmidt, Captain Walter 202
'schu' mine 286, 287, 296
Scobie, Lieutenant General Sir Ronald 323, 324, 326

Scott, Brigadier Pat 357–8
Scriven, Albert 136
Second World War (1939–45)
    atom bomb dropped on Japan 366–7
    battles *see individual* battle name
    Eastern Front 105, 174, 216
    end of 351–4
    Greece and *see* Greece
    North African theatre 44–90
    operations *see individual operation name*
    Victory in Europe (VE Day) (8 May 1945) 353–4
    Victory over Japan Day (VJ Day) 367
Sedjenane, Tunisia 45–57
    battle of (1943) 1–4, 58–77, 78, 79, 80–1, 84, 85, 87, 162, 378, 385
self-inflicted wounds 25, 33–4, 54, 299
sentry guard 295
Serra Ridge, Italy 231
shellshock 68, 78, 136, 236, 249, 298–300, 339, 345
Sherlaw, Major Ronald 145
    Athens, on navigational errors in 325
    Athens, on negotiating with ELAS in 328
    Austria, tensions between Croatian and Yugoslav forces in and 357
    Corpo di Cava advance and 147–9, 150
    Cowans and 137–8
    'Dryden' assault and 248, 249–50
    Gemmano Ridge battle and 243–4
    Hospital Hill battle and 128–30, 131
    Italy landings and 112, 117–18
    'Johnson' assault and 248
    joins 16th DLI 95
    Military Cross (MC) 150
    Monte Camino fighting and 180
    Petriano fighting and 218
    rest period after wounding, on 301–2
    16th Durham Light Infantry Association and 386
    singing 327
    Teano river crossing 168–9, 171
    Victory in Europe – VE Day (8 May 1945) and 352
Shingle, Operation (1944) 193–4
Shutt, Maria 378–9
Shutt, Private Sidney 8, 66, 67, 71, 378–9
Sicily 105–6, 107, 137, 139, 140, 175
Sidi Barka Hill, Tunisia 85–9
Sidi Nsir station, Tunisia 84
ski patrols 370–1
'Sleep', Italy 308–9

snipers 61, 62, 66, 76, 164, 180, 184, 185, 217, 221, 288, 309–10, 327
Sobieski 202, 211, 213
Special Operations Executive (SOE) 322
Staffordshire 37, 38, 40
Stalag IV B prison camp, Germany 69
Stern, Sergeant Harry 11
Stoll, Sergeant 88
Streeton, 'Yorkie' 321
Stringer, Major Laurie
    Athens, wounded in 335, 336, 346
    Balignano spur battle and 262–7, 269–70, 271–2
    'battle drill' tactics, on 306
    Cesena fighting and 274–8
    command of 'B' Company, given 260–1
    Cosina river crossing and 314–16, 318–19
    Cossack Kononoff Brigade, on forcible disarmament and repatriation of 360–1
    demobilisation 373–4
    History of the Sixteenth Battalion: The Durham Light Infantry 163, 373–4, 388
    letters of condolence, on writing 304
    pride in achievement of men, on 388–9
    shellshocked men and 299
    'Sleep' attack and 307–11
Strothart, Lieutenant Fred 148, 177
Sugar Loaf (Djebel Azag), Tunisia 45
Sykes, Sergeant Ray 154, 156, 157, 158, 164, 298
Syria 124, 137, 209–10

T
tanks 15, 16, 20, 75–7, 87, 107, 115, 147, 148–51, 171–2, 217, 221, 222, 223, 226, 229, 231, 247, 250, 251, 252–3, 266, 273–7, 280, 285, 286–7, 306, 307, 308, 309, 310, 311, 317, 319, 324, 326, 337, 367
    anti-tank guns 16, 20–1, 115, 147, 148, 160, 252, 266, 287, 306, 338
    Churchill tank 75
    infantry-tank co-operation 20–1, 76, 171–2, 209–10, 273–4, 306
    Landing Ship Tanks (LST) 107
    Tiger tank 276
Taranto, Italy 106, 349, 350
Tavernia, Italy 246
Teano river, Italy 168–72
Telegraph Hill, Italy 175–6
Termoli, Italy 153
Terrace Hill, Italy 175–6

Index

Thomasson, Regimental Sergeant Major 24, 81, 137, 346
Thompson submachine gun 15, 20, 126, 128, 129, 130, 160, 168, 182, 191, 195, 198–9, 227, 237, 242, 247, 254, 264, 277, 284, 307, 316, 317
Thornton, Company Sergeant Major Leslie
   artillery fire, on being under 291
   Athens, confrontations with ELAS fighters in 333–4, 336–8
   Austria, on British soldiers' relations with women in 365
   Austria, on rounding up SS in 366
   'base wallahs', on 210
   Cairo, on arrival in 202, 203
   Cesena street fighting and 276
   desertion, on 300–1
   Gemmano Ridge battle and 234–5, 237, 238–40
   latrines, on 260
   Monte Camino fighting and 178–9, 185–7
   Monte Siola fighting and 200–1
   officer, on what makes a good 280
   redeployment as 'C' Company sergeant major 232
   rejoins army after demobilisation 384–5
   snipers, on 288–9
   toilet use under heavy fire, on 292
   VE Day (8 May 1945) and 350–1
   wine drinking 257–8, 346
Tiffin, 2nd Lieutenant Douglas
   anti-personnel mines, on 286–7
   casualty levels, on 296
   joins 16th DLI 208–9
   Petriano village fighting and 217–19
   reliability of men, on 297
   return home 383–4
   'The Triangle' fighting and 227–30
Tiger tank 276
Tito, Josip 354, 355, 357, 358–9
'The Triangle', Italy 221, 227
Tuck, Private Joseph 163, 228, 229
Tunis 44, 45, 59
   advance to 78–104
Tunisia 44, 45, 59, 78–104, 137, 154, 171
Tunney, Thomas xi, 26, 27, 65–6, 67–8, 69
Tunney, Private Tom xi, 26–7, 65–6, 67–8, 69
Turnbull, Corporal Tom
   Corpo di Cava fighting and 148, 149
   kit inspections 5
   mental effects of war, on 345
   Monte Siola fighting and 198–9
   mortar fire, on 291
   NCOs, on 281
   North Africa, on deployment to 33
   Sedjenane battle and 59, 61, 64–5
   Sedjenane relief operation and 46–7
   Teano river crossing and 171
   training 18–20
   Volturno crossing and 163–4
25-pounder guns 48, 149, 150, 179, 184, 292–3

U

US Army units
   II Corps 45, 58
   Fifth Army 106, 142, 153, 174, 175, 193, 194
   VI Corps 106
   82nd Airborne Division 106
   See also Allied units
USAAF 110

V

venereal diseases (VD) 25, 167, 205, 341
Verrucchio, Italy 246–7, 256, 260, 261
Vick, Corporal Harry 263–4, 266
Vickers 1, 2, 3, 80, 94, 326
Victory in Europe (VE) Day (8 May 1945) 350–2
Victory over Japan Day (VJ Day) (15 August 1945) 367
Vienna, Austria 216, 367–74, 384
Vietri valley, Italy 145, 153, 161
Viktor line, Italy 153
Vile, Jack 199
Villa Literno, Italy 153, 154
Villach, Austria 355–6
Ville d'Oran 349
Virr, Sergeant William 94
   Atlas Mountains tactical exercises and 96
   Balzanino river nuisance patrol 307–8
   Cairo, hires local guide in 204
   Calabritto advance and 176–7
   desert sores 97
   Gemmano Ridge battle and 235–7, 278–9
   joins 16th DLI 94
   La Crocella advance and 146
   mepacrine, on 103
   minefield, marooned in 220–1
   PIAT anti-tank weapon, on 287
   prisoners, on taking 294
   resorting to religion or superstitions/ making 'bargains', on 297

Salerno landings and 105, 113
  Siola advance and 199
  'Sleep' attack and 309–10, 311, 313–14
  sunburn 98
  2-inch mortars, on 288
  Volturno crossing and 160
  weather, on 193
Vizard, Major Arthur
  ack-ack gunners joining regiment, on 214
  adaptability of British soldier, on 344–5
  Athens, on Christmas in 335
  Austria, on Christmas show in 371
  Austria, on finding billets in 364
  best soldiers in the thick of the fighting, on habits of 342
  burials of soldiers, on 303–4
  Cairo, on local Arab salesmen in 204–5
  calls on wives and mothers of fallen 377–8
  'Dear John' letters, on 259
  demobilisation, on 372–3
  ELAS organisation, on 323
  fanatical nature of some Germans soldiers, remembers 277
  Gothic Line assault and 216
  Hospital Hill battles and 114–15, 120–4
  Italy landings and 101–2, 107, 108–9, 110, 111–12
  joins 16th DLI 80
  POW camp at Ghardimaou, on 91–2
  Preston, on 92
  promoted to major 84
  Sidi Barka fighting and 87–8
  16th DLI coming to the assistance of other units, on 85
  16th Durham Light Infantry Association and 386
  Tamara fighting and 81–3, 84
  wounded and evacuated 123–4, 132
Volturno river, Italy 153–68

W
Wade, Bill 290
Walcheren Expedition (1809) x
Wales, Sergeant Major Wilson 86
Ware, Lieutenant Colonel Richard 23, 29–30, 59, 63, 66, 72–3, 79
War Office 305
Waylen, Captain 106
Waymark, Lieutenant Stanley 263, 266, 271
Webley pistol 129
Weir, Major General Stephen 306
Welch, Major 76–7
Wells, Jackie 244, 255, 273
Whitehead, Lieutenant Wilson 156
Wildon, Austria 364, 370, 372–3
Wilson, General Sir Henry Maitland 193
Wilson, Company Sergeant Major S. A. 121, 124, 153–4, 161, 183
Winchelsea 22–6, 31, 32
wireless sets 70, 87, 120, 133, 223, 251, 285
Woodlands, Lieutenant 109, 125, 126
Worrall, Lieutenant Colonel Dennis
  Athens, takes break during posting to 330, 332
  Athens, on distribution of food in 334
  Balignano spur attack and 265, 271–2
  Corpo di Cava operations and 150, 211
  friendly fire and 309
  Gemmano battle and 238
  Gridolfo Ridge fighting and 222, 226
  Hay criticises 222, 226
  joins 16th DLI 80
  La Crocetta fighting and 262–3
  MC 150, 211
  promotion to lieutenant colonel 211
  respect of men for 280–1
  16th Durham Light Infantry Association and 386
  Tamara fighting and 81
Wright, Sergeant Harold 32

Y
Yalta Conference (1945) 335
Yugoslavia 354–9